CW00693560

Wellington and the Siege of San Sebastian 1813

Wellington and the Siege of San Sebastian 1813

Bruce Collins

Pen & Sword
MILITARY

First published in Great Britain in 2017 by
Pen and Sword Military
an imprint of
Pen and Sword Books Ltd
47 Church Street
Barnsley
South Yorkshire S70 2AS

Copyright © Bruce Collins, 2017

ISBN 978 1 78383 114 2

The right of Bruce Collins to be identified as the author of this work
has been asserted by him in accordance with the
Copyright, Designs and Patents Act 1988.

A CIP record for this book is available from the British Library

All rights reserved. No part of this book may be reproduced or transmitted
in any form or by any means, electronic or mechanical including photocopying,
recording, or by any information storage and retrieval system
without permission from the Publisher in writing.

Printed and bound in England
by CPI Group (UK) Ltd, Croydon, CR0 4YY

Typeset in Times New Roman by Chic Graphics

Pen & Sword Books Ltd incorporates the imprints of
Pen & Sword Archaeology, Atlas, Aviation, Battleground, Discovery,
Family History, History, Maritime, Military, Naval, Politics, Railways,
Select, Social History, Transport, True Crime, Claymore Press,
Frontline Books, Leo Cooper, Praetorian Press, Remember When,
Seaforth Publishing and Wharncliffe.

For a complete list of Pen and Sword titles please contact
Pen and Sword Books Limited
47 Church Street, Barnsley, South Yorkshire, S70 2AS, England
E-mail: enquiries@pen-and-sword.co.uk
Website: www.pen-and-sword.co.uk

Contents

List of Plates

View of San Sebastian by James Webb, 1870s
San Sebastian, 1874 by James Webb
Depot Generale de Marine, Baie, port et ville de St Sebastien, 1793
Storming of the town and castle of San Sebastian
British troops advancing, San Sebastian
The Storming of San Sebastian by Denis Dighton
Bridge of boats across the Adour
Bayonne from St Etienne
Captain Sir George Ralph Collier by William Beechey
Joseph-Désiré Court, Le Maréchal Soult

Preface

Sir Michael Howard records that when, in the mid-1950s, he cast around for a research project, 'The Napoleonic period seemed to have been flogged to death by operational military historians'.[1] Subsequent work, he freely admits, revealed the erroneous nature of this initial judgement. But something similar might be thought today, especially as bicentenary publications have climaxed with numerous re-workings of the battle of Waterloo.

In fact, the subject continues to be open to fresh approaches and re-appraisals. Distinguished work has provided new insights into, among other topics, the British government's policies and strategic directives, the operational skills demonstrated by Wellington, the recruitment of troops and the creation of the army, the conditions under which the British soldiers campaigned and fought, and the Spanish experience of the war.[2] Recent publications, however, leave open the question of how useful operational studies might still be to understanding the British army in this period.

This study arose from a broader interest in British siege warfare from the late eighteenth century to the South African War of 1899–1902. One aspect of that interest is the conduct of three sieges of the capital of Mysore, Seringapatam (Srirangapatnam), during the 1790s. The campaigns against Mysore involved the future Duke of Wellington who served in neighbouring Madras from 1796 to 1805. I offered some preliminary observations on possible connections between Wellington's Indian experience of sieges and his conduct of sieges in the Peninsular War in November 2005 at a conference organized by the British Commission for Military History on 'Land and Sea Warfare in the Age of Nelson and Wellington'. That interest was subsequently developed at the Third Wellington Congress at the University of Southampton in July 2006 in a paper published in C.M. Woolgar (ed.), *Wellington Studies IV* (2008). From that point, I decided to re-examine the longest and most difficult of Wellington's sieges, that of San Sebastian.

Any study of the British experience of the Peninsular War will recognize the importance of Charles Oman's monumental history. I have chosen not to pick my way through his chapters on the siege but to explore the subject with different questions in mind. By re-working the history of the siege, I hope in particular to demonstrate the overriding and unremitting demands of managing an army and its operations. This perspective is intended to qualify the importance so often attached to strategic insight and charismatic leadership in the history of campaigning. It is difficult to do justice to the actions and skills of senior battalion and brigade officers, because evidence is limited and events are opaque. What follows is therefore an exploration of a particular campaign highlighting the challenges of managing complex operations.

The sacking of San Sebastian after the siege created a great deal of controversy in Spain and a cultural history of the nature and bounds of that controversy could be written. One footnote to that cultural history might be added. Oman concluded his account of the siege by regretting 'the disgraceful sack which followed the storm', but also by describing a ceremony of Anglo-Spanish reconciliation in 1925. Demonstrating for Oman that 'the present generation has forgotten and forgiven that sad story', a monument to the British dead was erected on the mountain where the castle stood overlooking the town itself.[3] According to the regimental history of the King's Own, the memorialization of fallen British soldiers on Mount Urgullo was a unique occurrence in Spain.[4] Sadly, however, the monument was constructed from stones from earlier memorials. The nature of the stones used and the exposed situation of the cemetery meant that by 1935 the monument was in Oman's words 'much injured and mutilated'. The British government felt unable to press for its restoration since the monument was Spanish property; local representations, it was suggested, might lead to locally initiated repairs.[5] Eighty years later, the site remains sad and neglected, even disturbingly so. In many various ways, the response to the siege within the Basque country and in Spain more generally would make an intriguing subject for research.

But my concern here is with British military history and with the implications of a close examination of one siege for our understanding of early nineteenth-century warfare more generally. Sieges had once been central to the conduct of war. By the 1800s the conduct of sieges was not seen as a vital component of Napoleonic warfare. Yet siege operations proved important in the Peninsular War and posed major military and moral challenges. This study offers a contribution to the re-examination of the British engagement in sieges during their long wars of 1790–1815 and indicates that the nature of siege warfare in the nineteenth century is open to re-appraisal.

Notes

1. Michael Howard, *Captain Professor* (London, 2006), 145.
2. See, for example, the books by Rory Muir, Roger Knight, Huw Davies, Kevin Linch, Edward Coss and Charles Esdaile in the Guide to Reading. Among others, Rory Muir, *Salamanca 1812* (New Haven, 2001), Thomas Munch-Petersen, *Defying Napoleon: How Britain Bombarded Copenhagen and Seized the Danish Fleet in 1807* (Stroud, 2007), and Andrew Bamford, *A Bold and Ambitious Enterprise: The British Army in the Low Countries, 1813-1814* (London, 2013) demonstrate the continuing value and scope of operational histories.
3. Charles Oman, *A History of the Peninsular War*, 7 vols (London, 2005 reprint of 1930 edn), vii, 62.
4. Colonel L.I. Cowper, *The King's Own. The Story of a Royal Regiment*, 2 vols (Oxford, 1939), I, 423.
5. *House of Commons Debates*, vol 301, 16 May 1935, c 1893.

Acknowledgements

This book arose from an interest in the understudied subject of British siege warfare from the siege of Gibraltar in 1779–83 to the dramatic sieges of the South African War in 1899–1900. I gave a paper on San Sebastian to the Fifth Wellington Congress at the University of Southampton in 2013 and Rupert Harding of Pen & Sword Books asked me whether I would like to prepare a book on that siege. I am most grateful for his invitation and for his patience, encouragement and support in the intervening years. In general terms, I owe much to the participants in Wellington Congresses since the third one in 2006 when I gave a paper on siege warfare in the age of Wellington and began working on this subject. Although I have not presented papers on this topic to meetings of the British Commission for Military History, I have gained much from its conferences and from conversations with fellow members, particularly Richard Tennant and John Peaty who both know a great deal about this period. The Commission is an excellent forum for bringing together academic historians, research students, non-university researchers and retired officers with expertise in military history. I have learned a lot from seminar discussions, fleeting comments and corridor conversation at its meetings over many years.

Any scholar working on material involving the first Duke of Wellington is indebted to Christopher Woolgar and Karen Robson for their exemplary work on the Wellington Papers at the Special Collections in the Hartley Library, University of Southampton. I am grateful for their helpfulness and support and for permission to quote from and use maps in the Wellington Papers. I owe a great deal to a strategic research investment fund at Sheffield Hallam University in 2014; it provided a research grant which enabled Dr Wilfred Jack Rhoden, a historian of nineteenth-century France, to undertake a documents search for me at the Service historique de la Défense, Château De Vincennes. His highly professional work in locating and photographing sets of files relevant to this study have enabled me to broaden the scope of my research. The Faculty of Development and Society at Sheffield Hallam University has supported individual research in the Humanities through the Humanities Research Centre in an enlightened and effective way; and I am grateful to the faculty's HRC for steady funding for conference attendance and short research visits. It has been good to work throughout the evolution of this project in the History group at Sheffield Hallam; every member of the group submitted successfully to the 2014 Research Effectiveness Framework and that level of commitment to research continues.

The book was greatly improved by the comments, critiques and positive suggestions of two anonymous readers. As I had virtually no quibbles or disagreements with their reports, and indeed was stimulated by their reactions, I asked Rupert Harding if they would agree to waive their anonymity. Charles Esdaile and Rory Muir agreed to do so, and I am delighted to be able to thank them for their trenchant assessments and suggestions for further work. Rory Muir helped enormously in pressing me to explain more fully and, I hope, more clearly numerous points in the original text. His eagle eye saved me from various slips and misjudgements, though he may feel that one or two conclusions are still contestable. Their reports together stimulated me to expand the range of issues covered in the book, and the detail with which I treated them. I hope that the consequent expansion of the book's scope has strengthened its value. I have benefitted over the years from conversations with Huw Davies. We share an interest in exploring how tactical thinking and practice was disseminated in the British army across its many divergent spheres of operation. Tessa Dunlop, who is intermitting her PhD research with me to write her third book, kindly read two chapters; her incisive comments encouraged me to clarify my arguments and trim my prose. Finally, my wife, Dr Linda Nash, read through various drafts, offered the most tactful criticism and repeatedly reminded me of the need to develop the points made rather than rush on to the next section of an ever expanding text. I am responsible for whatever lapses and errors remain in what follows.

Bruce Collins
Sheffield, June 2017

Maps

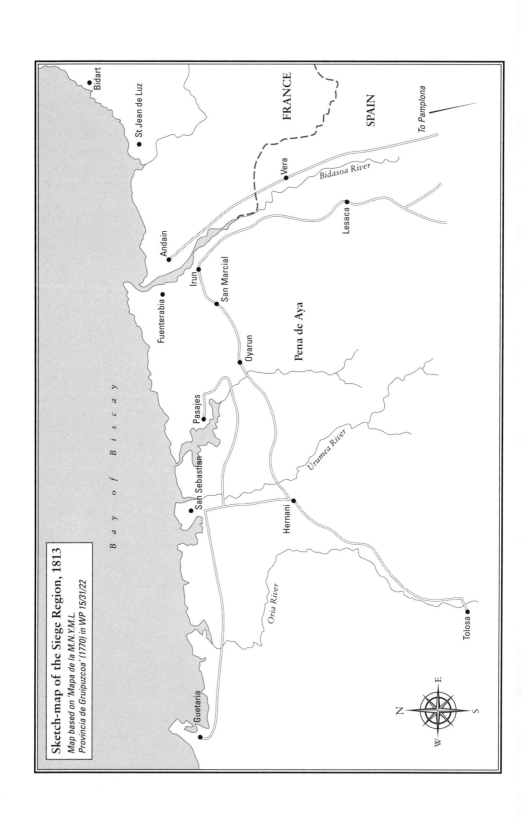

Sketch-map of the Siege Region, 1813

Map based on 'Mapa de la M.N.Y.M.L. Provincia de Gruipuzcoa' (1770) in WP 15/31/22

Bidart

St Jean de Luz

FRANCE

SPAIN

To Pamplona

Vera

Bidasoa River

Andain

Lesaca

Irun

San Marcial

Fuenterabia

B a y   o f   B i s c a y

Oyarun

Pena de Aya

Pasajes

Urumea River

San Sebastian

Hernani

Oria River

Guetaria

Tolosa

N
E
S
W

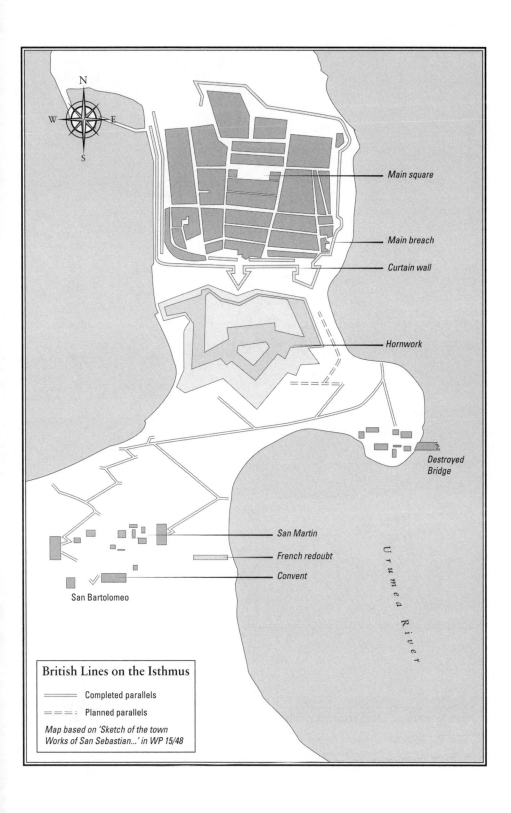

Main square

Main breach

Curtain wall

Hornwork

Destroyed
Bridge

San Martin

French redoubt

Convent

San Bartolomeo

U r u m e a   R i v e r

British Lines on the Isthmus

Completed parallels

Planned parallels

*Map based on 'Sketch of the town
Works of San Sebastian...' in WP 15/48*

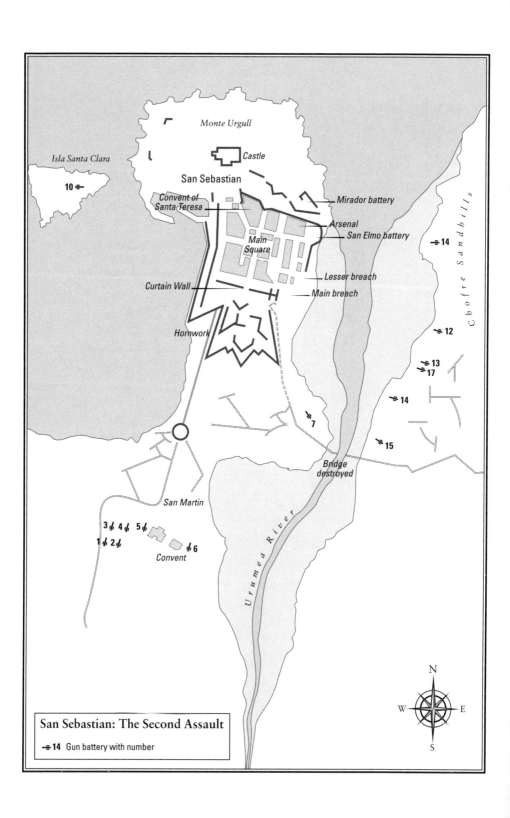

Monte Urgull

Isla Santa Clara

10

Castle

San Sebastian

Convent of
Santa Teresa

Mirador battery

Arsenal
San Elmo battery

Main
Square

14

Curtain Wall

Lesser breach

Main breach

12

Hornwork

13
17

14

7

15

Bridge
destroyed

San Martin

3 4 5

1 2

6

Convent

Chofre Sandhills

Urumea River

N

W   E

S

San Sebastian: The Second Assault

14   Gun battery with number

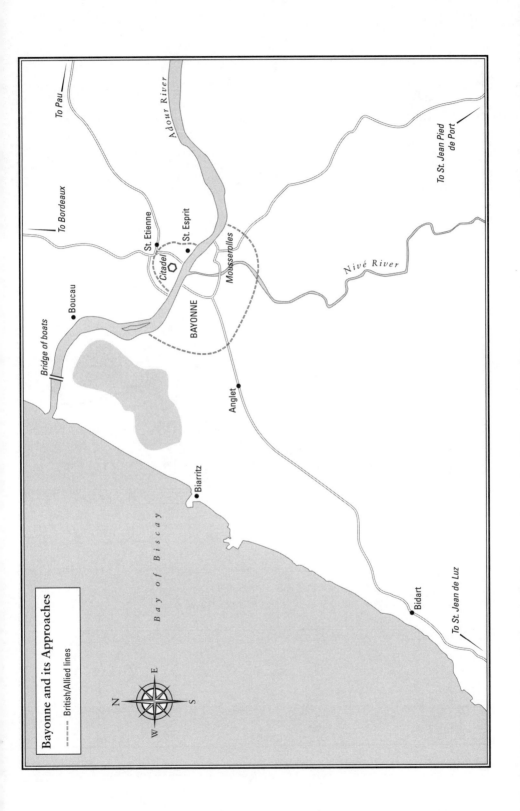

Bayonne and its Approaches

----- British/Allied lines

To Pau

To Bordeaux

Adour River

St. Etienne

St. Esprit

Citadel

Mousserolles

BAYONNE

Boucau

Bridge of boats

Nivé River

To St. Jean Pied de Port

Anglet

Biarritz

Bay of Biscay

Bidart

To St. Jean de Luz

N
W E
S

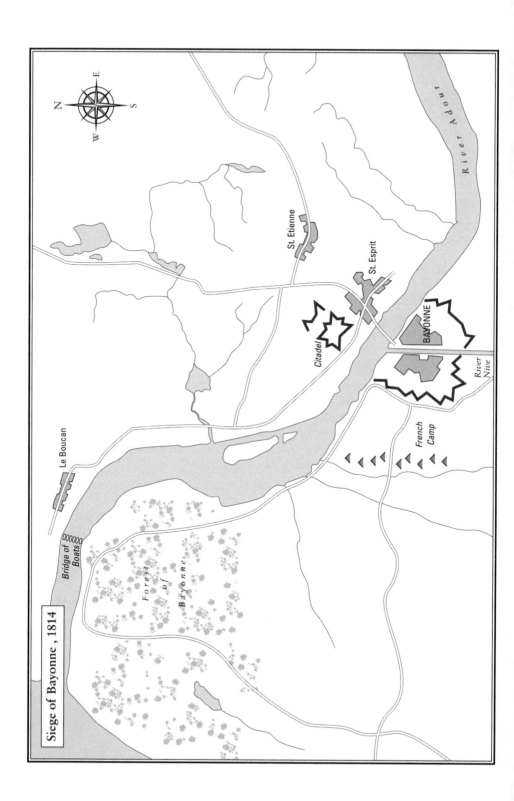

Siege of Bayonne , 1814

River Adour

St. Etienne

St. Esprit

Citadel

BAYONNE

River Nive

French Camp

Le Boucan

Bridge of Boats

Forest of Bayonne

N
E
S
W

Chapter 1

Siege Warfare and Wellington's Generalship

Siege Warfare as a Challenge

On 31 August 1813, the northern Spanish port of San Sebastian was stormed and sacked by British and Portuguese forces. A senior artillery officer, Lieutenant Colonel Augustus Frazer, described the town a few days later:

> The scene is dreadful: no words can convey half the horrors which strike the eye at every step. Nothing, I think, can prevent the total destruction of the unhappy town. Heaps of dead in every corner; English, French, and Portuguese, lying wounded on each other; with such resolution did one side attack and the other defend. . . . The very few inhabitants I saw, said nothing. They were fixed in stupid horror, and seemed to gaze with indifference at all around them, hardly moving when the crash of a falling house made our men run away. The hospitals present a shocking sight; friends and enemies lying together, all equally neglected.[1]

Amidst this devastation, the British still confronted the French defending the castle which dominated the town. The intensity of the conflict and the suffering of the traumatized population ignited considerable controversy. Within weeks, the British were charged with deliberately destroying the town, an accusation which has been repeated down the centuries.

This outcome was not what Wellington had expected six weeks before the assault. On 20 July, he wrote to Lord William Bentinck, commanding a force on Spain's eastern coast: 'In the course of a few days I hope to have possession of San Sebastian, and I propose then either to move forward into France, or to make myself master of all the garrisons of Aragon, so as to connect myself more closely with you.'[2] In reality, San Sebastian had to be attacked twice and at great cost in British casualties before Wellington's troops captured the town on 31 August and its castle on 8 September. The advance into France, sternly resisted by an effective French army, did not begin until October. And no swing towards Spain's eastern coastal belt ever occurred.

The siege of San Sebastian was significant for many reasons. It took up far more time and effort than Wellington had expected, testing British military resolve and effectiveness in the process. Questions were raised about the British army's ability to conduct such demanding operations. The British management of the siege led to arguments about the limits of 'scientific' warfare and especially the role played by engineering and artillery officers. From the historian's perspective, it has been unclear why San Sebastian figured so significantly in both the French defenders' and the British assailants' calculations. The siege's strategic significance and Spanish reactions to the siege need therefore to be set in the wider context of uncertainties about the direction of the war against France during July–October 1813.

There is also the larger question of why sieges rarely figure in the history of Revolutionary and Napoleonic warfare. In the late seventeenth century intricately fortified cities and sieges dominated military planning. For Louis XIV, sieges were the stuff of campaigning, with besieged towns offering tangible objectives and siege operations being subject to rationale planning and definable timetables. They were also far less bloody than unpredictable battles.[3] Sebastien de Vauban was the king's engineer expert and took formal charge of French fortifications from 1678 to 1707. Attaining the rank, unprecedented for an engineer, of general and eventually Marshal of France, Vauban participated in 48 sieges and planned 160 fortresses. His lines of forts and fortified towns from the Swiss Alps to the English Channel included forty major works, some of which – such as Verdun, Metz, Belfort and Besançon – acquired a long and resonant history.[4]

For Napoleon, however, sieges were of minor significance. David Chandler in his classic study of Napoleon's campaigns mentions a few instances, but in 1,100 pages of text offers no assessment of siege warfare. So, too, Rory Muir's excellent study of tactics and battle in this period omits a separate analysis of siege warfare. Bruno Colson's extensive study of Napoleon's writings on war provides just two index references to siege warfare as a specific type of conflict.[5] Donald Horward, in his study of the French sieges of Ciudad Rodrigo and Almeida in 1810, noted the lack of development in siege warfare since Vauban's time. Whereas 'the science of warfare' was in many aspects 'transformed' in the eighteenth century, and especially from the 1790s, siege warfare relied on 'the same time-tested Vauban tactics that were common knowledge to all military men'.[6]

Many explanations for the decline of siege warfare may be offered. Sieges were very expensive to stage. The standard eighteenth-century approach was to isolate a besieged town until its defenders were starved into submission. Such an approach was feasible where a besieging army could advance on adequate roads, could maintain its supply lines and could insulate the besieged town from sources of food. But there were still real risks. When the Spanish and French besieged the British port and base at Gibraltar from 1779 to 1783, the Spanish held all the advantages as they ruled the territory abutting the isolated isthmus and had ample facilities at the nearby port of Algeciras. But the besieged were able to secure supplies, regularly through small-scale blockade-running and annually through the arrival of Royal Navy fleets accompanying large transport convoys. For the French and Spanish, Gibraltar tied down blockading fleets and eventually sucked in armies totalling 40,000 men, all to no effect. From a military planner's perspective, such costs in resources and pay provided a convincing argument against mounting sieges of well-defended positions in the first place.

The alternative to waiting for the besieged to starve was to mount a direct bombardment followed by a summons to surrender. That approach required expensive cannon, whose conveyance depended upon plentiful transport animals and manpower, and food for both. Great stockpiles of munitions were also necessary. Yet, even when the difficulties of access were overcome and a bombardment was launched, a refusal of the besieged to capitulate might lead to an assault, almost certainly inflicting heavy casualties on the attackers. Both approaches inevitably inflicted sickness, starvation and death on besieged civilians. That went counter to Enlightenment efforts, at least in thinking about and planning for wars, to confine warfare as far as possible to the clash of professional armies.

Such drawbacks had long provoked criticism of siege operations. Sun Tzu's *The Art of War*, compiled in about 400–320 BC, gave a stern warning: 'The worst policy is to attack cities'. The disadvantages were so alarming that sieges should be resorted to 'only when there is no alternative'. Preparations for an assault would take at least six months, creating an undesirable burden when any government's aim should be to avoid 'protracted war'. The alternative to costly preparation was immediate attack. But impetuous assaults were disastrous: 'If the general is unable to control his impatience and orders his troops to swarm up the wall like ants, one-third of them will be killed without taking the city'.[7]

Given such logistical and ethical challenges, any decision to besiege a town should, in theory, have been informed by a careful assessment of the costs involved. Responding to his experience of the long wars of 1792–1815, Carl von Clausewitz insisted that deciding whether a siege was worthwhile or not depended upon the state of the wider campaign. In limited campaigns, a fortress might be the objective, 'a small, independent conquest'. A siege in such circumstances was not risky, and the captured fortress could be useful as an asset in itself or as a 'bargaining counter' in subsequent peace negotiations. Secondly, sieges which consolidated a campaign after a decisive battle had been won might absorb resources, but would not involve great risks. The third type of siege, however, was extremely dangerous for the attacker. In a campaign directed at achieving a decisive victory over an opposing army, a siege would divert manpower from the campaign's main objective and reduce the attacker's advantages. It was, therefore, 'a necessary evil', because 'any kind of interruption, pause, or suspension of activity is inconsistent with the nature of offensive war'.[8] While Wellington initially regarded San Sebastian as an easy conquest, the subsequent siege quickly became an operation of this sort.

Clausewitz further stressed that any decision to besiege a town partly depended on what purpose a fortified place served. A retreating army needed fortified positions as depots for supplies, whereas an advancing army lived off the land or on supplies from an expanding domain in its rear. Fortresses might defend large centres of population, or key roads and especially river crossings, or serve simply as staging posts for recuperation and resupply to armies on the march, or as places where retreating forces could seek temporary refuge and respite. In the Low Countries and northern Italy, they often formed interrelated points in a network of defences, less important individually but essential links in defensive chains. They could be designed as garrisons for troops who did not actively or normally occupy a territory. Conversely, they could be used by insurgents as rallying points and centres of authority, political power and supply.[9]

One explanation for the reduced incidence of siege warfare was therefore that fortresses themselves had lost their significance. In 1781 the Habsburg ruler, the Emperor Joseph II, dismissed the seven great Barrier Fortresses in the Austrian Netherlands, roughly speaking modern Belgium, as obsolete. They had not prevented the French from overrunning the country in the 1740s and they were poorly maintained and in some cases dilapidated by the 1780s. Austria had allied itself with France in 1756 and Joseph saw no need for defensive measures against his brother-in-law Louis XVI.[10] Those heavily fortified towns had been the objective of French armies for over a hundred years. When the new French republic attacked the Austrian Netherlands in 1793, the French therefore had no major sieges to conduct.

The decline in the value of fortified positions flowed in part from profound changes in the composition and size of armies. As Christopher Duffy has indicated, armies became far larger in the eighteenth century, providing the means to defend wide expanses of frontier with dispersed troops. Armies were no longer huddled in fortified towns. Moreover, the rise of mainly large, partially conscripted regular armies reduced the need to control potentially mutinous or disaffected mercenaries in confined spaces.[11] Napoleon did not dispense with fortified places, but he tended to use them to support his operations, as major military depots, as protective defensive posts and as places into which forces might retreat.[12] He prioritized mobility, with French armies unencumbered by traditional support and baggage trains. One of his generals, Maximilien Foy, later enthused: 'We have shaken off the yoke of useless fortresses'.[13]

A further factor may have been the fevered political climate of the mid-1790s. Reform-minded urban elites in the Low Countries and northern Italy often welcomed the arrival of French 'liberators' as a viable means of achieving political and social change. The systematically fortified cities created in the seventeenth century had been instruments of absolutist rule, imposing order among the civilian inhabitants as well as providing them with much-needed security. This function became less important when population growth saw cities spill out beyond their walls and when absolutism came under attack. Moreover, campaigning, especially in the 1800s, flowed far beyond those areas of the Low Countries and northern Italy where elaborately fortified towns were most commonly found.[14]

There were additional reasons for the declining significance of siege warfare. Apart from reviewing how strategic calculation weighed against besieging a fortified city, Clausewitz warned that an effective siege required far more manpower than the numbers needed simply to isolate an enemy town. A besieging army had to guard its front against possible surprise sorties by the besieged garrison. But it also had to protect its rear from possible attack by an enemy's relieving army. For example, Louis XIV's siege of Namur, in what is now Belgium, from 25 May to 30 June 1692 absorbed 60,000 troops and 151 guns to crush a defending garrison totalling 6,000 troops. Even so, the besieging army had to be protected from attempts to relieve Namur by an army of observation consisting of another 60,000 men. In classic, late seventeenth-century sieges the outer rim of trenches faced away from a besieged town to give direct security to the besieging army. Such outer lines might extend to 15 miles in length, thereby absorbing many thousands of men in both constructing and defending them.[15] By the late eighteenth century, as Clausewitz indicated, entrenching the besieging force, to protect it in this elaborate way, had become increasingly rare. Such methods would only be applied if the siege itself was the campaign's strategic objective, and, given the time required to dig long trenches, only if a 'fairly weak' enemy field army was not the campaign's strategic objective.[16]

States' ability to raise increasingly large armies and, after the Seven Years War, organize those armies into self-sufficient divisions meant that fortified towns could be besieged without needing to commit the entire strength of a warring country's field army to the task. By tying down a declining proportion of an invading state's manpower, besieged cities became less dominant, and often less important, strategic targets. Moreover, the conduct of siege operations became more efficient and speedier than it had been earlier in the eighteenth century. By the late eighteenth century, engineers were more widely accepted as soldiers, as distinct from mere supplementary technical experts, and there was a broader dissemination of technical training and knowledge among officers in general. Engineers' and artillerists' enhanced status meant that sieges could be left to subordinate commanders and senior technical officers rather than remaining, as they had been in the preceding 150 years, the central preoccupation of kings and commanders-in-chief.[17]

But the key shift remained Napoleon's focus on his enemies' main armies as the overriding objective in any campaign. Once such principal armies had been crushed, the expectation was that a political settlement would rapidly follow. Even if campaigning continued for a while, pockets of resistance would be mopped up or soon collapse. For example, in the Italian campaign of 1796, Bonaparte laid down a siege of the great fortified city of Mantua. This was a relatively straightforward task since Mantua is almost entirely surrounded by water and marsh. But the exigencies of the campaign pressed the French into trying to seize the city. They had no siege train and so gathered in 179 guns from captured Italian cities. A hurried assault failed on 17 July and they had to withdraw, abandoning the guns on 31 July in the face of major Austrian troop movements in the region. The siege was resumed by 10,000 troops in September, but Bonaparte concentrated with his main army upon Austrian relieving forces. Despite fighting en route, he failed to prevent them entering Mantua on 12 September. However, the siege bottled up perhaps 30,000 Austrian troops who lost increasingly large numbers to illness and starvation as the siege dragged on. Meanwhile Bonaparte won further victories – notably at Rivoli on 15–16 January 1797 – in campaigning against the Austrians elsewhere in the region. With the Austrian war effort sagging, the prospect of relief disappeared and Mantua surrendered on 2 February. The results of food shortages were so severe that only about 16,000 Austrians were able to march out of the city.[18] The siege of Mantua demonstrated how a significant strategic objective remained subordinate in Bonaparte's thinking to pursuing and defeating Austrian armies in the field. Subsidiary

French forces blockaded those Austrians in Mantua while the main campaigning and fighting occurred elsewhere.

A second example underscores this shift. During his campaign in Poland against Russia, Napoleon decided in February 1807 to prepare to besiege Danzig, both for the ample resources of food and other supplies which it held and because it was a major port in his enemies' hands. Marshal Lefebvre invested the city on 18 March and positioned his batteries by 24 April. The Russians tried to break the siege but a relief force was beaten back by the besiegers on 15 May. When the final French dispositions for a bombardment were completed, the Russians agreed to the French summons to discuss terms. On agreeing not to fight France and its allies for twelve months, the defenders were allowed to surrender with the honours of war on 27 May. Despite possessing 16,000 men, 303 guns and 46 howitzers and mortars, they chose to save the city from destruction and to keep their force in being. Napoleon wanted a quick solution since he needed the supplies in the city and the troops assigned to the siege for his main campaign. He advanced with 80,000 men to a stunning victory at Friedland on 14 June. This proved enough to pressure Alexander I to seek an armistice on 19 June.[19] The generous terms offered to the Danzig garrison probably eased the path to a wider settlement and clearly had no negative impact on the French, who ended the war far ahead of the twelve months' parole given to the garrison. Although the siege of Danzig differed from that of Mantua, the role it played was similar. Both sieges pinned down enemy forces and led the enemy to attempt to relieve the besieged garrisons. But in both cases Napoleon left siege operations to subordinates and conducted more fluid and dynamic campaigns against his enemy's main armies.

The same priorities applied when Napoleon was on the defensive in 1813. As the Continental allies prepared to invade France, their armies were so large that Napoleon had to concentrate his forces to oppose them. This meant, as General August Gneisenau informed Tsar Alexander in November 1813, that the estimated 100 to 140 fortresses surrounding France's eastern borders were an 'immeasurable burden'; Napoleon could not conceivably man them to anything approaching full strength. The allies, therefore, only had to march with overwhelming numbers into the midst of them and choose those which could not be defended to use as bases supporting their further advance.[20] Sieges formed no significant part of the allies' grand strategic plan for invading the most heavily fortified area in the world.

Given such developments and given scepticism about siege operations long predating the early nineteenth century and reiterated in it, historians have unsurprisingly paid limited attention to siege warfare in this period. Battles, with their displays of individual and collective heroism, determination and initiative on the one hand and haplessness, demoralization and incompetence on the other, were the trademark of Napoleonic warfare and have appealed far more to modern military historians than the undramatic process of building fortifications, operating siege weapons and managing the logistics of prolonged blockades.[21]

Yet despite contemporaries' and later military historians' fascination with the more dynamic aspects of war-fighting, siege operations continued to play a role in Napoleonic warfare. Gunther Rothenberg listed twenty-two 'selected sieges, assaults, blockades, 1792–1815' in his classic study, *The Art of Warfare in the Age of Napoleon* (1980). Although Rothenberg omitted San Sebastian, his list demonstrated that few sieges culminated in dramatic battles. Among his twenty-two, four towns surrendered when they were formally summoned to do so. Six surrendered after some resistance. Danzig, then in French hands, surrendered on 29 November 1813. Its people were starving after months of blockade and bombardment by the Russians, Prussians and, off the coast, the Royal Navy. Another two besieged garrisons were allowed a free evacuation. On three occasions a siege was lifted. Four towns survived blockade or siege, although the siege of Hamburg from 24 December 1813 to 12 May 1814 caused heavy losses for both the Russian besiegers and the French besieged. One town, Burgos, survived assault. Zaragoza was besieged twice in 1808–9 and surrendered only after intense fighting within the city itself. Gerona in 1809 also inflicted very heavy casualties on the French attackers. Defining a category for Zaragoza and Gerona is difficult because those towns surrendered only after prolonged fighting following assaults. Finally, of the twenty-two sieges listed by Rothenberg, only two were described as having been taken by assault and both – Ciudad Rodrigo and Badajoz – fell to Wellington in 1812.[22] Most sieges did not provide the dramatic or even uplifting outcome of 'decisive' battle. Even when they did, limited historical attention has been paid to them. Thus five of Rothenberg's twenty-two occurred during the Peninsular War and three of them – Zaragoza, Gerona and Badajoz – were among the most bloody of the whole period 1792–1815, with Zaragoza suffering more casualties than any other siege in Rothenberg's list. Yet such sieges have not been studied as a distinctive phenomenon of the war.

If Wellington operated in a military culture which did not prioritize siege warfare, the Peninsular War failed to conform to Napoleonic expectations because Spaniards resisted French conquest so widely and for so long. Between 1808 and 1813, the French conducted twenty sieges in the Iberian Peninsula, aimed mainly at pacification rather than at crushing Spanish field armies. From 1811, Wellington's forces undertook ten sieges, including three attempts upon Badajoz and two against San Sebastian; the others were directed against Ciudad Rodrigo, the Salamanca forts, Burgos, Pamplona and Bayonne. These fortified towns (with the exception of the minor Salamanca forts) were not strategic objectives in themselves, but had to be taken because they dominated essential lines of communication or because they held out as centres of French resistance.[23]

Criticisms of Wellington's Siege Operations

To secure those fortified towns, Wellington was obliged to commit his main army, which rarely numbered more than 60,000 troops. He had too few men to despatch separate corps to undertake sieges as sideshows, as the French did at Mantua and Danzig and when they assigned 44,500 soldiers to besiege Zaragoza in December 1808, while maintaining other large armies in operations farther afield.[24] Siege operations for Wellington detracted from the 'Light and Quick' approach which he had developed from his experience in India and which drove his campaigns from January 1812 to July 1813. During that short period he staged four sieges – of Ciudad Rodrigo, Badajoz,

Burgos and San Sebastian – which proved surprisingly problematic, bloody and controversial. Wellington's commitment to dynamic advances in Spain led him to press for the speedy resolution of sieges more typically associated with a more deliberate, if not ponderous, form of warfare.[25] Consequently, at the very time when his army's battlefield reputation rose, its siege operations provoked intense criticism. A final siege operation, against Bayonne in 1814, provided an embarrassing finale to Wellington's campaign in south-west Europe.

For the British, Wellington's campaigns provided plenty of battles to describe and assess. Wellington sought to outmanoeuvre or break French armies and assist Spanish resistance, not to gain territory per se. While he attacked towns when and where they impinged on his lines of advance and communication, he did not wage war in the Peninsula in order to conduct sieges. Such towns as he assailed were incidental to his broader strategic objectives. Moreover, the places besieged in 1812–14 were not defended by elaborate eighteenth-century fortifications. They were old walled towns with modern defensive components inserted into structures which pre-dated the rigorously geometrical defences developed from the mid-seventeenth century. This fact encouraged Wellington's optimistic belief that he could seize such towns without prolonged preparations.

His decisions to do so have been criticized on five counts. Together these critiques suggest that the conduct of sieges was a distinctly weak aspect of the British way of war in Continental Europe. Wellington's Judge Advocate General, Francis Larpent, despaired in July 1813, 'The French certainly understand sieges better, I think, than we do'.[26] First, it is claimed that Wellington engaged in sieges when the British lacked experience and expertise in that specialist form of warfare. Wellington's first, brief siege of Badajoz in June 1811 represented, according to Gunther Rothenberg, 'the first major siege operation undertaken by the British since 1793'.[27] This may have been true of campaigning in Europe, but the British had in fact conducted significant sieges farther afield. Wellington himself had served prominently at two major sieges in India, in 1799 and 1803, to which we will return later in this chapter.

If we go back a little before 1793, we find that the British were not quite as inexperienced in siege warfare as Rothenberg's comment implies. The prolonged and successful defence of Gibraltar in 1779–83 left a significant legacy. The siege of Gibraltar is now largely forgotten but remained in the collective memory in the 1810s. It provided a rare British success in the wider conflicts sparked by the American War of Independence. When Spain in 1779 joined France in warring upon Britain, its objective was not to promote American independence but to recover Gibraltar, which had been lost to Britain in the 1710s. Spain laid siege to the garrison town and eventually secured substantial French assistance to mount a prolonged naval blockade and to threaten and then stage a land assault. With France, the dominant European power of the eighteenth century, providing substantial naval and military support to the Spaniards, British defiance against the naval blockade and the military and naval assaults readily stimulated patriotic pride at the defenders' stoicism and courage.

The siege was strikingly memorialized in print and paintings. A full account of the siege was published by Captain John Drinkwater in 1785. Drinkwater volunteered for the 72nd Regiment, raised in 1777 in response to wartime manpower needs. Having served in Gibraltar throughout the siege, he devoted himself to writing up his detailed notes after his regiment was disbanded and he returned to England in 1783. The book went through four editions by 1789. Its reputation endured. In 1844, an obituary of Drinkwater in *Colburn's United Service Magazine*, aimed at a naval and military readership, described it as 'a graphic' history which 'attracted great attention on its appearance' and 'which has been long looked upon as a standard work in the military history of Great Britain'.[28]

The siege, prominently depicted in pictures and prints, also attracted much public interest during the ten years between its end and Britain's entry into the war against republican France. A print of one of the most important confrontations of the siege appeared as early as February 1783 and that year saw 'at least half a dozen pictures related to Gibraltar exhibited', notably at the Royal Academy's annual show. Two of the finest paintings proved very popular. In 1789, John Turnbull exhibited a canvas involving a dying Spanish officer refusing assistance from senior British officers. It was highly rated by *The Times*. The most celebrated depiction of the siege, by John Singleton Copley, was not completed until 1791. It was first exhibited in a large marquee in Green Park, where visitors paid 1 shilling each to view it; 60,000 were said to have done so. Copley's vast painting was then placed in a dominant position in the Common Council Chamber at Guildhall. There it was seen by all who attended meetings of the City of London's governing body, which commissioned the work.[29] In addition, four paintings of the siege done by George Paton in 1783 were donated in 1792 to be hung in the Council Chamber; the donor was the print publisher John Boydell, who had recently completed a term of office as Lord Mayor of London and had made a fortune from publishing engravings.[30]

Turnbull's and Copley's pictures were prominent, popular and painted with a purpose. Both depicted the British generously offering humane assistance to enemy soldiers and sailors wounded when Gibraltar's defences were assaulted, once by land and once across the bay of Algeciras. Such generosity was commemorated because the British held Gibraltar until the end of the war and suffered few casualties in the siege. They endured without rancour because the besieged were dramatically re-supplied in late 1779, April 1781 and October 1782. Transport ships – in 1781 nearly a hundred of them – were convoyed by powerful Royal Navy fleets which broke through the Franco-Spanish naval blockade.[31] All this created a reassuring mix for the British: although the besieged survived four years of privation, they suffered few casualties, were sustained by the Royal Navy and showed compassion in their treatment of the enemy. Such carefully crafted commemorations of British military and naval prowess helped boost a patriotism tempered by non-militaristic restraint.

Commemorating the siege was important in London's contested and often radical politics in the late eighteenth and early nineteenth centuries. The City of London – 'the square mile' – contained an extraordinary concentration of people by any contemporary yardstick, some 222,000 of them in 1801. One of its four MPs in 1813, Harvey Combe, opposed the government and supported Constitutional Reform. The neighbouring city of Westminster, with 158,000 people in 1801, returned Charles James Fox as one of its two MPs from 1780 until his death in 1806. Fox opposed the American war and the wars against France from 1793. The Westminster MPs in 1813 were Captain Lord Cochrane, RN, KB and Sir Francis Burdett, 5th Baronet. Cochrane constantly agitated against the Admiralty establishment and opposed 'internal warfare' in the Peninsula. (He eagerly advocated naval raids on the French and Spanish coasts, having enjoyed some success and even more celebrity in conducting some of them.) Burdett was an independent-minded radical, who often won Combe's support. He formally opposed the Peninsular War as late as February 1812. However strong their current support in the rest of the country might be in 1813, ministers could not ignore often critical and sometimes radical 'public opinion' in London.[32]

Disseminating images of British military and naval success, while playing down overt militarism, contributed to the necessary work of building public support for the war effort in the capital. In public image-building, therefore, the siege of Gibraltar provided a positive role-model. Moreover, the siege of Gibraltar contradicted Rothenberg's view of British inexperience in siege warfare. As this study of the siege of San Sebastian will demonstrate, the siege of Gibraltar – and not just selective images of it – was familiar to serving officers in the 1810s. Siege warfare was scarcely *terra incognita* to the British.

A second criticism more specifically highlighted the British lack of equipment for major siege operations in Europe. A leading American military historian, Russell Weigley, concluded:

> Wellington's army was never adequately stocked with the tools and skills of military engineering. It never possessed an adequate siege train, so that conducting sieges was always a more troublesome endeavour than it should have been, and it was partly for this reason that premature assaults occurred so often. . . . Amateurism and penny-pinching together conspired against the effectiveness of the army in its technical branches.[33]

This conclusion follows Charles Oman's dismissive views in his great history of the Peninsular War. The first brief attempt at Badajoz, in May 1811 – 'this mismanaged fragment of a siege' – was scarcely bettered by a more serious effort a few weeks later. The artillery for this second attempt 'was still utterly inadequate' and the engineers, 'few and unpractised in their art', selected wholly inappropriate targets for the assault.[34] Wellington repeatedly complained of the inadequacy of his ordnance. In January 1813, he informed Lord Bathurst, the Secretary of State for War and the Colonies, that his artillery allocation was 'lower than that of any army now acting in Europe . . . and below the scale which I have read of for an army of such numbers'.[35] Wellington could, therefore, be criticized for pushing ahead despite inadequate resources. The Victorian historian of the Royal Artillery concluded that the siege of Burgos was 'a blot on the military reputation' of Wellington, arising from 'an ignorance of what artillery could and could not do, which every now and then manifested itself in his military operations'.[36]

A third, related criticism claimed that by force of circumstance or military temperament the British did not have the appropriate mental attitude for prolonged siege operations. A junior engineer officer who had served for many years in India and the Peninsula asserted in 1829: 'A siege does not suit the temper of a British army. It is a slow tactic which they do not like; and that spirit which achieves such wonders in the open field, when it finds itself checked by stone walls, either evaporates in disappointment, or wastes itself in delay.'[37] One careful scholar of the Peninsular campaign concluded that 'The British had shown themselves inept and untrained in all their sieges, relying for success on the sheer courage of their men . . .'.[38] Huw Davies, in his stimulating re-appraisal of Wellington, argued that the siege of Burgos 'mainly failed because of Wellington's caution and reluctance to engage in sieges properly. . . . Wellington was . . . accruing a seriously poor record in siege warfare'. Influenced by criticism of the heavy casualties his army suffered in assaulting Badajoz, Wellington over-compensated by deploying too few troops in the action against Burgos, while failing to assemble an artillery battery adequate for the task.[39]

Whether or not national temperament shaped attitudes, the British faced very adverse odds in challenging the French in siege warfare. After all, the French had been planning and building fortresses and launching sieges on a scale unimaginable for the British since at least the late seventeenth century.

A fourth criticism of Wellington's sieges arose from British soldiers' conduct when they stormed into besieged towns. At the third and successful attempt on Badajoz, in April 1812, and at San Sebastian they engaged in unbridled plundering and committed atrocities against men, women and children. Oman stressed that 'the outrages of all kinds passed belief' at the former.[40] Charles Esdaile concluded after reviewing events at San Sebastian, 'What took place was simply a disgrace – a war crime indeed'.[41] The insistence that soldiers had the right of conquest if a town refused to surrender made it extremely difficult to police the behaviour of troops who had come through the horrors of assailing well-defended fortifications. The eighteenth-century desire to differentiate between soldiers and civilians clearly broke down completely in these contexts. Sieges thus affronted Enlightenment efforts to confine war-fighting as far as possible to professional armies.

A fifth criticism concerns the risks of fighting within a stormed town if the defenders refused to capitulate once a city's walls had been successfully assaulted. A densely packed urban environment was an even less manageable fighting space in the late eighteenth century and early nineteenth century than it is today. Soldiers of this period had no training in street fighting or house-to-house combat. Most soldiers were drilled only for battle. The Boston Tea Party of 1770 and the Gordon Riots of 1781 in London showed the dangers involved when troops policed city disturbances. The suppression of Wexford in 1798 during the Irish Rebellion highlighted the difficulties of more extreme military interventions.

Given such criticisms and reservations, it is not surprising that siege operations have attracted limited interest as an aspect of Britain's conduct of war during 1793–1815. A re-assessment of these diverse and long-standing criticisms is overdue.

Scientific Warfare and Officer Professionalism

In conducting the campaigns of 1812–13 and in undertaking four sieges, Wellington had to manage diverse and complex operations which cast significant light on two of the five criticisms of his decision-making which have been noted. Those two criticisms concerned the British army's capability in the more distinctly scientific branches of war-fighting and the British officer corps' ability to deal professionally with the challenges of specialist operations.

The creation from the late sixteenth century of ever more elaborate defensive fortifications inevitably involved detailed and expanding scientific work. Cartography and surveying, the use of mathematics, the calculation of the range and impact of cannon fire, the intricate planning of defensive walls and street lay-outs, and the emergence of the engineer were all facets of the development of fortified cities.[42] Besieging such cities naturally demanded increasing attention to heavy artillery and the guns' calibre, range and resilience as well as to the construction of complex approach parallels and the management of manpower in a suddenly expanded diversity of tasks.

Yet the four sieges Wellington undertook in 1812–13 exposed him to charges that he had inadequate siege trains poorly prepared for the challenges of scientific siege operations. This impression that Wellington lacked awareness of scientific approaches to sieges or the ability to manage specialist operations runs counter to the fact that he had participated in logistically challenging sieges.

The attack in 1799 on Seringapatam, Mysore's capital, was Wellington's second exposure to war-fighting, following his posting to Flanders in 1794–5. Seringapatam was the capital of the kingdom of Mysore, in southern India. The state had been taken over in the 1760s by Haidar Ali who created a strong modern army and attacked the British-held territory of Madras in the 1780s, threatening on one occasion to seize the port of Madras itself. His son and successor, Tipu Sultan, was widely demonized in Britain by the late 1790s as an aggressive expansionist who had seriously mistreated British prisoners of war. The British mounted elaborately organized invasions of Mysore twice in 1790–2 and again in in 1799. The siege of 1799 was brief and ended with the storming of the city's walls and Tipu Sultan's death. The campaign was celebrated as a well-executed act of retribution which removed a vicious and long-standing enemy.

The campaign against Seringapatam was warmly and variously celebrated. A public report of 1 March 1799 predicted that the city would be taken within two months and an account published in 1800 declared that 'No contingency . . . which human wisdom could foresee, or human care and diligence could provide for, was neglected in the various and complicated arrangements made for the success of this important enterprize'.[43] When George III presided at the state opening of Parliament in September, news of Seringapatam's fall was only ten days old in London. Ministers used that victory, together with allied successes in Italy and the United Provinces and the impending parliamentary union with Ireland, to give an optimistic up-date on their conduct of the war. At the same time, Sadler's Wells staged a new play, *The Tyrant of India or Tipoo Sultan*.[44] Attention was sustained with reports on how the East India

Company's revenues would be boosted by the territorial gains made, on tales of daring at the storming of the city, and on the division of fabulous items taken as prize worth in all £1 million.[45] The enduring collective British memory of Seringapatam's downfall was suggested in 1829, when the author of an extensive military memoir commented that 'most of my readers have doubtless perused the histories of the wars of Hyder and Tippoo'.[46]

The key to success at Seringapatam lay in the logistical operation which underpinned the offensive. The expedition started in February from the Madras presidency and involved 36,000 troops under the East India Company, later joined by nearly 10,000 allied troops provided by the Nizam of Hyderabad. The British invaders brought with them 40 siege guns, 57 light field guns and 7 howitzers, with nearly 53,000 shot. Depots of grain, notably rice, were established in the rear to supply 40,000 men for 182 days.[47] Despite Hew Strachan's conclusion that 'In India, sieges were undertaken in a somewhat cavalier fashion', some sieges in the sub-continent were major operations.[48] In a thoroughly methodical manner, the British began their trenches at 750yd from the town's walls and dug more trenches at 400yd, approaching their target by cautious stages. The bombardment of the guns and infantry on the walls, as distinct from the breach, took days, but did not require the use of heavy artillery. A great deal of work had been done to extend and improve the fortifications after 1792, but that work concentrated on the north, north-west and east of the perimeter. The British changed their direction of attack from the northerly approach used in 1791–2 and advanced from the west to the defenders' 'surprise and disappointment'. The assault on the breach progressed quickly in the face of limited artillery fire from the defenders.[49] All this was familiar to Wellington who commanded in the trenches in the siege and, as a colonel, had charge of three battalions in reserve when the assault was launched.

During his dynamic campaign of 1803 in central India, Wellington besieged and stormed Gawilgarh (Gwalighur), a fortress held by one of the leading Maratha princes, the raja of Berar. The fortress has been described as resembling a figure 8 with the southern end built on a high and steep escarpment and the northern end being the only accessible part, linked by an isthmus to high tableland. The defensive walls across the isthmus and at the junction of the two portions of the fortress were 'strong and high, and well flanked with towers'. When Wellington's engineer officer, Captain Johnstone, and John Blakiston, an artillery officer, decided to reconnoitre the northern wall, they needed 'two days of hard marching' to reach it from the plain below. Their advance was delayed by a road 'extremely rugged and difficult, in many places not more than a footpath, and at the same time very circuitous'. Wellington decided that this northern wall would be the main objective. According to Blakiston, 20 miles of road had to be built by the army's pioneers in order to haul artillery to the northern entrance. The ground in front of the entrance was level enough to allow trenches to be dug. The batteries opened fire on the walls on 13 November, but could not create a breach until three days later. By then guns had also been dragged up a steep hill to the south of the fort to lay down diversionary fire which began on 15 November. The assault occurred at 10.00 a.m. on the 17th, with two feints accompanying the main northern attack. The breach was readily gained but there was some fierce fighting within the fortress.[50] Blakiston attributed victory in part to the campaign-hardened superiority of the British troops in India, and the unequalled application, as well as high ability, shown by Johnstone. In general, Blakiston concluded 'of the officers of the Indian army generally, whether of the King's or Company's service, that in no part of the world . . . have I witnessed so much zeal in their professional duties as is displayed by them'.[51]

These two sieges demonstrated that British armies in India could plan and conduct sieges at considerable distances from their bases and launch carefully prepared final assaults. But transferring this expertise to European warfare entailed two difficulties. Siege operations were labour-intensive and success in India partly depended on access to plentiful labour supplies; clearing 20 miles of passable road was no light task. Were such resources similarly available in Europe? Secondly, when a city was stormed there were four layers of defence: the walls themselves; the breaches and the lines behind them; the streets and buildings inside the walled town or city; and a fort or castle for the garrison within the city. The defenders at Seringapatam and Gawilgarh resisted at the walls and inside the city, but seem to have offered limited defence-in-depth of the breaches and the areas immediately behind them. Were the French likely to replicate that omission?

The Military Revolution and the Management of Armies

If sieges continued to pose challenges in this period of rapid transformation in war-fighting, they also raised questions about the effective management of armies and their operations. The French Revolutionary and Napoleonic wars have typically been treated as a transition phase in European warfare. Over the centuries, mediaeval warfare, very often conducted through long sieges of fortified towns and strategically placed castles, was transformed by the application of gunpowder and the development of artillery. Open battle steadily, during the seventeenth century and in the eighteenth century, displaced siege operations as the decisive aspect of warfare. It was often claimed that the expansion of artillery added enormously to the costs of warfare and therefore to the pressures on states to expand revenues required for war. In fact, the greatly increased cost of war in the eighteenth century resulted from the growing size of armies. Armies grew even more dramatically in size in the 1790s and 1800s. This development depended upon the expanded mobilization of civilians into armies, increasing state acquisition of the necessary resources for war, and the articulation of ideological and nationalistic rhetoric to arouse mass public commitment and to demonize an enemy. The growing size of armies and the extending scope and scale of military operations from the early 1790s has led to the claim that the period 1792–1815 saw the origins of 'total war'. This emphasis on total war highlights changes in the period which led to or foreshadowed future developments, but military historians have been sharply divided over the extent to which total war describes states' control over their societies and their resources in these years.[52]

There is a continuing debate between those who see mass mobilization and ideological polarization as the key stimuli to the emergence of modern war and those who see the critical developments of the period in the growing size of armies, the increasing speed and geographical spread of campaigning, and the scale of battles fought. Both sides, however, tend to overlook the organizational consequences of the changes they highlight. The mass mobilization of societies for war required the extension of state authority and control over people and resources. That in turn depended not simply upon ideological fervour but more importantly upon significant improvements in bureaucratic efficiency. Such improvements occurred in Britain, but they were hard-won.[53] Moreover, the new intensity, frequency and widespread nature of campaigning and the political expectations that decisive battles would be fought and won required the improved management of armies.

The importance of effective military management in this apparently transformative period has typically been overlooked. The reasons for such oversight are three-fold. First, non-military historians have been excited by the ideological and political implications of the expanded scope and scale of Revolutionary and Napoleonic warfare. Historians of ideas and popular culture see participation in and enthusiasm for mass mobilization as the main characteristics of this new age of 'total war'. Secondly, military and naval historians have often concentrated on charismatic leadership as the key factor in galvanizing and channelling this spirit of mass popular involvement in and support for extended warfare. The management of armies was not supported by grand strategic theory in the early nineteenth century. Brian Bond has succinctly assessed the impact of Jomini and Clausewitz by stressing how Jomini saw victory in war flowing from the pursuit of clear strategic precepts, especially concerning 'lines of operation'. Clausewitz was less rigid in operational precepts, but proclaimed the overriding importance of seeking decisive battle against an enemy's army and concentrating forces to that end.[54] While describing how a commander set the direction in which his army moved and the objectives which it pursued, neither Jomini nor Clausewitz gave much weight to the management of armies as diverse and potentially highly unstable organizations. Instead, successful generals focused on bringing their opponents to battle and inspired their men to follow them through their ability to envisage and organize a rapid campaign and their boldness and courage in bringing that campaign to its culminating point in battle. The Jacobins' mass mobilization in 1793, Napoleon during much of his career and the use of Nelson as symbol and model – 'the Nelson touch' – were the most obvious examples of this style of leadership.

Thirdly, military management for historians typically becomes a matter of organizational structures or of resolving disputes among hot-blooded or strong-willed subordinates and rivals. Dennis Showalter reminds us that more general military management was weak: 'eighteenth-century armies had to fight with an underdeveloped nervous system. . . . Even brigades were frequently improvised from operation to operation. Higher formations were entirely *ad hoc*'.[55] Napoleon, of course, worked hard to fill this organizational gap. Taking as his base the C3 notion of command, control and communication, Martin van Creveld describes how Napoleon organized large and interlocking staff systems to co-ordinate his corps within the imperial army. He explains how the system worked in directing the army on campaign.[56] But staff systems, while vital in positioning the imperial army, did not manage armies on the ground, which is where, ultimately, they have to be effective. No one studying this period will be left in doubt that the vastly enlarged French armies benefitted from Napoleon's innovative organization of army corps. But to stress the vital significance of that initiative does not exhaust the matter.

Trying to assess the management of British armies in this period is bedevilled by the default assumption that the British army was 'managed', if that is the appropriate word, mainly by amateurs. For example, the French General, Foy, a very experienced Peninsula veteran, provided in the mid-1820s a lengthy assessment of the British army's recent achievements and character. He argued that it was unique and praiseworthy in 'its deference to the power of the law', but flawed in its refusal to regard war as a highly complex challenge. Admittedly, the infantry were exceptionally brave and fiercely determined in battle, and NCOs were excellent. But military effectiveness typically depended upon stern discipline rather than widely disseminated skills; 'The English soldier is stupid and intemperate'.[57] According to Foy, the British viewed their army as a necessary evil and only began to train their junior officers in the midst of the long wars of 1793–1815. Some staff work impressed, but the typical divisional commander in the Peninsula, in contrast to his hard-working French counterpart, 'divided his time between hunting, horse exercise, and the pleasures of the table'. The specialist officers compared unfavourably with their French equivalents. Artillery officers had a far narrower range of expertise and responsibilities and in the Peninsula 'have shown their want of skill in the attack of strong places'.[58] Royal Engineer officers were 'inferior in theory and practice to those who exercise the same profession elsewhere'. Given the absence of modern fortifications in Britain, 'It is not unreasonable to suppose that engineers who never build fortresses, and who never even see any, have nearly the same knowledge of fortification that sailors would have of naval tactics who had never seen the sea.'[59] These reflections were recorded before Foy died in 1825. He had been elected to the Chamber of Deputies 1819 and had good reasons to play down the British army's competence. The French in 1823 sent 100,000 troops into Spain to restore Fernando VII's absolutism. This intervention and flexing of French military muscles met strong opposition in the British press and Parliament, and the possibility of British involvement was canvassed. Although Foy objected to French action, he also asserted that British military interventions in Continental Europe posed no threat. The British public would not stomach the high costs customarily incurred in sending an army overseas and recruiting significant numbers of soldiers was always difficult. Britain would at best field only a small army, which would depend upon supply and re-supply by sea and prove incapable of speedy operations and indeed any major operations at a distance from the coast.[60] Foy thus proclaimed politically liberal principles while remaining patriotically French. It was doubly comforting that the British distrusted militarism and that any armies they raised for Continental service were small and not particularly talented.

Claims such as Foy's have long influenced serious historians. The French historian Elie Halévy, introducing his monumental account of nineteenth-century Britain, argued in 1913 that the army's 'defective organization' and lack of disciplined professionalism meant that it posed no threat to the 'the nation's traditional liberties'. 'The English officer was a man of fashion, who regarded war as a sport, not a science.'[61] According to S.G. Checkland, a leading economic and social historian, in 1964, the British ruling classes viewed war as 'an amateur game, a matter for lords and gentlemen, not very different, though on a grander scale, from the duel. Men and their spirit meant more than arms and technology'.[62]

Military historians have been less dismissive, but not exactly flattering. In the 1970s, Michael Howard depicted a somewhat ossified officer corps possessing few reforming leaders whose work was largely thwarted by Wellington's influence over the army.[63] At the same time, Gunther Rothenberg claimed that the British army's improved performance from its dire position in 1793 was 'all the more remarkable because it essentially retained its eighteenth century character. Officers were neither skilled professionals nor, with rare exception, dedicated idealists'.[64] Alessandro Barbaro, in his wide-ranging study of Waterloo, referred to 'the plodding management and slowness of movement that characterized British troops'. Cavalry officers remain favourite exemplars of the national military malaise. With them in mind, Barbaro concluded, 'To the defect of experience, the British officers added an educational background and a value system in which competence and professionalism did not receive pride of place'.[65] Alan Forrest has concluded in 2015 that Waterloo confirmed widespread complacency about 'officer-training and military education, where the very success of Wellington's army tended to become an excuse for . . . opposing any moves towards greater professionalization of the officer class'.[66] While there have been notable dissents from this view, and some fine studies of the growth of staff work, doubts about the professional competence of the British officer corps have proved exceptionally durable.

One problem is that professionalization is an ambiguous concept when applied to the late eighteenth and early nineteenth centuries. Clergymen, lawyers and medical doctors constituted the principal professional callings in this period. The requirement to meet specified educational standards applied to each, but they were not standardized or exclusionary. Barristers, for example, had to fulfil strictly defined, though not academic, criteria, but solicitors did not. Going beyond those established professions, the role played by formal education in manufacturing, where Britain became a world leader in this period, offers an interesting parallel to the place of scientific training in the army. Britain from the mid-eighteenth century was an industrializing country in which innovation in manufacturing and transport accelerated. Was it therefore a society in which Enlightenment thinking and scientific research inspired and spun out into technological developments and applications?

In fact, the manufacturing sector, like the army, did not uniformly develop through the application of scientific methods. While many of the great industrial inventors of the period 1660–1800 were indeed men who acquired formal scientific and technical knowledge, at least half of them had no links with formal learning. What distinguished the whole range of inventors, including those with scientific connections, was their direct involvement in experimentation. In particular, inventors in the metal trades advanced by trial and error in practical applications, not through scientific training or connections. The military preference for learning by serving and observing paralleled the ways in which so many British industrialists and manufacturers depended on deduction and instruction in the workplace rather than in the lecture-hall or laboratory. Artillery technology in particular was related to a branch of manufacturing, the metal trades, which were the least linked to formal learning.[67] This fact makes an understanding of the human role in the adoption and application of new technologies more complicated; as Don Leggatt has stressed for the introduction of new technologies in the Royal Navy, the influence and effectiveness of experts requires as much attention as the impact of technological developments themselves.[68]

We tend to see the rise of the expert and the spread of professional or scientific expertise and identity as indications of progress and modernity. But the growth of professions and the role of military experts were not straightforward in this period. Professional groups could be hide-bound, inward-looking and protective of their special interests. The development of professional status could lead simply to the creation of separate bureaucratic bodies filled with aggrandising specialists.[69] The growth of military engineering by the 1780s meant, for Christopher Duffy, that 'the new race of pedants and careerists had devised a "science" of engineering which seemed to outsiders at the same time unapproachable and unchallenging'.[70]

Important operational consequences flowed from the mental and organizational silos experts built for themselves. Siege warfare had been depicted from the mid-seventeenth century as a form of warfare especially liable to control, routine, rigorous timing and predictable outcomes. All aspects of it were subjected to repeated attempts at detailed measurement and calibration. For example, the slopes and thickness of defensive walls shaped the nature of any bombardment. Ideally for defenders, they would be impenetrable to cannonballs. But if they were too thick they restricted the use of defensive guns. On the other hand, wide and shallow apertures for the defenders' guns exposed a fortress's artillerymen to enemy fire. Besiegers for their part had to calculate the position of their artillery in order to neutralize the town guns without being dangerously exposed to those same guns' counter-fire.[71]

But what happened in practice demonstrated that scientific and technical expertise co-existed with experience-driven systems for transporting ordnance, supplying munitions, digging trenches, positioning batteries, suppressing enemy artillery defences and overcoming breaches. Well-developed scientific approaches had to be applied in conditions where technical exactitude often proved elusive. Engineer officers, unsurprisingly, did not agree on how regulated procedures should be applied in practice. Strategic principles, scientific techniques and the range of specialisms spanning transport, light artillery, heavy artillery, siege works, sapping, infantry tactics and the role of cavalry formed distinctive if closely inter-related elements in the organization of an effective siege operation. All these elements had to be co-ordinated and managed.

The campaigns in 1812–14 highlighted the difficulties Wellington faced. He did not command the military resources of a great state. The armies under his direct control were relatively small by Napoleonic standards. He did not have reserves of efficient troops to detach for independent siege operations against targeted towns. The troops undertaking sieges in 1812–14 constituted his main army, or component parts of that army continuing to work in tandem with the other divisions within it. The only exception was late in the campaign when a Spanish army was deployed to blockade Pamplona. The organization of Wellington's army in the field had become more formal by stages, with administrative structures still relatively recent in origin, mostly going back no further than 1809. Even so, much administration remained expedient and improvised, with senior officers having to adapt to rapidly changing circumstances.

Such improvisation was reinforced by two factors related to national identity and experience. First, the British did not feel that they had access in Iberia to responsive administrative or military infrastructures. British officers overwhelmingly concluded that the people of the Peninsula lacked the energy, efficiency and sense of national purpose which distinguished peoples living north of the Pyrenees. The Peninsula's natural resources were frequently admired, but their exploitation was regarded as lamentable.[72] Given his own deeply conservative social views, Wellington could scarcely criticize the Spanish class system for the shortcomings of regionally based armies mainly led by local landowners and aristocrats. He preferred to blame the liberals in the Regency government at Cádiz for failing to create an efficient army and to advance a clear national agenda dedicated to fighting the war.[73] Secondly, this critique of especially Spanish political and military failings in 1813 fed more generally among British officers and men into respect for French efficiency. As Gavin Daly has pointed out, British officers who opposed French rule in Spain conceded that it might be the only means of modernizing the country. The nearer the British approached to the French border with Spain, the more they felt they were about to enter a different and better world.[74] The challenge of running a large army on campaign was therefore compounded by uncertainties about the reliability of Britain's close allies and an awareness of French administrative drive and effectiveness. Moreover, in launching siege operations the British faced opponents who had led the development of modern fortifications and siege warfare since the seventeenth century.

In these circumstances, the management of the allied army under Wellington's direct command was particularly important. The word management is deliberate. One subaltern praised the 'truly admirable' conduct of all those involved at the climax of the siege of San Sebastian, but concluded also that 'we do not manage sieges well'.[75] The skills of military high command are varied and sometimes elusive, involving as they do charisma, leadership, risk-taking, personal courage, political credibility, resilience, decisiveness, tactical alertness and strategic insight. The list could be extended. The study of British armies in battle during this period readily generates examples of incompetence and blundering, but also ample evidence of charismatic and effective leadership. One purpose of this study, however, is to emphasize, first, that an army is not simply formed or forged as an instrument of military power, to be commanded as a defined entity with fixed characteristics or capabilities, and, secondly, that more attention needs to be paid to the management of an army's material and manpower resources in any given campaign.

Armies' volatility and campaigning's uncertainties required the effective handling of soldiers' individual and collective fears and expectations as well as their drilled responses. Armies were made up mainly of young men governed by wildly differing motives and impulses, displaying energy or indifference, headstrong courage or cynical risk-avoidance, warmed by comradeship or insulated by self-interest, driven by pride or riven with resentments, inspired by notions of honour or inhibited by fear of injury, intent on mastering their military trade or content to follow the drill-book. Attitudes and behaviour changed with circumstances, and the motivations and emotions of individuals influenced the mood and morale of an army. Armies' cohesion and capacity to march and fight were volatile because they were (and are) psychologically labile organizations and managing an army was (and remains) a demanding business. One theme of this study is, therefore, that the management of armies on campaign remains an important but elusive aspect of the history of warfare.

By briefly considering the British conduct of the three sieges of 1812 and by evaluating the conduct of the siege of San Sebastian in detail, this study will consider whether Wellington had a serious problem with siege operations. The siege will be analysed as part of a fluid and unpredictable campaign notable for the uncertain relationship between military planning, setting strategic objectives and maintaining an army's momentum and morale. The campaign and the significant sieges it involved also tested the army's logistical support and impact on local civilians. John Lynn has reminded us of the important distinction between war-as-event and war-as-process, that is, between battles and campaigns, the latter encompassing the inputs which shaped campaigns.[76] This study re-assesses the siege of San Sebastian as part of the campaign after Vitoria and of Wellington's management of his army in this final phase of the Peninsular War.

Notes

1. Edward Sabine (ed.), *Letters of Colonel Sir Augustus Simon Frazer, K.C.B.* (Uckfield, 2001 repr.), 243–4.
2. Wellington to Bentinck, 20 July 1813, Lieutenant Colonel Gurwood (ed.), *The Dispatches of Field Marshal the Duke of Wellington*, 12 vols (London, 1838) (hereafter abbreviated as *WD*), x, 553.
3. John A. Lynn, *The Wars of Louis XIV 1667–1714* (Harlow, 1999), 3, 75–8.
4. Christopher Duffy, *The Fortress in the Age of Vauban and Frederick the Great 1660–1789*, 2 vols, Vol. ii, *Siege Warfare* (London, 1985), 71, 85–94.
5. David Chandler, *The Campaigns of Napoleon* (London, 1966), 89, 121, 141–5; Rory Muir, *Tactics and the Experience of Battle in the Age of Napoleon* (New Haven CT, 1998); Bruno Colson, *Napoleon on War* (Oxford, 2015).
6. Donald D. Horward, *Napoleon and Iberia; The Twin Sieges of Ciudad Rodrigo and Almeida, 1810* (London, 1994 repr.), 80.
7. Sun Tzu, *The Art of War*, trans. and with an introduction by Samuel B. Griffith (Oxford, 1963), 73, 78–9.
8. Carl von Clausewitz, *On War*, ed. and trans. Michael Howard and Peter Paret (Princeton NJ, 1989), 551–2, 599.
9. Clausewitz, *On War*, 395–9.
10. Derek Beales, *Joseph II: II Against the World, 1780–1790* (Cambridge, 2009), 142, 165, 373–4.
11. Duffy, *The Fortress in the Age of Vauban and Frederick the Great*, ii, 292–3.
12. Janis Langins, *Conserving the Enlightenment. French Military Engineering from Vauban to the*

Revolution (Cambridge MA, 2004), 131, 451.

13. General Foy, *History of the War in the Peninsula under Napoleon*, 2 vols (London, 1827), i, 105.

14. Paddy Griffith, *The art of war of revolutionary France, 1789–1802* (London, 1998*)*, 248–51; Gunther E. Rothenberg, *The art of warfare in the age of Napoleon* (Bloomington IN, 1980), 40–1, 218–19; Donald D. Horward, 'Napoleon and the mighty fortresses of Europe', in R. Caldwell, D. Horward et al. (eds), *The consortium on revolutionary Europe 1750–1850: selected papers 1994* (Tallahassee FL, 1994), 306–14.

15. Lynn, *The Wars of Louis XIV*, 76, 224–6.

16. Clausewitz, *On War*, 403, 551–3.

17. Duffy, *The Fortress in the Age of Vauban and Frederick the Great*, ii, 294–5; Langins, *Conserving the Enlightenment*, 122–35.

18. Chandler, *The Campaigns of Napoleon*, 87, 92, 96–9, 120–1.

19. Chandler, *The Campaigns of Napoleon*, 560–4, 576, 582–3.

20. Gneisenau to Alexander, 7, 13 November 1813, Michael V. Leggiere, *The Fall of Napoleon: Volume 1 The Allied Invasion of France, 1813–1814* (Cambridge, 2007), 558, 561.

21. Bernard S. Bachrach,'Medieval Siege Warfare. A Reconnaissance', *Journal of Military History*, 58 (1994), 119–33.

22. Rothenberg, *The art of warfare*, 254–5.

23. Philip Haythornthwaite, 'Sieges in the Peninsular War' and 'A List of Peninsular War Sieges', in Paddy Griffith (ed.), *A History of the Peninsular War: Volume IX* (London, 1999), 213–29, 419–23.

24. Charles Oman, *A History of the Peninsular War*, 7 vols (London, 1900–30).

25. Huw J. Davies, *Wellington's Wars. The Making of a Military Genius* (New Haven CT, 2012), 249–52.

26. Sir George Larpent (ed.), *The Private Journal of F. S. Larpent, Esq, Judge Advocate General of the British Forces in the Peninsula*, 3 vols (London, 1853), ii, 10.

27. Rothenberg, *The art of warfare*, 221; some points made here were first aired in Bruce Collins, 'Siege Warfare in the Age of Wellington', in C.M. Woolgar (ed.), *Wellington Studies IV* (University of Southampton, 2008), 22–53.

28. *Colburn's United Service Magazine*, 1844, Part I, 438–9.

29. Peter Harrington, *British Artists and War: The Face of Battle in Paintings and Prints, 1700–1914* (London, 1993), 45–7, 50–4.

30. Vivienne Painting, *John Boydell* (London, 2005), 15–17, 22–3.

31. J.W. Fortescue, *A History of the British Army*, 13 vols (London, 1900–30), iii, 299, 345, 417.

32. R.G. Thorne, *The House of Commons 1790–1820*, 5 vols (London, 1986), ii, 263, 266–7; iii, 93, 302, 308–9, 463–4, 488–9, 545; v, 133–4.

33. Russell F. Weigley, *The Age of Battles: the Quest for Decisive Warfare from Breitenfeld to Waterloo* (London, 1991), 487, 500.

34. Oman, *A History of the Peninsular War*, iv, 287, 417.

35. Wellington to Bathurst, 27 January 1813, WD, x, 48.

36. Captain Francis Duncan, *History of the Royal Regiment of Artillery*, 2 vols (London, 1872–3), ii, 335.

37. Anon. [Blakiston], *Twelve Years' Military Adventure in Three Quarters of the Globe*, 2 vols (London, 1829), ii, 271.

38. W.F.K. Thompson (ed.), *An Ensign in the Peninsular War: the letters of John Aitchison* (London, 1981), 253.

39. Davies, *Wellington's Wars* , 165–6.

40. Oman, *A History of the Peninsular War*, v, 257.

41. Charles Esdaile, *The Peninsular War. A New History* (London, 2002), 470; also 386–7, 468–9.

42. Martha D. Pollak, *Turin 1564–1680: Urban Design, Military Culture, and the Creation of the Absolutist Capital* (Chicago IL, 1991), 19–30, 217–21.

43. *The Times*, 22 July 1799; Alexander Beatson, *A View of the Origin and Conduct of the War with Tippoo Sultaun* (London, 1800), 173–4.

44. *The Times*, 14, 25, 26 September 1799.

45. *The Times*, 17 September, 12, 13 December 1799.

46. Anon. [Blakiston], *Twelve Years' Military Adventure*, 98.

47. Beatson, *A View of the Origin and Conduct of the War*, cxix–cxx, 174.

48. Hew Strachan, *From Waterloo to Balaclava: Tactics, Technology, and the British army, 1815–1854* (Cambridge, 1985), 131.

49. Beatson, *A View of the Origin and Conduct of the War*, 99, 103, 107, 115–19, 125–8, 169–72.

50. Anon. [Blakiston], *Twelve Years' Military Adventure*, i, 213, 219–23, 225–6.

51. Anon. [Blakiston], *Twelve Years' Military Adventure*, i, 232–3.

52. See the excellent essays: Roger Chickering, 'Introduction: A Tale of Two Tales: Grand Narratives of War in the Age of Revolution'; Azar Gat, 'What Constituted the Military Revolution of the Early Modern Period?'; Ute Planert, 'Innovation or Evolution? The French Wars in Military History', in Roger Chickering and Stig Forster (eds), *War in an Age of Revolution, 1775–1815* (Cambridge, 2010), 1–17, 21–48, 69–84. See also: Geoff Mortimer, 'Introduction' and Alan Forrest, 'The French Revolutionary and Napoleonic Wars', in Geoff Mortimer (ed.), *Early Modern Military History 1450–1815* (Houndsmills, 2004), 1–5, 196–211.

53. Roger Knight, *Britain Against Napoleon: the Organization of Victory 1793–1815* (London, 2013).

54. Brian Bond, *The Pursuit of Victory from Napoleon to Saddam Hussein* (Oxford, 1996), 44–7, 52–6.

55. Dennis E. Showalter, *The Wars of Frederick the Great* (Harlow, 1996), 7–8.

56. Martin van Creveld, *Command in War* (Cambridge MA, 1985), 1, 62–78.

57. Foy, *History of the War*, i, 149, 157–8, 163, 178–9, 196.

58. Foy, *History of the War*, i, 146, 164, 177–8, 204.

59. Foy, *History of the War*, i, 207.

60. Foy, *History of the War*, i, 211, 214, 219–21, 224.

61. Elie Halevy, *England in 1815*, trans. E.I. Watkin and D.A. Barker (London, 1961 edn), 84, 94–5.

62. S.G. Checkland, *The Rise of Industrial Society in England, 1815–1885* (London, 1964), 285.

63. Michael Howard, *War in European History* (Oxford, 1976), 88–9.

64. Rothenberg, *The art of warfare*, 174.

65. Alessandro Barbaro, *The Battle. A History of the Battle of Waterloo* (London, 2006 edn), 186, 389–90.

66. Alan Forrest, *Great Battles. Waterloo* (Oxford, 2015), 128.

67. Robert C. Lewis, *The British Industrial Revolution in Global Perspective* (Cambridge, 2009), 242–57.

68. Don Leggatt, *Shaping the Royal Navy: Technology, authority and naval architecture, c1830–1906* (Manchester, 2015), 5–8.

69. Langins, *Conserving the Enlightenment*.

70. Duffy, *The Fortress in the Age of Vauban and Frederick the Great*, ii, 294–5.

71. Langins, *Conserving the Enlightenment*, 341, 350–1, 366, 369.

72. Gavin Daly, *The British Soldier in the Peninsular War: Encounters with Spain and Portugal, 1808–1814* (Houndsmill, 2013), 215–18.

73. Wellington to Bathurst, 5 September, 21 November 1813, *WD*, xi, 88–91, 306.

74. Daly, *The British Soldier*, 212–13, 218.

75. Thompson (ed.), *An Ensign in the Peninsular War* , 260.

76. Lynn, *The Wars of Louis XIV*, 367, 375–6.

Chapter 2

Wellington's Sieges in 1812

Introduction

The sieges of Ciudad Rodrigo and Badajoz and the failure of the month-long siege of Burgos highlighted tensions between scientific and traditional approaches to war and challenges in managing the army and its operations. Gunther Rothenburg noted that the sieges were costly and 'troubled by recriminations'; worse, 'success was compromised by atrocities that were a stain on the reputation of Wellington's normally well-disciplined army'.[1] Rory Muir has indicated that Wellington should have acted more quickly on 7 April to quell the disorder in Badajoz and that the grim casualties at the storming of the breaches lead to 'the impression that the siege might have been conducted more skilfully'.[2] General Sir Harry Smith, who fought in many battles across the empire from the 1810s to the 1840s, lamented of the appalling fighting and unspeakable atrocities at Badajoz that 'There is no battle, day or night, I would not willingly re[-]act except this'.[3] In 1871, when the siege of Paris briefly drew attention to historical sieges, one magazine noted that the 'disgraceful' excesses in Ciudad Rodrigo were later capped by 'the atrocities of an ungovernable army' at Badajoz.[4] Charles Oman, writing after the controversies over British treatment of Boer civilians in 1901–2, offered some mitigation for the violence at Badajoz in April 1812 by stressing that the French committed still greater excesses, and noting the long tradition of sacking towns which refused to capitulate when summoned to do so.[5]

If Badajoz was bad, the failed Burgos campaign was worse. According to one leading participant, the failure gave a life-line to the French; 'a beaten enemy gained time to recruit his forces, concentrate his scattered armies, and regain the ascendancy'.[6] In 1873, the official historian of the Royal Artillery, Francis Duncan, felt it had been 'a blot' on Wellington's military reputation.[7] David Gates described the campaign as 'a tragic farce' which 'served no useful purpose'.[8] John Keegan argued that gunpowder transformed sieges, making the creation of breaches far easier but rendering 'the assault on the breach an affair of horror'. All Wellington's Spanish sieges, but especially Badajoz and San Sebastian, inflicted 'appalling' casualties. His 'Peninsular battles, by contrast, were almost methodical affairs'.[9] In his forensic and generally favourable reassessment of Wellington's military genius, Huw Davies has qualified his overall judgement with the reservation that, by the end of 1812, 'Wellington was . . . accruing a seriously poor record in siege warfare'.[10]

Such assessments contradict claims that siege warfare was amenable to scientific management. Sir John Jones, the leading Royal Engineer of the early nineteenth century, emphasized the dual nature of sieges. In terms of fighting, 'A siege is one of the most arduous undertakings on which troops can be employed, . . . one in which the prize can only be gained by complete victory, and where failure is usually attended with severe loss or dire disaster'. For governments, it was therefore vital that 'sieges should be carried on in the best possible manner, that is, by a due union of science, labour, and force'. Since 'scientific perfection in carrying on sieges' was 'in great measure the result of superior wealth and civilization', European siege warfare over the previous two centuries had become more dependent on 'combination and expenditure than on individual exertion or heroism'.[11] Thus eighteenth-century practice had prioritized control and scientific method in war-making in general and siege operations in particular. After all, siege warfare sought to replace manpower with machinery, risk with certainty, and heroics with calibration. Yet the British, despite their economic strength and scientific capacity, did not attain Jones's 'due union of science, labour, and force' in their siege operations in the Peninsula. This was partly because eighteenth-century sieges, based on lengthy and tight blockading until defenders capitulated, did not meet the requirements of speed and decisiveness characterizing the ideal type of Napoleonic warfare. In his own campaigns, Napoleon generally avoided sieges in the pursuit of more decisive results. Wellington's conduct of siege warfare, therefore, needs to be re-examined in relation to contemporaries' arguments about the rise of scientific warfare. There were numerous logistical obstacles to delivering fluid and fast campaigns. While, as Keegan argued, battles as events could be managed to a high degree, prolonged sieges posed far more challenges than the application of scientifically calibrated firepower allowed for.

Technology
The first problem with the scientific approach to the analysis of war – and contemporary writers on siege operations insisted that sieges were ideally suited to scientific method – was that technological advantages can be patchy in effect and/or difficult to apply. The British conduct of sieges in 1812 was repeatedly undermined by failures to apply the available technology. The British withdrew twice from Badajoz in May–June 1811 because they had a small and obsolete siege train, consisting essentially of outdated Portuguese heavy guns culled from the border fortress of Elvas. Of the 30 heaviest guns used – the 24-pounders which made up the majority of the siege train totalling 46 guns – 18 were disabled during the 35 days of operations. Only three were rendered ineffective by enemy fire. Six of the twelve howitzers were also disabled.[12] Yet this technological deficiency did not necessarily trigger the eventual withdrawal, which in fact resulted from the threatened approach of a French army.

In contrast, at Ciudad Rodrigo in January 1812, the British, having now brought their own modern siege train of seventy-eight guns, mortars and howitzers from Lisbon to Oporto and then up country to the Portuguese-Spanish border, created a breach far more quickly than the French expected, and thus took the town before the French could begin planning to move troops to relieve the garrison.[13] At Badajoz in 1812, however, the naval commander at Lisbon did not provide the anticipated 24-pounder guns, but instead delivered a batch of 18-pounders from surrendered Russian warships at anchor in the Tagus estuary. Although the British secured heavy guns and created breaches, the work took a number of days. This allowed the French to construct elaborate and viciously inventive defences beyond the breached walls. When the British stormed the main breach, in formidable numbers, they suffered severe casualties and failed to penetrate into the town at their preferred point of entry.

This reverse at the main breach at Badajoz in particular stimulated later discussion about the techniques of siege warfare. Debate hinged on the nature of breaching and the prevention of repairs to damaged breaches. One contention was that the British had opened a breach some 150ft wide, when 90ft would have been sufficient for columns of thirty men abreast to storm, and such a narrower breach could have been made in one day. Any bombardment, it was argued, should take one day and never more than two, so that an assault would follow immediately, leaving the defenders no time to repair damage and/or install defences on or at the breach. John May, who was brigade major of the artillery at Badajoz, later calculated that fifty 24-pounder iron guns would be needed to make a breach 90ft wide in one day.[14] Breaching guns needed to be supported, according to engineer officers, by more effective howitzers and mortars to deliver vertical fire which would impair or prevent repair or retrenchment work.[15] At neither Ciudad Rodrigo nor Badajoz did the British have enough heavy guns to achieve such a speedy breaching, or effective vertical (mortar) fire to prevent the defenders repairing the breaches or constructing defensive works behind them. The battering train at Badajoz included only sixteen 24-pounders, one of which proved unserviceable.[16]

Wellington, however, was reluctant to accept such criticism of technological deficiencies. After Badajoz, he responded that the Royal Engineers should have placed batteries on the glacis and blown in the counterscarp, which caused such chaos early in the advance towards the breaches. Without more breaching guns and more vertical fire directed against the retrenchments and the defenders, this suggestion was rejected by engineers as wholly impractical.[17]

Technical explanations of failure were undeniable at Burgos where the British took only three high-calibre guns and five large howitzers; two of the guns were *hors de combat* within days of the beginning of the siege. The first task facing the British was to seize a defensive outlying horn-work which commanded a small hill opposite the north side of the castle, from which it was separated by a narrow but relatively deep valley. This operation cost 421 casualties and involved some fierce fighting, especially by the 42nd. The horn-work had to be secured, but it offered a very exposed platform for British artillery, since its open side faced the castle across the valley within full view and easy range of the main French battery of nine heavy guns. The day after commencing the attack, Wellington wrote that 'I doubt . . . that I have the means to take the castle which is very strong'. He remained uncertain, writing on 2 October that 'I am very much afraid that I shall not take this castle'.[18] When attempts were made to mine small sections of the defensive perimeter, notably under a church, they failed to open breaches which the British could take. The engineers received further criticism for not mining more directly.

The lack of siege guns available for all three sieges was obvious. The British had captured a great deal of artillery in the first eight months of 1812. An official assessment of the ordnance taken in the Peninsula from 1808 to April 1814 valued it at £283,008, of which ordnance worth £144,341 was seized at Ciudad Rodrigo, Badajoz and Madrid between January and August 1812.[19] At Ciudad Rodrigo they took thirty-four French 24-pounder guns, and a further thirty-nine such heavy artillery at Badajoz.[20] The real challenge, however, was in moving them to the siege site.

Traditional Constraints
Despite arguments about applying technology, the British were constricted by pre-modern means of land transport. It has been pointed out that Wellington's logistical system was far more defective than he claimed.[21] The issue of logistics has become excessively intertwined with theorizing about 'total war', and too much removed from the practical experience of moving armies on pre-modern roads with ill-fed animals.

When the initial British expeditionary force landed in Portugal in August 1808, the commanding Royal Artillery officer was indignant at the lack of horses. The only transport provided consisted of 300 horses described as 'old, blind, and casts from the Cavalry' of whom 75 died soon after arrival.[22] Although the supply improved by the end of the year, the flow of animals was irregular. In January 1812, the Royal Artillery needed 1,400 horses for its heavy guns (excluding, that is, field artillery with the infantry) and had only 1,100, at a time when impending losses were expected at Ciudad Rodrigo.[23] The requirement for all forms of artillery and for the ammunition wagons and carriages totalled 2,100, yet only 1,785 were available on 1 January, of which 100–200 were sick. Only 200 horses were apparently ready at Cork for shipment to Portugal, yet delays of 'several months' in securing transport ships were typically encountered. Moreover, procuring animals took too long; Major General Borthwick, commanding the RA in the Peninsula, urged that the process should become more like that used in ordering ammunition.[24] Some 719 horses were shipped from Portsmouth and Cork to Portugal between March and June. But they were despatched in three consignments. One convoy, for example, consisted of nine vessels of between 210 and 427 tons sailing from Portsmouth and Cork.[25] For all the claims about Britain's command of the oceans, this was a fragile supply line. In early March 1812, Borthwick noted that 'almost all' troops and brigades faced shortfalls in the number of horses and mules. Such deficiencies endangered the viability of units, which would have to be broken up or sent to the rear. Since horses expected from Ireland had not yet arrived, RA officers would have to purchase horses locally, sending their acquisitions to headquarters for inspection by veterinary surgeons and approval by commanding officers before being used. Local horses were unlikely to be of sufficient size, strength and condition for use by the Royal Artillery.[26] In September 1812, the RA complained of the 'shameful' condition of remounts, with under half of one batch at Salamanca being fit for duty.[27] By the end of the retreat from Burgos, the artillery's horses had suffered so much from the bad weather and the lack of food that only two brigades of artillery could be brought out for duty on 20 November; 'there is not a spare horse or mule with the army'.[28]

Sustaining and managing the 2,100 horses and 295 mules needed by the Royal Artillery in the Peninsula for 1812 provided an additional challenge. Borthwick recommended establishing a corps of drivers, consisting of 1,335 drivers, officers and NCOs, supported by 136 tradesmen, such as tanners, farriers, collar-makers, carriage-makers and wheelers.[29] Later in the year a request was made for one shoe-smith for every 200 horses and for increased attention to be given to the care of sick and convalescent horses, as well as more expert saddling.[30] On campaign, the horses – described as being in 'miserable' condition in early February – suffered from lack of forage.[31] When the campaign shifted to Badajoz, one RA unit, attached to the 6th Division, reported that no rations of corn for its horses had been received from 27 March to 6 April.[32]

Local transport was in short supply. The British used 1,100 bullocks assisted by 1,200–1,400 Portuguese militiamen to haul their heavy guns from Lamego, above the banks of the Douro, to the area around Almeida, the forward base for operations against Ciudad Rodrigo.[33] The siege train did not arrive at Ciudad Rodrigo until 11 January. It was accompanied by two days' worth of ammunition and depended upon additional supplies being hauled from the camp at Gallegos, about 9 miles to the rear.[34] Once Ciudad Rodrigo was taken, it proved impossible to transport the very heavy guns from Ciudad Rodrigo and Almeida south to Badajoz in February–March 1812. The carts used for the heavy guns were in poor condition; bad weather, the high mortality rate of bullocks and the desertion of local bullock drivers added to the delays. Instead, 24-pounder guns were shipped from Lisbon to Setugal, and then by road 115 miles to Elvas, in a complex and slow process. Locally recruited labour, consisting of 200 Portuguese militiamen, supported the move from Setugal to Elvas.[35] In another example of reliance on local labour, in August with one-fifth of the RA's drivers on the sick list and no replacements forthcoming, Wellington approved the appointment of Spanish drivers, although they were confined to the reserves, ensuring that only British drivers served with the artillery's active brigades.[36] Such transport difficulties also, of course, hampered the French, despite their control of most of Spain's administrative infrastructure. For example, the French advance from Salamanca on Ciudad Rodrigo in 1810 was delayed by problems in organizing a siege train and securing enough carriage animals, as was Soult's move upon Badajoz in early 1811.[37]

The army, therefore, had to function with limited artillery partly because transporting guns was so difficult. The commanding engineer at Burgos, Lieutenant Colonel John Burgoyne, had earlier in the year noted the challenges of transporting heavy loads in Spain. For the Burgos campaign, Wellington rejected the idea of bringing extra guns from the coast through Santander or from Madrid on the grounds that demands on transport 'are so extensive, that the attempt would be impracticable'.[38] Moreover, transporting heavy guns would have been interrupted by heavy rains which affected the Burgos area on seven of the fourteen days between 2 and 16 October.[39] The inadequacies of the siege train resulted, therefore, not from defective knowledge or skill but from limitations on transport.

Given such difficulties, siege operations had to depend upon forward bases as hubs for wide-ranging activities. Any invasion of Spain from north-eastern Portugal relied on Almeida, whose defences the British reconstructed in 1810–11. During December, for example, the engineers at Almeida used 148 soldiers selected from the army to construct a trestle bridge allowing the British to cross the Agueda River to the north-west of Ciudad Rodrigo, avoiding the main bridge commanded by that town's defences. Again, from 19 December, 1 officer and 43 men from each battalion worked on making 4,300 fascines, 2,030 gabions and numerous pickets to support and protect the gun emplacements during the siege.[40] This work depended on securing enough suitable timber from the surrounding area and highlighted the value of a secure base at Almeida.

The advances on Badajoz were anchored in Elvas, only 14 miles behind the Portuguese border. Troops and weapons began to be despatched southwards to Elvas almost as soon as Ciudad was won. Howitzers, twenty-four 18-pounder guns and carriages for heavy guns took four weeks to travel overland from Almeida to Elvas. The 24-pounders essential for breaching went by sea from Lisbon to Setubal and were then drawn by oxen to Elvas, where an artillery park of fifty-two guns and howitzers was built up by 8 March. A pontoon bridge was constructed in Lisbon and taken up country. A party of trained artificers was eventually transferred from Cádiz to the front to supplement 115 Royal Military Artificers already with the army. In total, a specialist body of 328 men from the Royal Artillery and 626 Portuguese artillerymen was assembled.[41] This was substantially fewer than the 2,000 artillerymen and sappers Soult had taken for his advance on Badajoz a year earlier.[42] Moving materiel from the base required significant local labour supplies; for example, 1,000 Portuguese militia soldiers hauled 500 gabions from the stock which had been produced by the Portuguese at Elvas to Badajoz.[43]

No forward base supported Burgos, however, and this was one reason for the lack of a siege train there. Wellington had not defined where his campaign would end in September/October 1812, hoping that it might be on the Ebro River, in which case he expected the French to evacuate Burgos as part of their general withdrawal. However, the nearest main base remained Madrid, 130 miles to the south of Burgos.

If siege trains depended upon transport resources which often proved inadequate, siege operations themselves required substantial supplies of scarce labour. In each of the three sieges under review, an existing defensive outwork, situated at about 500–600yd from the main fortifications, was seized from the French and used as a base for the construction of trenches directed towards enemy lines. The work involved was heavy and unpopular. At Ciudad Rodrigo each of the four infantry divisions was assigned to trench duties for 24 hours in rotation, with the result that, during the course of the siege, three divisions worked in the trenches for three days and the Light Division worked for four, including the day of the assault when two divisions were deployed. A maximum number of 1,200 troops was engaged in digging on any one night and fewer were detailed for daytime tasks. The working parties also needed protection from possible sorties launched by the defending garrison.[44] At Badajoz, 1,200–1,400 troops were assigned to working parties for 11 of the 14 nights to 31 March, while for 7 days at least another 1,000 did daytime work in the trenches. These working parties were covered by up to 2,800 troops in any one day. Thus, the preparatory stage of the siege involved assigning somewhere between 4,000 and 5,000 troops (out of 12,000) to working on and protecting the trenches each day.[45]

The siege of Burgos required less extensive effort, as the fortifications were more limited in extent. Working parties of up to 650 men were deployed, typically at night, to dig trenches and construct approach routes and lines of defence. Men at work were exposed to French fire from the defences. They also suffered from 2 sorties from the garrison on 5 and 8 October, resulting in 326 British casualties.[46] In addition tools were lost and some of the British works destroyed. Perhaps more galling was the expenditure of scarce British ammunition. The discharge of what Wellington called 'an unconscionable quantity of musket ammunition', particularly on the nights of the two French sorties, meant that his army could not launch any attacks from 9 October until more ammunition arrived from Santander.[47]

The quality of the work on the trenches proved controversial. Even without the damage inflicted by the French, Burgoyne complained of the 'neglect and misconduct of the working parties' and considered that delays in trench construction resulted from British soldiers not working nearly as hard as their French counterparts in digging and similar chores.[48] Wellington speculated that the men's commitment may have declined because their pay was long in arrears.[49] Despite that defect, commanders at Burgos insisted that the nocturnal working parties, assigned to their duties for 6 to 8 hours, were well enough treated. During the last 11 nights of September, working parties of at least 300 men, and of 600 men on 3 occasions, had gone out on 7 nights. But only 350 reported on the night of 27–8 September, far short of requirements and expectations.[50] This poor attendance triggered Wellington's first General Order, of 1 October, declaring that he would receive morning reports on the previous night's work, including the names of officers in command of working parties.[51] Divisional officers were instructed to check carefully whether all men were present with the working parties and report on arrival in the trenches to the field officers there. Each working party in the 6th Division was to post a corporal and three sentries at their trench's entry, and permit no soldier to leave unless he was wounded.[52] Somewhat later in the war, on the approach to Bayonne in March 1814, one commander hit upon an apparently novel method of tackling slackness. Major General Frederick Robinson, notorious for bluntness, used underemployed drummers and fifers to play music while working parties applied themselves to their tasks.[53]

If a successful siege required effective ordnance and transport and the thorough preparation of trenches and their approaches, the culminating point in these sieges involved storming breaches in traditional style. In rebutting Wellington's criticisms of the Royal Engineers' performance, Burgoyne claimed that the failure at Burgos resulted from insufficient troops assaulting the breach. A larger force, in his view, would have boosted the assailants' self-confidence and spirit of emulation.[54] This criticism is difficult to assess. Only 960 troops were assigned to positions for the attack. But the rest of the 6th Division had marched from their encampment into the town on the morning of the planned assault. Although the total force available fell short of the 6,500 troops ordered to the main breaches at Badajoz, it was still substantial in relation to the small size of the castle at Burgos, which measured only about 200yd by 150yd at its greatest extent, and in relation to the garrison whose initial 2,000 troops had been reduced by casualties and sickness. If the first wave of the assault had succeeded, it seems likely that sufficient back-up was available to secure victory.

Although the problems at Burgos raised issues of both morale and tactics, Wellington paid scant attention to the former. By October, Wellington's army had been in motion since January, whereas the normal expectation was that the army would recuperate from the rigours and sickness of summer campaigning by spending from October–November to April–May in winter quarters. Campaigning had not only begun earlier than usual in 1812; it had covered a wide geographical area and involved two major sieges, the battle of Salamanca, and operations upon Madrid, as well as skirmishes with the French during the British advance in September–October. As well as arrears of pay, general exhaustion intensified demoralization and poor performance. Nor did it require much imagination for ordinary soldiers to see that the task at Burgos was daunting. The castle commanded a highly defensible hill and the French were well provided with artillery, munitions and food. To overcome this, the British had 3 18-pounder guns, which were lightweight for the task and 2 of which were swiftly taken out of action, and 5 24-pounder howitzers, supported by only 2,740 rounds of shot when the siege began.[55] The obvious way to make up for the weapons gap was to mine the castle wall, but mining failed to create a viable breach. The key to success at Ciudad Rodrigo and Badajoz had been attacks at a number of points on the defences, and that was not possible at Burgos.

The balance between traditional fighting and scientific warfare was clear. The breakthrough at Badajoz, which possessed the most complex, extensive, and formidable defences of the three towns attacked in 1812, was achieved by the least scientific method – scaling the castle wall by ladder – after numerous failed attempts at escalation along a more exposed section of 120ft of the castle's wall. At Ciudad Rodrigo the breakthrough was made by flanking attacks on the main defensive walls; these enabled the British to advance through the main breach while also hitting the French at their left flank within the defensive walls. Two additional subsidiary attacks broke into the town at widely separated gates, deepening the sense of vulnerability, and indeed panic, among the defenders. Even where scientific methods were applied, success owed much to decidedly old-fashioned approaches. This is consonant with Huw Davies's argument that Wellington brought back from India a commitment to 'Light and Quick' methods of campaigning, and that his key battlefield victories resulted not from superior technology, training or tactics, but from sheer determination and willingness to sustain high casualties.[56]

At Burgos, where even small-arms ammunition ran low, improvisation was taken to extreme lengths. The British compensated for the shortage of shot by retrieving French shot fired at their own works. Soldiers were paid for each projectile thus salvaged, and were rewarded even if the shot gathered was of different calibre and thus useless in British guns; the payments remained to stimulate the soldiers' initiative. This was a widespread practice. The British arrived with 2,740 shot, shell and case assigned to the siege train; they gathered 2,911 French shot and used 1,329 in British guns, thus increasing their initial stock by 50 per cent.[57] The decision to mine the walls and then the church of San Roman on the castle's southern edge, away from the two main breaches, was taken because of the shortage of gun ammunition and the relatively ready availability of gunpowder, sent by the Royal Navy from Santander.[58] The mining failed, however, because there were few British engineers and troops trained in the technical skills of sapping and mining. An attempt was then made to fire 'hot shot', using the five heavy howitzers, on to the roof of the church of Santa Maria la Blanca, which served as a store within the fortifications. It was hoped that vital supplies would be destroyed if the church could be set on fire, and that privation and demoralization would induce the garrison to surrender. This also failed. The howitzers were inaccurate; shot could not be heated quickly enough to create a hail of projectiles; and the roof did not burn significantly when it was hit.[59] Another tactic was for officers who were good shots to try to take out individual French marksmen firing on troops in the works; again, this yielded negligible results.[60] Such improvisations demonstrated the army's initiative and dedication, but little scientific application.

Discipline

To represent siege operations as 'scientific' warfare became even more difficult when considering the consequences of storming defended towns. The very misconduct which scientific methods of warfare were supposed to suppress was all too evident in the savagery which followed Wellington's assaults of besieged towns. Yet explanations for the rampant indiscipline at Badajoz have not progressed significantly from Napier's work, and how order was restored has not been satisfactorily explained, beyond suggesting a combination of exhaustion among the drunken troops and a belated and rough-and-ready crackdown on egregious offenders. Nor has the collapse of discipline in the retreat from Burgos been explained other than in terms of drunkenness.

At Badajoz, discipline in fact broke down because the dramatically enhanced defences destroyed the attacking forces' cohesion. When RE officers who accompanied the assault, to guide the advancing battalions, became casualties, many British units lost direction. Heavy losses among officers and sergeants left the men leaderless, and the congestion and chaos in the trenches meant that battalions and companies were dispersed and divided. One senior officer estimated that no party of more than fifty men attempted to ascend the breach, while Oman suggested that perhaps forty separate, small-scale efforts were made to attack the main breach. One contemporary military conclusion was that no attack could succeed in such fragmented fashion.[61] This fragmentation led to dramatic consequences. The town fell to two flanking attacks which forced the garrison's surrender and allowed the full British force's entry into the town at about 2.00 am on 7 April, 4 hours after the assault began. The largest contingent among the victors consisted of the thousands of men who had failed to take the main breach and had suffered appalling casualties. About 2,000 French troops laid down their weapons and surrendered in the middle of town in the early hours of 7 April. By dawn, there may have been 10,000 British troops inside the walls. Most of them had been under great strain for up to two days: the assault had been planned initially for 5 April, then for 7.30 pm on the 6th, and finally began just before 10.00 that night. Adding to the tensions created by the long wait before the impending assault, most of the men had been involved in or witnessed scenes in which their fellow soldiers had been wounded or killed in horrifying circumstances. Their predictable response was to drink to excess. Drink and anger led to plundering, rape, assaults upon individuals irrespective of nationality, age or gender, and to random killing.

But the descent into chaos resulted also from the breakdown in the army's management system. The officer corps was profoundly disrupted by the assault. Of the 72 officers killed during the siege, 59 fell on the night of 6–7 April; some 258 of the 306 officers wounded during the siege were struck that night.[62] Since the total complement of officers for the attack was probably about 600, allowing for one officer for every twenty men, half the officer corps for the troops engaged was hit. As 268 sergeants were also killed or wounded during the siege, and mostly on 6–7 April, the problem of managing the troops who had participated in the assault, and who by the morning of the 7th were ranging freely in a defeated and open town, became even more acute.

In the midst of post-battle chaos, senior commanders were also distracted. Captain Harry Smith came across Colonel Allen in tears and holding a pair of scissors; the colonel asked Smith to cut a lock of hair from the body of his dead brother, an officer in the Rifle Brigade, so that it could be sent home to their mother. He was unable to complete the task himself.[63] Wellington composed his formal, publishable despatch, which takes up eight tightly packed pages in print, during the day. Time had to be devoted to filling gaps in the army command. Six generals were wounded on 6–7 April, and three battalion commanders had been killed and three more wounded.[64] Acting senior officers and brevet officers had to be assigned to new duties. Among some officers at least, the prospect of promotion without purchase to fill over sixty vacancies caused by death, and brevet vacancies occasioned by serious injuries, presumably attracted as much attention as the misdemeanours of drunken troops in the centre of town. Edmund Wheatley, in the midst of fighting at the siege of Bayonne, instantly greeted the death of a lieutenant in his regiment by announcing his impending promotion to fill the vacancy; 'Interest is the impulse in these our modern wars'.[65]

With the management of the army at least temporarily in disarray, how was discipline re-asserted and the army directed back to its duties? One task was to collect the wounded and get them to makeshift hospitals or back to camp. This effort seems to have been only partially successful, at least in the short term. William Surtees could persuade passing soldiers to participate in carrying wounded men to the field hospital for one or two journeys only; and he himself was too exhausted to continue this work beyond noon on 7 April. At some point during the day, Wellington recognized that continuing lawlessness had to be stopped and ordered the troops on parade and under arms. Subsequently, the men were ordered back to their encampments, miles from the town. The following day, by which time bacchanalian excess had subsided, Power's Portuguese brigade entered the town to take on garrison duties and restore order until relieved by 3,000 Spanish troops. The Portuguese consisted of two battalions from the garrison at Elvas and one from Abrantes which had played a minor role during the siege.[66] Portuguese troops could be clearly distinguished from the British, and probably had little compunction in dealing with any remaining dissolute British soldiers. On the other hand, British soldiers may have found it provoking to be displaced by troops who had played a minor part in the intense fighting of 6–7 April and who were often held in low esteem by the British. The Portuguese also are recorded as joining in the looting.[67]

Practical concerns re-focused the army. Work began on 9 April to fill the extensive trenches, and 2 working parties of 500 men each spent the next few days completing the task. More importantly, Wellington resumed campaigning. Throughout the siege, he had paid careful attention to the potential threats from Soult to the south and Marmont to the north. On 11 April, he decided that Marmont might menace Ciudad Rodrigo, which was short of food and other supplies. On 12 April, the divisions involved in storming Badajoz left their camps around the town and began a relatively speedy march to Ciudad, which they reached by 22 April.[68] Thus during 8–11 April the army was diverted from the horrors of sacking Badajoz to the transfer and care of the wounded and the re-organization of the garrison within the town, to filling in the trenches and preparing for a resumption of campaigning. Returning to the demands of campaigning in an active and highly mobile army obliged the men to move on from scenes of non-combatant violence.

Scientific Officers

Specialist skills were of increasing value to early nineteenth-century armies, but the status and training of specialist officers remained ambiguous if not contested. Tracing the development of expertise is made problematic by the absence of formal training for many functions and, equally important, the typical lack of written records concerning the acquisition and transmission of technical skills. In many instances, the only way professional development can be suggested is by demonstrating that particular officers continued to be deployed over sustained periods in demanding postings. Only occasionally were evaluations of technical expertise offered. For example, one officer complained in a letter published after the retreat from Burgos that officers trained at the recently established Military Academy were ill-suited to executing such practical tasks as arranging billets for exhausted troops. They regarded themselves as budding heads of military departments rather than as practical organizers. Such young 'pedants may be well viewed in the theory, but many of them are incompetent to the practical part, either in respect to ability, or activity; . . . a youthful Staff is the ruin of an army'.[69] Another officer made a rare comparison in citing Wellington's comment in India 'that Lord Lake's army, was the best school that a young officer could be with, because he would [,] he must perceive the want of an effective commissariat'.[70]

A recurrent complaint was that the shortage of expert technical officers restricted the practice of scientific warfare in the Peninsula. Of the twenty Royal Engineer officers available at the beginning of the siege at Badajoz, eight were killed or wounded by 6 April and a further five fell – killed, mortally wounded or severely wounded – during the assault.[71] At Burgos, the Anglo-Portuguese army of about 24,000 officers and men included only 5 Royal Engineer officers. The specialist service depended on improvised volunteering. At Badajoz, for example, two members of the Royal Military Surveyors and Draftsmen offered to act as assistant engineers, and were subsequently recommended for commissions as second lieutenants in the RE, since there were no promotion prospects in their own department, whose work was not regarded as of officer calibre.[72] In the absence of formal training beyond initial instruction, it was particularly difficult for officers to disseminate good practice when so many of them were so rapidly incapacitated.

The Royal Engineers contained no other ranks and had to draw soldiers from line regiments. At Burgos, line troops were designated for basic work such as constructing gabions and fascines. (These were sand-filled baskets or casks and bundles of wood respectively and were used to protect gun emplacements.) Another eighty men who had skills as masons, carpenters and miners were gathered from the ranks.[73] The effectiveness of RE officers, according to *The Times*, was reduced by their lack of numbers and the labour and danger in supervising troops unskilled in siege operations. By contrast, not only did the French have a strong engineering corps, but Marshal Soult, when he arrived in Andalucia, established a Spanish corps of sappers and miners who then accompanied him on his withdrawal from the south. No equivalent effort to create such a labour force had been made by the British.[74]

Unlike the Royal Engineers, the Royal Regiment of Artillery recruited gunners and drivers and incorporated foreign units as well. But it struggled to keep pace with the wartime demand for manpower. The total strength of the Royal Artillery was 24,498 in June 1812. During the 3 years 1809 to 1811 inclusive, the service had lost 5,117 gunners to age, illness, disabling wounds and death from natural causes as well as from fighting. Recruitment in those 3 years reached 5,200. Only in 1812 did new recruits outnumber permanent losses, and even then only by 1,161 men. The scale of turnover meant that about 30 per cent of the Royal Artillery in mid-1812 had joined since the beginning of 1809.[75] The entire regiment had little experience of scientific sieges before 1812.

The Royal Artillery had more officers available than the Royal Engineers, but the attrition rate was quite high. There were fourteen RA officers at Ciudad Rodrigo, of whom six had been wounded by the end of the siege of Badajoz three months later. Only three of the thirteen RA officers at Burgos had been present nine months earlier at Ciudad Rodrigo; one of those three was wounded, thus bringing to 50 per cent the proportion of RA officers at Ciudad Rodrigo who became casualties in 1812's three sieges. Losses so disrupted the senior command that there were no fewer than four successive commanding officers of the RA within Wellington's army during 1812. The first, Major General Borthwick, returned to England having been wounded at Ciudad Rodrigo, though difficult relations with Wellington may have encouraged him to leave. Another, Lieutenant Colonel William Robe, was severely wounded defending a bridge on the retreat from Burgos.[76]

The pressure on these scientific officers was considerable. They were expected to fulfil numerous tasks not directly connected with war-fighting. For example, in planning for the advance upon Ciudad Rodrigo, the Royal Engineers undertook an extensive exploratory survey in 1811 of the Douro River to establish how far it was navigable, as a way of approaching the northern section of the eastern frontier with Spain and the road to Ciudad Rodrigo and onwards to Salamanca and Madrid.[77]

Moreover, their training and professional experience at home heavily emphasized regulation and inspection. While testing and assessing new weapons and munitions absorbed some attention, tight administration – a necessary safeguard against corruption and an essential precaution against parliamentary inquiry – dominated professional practice. The business of the Board of Ordnance, which controlled the engineers and artillery, focused on the detailed allocation of resources and virtually ignored field conditions and operations.

This system dealt with an impressive wartime expansion in the volume of activity, delivering, most notably, millions of muskets and tens of millions of ball cartridges to the Peninsula. But the experience provided for its officers was deeply rule-bound rather than practical and it did little to promote co-operation between the military services or on campaign. While Wellington struck effective working relationships with some technical officers, he clearly subordinated technical advice to other military priorities.

The nineteenth-century historian of the RA, Francis Duncan, stressed that sieges were 'mere episodes in Wellington's general operations, not goals to which these operations tended'.[78] Wellington's approach to siege operations reflected an impatience to maintain the tempo of his campaigning, even at the cost of heavy casualties when enemy defences had to be stormed. After Badajoz, with its grim casualties, his comment to his brother, the Foreign Secretary, was characteristically detached: 'Our loss was severe, but it is impossible to perform services of this kind without heavy loss'.[79] Although he sought to expand his capability to undertake sieges, pressing for more specialist troops in an expanded contingent of RA, and for the establishment of a branch of Sappers and Miners, he never besieged towns which were strategic objectives in themselves. Their capture was vital to securing lines of communication and as catalysts to induce the French to re-group their armies and thus give breathing space to those Spaniards continuing to resist the French. In order to secure such relatively peripheral objectives, Wellington predictably subordinated scientific expertise to an ultimate reliance on fighting skill and determination.

Scientific siege operations depended on the time available to force a besieged town's surrender. The steadily planned approach could take months to force the besieged to capitulate. If a town had to be taken fairly quickly and therefore stormed, the engineers' and artillery officers' technical expertise confronted the usual challenges created by the friction and fog of battle. Storming a town was part of siege warfare but it was a distinctive aspect of it. There was far more pressure to improvise, but improvisation became difficult when the defenders responded rapidly, imaginatively and even unpredictably to impending threats. At Badajoz, most notably, the French dug the defensive ditches deeper than the British realized, flooding parts of them and laying hidden mines and barrels of explosives in the dry parts to ensure that many attackers were either drowned or burned alive. The ascent from the ditches towards the breach was covered with impassable *chevaux-de-frises*, or wooden beams riddled with sword blades, as well as other lethal devices. Of the 6,500 men attacking the main breaches, some 1,854 were killed or wounded in less than 3 hours of fighting. No British forces reached the top of the breaches until after the town walls were scaled elsewhere and the defenders withdrew into the town.[80] Although the British lacked both sappers and miners to break down the counterscarps and the appropriate artillery to destroy the retrenchments behind the breaches, they also encountered a lethal mix of improvised defensive measures. Thus when the 'modern' emphasis on speed and the offensive took precedence over the equally 'modern' quest for scientific system and certainty, an old-fashioned bloodbath in close-quarter fighting resulted.

Burgos

After returning to Ciudad Rodrigo by late April, Wellington's army then advanced to Salamanca, Madrid and, in September, Burgos. Wellington had hoped the French army of Portugal would retreat beyond the Ebro, but when it settled into a defensive position about 25 miles north-east of Burgos, he divided his army, leaving about two-thirds of it to cover and watch the French position while the remainder moved to besiege the castle at Burgos.

It has long been argued that he should have summoned up heavy guns from Madrid, where there were plenty of them, or secured a few heavy guns from the Royal Navy squadron operating on the northern Spanish coast. The inhibiting factor for Wellington was that he had no intention of lingering at Burgos – a strategic point, not a strategic centre. Its population was estimated at about 8,000 to 9,000 and the surrounding countryside was agriculturally productive.[81] However, the town was significant because it commanded three bridges across the Arlanzon River and because the French had repaired and extended its defences after attacking it in 1808 and held substantial munitions and stores there. Wellington hoped that the fortress – the town was undefended – would be taken by *coup de main*. By the time he had failed in this objective, the two French armies of the North and of Portugal threatened to advance back towards Salamanca and Madrid, and began to do so on 21 October.

Burgos posed great difficulties for bringing up a siege train. Wellington's nearest forward base was 130 miles away, at Madrid. Drawing naval guns from Santander was not straightforward and its harbour could take only a small number of larger warships. The main port for naval operations was far to the west, at La Coruña. Wellington's confidence in the navy had already been dented at Badajoz, when 24-pounder guns which were promised failed to materialize. Santander had fallen to the Royal Navy only in August, and the squadron commander, Sir Home Popham, focused on supplying Spanish guerrilla leaders and in landing farther east along the coast, at Bilbao and, from the end of August, at Guetaria, a very small but strongly defensible port. The naval squadron blockaded Guetaria during 18–23 September, just as Wellington began his siege of Burgos, some 120 miles south-west of that tiny port. There was thus limited co-ordination of operational plans between Wellington and the naval squadron. When Popham supplied Wellington with additional gunpowder, it took seven days to cover the 70 miles across the mountainous route from Santander to Burgos. [82] Moreover, the road was vulnerable to French raiding. Late in the siege, Wellington informed Popham that Santander could not become a point of communication with England until the British army was 'firmly established' on the Ebro or possibly farther east. The fluidity of the fighting fronts in the region vindicated such caution. Moreover, Wellington doubted the 'practicality' of Santander's being a major link at any time, because land transport in the neighbouring country was scarce.[83]

The Royal Navy's strategic commitment to operations on the northern Spanish coast was far from clear. Lord Keith, the Commander-in-Chief of the Channel fleet, whose responsibilities covered the Bay of Biscay, had limited means with which to reinforce the squadron and probably even less inclination to do so. Wellington seems to have ignored naval sensitivities. Popham resented the fact that during November he had held station in rough seas without being informed by Wellington that the army had withdrawn to the south-west. His squadron itself left the Spanish northern coast by the end of the year.[84]

The retreat from Burgos was as humiliating as the failed siege had been. Of course, the town had not been captured and sacked, with the subsequent breakdown of discipline in an orgy of looting. But, within days of the beginning of the retreat, insubordination became problematic. On 28 October, for example, orders for the 6th Division stressed that the men should not straggle or get drunk, and officers and NCOs were instructed to tighten discipline. Somewhat desperately, the troops were to be reminded that men who were drunk and unfit for duty were cowards, since every soldier needed to be capable of bearing arms at all times. Major General Henry Clinton, commanding the division, believed that such reasoning would be understood, since the army was retreating in close proximity to the enemy. On 3 November, officers were reminded that foraging parties had to be organized at brigade level and that officers were responsible for discipline within foraging parties and for preventing straggling. A further order insisted that soldiers leaving the ranks for ordinary purposes should obtain permission for absence and should leave their arms with their comrades.[85] None of this established control. From 23 October to 29 November, 4,752 rank and file of the retreating British and Anglo-Portuguese armies went missing and about 951 more were killed and wounded in running engagements with the French. About 3,000 casualties were suffered between 15 and 19 November when terrible weather and acute food shortages devastated the last stage of the retreat to Ciudad Rodrigo, where the troops began arriving on 19 November.[86] On 28 November Wellington issued a blistering denunciation of his officers and men for their repeated failure to stamp out indiscipline, straggling and marauding. Starting out as a printed circular sent to the commanding officers of divisions and brigades commanders, it was swiftly disseminated more widely.[87] Wellington then blamed virtually everyone but himself for the ignominious finale to the campaigning of 1812.

Wellington's anger at the fragmentation of his army had an immediate political as well as an understandable professional cause. On 17 October, Wellington informed the Secretary of State for War and the Colonies that he wished to have British officers appointed to commands in the Spanish army, in order to improve its fighting effectiveness. He conceded that the Spanish government and Spanish officers were unlikely to accept British officers in order to stiffen discipline because 'they do not admit the superiority of our discipline, and do not attribute to that cause our success'.[88] The breakdown in discipline in the retreat from Burgos could not therefore have come at a worse political moment. While the excesses at Ciudad Rodrigo and especially

Badajoz might be dismissed as exceptional, the army's behaviour during the retreat undermined Wellington's claims to superior British military management at the very time when he took up the command-in-chief of the Spanish armies in the field.

Assessments of Wellington's Sieges in 1812
Typically analysed as the most 'scientific' form of warfare, siege warfare involved ill-discipline, the breakdown of unit cohesion, atrocities against civilians, and widespread marauding and desertion. This was explained away on various grounds. Among those entering Ciudad Rodrigo after the assault was Major William Gomm who initially noted that there had been 'less bloodshed than is usual in such extremities'. A week later, he wrote home that the British were not naturally bloodthirsty, but were rapacious for plunder and had suffered more casualties than the defenders. He added that the town was full of powder, and that many houses set on fire on the first night simply continued to burn. For someone accustomed to terrible scenes, this was all part of war.[89] From Badajoz, Gomm insisted that British soldiers were less bloodthirsty than others but misbehaved when drunk.[90] In published accounts, most notably those of William Napier in 1828, which became much quoted, and William Surtees in 1833, the excesses of Badajoz were explained as the reaction of troops who had come under extraordinary pressure and suffered horrific casualties; the excesses and the suffering demonstrated to Napier that 'a British army bears with it an awful power'.[91]

In Britain, the government's critics did not attack the army's behavioural lapses, but concentrated instead on the sieges' strategic implications. For example, opposition newspapers queried the value of taking Ciudad Rodrigo. The *Morning Chronicle* hoped that it would deter a French invasion of Portugal or 're-animate the Spanish to prevent their subjugation'. It would not, however, deflect the French from their campaigning in southern Spain and indeed might even play into French hands, allowing Marmont's and Dorsenne's armies of Portugal and the North respectively to hold Wellington in place at Ciudad Rodrigo, some 320 miles from Lisbon, while Soult advanced on the Tagus River and into Portugal from Badajoz, only 120 miles from the Portuguese capital.[92] An even more sceptical newspaper, the *Liverpool Mercury*, argued that the French in taking Valencia, on the east coast, created more strategic opportunities than Wellington's capture of Ciudad Rodrigo had closed off. It also claimed that Wellington's further advance into Spain required the organization of a more efficient Spanish army.[93] The later failure at Burgos reinforced this insistence that British advances depended upon more concerted Spanish action. Yet, 'Of the Spanish patriotism, which our ministers and their venal prints told us we might expect to find re-animated by the victory of Salamanca, and by the possession of Madrid, we have perceived no symptom.'[94] According to this newspaper, British generals in Spain acted within guidelines laid down from home; British troops did 'all that could be expected of them'; 'the fault is not in them, but in that system . . . in which the object, in the present state of the Spanish people, is unworthy of their efforts'.[95]

The opposition press attributed failure in late 1812 to ministerial incompetence. When Wellington requested extra troops after Salamanca, ministers had 'an opportunity that was unexampled in the history of wars'. Although sufficient manpower and the requisite support of the Prince Regent were available to meet Wellington's needs, ministers merely redistributed troops to the Alicante front in east-central Spain, thus dispersing rather than concentrating military assets. The *Morning Chronicle* concluded, 'We sicken at the thoughts of the manner in which the war has been conducted'. *The Times* insisted that Wellington had held British forces together and conducted the retreat from Burgos skilfully in the face of a superior French force. But the retreat was a terrible political disappointment, highlighting ministers' failure since June to act vigorously and press for victory.[96]

Despite such criticisms of government policy, one unexpected outcome of the sieges of 1812 was the belief, as expressed in public discourse, that British soldiers had reached French levels of military effectiveness. *The Times* insisted that Ciudad Rodrigo was 'the most brilliant success with which our arms have been favoured during the whole war'. British soldiers had defeated the French despite all the advantages lying with the latter.[97] Lieutenant Colonel Jones, an engineer, insisted that 'the reduction of Ciudad Rodrigo . . . must be ranked as one of the happiest, boldest, and most creditable achievements recorded in our military annals'.[98] For Francis Duncan, in writing the history of the Royal Artillery, the attack on Badajoz was 'a night in which the most cruel death was fair to look on, – because hallowed by marvellous courage and rare devotion'. Duncan insisted in 1873 that the troops' 'irregularities and license' after the siege were 'dimming' but not injurious to their reputation. Inspirational acts of self-sacrifice counter-balanced such lapses, setting an example to future generations; 'The story of the storming of Badajoz is one which will thrill the heart of every Briton for all time'.[99] Jac Weller later emphasized the strategic triumph of taking Badajoz, as well as the loss to the French of 5,000 troops who were killed, wounded or taken prisoner.[100] More recently, Allan Mallinson has restated the duality of Badajoz's legacy as 'one of the greatest fighting feats of the British army and one of its worst instances of indiscipline'.[101]

Such conclusions do not sufficiently illuminate the ways in which Wellington's sieges offer a model for the study of siege warfare. The first lesson was that scientific warfare could not be sustained with pre-modern transport systems. British failure to secure adequate transport could be ascribed to the lack of heavy-duty horses in Portugal and Spain, where the mule was the more common beast of burden. The French suffered similar problems in organizing siege trains and supplies for their sieges of Ciudad Rodrigo and Badajoz in 1810–11. But the British made no long-term provision for planning and delivering basic transport requirements for future campaigns.

The second lesson was the need in more complex operations for the British army to work closely with the indigenous population. The case against using vertical fire and more widespread bombardment of French-occupied towns was that the British should not inflict casualties and damage upon allied civilians and their property. But storming towns may well have inflicted even worse suffering upon their inhabitants. Moreover, the conduct of sieges placed major demands upon local resources of manpower and materiel. Such resources were scarce and their utilization created additional friction between the British and the Portuguese governments. Although Wellington frequently expressed irritation with the Portuguese and Spanish authorities, there appears to have been little planning for these resource demands. British sources were extremely reticent about their dependence on Portuguese militiamen in transporting their siege trains and on the Portuguese more generally for logistical support.

The labour requirements of siege warfare provided a third lesson. Digging and safeguarding trenches and parallels involved rigorous, repetitive and much-resented work. This experience may well have contributed to the aggression expressed by troops when they stormed besieged cities. Soldiers' fighting instincts may have been intensified by the desire to quit the trenches, and their insistence on indulging themselves once inside captured towns compensated not only for the horrors of the assault but also for the miseries of trench digging and the associated preparatory work for siege operations.

Beyond these operational lessons were two more general lessons about siege warfare. The 'scientific' mode of warfare was difficult to reconcile with the pace of 'modern' campaigning. Conceptually, two different kinds of modernization – the development of deliberate, experimentally tested, and technologically sophisticated methods of taking defended towns and the drive for speed and dynamism in campaigning – were at odds. When pressures of time and the need to maintain the pace of 'modern' warfare prevailed, then old-fashioned breaching and heavy casualties were the preferred options in siege warfare. The final lesson therefore was the most difficult to articulate. The sieges of 1812 proved to be improvised parts of a fluid process of campaigning, not exercises in highly scientific warfare. They involved relatively little strategic planning but required detailed and intense management. The scale and range of logistical requirements was challenging. Local labour inputs were required. British troops had to be assigned to diverse, unfamiliar and short-term tasks. The mix of weaponry and technical calculations involved in siege operations differed from that required by an army on the march or engaging an opponent in battle. Perhaps the real significance of these sieges is that we should shift our attention from arguments about whether or not this period witnessed the inception of 'total war' to how far improvisation, the management of a changing mix of technologies and war-fighting techniques, and the capacity of soldiers to engage in operational multi-tasking were the hallmarks of an effective army. Wellington's army in 1812 experienced significant changes in fortune. It demonstrated an ability to improvise and adapt to divergent roles, and, whatever its lapses in discipline, to be resilient in fighting despite heavy casualties. Improvisation and a determination to fight, however, have been played down because they scarcely manifested that 'due union of science, labour, and force' which John Jones defined as the hallmarks of siege warfare as conducted by states possessing 'superior wealth and civilization'.[102]

Notes

1. Rothenburg, *The art of warfare*, 220.
2. Rory Muir, *Britain and the Defeat of Napoleon, 1807–1815* (New Haven CT, 1996), 201–2; Esdaile, *The Peninsular War*, 386–8.

3. Harry Smith, *The Autobiography of Sir Harry Smith 1787–1819* (London, 1999 repr.), 66–8.

4. 'Three Modern Sieges', *All the Year Round*, 5, 25 February 1871, 296.

5. Oman, *A History of the Peninsular War*, v, 256–64.

6. Lieutenant Colonel Harry Jones (ed.), *Journals of the Sieges Carried on by the Army under The Duke of Wellington in Spain . . .*, 3 vols (London, 1846, 3rd edn repr. 1998), i, ix.

7. Duncan, *History of the Royal Regiment of Artillery*, ii, 335.

8. David Gates, *The Spanish Ulcer* (London, 1986), 371.

9. John Keegan, *The Mask of Command* (London, 1988 edn), 149–50.

10. Davies, *Wellington's Wars*, 166.

11. Jones, *Journals*, i, ix–x.

12. Jones, *Journals*, i, 18, 25–8, 30, 33, 67–8.

13. Jones, *Journals*, i, 80–4.

14. Sir John May, *A Few Observations on the Mode of Attack, and Employment of the Heavy Artillery* (London, 1819), 5, 7, 25–6, 40, 42.

15. May, *Observations*, 7, 41.

16. Jones, *Journals*, i, 185.

17. Jones, *Journals*, i, 223–4.

18. Wellington to Paget, 20 September, to Popham, 2 October 1812; also to Mulgrave, 27 September 1812, *WD*, ix, 437, 454, 465.

19. 'Abstract Account of the Valuation of Ordnance . . . Captured in the Peninsula 1808– April 1814', WO 44/503.

20. 'Return of Ordnance taken 21 January 1812', WO 1/253; 'Return of Ordnance and Ammunition taken at Badajoz 8 April 1812', WO 1/254.

21. Davies, *Wellington's Wars*, 251.

22. Duncan, *History of the Royal Regiment of Artillery*, ii, 197–8, 212.

23. Borthwick to Macleod, 8 January 1812, WO 55/1544.

24. Memorandum from Borthwick to Wellington (received 26 January 1812), WO 1/253.

25. J. Macleod, 11 March, 1 May, 27 June 1812, WO 55/1316; R. Crew to Macleod, 26 May 1812, WO 55/ 1278 .

26. Borthwick to field officers of artillery, 7 March 1812, WO 55/1544.

27. Robe to Fisher, 12 September 1812, WO 55/1545.

28. Waller to Macleod, 29 November 1812, WO 55/1545.

29. 'Proposed establishment of a corps of drivers . . .', 26 January 1812, WO 1/253.

30. Fisher to Macleod, 9 December 1812, WO 55/1545.

31. Borthwick to Douglas, 5 February 1812, WO 55/1544.

32. May to Elige, 8 April 1812, WO 55/1544.

33. Duncan, *History of the Royal Regiment of Artillery*, ii, 310–11.

34. Jones, *Journals*, i, 111–12, 136, 141; Francis Culling Carr-Gomm (ed.), *Letters and Journals of Field Marshal Sir William Maynard Gomm* (London, 1881), 246.

35. May to Dundas, 2 February 1812; Borthwick to Framingham, 4 February 1812, WO 55/ 1544.

36. Robe to Macleod, 30 August 1812, WO 55/1545.

37. Horward, *Napoleon and Iberia*, 81, 101, 111–12; Oman, *A History of the Peninsular War*, iv, 30, 36.

38. Wellington to Popham, 2 October 1812, *WD*, ix, 465.

39. Jones, *Journals*, i, 302, 311, 317, 319–20.

40. Jones, *Journal*, i, 89, 95.

41. Oman, *A History of the Peninsular War*, v, 223–5; Duncan, *History of the Royal Regiment of Artillery*, ii, 318.

42. Oman, *A History of the Peninsular War*, iv, 30.

43. Jones, *Journals*, i, 148, 155.

44. Jones, *Journals*, i, 104–20; Oman, *A History of the Peninsular War*, v, 169.

45. Jones, *Journals*, i, 155–6, 158–95.

46. Oman, *A History of the Peninsular War*, vi, 741.

47. Wellington to Beresford, 9 October 1812, *WD*, ix 478.

48. George Wrottesley, *Life and Correspondence of Field Marshal Sir John Burgoyne*, 2 vols (London, 1873), i, 233.

49. Wellington to Beresford, 5 October 1812, *WD*, ix, 470.

50. Jones, *Journals*, i, 281–99.

51. Wellington, 1, 3 October 1812, Duke of Wellington (ed.), *Supplementary Despatches and Memoranda of . . . Arthur, Duke of Wellington*, 9 vols (London, 1858), vii, 436–7.

52. Order, 1 October 1812, 'Orders for the VI Division 12 Feb – 6 Nov 1812', Clinton Papers, Box G13, John Rylands Library, University of Manchester.

53. Gareth Glover, *An Eloquent Soldier* (Barnsley, 2011), 241.

54. Wrottesley, *Life and Correspondence*, i, 235–6.

55. Jones, *Journal*, i, 331.

56. Davies, *Wellington's Wars*, 20, 51, 61–4, 73–5.

57. Jones, *Journals*, i, 298, 331.

58. Wellington to Popham, 5 October 1812, *WD*, ix, 471.

59. Jones, *Journals*, i, 314–15.

60. Jones, *Journals*, i, 301.

61. Jones, *Journals*, i, 212, 215; Oman, *A History of the Peninsular War*, v, 250.

62. Jones, *Journals*, i, 208.

63. Smith, *The Autobiography*, 67.

64. Wellington to Liverpool, 7 April 1812, *WD,* ix, 40–1.

65. Christopher Hibbert (ed.), *The Wheatley Diary* (London, 1964), 48–9.

66. Jones, *Journals*, i, 220; Oman, *A History of the Peninsular War*, v, 261, 264; William Surtees, *Twenty- Five Years in the Rifle Brigade* (London, repr. 1833), 144–5, 149.

67. G.O., 8 April 1812, 11.00 p.m., John Gurwood (ed.), *The Dispatches of Field Marshal the Duke of Wellington*, enlarged edn, 8 vols (London, 1845; repr. Cambridge, 2010), v, 583.

68. Jones, *Journals*, i, 221; Oman, *A History of the Peninsular War*, v, 289–94.

69. *The Military Panorama or Officers' Companion*, March 1813, 556.

70. Glover, *An Eloquent Soldier*, 244.

71. Jones, *Journals*, i, 154–5.

72. E. Shipps to Lieutenant General Mann, 14 May 1812 (+ enclosure from Lieutenant Colonel Fletcher), WO55/ 981.

73. Jones, *Journals*, i, 272.

74. *The Times*, 19 October (p. 3), 26 October (p. 2) 1812.

75. Returns from J. Macleod, 20 December 1812; 20 February 1813; 3 March 1813; 7 March 1813, WO 55/ 1316.

76. Jones, *Journals*, i, 112, 129, 156, 273; *The Royal Military Calendar or Army Service and Commission Book*, 5 vols (3rd edn, London: 1820), iv, 166–8.

77. Report of Captain G. Robe on the navigation of the Douro, 26 November 1811, WO 55/1561.

78. Duncan, *History of the Royal Regiment of Artillery*, ii, 306.

79. Wellington to Wellesley, 8 April 1812, *WD*, ix, 47.

80. Oman, *A History of the Peninsular War*, v, 244–50.

81. *The Times*, 14 October 1812, p. 3. T. Sydenham to Henry Wellesley, 28 September 1812, Wellington (ed.), *Supplementary Despatches*, vii, 430.

82. Christopher Hall, *Wellington's Navy. Sea Power and the Peninsular War, 1807–1814* (Manchester, 2004), 201–7.

83. Wellington to Popham, 17 October 1812, *WD*, ix, 495.

84. Kevin D. McCranie, *Admiral Lord Keith and the Naval War Against Napoleon* (Gainesville FL, 2006), 154–6.

85. Orders for the VI Division, 28 October, 3, 4 November 1812, Order book, 12 February– 6 November 1812, Clinton Papers, Box G13.

86. Oman, *A History of the Peninsular War*, vi, 143, 152–5, 747–8.
87. This reprimand was issued in a printed circular; I saw a copy in, I believe, Clinton Papers, Box G13, which contains divisional order books.
88. Wellington to Bathurst, 17 October 1812, WD, ix, 496.
89. Carr-Gomm (ed.), *Letters and Journals*, 245–8.
90. Carr-Gomm (ed.), *Letters and Journals*, 250, 262–3.
91. Surtees, *Twenty-Five Years*, 138–49; 'A Picture of War', *Chambers's Edinburgh Journal*, 16 February 1839, 32.
92. *Morning Chronicle*, 5, 6, 15 February 1812.
93. *Liverpool Mercury*, 7 February 1812.
94. *Liverpool Mercury*, 30 October 1812.
95. *Liverpool Mercury*, 13 November 1812.
96. *The Times*, 23 December 1812, p. 2.
97. *The Times*, 5 February 1812.
98. Jones, *Journals*, i, 135–7.
99. Duncan, *History of the Royal Regiment of Artillery*, ii, 317, 320.
100. Jac Weller, *Wellington in the Peninsula* (London, 1999 edn), 204.
101. Allan Mallinson, *The Making of the British Army* (London, 2009), 228.
102. Jones, *Journals*, i, x.

Chapter 3

The Campaign to July 1813

Wellington's Campaign in 1812–13

The end-game of the Peninsular War began with modest British ambitions. From 2 October 1811 until 6 January 1812, Wellington commanded his army from the north-central Portuguese border at Freneda. 'This small town or village' lying in a plain about 4 miles from Fuentes de Oñoro enjoyed ready access to the fortress town of Almeida, 10 miles to the north, and to the road into Spain commanded on the Spanish side by Ciudad Rodrigo. Its small population, according to one officer, limited the opportunities for local people to spread information about British movements and preparations.[1]

This position commanded a wide gap between two French armies in western Spain. The French Army of the North had retreated from the fortified town of Ciudad Rodrigo towards Salamanca, with its ultimate destination rumoured to be Valladolid, 70 or so miles to the north and east of Salamanca. To the south, the French Army of Portugal was marching towards Baños and Plasencia, 40 and 50 miles respectively as the crow flies to the south-east of Ciudad Rodrigo.[2] Those two towns were on the main road between Seville in the far south and Salamanca, allowing the Army of Portugal to march northwards to Ciudad Rodrigo or southwards to Badajoz, each dominating a major east–west road crossing the Spanish-Portuguese border.

This French withdrawal in divergent directions opened up opportunities for a British advance into Spain. As a first, tentative step, Wellington's forces organized a loose blockade of Ciudad Rodrigo from September 1811. The only significant French convoy to break the blockade, on 1 November, consisted of so many troops that two months' worth of the six months' food supplies it conveyed were consumed en route. Writing on 18 December 1811, Wellington informed Lord Liverpool, the Secretary of State for War and Colonies, that Ciudad Rodrigo's garrison would have 'neither bread nor meat' by 24 February. He had built up the fortified Portuguese border town of Almeida as a major forward base more than 25 miles from Ciudad Rodrigo and moved a siege train there. But he planned to attack Ciudad Rodrigo before the garrison's supplies ran out because he wished to march southwards against Badajoz in February–March. At that time, the weather farther south was agreeable to his men and forage would be available for his animals. Taking Ciudad Rodrigo was not a certainty, but he was confident of taking Badajoz as long as he concentrated his entire field army upon that objective.[3]

These moves had specific, short-term objectives. Seizing control of two of the main routes across the Spanish-Portuguese border would enable the British to assist the

Spanish forces opposing French occupation with greater ease and flexibility. A further objective was to relieve pressure upon Spanish forces fighting the French elsewhere. On 1 January 1812, Wellington noted that French forces in northern Spain were being regrouped. The larger aim was to strengthen the drive against Spanish guerrillas who opposed Marshal Suchet's efforts to capture Valencia on the east coast. Wellington argued that by attacking Ciudad Rodrigo, even if he did not seize it, he would force the French to redirect significant numbers of those troops back to the Spanish-Portuguese border, thereby sapping their ability to reinforce the hard-pressed Suchet.[4] Wellington, therefore, planned an extensive border raid, using the artillery and siege equipment steadily accumulated in the last months of 1811 at Almeida.

What followed went far beyond the incursion originally intended. From Portugal, Wellington besieged and took the two fortress towns, Ciudad Rodrigo and Badajoz, as he had hoped. He then pursued French forces, driving them from Madrid and pushing them as far north as the fortified town of Burgos, well beyond any objective initially envisaged. There, in November, his offensive collapsed and he beat a hasty retreat back to the border region. As of 25 January 1813 he was back in Freneda where he had started sixteen months earlier.

In early November 1812, Wellington reflected on the strategic priorities facing him:

> It is scarcely necessary to consider what we shall do with our army after the French withdraw from Spain; as that event is not at present very probable, unless Buonaparte should be so pressed in the North as to be induced to weaken his force. . . . My opinion is, however, that if we should get the French out of Spain and the war should continue, we should carry on our operations on the southern frontier of France. . . . our means would be much greater than they would be on any other scene, would be applicable at a much earlier period, and would, moreover, be applied on the most vulnerable part of France.[5]

He saw no point in sending an army to Italy or transferring his own army to Germany, where it would be used simply as a pawn in the interests of the continental powers.

Wellington was soon proved wrong in his assessment of French manpower deployments. As 1813 opened the French dramatically cut their forces in Spain to meet the demands of Napoleon's invasion of Russia. Exploiting this shift in the balance of military power, Wellington once again went on the offensive in May 1813. A spectacular advance drove the French army to Vitoria, broke their army there on 21 June, and pushed its remnants back to the Pyrenees. In what looked like a footnote to his decisive victory at Vitoria, he then besieged the small port of San Sebastian.

Preparations in Early 1813

San Sebastian did not figure in British planning for the campaign of 1813. At the beginning of the year, Wellington learned of the latest events in Napoleon's disastrous Russian campaign. He immediately sent information about the state of the war in Spain to Vienna, knowing the importance of drawing Austria back into a coalition against France. He defined his strategic objective – 'to give employment to between

150,000 and 200,000 French troops in the next campaign' – in the most graphic terms to encourage Austria's re-entry into the war.[6] Given that priority, Wellington focused single-mindedly in the spring on pursuing his enemy's main army, not on specific territorial acquisitions. The earliest reference to San Sebastian in Wellington's official papers merely mentioned, in one sentence, an inquiry he would make in late February about the port's trade.[7] Whether this inquiry sought information on potential French supply routes if they were pushed back to the Franco-Spanish border or on possible British uses of the port if their campaign advanced that far remains unclear. It was, however, abundantly obvious that siege operations against San Sebastian, or anywhere else, did not dominate planners' thoughts for the new marching season beginning in May 1813. At his winter headquarters at Freneda in February, Wellington worried not about the possibility of yet another debilitating siege but about logistics, maintaining discipline on campaign and the diversion of resources to a British expeditionary force which the government in London planned to deploy on Spain's east coast.

Mounting a new campaign from Portugal required replenishing the army's weapons, clothing, transport support and finances, and these needs dominated planning in late February and early March. Wellington requested 60,000 muskets from Britain for his own and the supporting Portuguese armies. Within a week, this total had risen from 50,000. His request for suits of clothing also rose, from 50,000 to 100,000 for 1813, to allow for clothing to be distributed to the Spanish. He reassured the government in London that he would control the issuance of clothing tightly and that 'none shall be issued, the issue of which can be avoided'. Transport remained a concern. Although 1,500 extra horses for the artillery had been requested in October, only 800 had arrived for the spring campaign, and 100 of those were assigned to the Mediterranean coast.[8] As usual, the supply of money from the treasuries in Lisbon to the troops at the front was much delayed. The Portuguese authorities received their subsidy from Britain, but delayed paying their soldiers. In early March 1813, British troops had been paid to late November 1812, whereas the Portuguese had not been paid beyond June of that year, leaving them eight months in arrears. Wellington noted that 'serious evils' had resulted from major delays in payments in 1812, and warned that they would recur in 1813 unless payments were speeded up.[9] While the general did not spell out those consequences, long-delayed pay intensified soldiers' normal appetite for plundering local people on the march.

Wellington saw plundering and the mistreatment of civilians as persistent defects in his soldiers' conduct. On 10 February 1813, as the army recovered from the exhausting campaigning of the previous year, he reported to the secretary of state, 'Scarcely a post arrives that does not bring an account of some outrage committed by a British soldier on the inhabitants of Portugal.' He suggested various measures to increase the likelihood of punishment for misbehaviour and to reduce the abuse of civilians. For example, he recommended that courts martial should be conducted by panels made up of fewer officers in order to make them easier to convene. He urged that written evidence should be acceptable at trials, to overcome the difficulties in getting witnesses to attend courts, which were often held at some distance from the scenes of alleged crimes. He also wanted to expand the Corps of Guides for the campaign of 1813 in order to use them not just for reconnaissance and guarding lines of communication but also for policing the army on the march. Wellington was particularly concerned with policing roads used by soldiers to and from general hospitals, which were farther back from the front than regimental hospitals. A good deal of misconduct, he believed, occurred as soldiers went to or returned from such hospitals. A separate corps was necessary because 'our English non-commissioned officers and soldiers are not very fit to be trusted alone, and out of the view of their officers, in detached stations at a distance from the army'. Wellington expressed the recurrent wish to improve the army's internal discipline, especially through its non-commissioned officers.[10] His correspondence with the minister in London reminds us that planning concentrated as much on the basics of managing the army as it did on strategic assessments.

As for planning siege operations, Wellington noted on 10 February that 'it is possible that the events of the next campaign may render it necessary for the army to undertake one or more sieges in the north of Spain'. He presented no suggested objectives, but wanted the capability to mount a siege. The problem was that his army's larger guns, with the ammunition and supplies to support them, had been shipped to Alicante, on Spain's Mediterranean coast in June 1812. This disposition was to support an expedition to be launched from the British forces in Sicily. The British had occupied Sicily with about 10,000 men, as guarantors of the Neapolitan Bourbon monarchy, since 1808. Wellington retained artillery guns and supplies and he requested in February that they be shipped to La Coruña. He also asked that twice the amount of this equipment should be made ready in England for despatch to Spain when he needed it.[11] This was the only suggestion that he might need to take fortified towns.

But while Wellington prepared for the contingency of siege operations, he devoted more attention to opposing the government's planned expedition to eastern Spain. He informed Lord Bathurst:

> I doubt very much that the resources of the British Government are capable of equipping two armies for the field in the Peninsula, as they ought to be; and the attempt will only tend to cripple this army, upon which every thing depends, and which ought to be well equipped in order to be able to effect any thing, without doing much good to the other.

An army landed on the east coast should, he urged, simply cling to the coast, since any movement inland would require resources needed by his own army.[12] Looking forward from February, Wellington specified no geographical objectives for the year ahead. He simply wanted whatever heavy artillery was available in the Peninsula to be shipped to La Coruña, even though the westerly on-shore winds and heavy seas which battered that stretch of coast made it a difficult port from which to operate flexibly or quickly.

For their part, the French were certainly aware by May of a possible British offensive aimed at expelling them from Spain.[13] But their main preoccupations in March throughout the broad region from Burgos and Santander to the Franco-Spanish border were the protection of lines of communication and combating the threat from guerrilla bands. These remained their military priorities in May.

Controlling the towns, guarding the lines of communication and countering the guerrillas absorbed over 52,000 troops in March 1813 across this region, including the route south from Pamplona to Zaragoza. The coastal towns from Santander to the French border were guarded by 10,150 of those men. The stretch of the great royal road to France from Burgos to the French border on the Bidassoa River was guarded by 9,980 troops in 31 garrisons or small posts. Mobile columns accounted for 8,000 men in Navarre and 14,000 in the Biscay region and just beyond its western boundaries. Thus the two major east–west transport and communications routes and offensive operations against the guerrillas absorbed 42,000 troops.[14]

The distribution of garrisons along the coast indicated that in March the main French security focus was on Santander, where 4,000 of the 10,150 troops assigned to coastal towns were stationed, and Santona, with Laredo, where the garrisons totalled 3,000. The ports farther east, which became more important in July, were less well defended in March: Deba had a garrison of 300, Guetaria one of 800, San Sebastian 600 and Pasajes 150.

For the French in March 1813, San Sebastian was a useful port but not a garrison town on the scale of Pamplona, Bilbao, Vitoria or Burgos. It was a depot for munitions and food which could be drawn upon to supply ports to its west during the winter. One supply route ran from Bayonne to San Sebastian to Santona. Once the spring came, however, cruising in the Bay of Biscay by Royal Navy ships exposed French coastal traffic to attack. Indeed, French army officers assumed that the Biscayan coast, apart from Santona, Guetaria, San Sebastian and Pasajes, would also be open to the British to land munitions, arms, equipment, military clothing and merchandise.[15]

Large numbers of troops were assigned to defending lines of land communication. Of the 9,980 men assigned to the royal road between Burgos and the Bidassoa, 1,500 each were located at Burgos (including the fort de Burgos) and Vitoria. There were 700 men at Villareal and 600 at Tolosa. The road where it ran south and east of San Sebastian was protected by 300 troops at each of Hernani, Oyarzun and Irun, which became important in July and August. Two road routes other than the royal road were well protected. Branching off to the north-west, the road from Mondragon to Castro Urdiales on the coast absorbed 2,350 troops and the long road from Tolosa to Zaragoza via Pamplona was guarded by garrisons manned by further 4,300 soldiers.

The major immediate challenge came from Spanish insurgent bands whose threat was increased when they joined forces with regular Spanish divisions. In March, for example, Marshal Jourdan, King Joseph's chief of staff, was informed that the French were on the defensive in the region, whereas the Spanish guerrilla bands were on the offensive, most recently south of Santander and in the Bilbao area.[16] Although smaller towns and military posts were protected by yet another 6,500 troops, mobile columns were formed to pursue guerrilla bands. These took to the field once the weather improved. By the end of May, for example, columns actively pursued insurgent bands north-east of Pamplona, across the Biscay region and around Bilbao.[17]

The Aftermath of Vitoria

Wellington's shock advance in May–June pushed Joseph's main army into headlong retreat and destroyed French troop dispositions and operational focus in a region where complex security arrangements had been established. But the defeat and disintegration of the main French army in Spain on 21 June at Vitoria did not ease Wellington's difficulties in deciding his next moves. He faced a dilemma later described by Marshal Marmont:

> I have commanded armies of different numerical strength, and corps d'armée, under Napoleon: but 10,000 men alone, abandoned to the combinations of their own chief, cause him much more trouble and anxiety than the command of 50,000, forming part of an army of 200,000. For the latter to move, march, and engage according to orders, and in a determined direction, is easy. When the action is over, or the march terminated, when the camp is pitched, the General may repose as tranquilly as the private, until he receives further orders. But this is the moment of anxiety for the Commander-in-Chief, and which calls for his utmost vigilance and foresight.[18]

Wellington faced acute and immediate dilemmas as commander of a victorious army. He was forced by geography to follow the French up the royal road if he sought to invade or at least threaten to invade France itself. And he knew the French held a string of ports on the northern coast. In the days following the battle, Wellington had four objectives to consider, while also being distracted by events on the east coast. First, he sent Spanish forces to press the retreating French baggage train as it withdrew into France, expecting that it might flee as far as Bayonne. Secondly, he toyed with pursuing the separate French division under Clausel. That force comprised 11,000 infantry, 500 cavalry and 6 light mountain guns.[19] It had approached Vitoria on the day after the battle and then marched back along the Ebro valley, operating to the south-east independently of King Joseph's battered army.[20]

The latter offered the third and most immediate objective. Wellington sent Karl von Alten's brigade of cavalry, the Light Division and a troop of horse artillery in pursuit of Joseph's army. The British horse artillery inflicted such severe casualties on the rear-guard that the wounded begged the advancing hussars 'to put an end to their torments by at once depriving them of life. This could not, of course, be complied with, and the whole road presented a frightful spectacle of mutilated human beings in the most excruciating endurance'.[21] The pursuing force pressed fast enough to prevent the French rear-guard from destroying any of the numerous bridges along their line of retreat – an important achievement. It got to within 4½ miles of Pamplona on 24 June.[22] This pursuit compelled Joseph's army to continue its retreat on 25 June, leaving a garrison in Pamplona.

Fourthly, the British now had in Pamplona a new objective and they invested the town on the following day.[23] Pamplona loomed large in Wellington's calculations in the week after Vitoria. His first reaction, on 25 June, was to besiege it. Since the Anglo-Portuguese army which triumphed at Vitoria had no heavy guns, the British dragged twenty-eight French 12-pounders taken at Vitoria to Pamplona. Guns of that calibre were useful only in suppressing enemy movements in and out of the city as well as defensive fire from the city walls. They were quite inadequate for breaching the walls. In addition, the British appear to have had limited shot to service the guns. On 26 June, Wellington therefore ordered 28,000 round shot to be sent by the commanding officers from their arsenals at La Coruña and Ferrol and in Galicia. At the same time, he requested the commander of the naval squadron to make a Royal Navy warship available to carry those munitions from La Coruña to Deba, a tiny port east of Santander along the coast of northern Spain, or to convoy any transport ships which could be hired.[24] For the latter task, he asked for at least a small warship. More significantly, he asked for the siege train, which he had requested on 10 February to be readied in England, to be brought to Santander and then transferred to shallow craft and delivered to Deba. Thus siege operations moved back onto the agenda on 26 June, when Wellington informed the commander of the naval squadron:

> After having taken Pamplona, it will not be difficult to make ourselves masters of Santona, Castro Urdiales, and even San Sebastian; and it is not impossible that the measures to take those places might hereafter, with your assistance, go hand in hand with those for the capture of Pamplona: but at present we must direct all our efforts to the latter.[25]

Santona and Castro Urdiales were small ports about 15 miles and 30 miles respectively east of Santander; the larger port of Bilbao was another 15 miles farther east of Castro Urdiales. Wellington's thinking about progress along the coast at this stage therefore envisaged only incremental gains. San Sebastian, around 100 miles east of Santander, was at the outer limit of his ambitions.

Wellington's main objective, Pamplona, created a challenge which he expected to overcome without great difficulty. The town held at least three months' worth of food reserves, so that a blockade would have to be, and indeed turned out to be, a lengthy process. In late June, however, Wellington sought to maintain the momentum of his hitherto fast-moving campaign.

Meeting this need depended on the Royal Navy's ability to organize convoys from Lisbon to La Coruña and then on to recently accessible ports on Spain's northern coast. On 24 June Wellington expressed his doubts about the local naval squadron's effectiveness. He needed not only the guns, ammunition and equipment required for a siege, but also more basic munitions, as well as money. For example, he had so little musket ammunition after Vitoria that his army had to use captured French balls, which were smaller than British ones and not fully compatible with the British infantry musket. Yet convoying heavy loads of ordnance or ammunition from Lisbon proved very slow because there were so few naval vessels available. In a semi-private letter not intended for wider circulation, Wellington urged the Secretary of State for War and the Colonies, Lord Bathurst, to press for 'the protection of the navigation of the coast of Portugal, and of the north coast of Spain'. This was urgent, since 'For the first time I believe it has happened to any British army . . . its communication by sea is insecure'.[26]

While addressing the logistical problems involved in besieging Pamplona, Wellington also sought to scatter and harry the defeated French armies. One of the four options already noted was to isolate Clausel's corps. By 27 June, Wellington had decided, with the 3rd, 4th, 7th and Light divisions, to press Clausel's force of 12,000–14,000 men towards Tudela. Meanwhile, Lieutenant General Sir Rowland Hill was tasked with investing Pamplona and shadowing the main French army towards Roncesvalles in the Pyrenees. Lieutenant General Sir Thomas Graham, farther north, was ordered to 'push' the French under Foy back towards the Franco-Spanish border and then establish a defensive position on the main road or royal road connecting France and Spain along the coast.[27]

These plans were then adjusted the following day. Clausel moved east 'by some extraordinary forced marches'. Although Wellington advanced to Caseda, on the River Aragon, on 28 June, he concluded that Clausel would 'get out of our reach'.[28] He called a halt, preferring to leave the route back to France across the Pyrenees via Jaca open to Clausel, in the hope that this would encourage the latter to withdraw in that direction, rather than join Suchet's army in Catalonia.[29] Wellington, as we have seen, had opposed sending a British force to the Spanish east coast. He did not want the eastern front to gain greater importance by the arrival there of additional French forces.

In the meantime, Wellington learned of Graham's progress to the north, where, by 25 June, the allies were well on the way to San Sebastian. Foy's rear-guard fought some stiff actions on 24–5 June, inflicting 422 casualties on Graham's forces and more among the Spanish under his command. Those actions were capped by an assault on Tolosa at 6.00–7.00 p.m. on the 25th. Graham reported favourably in his official despatch on his troops' behaviour in these operations, and particularly praised their conduct on taking Tolosa. His men had overcome various difficulties. The 'weather and the road were so extremely bad' on 23 June that initial progress was slow. His light troops worked hard to clear the French from fine defensive positions on the high ground on each side of the valley approaching Tolosa, while line troops, including Major General Bradford's Portuguese infantry brigade, pushed along the main road in the valley.[30]

The polyglot character of Graham's force, consisting as it did of British, King's German Legion, Portuguese and Spanish units, added to operational difficulties. When Spanish troops failed to arrive at the intended time to attack Tolosa, Graham reportedly instructed the commanding officer of the 1st Light Battalion of the King's German Legion to assault the town: '"you see the Spaniards do not go on as they ought, therefore your battalion must take the place. Go on."' Tolosa immediately proved to be 'much more capable of defence than was at first expected'. The gates were barricaded and protected by buildings flanking them outside the walls and manned by the defenders. Three companies of the 1st Light Battalion attempted to storm the Vitoria gate, but suffered very heavy casualties, with the 8th company losing twenty-one killed and wounded out of fifty men engaged. Some fell to friendly fire from Spanish soldiers who had by that point appeared to their left. The 2nd Light Battalion then arrived with a 9-pounder gun and the Vitoria gate was broken open. Pioneers from the King's German Legion line battalions forced the Pamplona gate and the French evacuated the town. Given the approach of nightfall, it was decided not to enter the town and face the confusion of possible fighting while the French left during the night. The King's German Legion suffered 19 killed and 128 wounded, losses which their early nineteenth-century historian believed 'would have been in a great measure, avoided, had a more matured plan of operation been adopted against the place'.[31]

Having apparently been casual in launching the assault on Tolosa, Graham next seemed similarly casual in writing to the Adjutant General that his Spanish and Portuguese troops had not been effective in pursuing Foy's army after Tolosa fell. Given the speed of the advance to Vitoria and the challenging conditions they had faced in the three days following the battle, the troops were naturally exhausted. But Wellington used Graham's comments as an excuse to drop his overly ambitious initial plan to besiege Pamplona. From Caseda, he wrote to Graham at 2.00 p.m. on 28 June:

> if we cannot depend upon the operations of the Spanish and Portuguese troops in pursuing a flying enemy, we certainly cannot depend upon them in those operations which must be carried on to cover the siege of Pamplona. I therefore propose to blockade that place rather than lay siege to it. We shall get the place at a later period . . .

Wellington's use of this criticism appears deliberate because he suggested on 28 June that Graham 'qualify . . . in some degree' his official dissatisfaction as expressed on the 26th 'with the conduct of some of the Portuguese and Spaniards'.[32] By 3 July Graham had corrected the impression that his troops had not performed to expectations.[33] But by then the plan to besiege rather than blockade Pamplona had disappeared.

Pamplona possessed imposing defences. Lieutenant Colonel Frazer visited the town in February 1814 and noted:

> We walked very attentively over the citadel and works, which were extensive and strong, in perfect repair, and well supplied with artillery. . . . The works are a great deal stronger than I supposed, and I have no doubt it is well we did not attack them, since I think we should have failed. . . . On two sides the river Arga runs under the walls, which are very high, and on these sides not accessible. . . . besides the numerous guns on the ramparts, there is on the esplanade a very complete park of about sixty pieces of artillery.[34]

The city's large fortress, the Ciudadela, was elaborately constructed in the seventeenth century to withstand and repel prolonged sieges. By 1813 the city, the capital of Navarre, had become a bastion of French support in a region of vigorous and often threatening guerrilla activity. It had historically been a major centre of Franco-Spanish trade and developed under French occupation as a vital base for the French army. The French garrison in the spring of 1812 totalled 4,500 and the French in the region depended on the city's hospitals. Its population was forcibly linked to the French by the occupiers' repression and then by guerrillas' treatment of alleged afrancesados when they blockaded the city for long periods in 1812–13.[35] A social and political alignment to the French added to its military strength.

The decision to blockade rather than besiege acknowledged Wellington's lack of heavy artillery. His 12-pounders were of limited use when 18-pounders were needed to suppress the defenders' artillery and 24-pounders were required to breach well-constructed fortified walls. The curious lapse in planning was that Wellington had contemplated a siege with the same complement of firepower only days earlier. Graham's suggestion of under-performance by Portuguese and Spanish troops appears, therefore, to have been a convenient pretext for a decision taken for different reasons which obtained before the events at Tolosa.

Wellington's forces' movements in four different directions during late June were hampered by two interrelated managerial problems. While his plans involved dividing his army, they also depended upon the closer integration of Spanish forces into his operations than was previously customary. The French retreat released Spanish forces from regional operations against the more numerous and more widely distributed French corps of 1810–12, and gave Wellington greater confidence in deploying them against the demoralized French. But, as Spanish stock seemed to be on the rise, Wellington's own army lost some of the glitter acquired in the campaign to Vitoria.

Wellington, writing to Bathurst, attributed his relative lack of military progress after Vitoria to the fragmentation of his army; tight-knit in the advance to Vitoria, it lost its cohesion afterwards. Territorial gains in the week after Vitoria followed painlessly from French withdrawal, but opened up opportunities for soldiers to plunder and drink without risk from French patrols. The battle of Vitoria had 'totally annihilated all order and discipline'. Instead of resting and re-supplying overnight after the battle, the soldiers searched for plunder and were in no condition to chase the retreating French the next day. They continued to plunder and desert on the subsequent march, which was also hindered by rain.[36] In early July Ensign George Hennell reported that Wellington 'is in a tremendous rage with the cavalry who behaved very bad with respect to plunder. He saw some of the 18th Hussars . . . plundering instead of pushing the enemy'. Indiscipline spread more widely. For example, at the end of the month, Hennell spent the day at a court martial of 16 soldiers, 14 of whom got 50 or 100 lashes that night for plundering.[37] One correspondent complained on 26 June of terrible weather, with heavy rain and muddy roads, made worse by the rapidity of the march and the frustration of not catching the fleeing French. By 30 June, he described 'scenes of drunkenness I never witnessed, of riot and disorder', with the soldiers 'swelling themselves with wine until they have no longer power of action, either mental or bodily'. Such abandon was sustained by the army's reportedly seizing 1 million dollars at Vitoria, which he suspected was nearer 10 million.[38]

A week after the battle, Wellington reckoned that he had lost 4,186 British and Portuguese troops at Vitoria and 4,156 to straggling and absenteeism since then. Of the 41,547 rank and file in the *British* regiments in his army on 17 June, some 3,164 had become casualties by 29 June but another 2,733 were missing as stragglers. He partly attributed a lack of discipline to the closeness of his NCOs to their men in both pay and situation. But junior officers also failed to control the ordinary soldiers, 'the scum of the earth'.[39]

He returned to this problem on 9 July, bemoaning the disappearance of thousands of 'our vagabond soldiers'. Having sent 'officers with parties of the Cavalry Staff corps in all directions after them', he could only guess that 'they are concealed in the villages in the mountains'.[40] By 19 July, with 5,892 troops sick and 'many stragglers still out', Wellington estimated that his Anglo-Portuguese army had 9,626 fewer men than before the battle of Vitoria, one month earlier.[41] To reinforce his own authority, he secured the support of the Commander-in- Chief, the Duke of York, in sending back to Britain those officers who had failed to maintain discipline after Vitoria. The duke promised to dismiss such officers with no further inquiry.[42] Although Wellington insisted that British troops would 'always fight', he worried that their health and behaviour depended upon regular pay which was not forthcoming as the campaign advanced.[43]

Such problems added to the confusion facing Wellington's army in late June. Wellington's own movements underlined this sense that no achievable objective had been defined. He was near Pamplona on 25–7 June inclusive, making his dispositions for the intended siege. He then pursued Clausel to Caseda on the Aragon River on 28–9 June. He failed to achieve his main aim of 28 June to engage Clausel because he could not catch Clausel where he wanted to fight him. However, his lesser objective of driving Clausel eastwards without pushing him into Catalonia was attained. On the 30th, Wellington therefore pulled back to Monreal, south of Pamplona, and then moved to Huarte, just to the east of Pamplona, on 1 July.[44]

On that day, Wellington learned that Lieutenant General Sir John Murray had broken off siege operations at Tarragona, on the east coast. Wellington was furious. In withdrawing on 14 June Murray abandoned his siege artillery and munitions. Wellington informed Murray that such a loss 'weighs most upon my mind in all this'. It boosted French morale, 'entirely cripples our operations on the eastern coast', and opened up the possibility that Suchet, no longer under threatening pressure in his sector, might move his army against Wellington's right flank. He was also irritated that Murray, in his despatches, had treated the loss of artillery as a matter of little note.[45] This reaction demonstrated Wellington's acute anxieties over the artillery available in the Peninsula. But it did not impress senior generals at home. The court martial held later in London upheld Murray's decision to abandon 'some battering guns and mortars, and stores of no great value' in preference to exposing troops to attack during their evacuation. He was found guilty only of an error of judgement and further action against him was left to the discretion of the Commander-in-Chief, the Duke of York.[46]

Having let off steam over the abandoned artillery, Wellington made his new dispositions for a blockade of Pamplona. On 2 July he put Lieutenant General the Earl of Dalhousie in charge of a 'light' blockade pending the arrival of Spanish forces to take on the task. The British would construct redoubts at 1,000–1,200yd from the town, so as to enable their soldiers to encircle it. Corn was to be cut, or burned, as close to the fortified walls as possible, so as to deny the defenders a continuing supply of food.

But Dalhousie's only artillery consisted of his divisional field guns. Nothing more effective in repelling French sorties against the encircling allies would be available until French guns captured at Vitoria arrived.[47]

The decision to blockade and wait for food shortages to force Pamplona's surrender reflected British logistical problems. The difficulties can be illustrated by the efforts made to bring heavier artillery from Deba. On 25 June, Lieutenant Colonel Augustus Frazer of the Royal Horse Artillery was just outside Pamplona when he was despatched to Santander, via Vitoria, to collect heavy artillery shipped from Lisbon via La Coruña for the siege. At Santander, he was to supervise the transfer of the heavy guns to smaller vessels, which would sail east along the coast to the tiny harbour at Deba. From there he was to find the means of transporting the guns to Pamplona where the trenches would in the meantime be dug. Frazer made light of the objective; 'I cannot imagine the siege of a little place like Pampelona will arrest the progress of such an army as ours'. The town was believed to be only 1,200–1,400yd by 1,000–1,200yd in size.[48] This comment showed how little information this relatively senior officer possessed and how cursorily he evaluated the challenge ahead.

Setting off the following day, he reached Santander on the morning of the 29th having travelled back to Vitoria and then across the mountains through Berberana and Espinoza. Securing horses and mules, and replacing those exhausted by the mountain tracks delayed his progress. But Frazer's arrival conveniently coincided with that of the heavy guns from La Coruña, which reached the port on the same day. He then sailed eastwards, by a Royal Navy brig, to Deba, where stores and ammunition were unloaded. By the afternoon of 1 July the squadron commander, Captain Sir George Collier, had landed and reviewed the position with Frazer. Collier concluded that the bar at the harbour would make it difficult to land the heavy guns and suggested that they be landed at a harbour farther east. Frazer felt unable to change his orders in that way. In the absence of soldiers, the sailors – 'famous fellows in all cases of energy and exertion' – did the heavy lifting. Disembarking and transporting the munitions proved to be no easy matter. There were no docks as such and so munitions had to be brought ashore by small boats. Landings were impossible at low tides. Meanwhile the weather intervened and Frazer noted on 3 July: 'It blows very hard. We cannot get our guns on shore . . .'[49] Deba's lack of facilities indicates how desperately the British would need a far larger and properly developed harbour if they were to operate well east of Santander and Bilbao.

Despite this failure, work proceeded at the harbour in getting small carts and loading them with stores, including barrels of gunpowder. Local labour was used and on 2 July four officers and ninety men of the British and Portuguese artillery arrived to work at the wharf and on repairing a suspension bridge. Frazer assembled about 100 carts and a pair of oxen for each cart. Apart from the difficulties in landing the ordnance, there was the challenge of conveying it about 66 miles to Pamplona. Although the main road from Tolosa to Pamplona posed no problems, the road from Deba to Tolosa, stretching for 36 miles, was 'bad'. An artillery officer, Captain William Webber, was tasked with repairing it, 'applying for that purpose to the civil authorities for the assistance of the peasantry'. On 3 July, however, orders arrived at Deba to re-embark the stores and ship them out of the tiny port. Pamplona was not going to be besieged after all.[50]

In justifying this decision, Wellington ignored earlier reservations about the reliability of Spanish soldiers. His despatch to the secretary of state commended their behaviour, following Graham's suppression of his initial criticisms. Wellington instead claimed that his decision followed Murray's evacuation from Tarragona. The French held Catalonia and Valencia by maintaining numerous fortresses. If the British no longer possessed the means to threaten those positions, Suchet could use his field army flexibly. By jettisoning so much artillery, Wellington asserted, Murray gave Suchet the option of marching west, linking up with Clausel and advancing upon Wellington's right flank. If Wellington's scenario seems exaggerated, he was disingenuous in stating that 'The disasters at Tarragona, and my view of their probable consequences, have induced me to determine only to blockade Pampluna'. In fact, news of Murray's retreat reached him on 1 July, *after* his change in thinking about Pamplona. A generous interpretation might be that the decision was confirmed by events to the east. But the key factor, as he explained to Bathurst, was a truer appreciation of Pamplona's strengths:

> the place was of such a description, and in such a state of defence, as to require a much larger equipment of heavy ordnance than I had immediately at command; and . . . it would require an operation of from five to six weeks' duration which could not even be commenced for a fortnight or three weeks, and the employment of from 15,000 to 20,000 men of our best troops; whereas the blockade could be held by troops of inferior numbers, and of not so good a description; and it is probable that, in point of time, the place would be obliged to surrender within twelve weeks.

By not tying 15,000–20,000 good troops down to besieging Pamplona, and by leaving the lighter blockade to what he regarded as less battle-ready Spanish troops, Wellington held his whole Anglo-Portuguese army in readiness to meet any French response to the circumstances changed by the British 'disasters at Tarragona'.[51]

The new plan for Pamplona won approval in some quarters. One officer, describing Pamplona as 'the strongest place in Spain' – a fact not apparent to Lieutenant Colonel Frazer a week or so earlier – welcomed rumours on 9 July that Spanish troops would conduct a blockade. His reasoning was curious. The French, he conjectured, were more likely to surrender quickly to the Spanish than to the British because the French feared that Spanish troops would treat the French more violently the longer the siege lasted and the longer therefore the eventual French surrender was delayed. British soldiers, by contrast, were so readily diverted by the prospect of plunder that thoughts of vengeance disappeared once an opportunity to go on the rampage opened up. By this reasoning, the French would conclude that it was ultimately more risky to prolong resistance against the Spanish than against the British.[52]

An additional advantage to Wellington's chosen course was that the blockade did not require large quantities of heavy artillery. Oman noted that the defensive walls carried about eighty guns, but one official British return stated that the largest guns taken at Pamplona when the siege ended were 12-pounders. The French did not possess the means to engage in a long-range and destructive artillery duel. The British began to move eighteen captured French 24-pounders from Vitoria on 26 July, followed later by six more of the same size. The initial complement of eighteen heavy guns was distributed in pairs to nine posts established in an outer ring around the town. Such a distribution indicated that the allies did not intend to breach the defensive walls. Wellington planned to deploy about 11,000 mainly Spanish troops against a French garrison of 3,600.[53] With the artillery provided by French guns captured at Vitoria, the British siege train shipped to Deba was available for use elsewhere. According to Lieutenant Colonel Hew Ross on 10 July, 'the opinion is general that we shall have it without a siege'.[54] But the blockade would last months before the garrison was starved into capitulating.

Notes

1. Anon. [Blakiston], *Twelve Years' Military Adventure*, ii, 157–8.
2. Wellington to Liverpool, 2 October 1811, *WD*, viii, 316.
3. Wellington to Liverpool, 18 December 1811, *WD*, viii, 471–2.
4. Wellington to Liverpool, 1 January 1812, *WD*, viii, 524.
5. Wellington to Bathurst, 7 November 1812, *WD*, ix, 542.
6. Wellington to Bathurst, 19 January 1813, *WD,* x, 32.
7. Wellington to Henry Wellesley, 25 February 1813, *WD,* x, 146.
8. Wellington to Bathurst, 17 February, 24 February, 3 March 1813; Wellington to Beresford, 27 February 1813, *WD*, x, 124, 140, 148, 163–4.
9. Wellington to Stuart, 7 March 1813, *WD*, x, 168–9.
10. Wellington to Bathurst, 10, 24 February 1813, *WD*, x, 106–7, 140–1.
11. Wellington to Bathurst, 10 February 1813, *WD*, x, 104–5.
12. Wellington to Bathurst, 17 February 1813, *WD,* x, 124–5.
13. General Buquet to the Prince of Wagram, 29 mai (1813), SHAT C8 343.
14. All French manpower numbers in this and the following paragraphs are in 'État des Troupes . . . sur la ligne de communication de Burgos à Yrun', SHAT C8 218.
15. Letter 10, 10 mars 1813, SHAT C8 213; letter 76, 12 mars SHAT C8 214.
16. Letter 10, 10 mars 1813 SHAT C8 213.
17. Rapport Pampelune, 23 mai 1813; 2 letters Pampelune, 29 mai 1813; letter, 18 juin 1813, SHAT C8 343.
18. *Colburn's United Service Magazine*, 1845, Part II, 357.
19. Clausel to the duc de Dalmatie, 12 juillet 1813, SHAT C8 248.
20. Wellington to Bathurst, 24 June; Wellington to Castanos, 26 Juin 1813, *WD*, x, 456–7, 462.
21. North Ludlow Beamish, *History of the King's German Legion*, 2 vols (London, 1837), ii, 220.
22. Ross to Sir Hew Dalrymple, 24 June 1813, *Memoir of Field Marshal Sir Hew Dalrymple Ross* (Woolwich, 1871), 40–1.
23. Wellington to Bathurst, 26 June 1813, *WD*, x, 463.
24. Wellington to Lieutenant Colonel Bourke, 26 June 1813, *WD*, x, 461.
25. Wellington to Captain Sir George Collier, 26 June 1813; Wellington to Bathurst, 26 June 1813, *WD*, x, 461–2, 464.
26. Wellington to Bathurst, 24 June 1813, *WD*, x, 458–9.
27. Wellington to Graham, 27 June 1813, *WD*, x, 464–5.

28. Wellington to H. Wellesley, 28 June 1813, *WD*, x, 472.
29. Wellington to Lord William Bentinck, 1 July 1813; Wellington to Bathurst, 3 July 1813 *WD*, x, 478, 501.
30. Graham to Wellington, 26 June, *WD*, x, 465–8.
31. Beamish, *History*, ii, 224–8.
32. Wellington to Graham, 28 June 1813, *WD*, x, 465–9.
33. Wellington to Graham, 3 July 1813, *WD*, x, 497.
34. Sabine (ed.), *Letters*, 397–8.
35. John Lawrence Tone, *The Fatal Knot: the Guerrilla War in Navarre and the Defeat of Napoleon in Spain* (Chapel Hill NC, 1994), 35, 42–3, 137–41.
36. Wellington to Bathurst, 29 June 1813, *WD*, x, 472–3.
37. Michael Glover (ed.), *A Gentleman Volunteer: The Letters of George Hennell from the Peninsular War, 1812–13* (London, 1979), 103, 113.
38. The *Royal Military Panorama or Officers' Companion*, ii, 545 (September 1813).
39. Wellington to Bathurst, 2 July 1813, *WD*, x, 495–6.
40. Wellington to Bathurst, 9 July 1813 *WD*, x, 519.
41. Wellington to Bathurst, 19 July 1813, *WD*, x, 544.
42. York to Wellington, 22 July 1813, Wellington (ed.), *Supplementary Despatches*, viii, 106.
43. Wellington to Liverpool, 25 July 1813, *WD*, x, 569.
44. Wellington to General Copons, 28 June 1813; to General Castanos, 30 June 1813; to Lord William Bentinck, 1 July 1813, *WD*, x, 471, 475, 477–8.
45. Wellington to Sir John Murray, 1 July 1813, *WD*, x, 488.
46. *Edinburgh Annual Register*, Vol. 8 (January 1815), 77.
47. Wellington to Dalhousie, 2 July 1813, *WD*, x, 489–90.
48. Sabine (ed.), *Letters*, 167.
49. Sabine (ed.), *Letters*, 169–72, 174, 178.
50. Sabine (ed.), *Letters*, 175, 177–80.
51. Wellington to Bathurst, 3 July 1813, *WD*, x, 506.
52. *Royal Military Panorama*, ii, 545, 547–8.
53. Oman, *A History of the Peninsular War*, vi, 528–9, vii, 150–1; 'Return of Ordnance, Carriages and Ammunition captured from the enemy on 21st Instant' in Dickson to Somerset, 5 July 1813, WP 9/2/2/10; Dickson to Somerset, 26 July 1813, WP 9/2/2/10.
54. Ross to Sir Hew Dalrymple, 10 July, *Memoir*, 42–3.

Chapter 4

San Sebastian as an Objective

French Re-organization

British attention shifted from Pamplona to San Sebastian, a prosperous port with a population of 8,400 situated on the north-eastern coast of Spain.[1] Its agricultural hinterland included some fine farming lands. As one officer noted from nearby Oyarzun, 'The country is very rich and well cultivated but very uneven, the hills are high and very rugged . . . – the valleys are consequently narrow, but produce very excellent crops of wheat and Indian corn, and the sides of the hills are planted with chestnut and apple trees'.[2] Its military significance lay not in commerce or wealth but in its position close to the more important of the two main northern roads from France into Spain (the other being on the east coast) and its ready accessibility on the Bay of Biscay to the southern French port of St Jean de Luz, 15 miles or so to the east.

The town itself had few assets of direct interest to the British; it was the French who chose to make San Sebastian a point of military significance. They did so as part of a broad defensive strategy which involved rethinking the leadership of the main armies in Spain, defining the available number of troops there and fixing upon key locations to be held.

Napoleon's first priority, as ever, was central Europe where he sought to delay and disrupt the new alliance of Russia and Prussia. On 25 May, the emperor proposed a truce with his Prussian and Russian enemies in central Germany and the French entered diplomatic discussions with the Prussians and Russians before the end of the month. Having failed to inflict a speedy defeat on their opponents, the French needed to replace manpower losses, and particularly to make up deficits in cavalry which suffered severely during the Russian campaign. People at home were weary of war. And Napoleon wished to appear ready to settle his differences with Prussia and Russia in order to encourage Austria to remain neutral. On 5 June, the three Continental belligerents signed a ceasefire to last until 20 July. On 30 June, from his base at Dresden, Napoleon agreed with Metternich, the Austrian foreign minister, to extend the armistice to 10 August. A peace conference, with Austria acting as mediator, would convene at Prague on 10 July. There were military advantages to this approach, allowing the French to embody and train fresh cohorts of conscripts and wait until the forthcoming harvest improved the flow of food to the French army. Having at least served those purposes, the negotiations duly failed. Austria, also using the time to build up its forces, joined the allies and set its main army on what turned out to be its momentous march to Leipzig on 17 August.[3]

On 17 June, Wellington knew that Napoleon had forced the Prussians and Russians into retreat at the battle of Bautzen, about 25 miles east of Dresden, on 20–1 May. The battle involved about 200,000 men on the two sides together, but the reports reaching Wellington suggested that the French victory was far from decisive and indeed cost the French 50,000 casualties. (The reality was still high but nearer 20,000.) Wellington at this time did not believe that Prussia and Russia would participate in a peace congress at Prague which Napoleon had proposed before Bautzen.[4] The situation in Germany did not therefore influence Wellington's advance to Vitoria. On 24 June, three days after the battle of Vitoria, Wellington informed his brother Henry that 'King Joseph and his army must quit Spain' and that the other French forces were vulnerable: 'I shall turn them out of Spain before they can be reinforced'.[5] When Lord Castlereagh, the Foreign Secretary, learned of the battle on 2 July, he had news of that triumph spread across Europe in the hope that it might stiffen Prussian and Russian resolve and help Vienna to decide in favour of war.[6]

Meanwhile, before news of the British victory at Vitoria on 21 June reached Paris, the minister for war, General Clarke, Duc de Feltre, who had headed the army's topographical department before being appointed minister in 1808, set out the objectives to be achieved in the light of Wellington's rapid advance across northern Spain. The minister asserted on 22 June that the fortified town of Pamplona, the Biscay coast and the lines of communication eastwards to France had to be 'conserved at all costs'. Of equal strategic importance was protecting the army of Aragon's lines of communication, at that time through Zaragoza, back to France. To begin this task the dispersed divisions of the Army of Portugal and the Army of the North had to be concentrated as a matter of urgency.[7] On 25 June, still unaware of Vitoria, Clarke informed Marshal Jourdan, Joseph's chief of staff, of Napoleon's 'astonishment' at Jourdan's mismanagement of the three armies at the king's disposal. The precipitate retreat had been confused, devoid of clear objectives or overall plan, and incompetent in failing to counter Wellington's outflanking movement on the French northern front. Co-ordination with the divisional generals had been poor.[8]

On 28 June, still ignorant of Vitoria but aware that the army was retreating east from that town, Clarke insisted in the 'strongest and most urgent' manner that the retreat had to stop and that King Joseph should initiate an offensive with the 'greatest vigour'. Presumably sarcastically, he assumed that this further retreat had been undertaken to enable the king to join up with Clausel's dispersed division operating to the south-east. He dismissed any excuses about the French being outnumbered in northern Spain by stating that 100,214 troops were available to the king, who ought therefore to be able to gather an army of 80,000 to halt Wellington's advance. Clarke further argued that Wellington's forces in the field were so depleted by garrison duties, consolidating lines of communication, sickness and convalescence that they could not exceed 45,000; the Spanish contingents, though significant in size, were widely dispersed in large numbers and could not add more than about 15,000 effectives to Wellington's fighting army. Moreover, the French were superior in courage, in their experience of war and in their awareness of past glories. Pressing for the restoration of 'the honour of imperial arms', the minister offered more practical, if very limited, assistance by ordering all troops at Bayonne who could be spared to be sent to the Spanish frontier, while the national guard in the French frontier departments would assume the active defensive duties hitherto fulfilled by those soldiers.[9]

The order to halt the retreat and consolidate in the area to the east of Vitoria suffered from two flaws. First, the instructions were issued before Paris knew of Vitoria. Secondly, the region into which the king and Clausel marched was particularly hostile to the French regime in Spain. As early as late 1811, guerrilla bands operated successfully in Aragon, Navarre and Guadalaxara. Referring to one leading guerrilla leader, Wellington had noted then that 'Mina's success in Navarre has . . . been extraordinary, and his numbers have rapidly increased'.[10] Navarre in particular offered little potential support for the French, since its people felt a limited sense of grievance against the old order and limited enthusiasm for the new dispensation. The local social structure was relatively flat, small-scale landowning was common, food was relatively plentiful and cheap, the church did not have large religious houses to support and taxes remained low.[11]

When Clarke learned of Vitoria, he insisted that King Joseph should demonstrate resolution and 'audace'. He reminded the king that he had 118,828 men (suddenly increased from his earlier estimate of 100,000) at his disposal, far more than Wellington commanded. Admittedly, the minister repeatedly ignored both regular and irregular Spanish troops confronting the French. Paris provided some extra resources for the battered army under Joseph's command. Four divisions under the Comte Reille were assigned to him. The minister promised to replace the heavy artillery losses at Vitoria. Biscuit, other food supplies and funds would be sent to Bayonne, and troops from the reserve would strengthen the frontier.[12]

If the first strategic priority was to keep a large French army in Spain and consolidate dispersed divisions, the next was to prepare the defence of the Bidassoa River frontier on the principal route into France. On 2 July, Clarke instructed Reille to co-ordinate the troops under his direct command at Irun with forces under Foy, then at Andoain, to create a corps of 20,000 men, sufficient to prevent the enemy crossing the Bidassoa. Reille's first duty was to stop the enemy at all costs and 'never permit him to set foot on the empire's territory'. Clarke may have feared that Wellington might try to outflank Joseph, if the king positioned himself at or near Pamplona, by marching north of Pamplona on the great or royal road towards the coast. Moving Reille's forces to block the coastal road into France would give the king time to bring up the main French army to thwart any such advance by Wellington. This assessment proved partly accurate because Spanish forces under Wellington's direction, though not his main army, moved up the royal road in early July.

It was now that San Sebastian entered French strategic thinking. Holding the town was part of these defensive arrangements to delay the enemy's progress and keep him out of France. Clarke, using figures already out of date, noted that the town was held by only 450 conscripts and 23 guns. It needed 3,000–4,000 troops and more guns and improved batteries. Strengthening San Sebastian should be a high priority and Joseph and Jourdan were to give Reille all possible support in meeting those needs.[13] Initially San Sebastian figured in a list of places to be defended, but by 6 July it was included simply with Santona and Pamplona among the emperor's priorities until a counter-offensive might be launched. Brigadier General Emmanuel Rey, having been appointed governor of the town a few weeks earlier, was commended for his energetic work in re-organizing the town's defences.[14] Meanwhile, Jourdan, criticized for three weeks of despatches full of 'gaps, contradictions and a kind of incoherence – inevitable, no doubt, in the confusion of the first moments' of a defeat – was asked how the British were able to invest and blockade San Sebastian without interruption 'in the vicinity and nearly in the sight of 80 thousand French?'[15]

The recurrent criticism from Paris indicated that Joseph's and Jourdan's days were numbered. Marshal Soult, Duc de Dalmatie, was transferred from a command in Germany to become the emperor's lieutenant in Spain, with command also of the French Pyrenean frontier. Clarke met Soult in Paris and issued him with his instructions on 6 July. He assured Soult that the marshal would receive artillery to replace the losses at Vitoria. But he also insisted that enough guns were available immediately to enable the French to resume the offensive as soon as possible, to occupy the province of Guipuzcoa – essentially the present Basque country – and 'by a single movement to relieve San Sebastian'.[16] Joseph was informed in a letter of 9 July that Soult would take over.

Why was so much importance attached to occupying territory in Spain? The most obvious advantage for the French was avoiding the costs of sustaining an army of over 100,000 men inside south-eastern France. The armies in retreat in June–July had long lived off Spanish resources. Men of the Army of Portugal had a particularly bad reputation for insubordination and plundering, which had been bridled by Clausel's stern measures in 1812. Clausel, however, had moved on and 'prodigious damage' had been inflicted on Navarre and Biscay by that army by late June 1813. Granted, this was a difficult area in which to feed large numbers of additional men.[17] But Napoleon pointed out in early July that the harvest there was not far off and that fact should encourage an offensive.[18] The war ministry secured one month's French supplies for Soult's army inside Spain, but the clear intention was that the army would enter areas of Spain which could support it. The converse of this was that a hard-pressed army would plunder in France as it was accustomed to plundering in Spain. Clarke emphasized to Joseph on 5 July that generals needed to restore discipline since there could be no ill-discipline on French soil.[19] For his operations on the Franco-Spanish border, Reille was told that 'the first obstacle' to be overcome was ill-discipline.[20] One aggravating cause of indiscipline was presumably the chronic delay in paying soldiers. Retreat into France meant that the burden of pay fell upon the already overstretched French treasury. Clarke's emergency measures of early July included the decision to pay the retreating troops from the French treasury; but that provision covered current pay, not the considerable amounts of back pay still outstanding.[21]

Thus the challenges which Wellington faced – in sustaining food supplies, maintaining regular pay, holding an army together, preventing soldiers' plundering, and acting cautiously when entering enemy territory to avoid alienating the local population – confronted French commanders as well. Their answer was to keep the war in Spain. Holding on to San Sebastian was one means of pinning British forces down, slowing the British advance, and retaining a base for French operations if the British were thrown into retreat.

San Sebastian entered French strategic thinking in early July. Napoleon's concerns were conveyed to Soult on 11 and 13 July. The emperor was amazed by the fact that the British had been allowed to blockade San Sebastian and to position themselves in front of the town, as well as operate on the main route into France between Tolosa and Irun. He wanted Reille, who had about 7,000 men immediately to hand, to cover the town. He also wanted Pamplona relieved as soon as possible and repeated the much-expressed insistence that Clausel, who commanded about 6,000 men east of Pamplona, should not be detached from the main army.[22]

Having communicated these concerns to Soult, Clarke wrote to Rey on 16 July informing him of the marshal's appointment, promising him that the marshal was getting the resources with which to relieve San Sebastian, and instructing him to defend the town with all means available since the emperor attached the highest importance to its retention.[23] San Sebastian had become a symbol of French resolve. Not for the last time, a siege was undertaken partly because the defenders sought to maintain national prestige and uphold French morale as much as they sought to retain a military asset. This was not one of the justifications for defending a fortress listed by Clausewitz, nor was it one that could readily be fitted into any models of scientific warfare.

Under firm instructions from Napoleon, Soult regrouped his forces from within France and focused on two principal lines of communication. He based his operations on the fortified town of Bayonne, near the coast and commanding the royal road into Spain. That road crossed the Bidassoa River, gave access to a branch road south to Pamplona and continued itself west through Hernani and then southwards to Tolosa. A second major route from Bayonne led via St Jean Pied de Port, in the mountains, across the Pyrenees through Roncevalles and down to Pamplona. Between these principal routes lay a lesser road through the Baztan valley. To Clarke's annoyance, Reille's forces had lost control of the valley to advanced parties of allied – and indeed Spanish – forces.[24] The Baztan valley was very long, quite broad in places, and useful as a source of supplies. But the allies made it difficult for the French to get into it and through it.

Soult began moving his armies on 23 July in a commendably quick recovery. Leaving a reserve on the Bidassoa, he pushed south from St Jean Pied de Port with the objective of lifting the allied siege of Pamplona. His plan was then to shift to his right and force the allies from their siege of San Sebastian and, much farther west, from the blockade of Santona. Once the threat from Wellington had been removed, Soult might be able to co-operate with Marshal Suchet, Duc d'Albufera, who was hard-pressed in Catalonia and Aragon.[25] The line of communication to the east from France ran through Jaca, in the Pyrenees, and Zaragoza, and had been kept open by Clausel's detached force of about 6,000 men.[26] The long valley to Zaragoza offered open country in which to move large bodies of troops. Whether these plans were thought to be realistic may be an open question. But Soult had certainly pushed Wellington into headlong retreat from Burgos in 1812. It is possible that the French believed that the British had over-extended themselves once more.

Soult's re-organization of the French army and his insistence on a counter-attack changed the nature of the campaign. As Soult initiated movements that opened an eight-month contest with Wellington, the whole front pulsed into action on 23 July. What lay ahead proved to be a grinding contrast to Wellington's dash to Vitoria.

British Preparations Against San Sebastian

While the French prepared to defend San Sebastian, Wellington had to satisfy himself on three counts before launching his operation against the town. Was a siege feasible? Would the port be sufficiently well blockaded to prevent French reinforcement from the sea? Which troops would be available for the siege? On the first and fundamental question, Wellington informed Graham on 3 July that he awaited 'Major Smith's report to determine upon the attack of San Sebastian, which appears to be an operation of a very different description from the attack of Pamplona'. Pending the results of Major Charles F. Smith, RE's deliberations, Wellington assigned pontoons and 18-pounders to Graham's command as part of the equipment for a siege.[27]

The second question, concerning naval support and sea power, remained open. Wellington's army had entered an entirely new theatre of war and had done so within one dramatic month. Was the navy able to adjust to this sudden shift in the direction of the land campaign? One advantage was gained with the rapid evacuation of other, smaller French-held ports on the north coast. The French garrison of 150 at Pasajes surrendered to the Spanish on 30 June. Guetaria was evacuated on 1 July. Similarly, the garrison at Castro Urdiales left for Santona.[28] Pasajes, about 2 miles to the east of San Sebastian, was an ancient and significant port and became the key to British operations against San Sebastian and in the region more generally. By mid-August, it was teeming with ships, supplies, soldiers and muleteers.[29] Guetaria was a smaller port, with a reported 300 inhabitants in 1797, lying to the west of San Sebastian. With its harbour well-protected from the sea by a rugged outcrop, it offered a minor base for French gunboats and privateers, but it was of no value to British naval operations or shipping.[30]

An immediate difficulty was the Royal Navy's shortage of ships for blockade and convoy duties. On 2 July, Wellington complained to Bathurst, 'You cannot conceive the inconvenience to which we are put for want of the sea communication with Lisbon'. Supplies ready for sailing from Lisbon on 12 May had still not left for Santander on 19 June. He estimated that hard currency would take two months to arrive from Lisbon by land, but could not be shipped by sea. Nor could captured French guns and stores be removed by sea. 'Surely the British navy cannot be so hard run as not to be able to keep up the communication with Lisbon for this army!'[31] In declaring to the secretary of state his intention to besiege San Sebastian, Wellington insisted that such a siege 'is one of quite a different description from that of Pamplona', but added that operations depended upon being 'secure at sea'.[32]

On 4 July, he asked the squadron commander, Captain Sir George Collier, to convoy the siege train from Bilbao to Pasajes and to suppress French seaborne communications to the east between Bayonne and San Sebastian. He recommended that the squadron be based at Pasajes, with one vessel covering Santona.[33] The latter port, some 85 miles to the west of San Sebastian, was still in French hands and the navy presumably feared attacks on coastal shipping by small French warships from it. On 3 July the Royal Navy sent a frigate, a corvette, two brigs and about fifteen barges to blockade San Sebastian. Overstretched, it failed to prevent nocturnal arrivals by sea from St Jean de Luz into San Sebastian. The replenishments received by the French garrison were not insignificant. For example, the French commissary Robert, who had left San Sebastian on 27 June, returned on 6 July with some soldiers from the 42nd and 22nd, a surgeon and large supplies of flour, rice, lard and brandy.[34] Anyone familiar with the siege of Gibraltar would have recalled the vital role played by privateers, schooners and trading boats in breaking the blockade to bring steady, if small-scale supplies of food to the garrison.[35] An early worry was that the French would be able to re-supply San Sebastian.

Vitoria and its aftermath opened up a new supply route for Wellington's army direct from England to Santander. For example, 3 million musket balls were shipped to the latter port in mid-July.[36] But on 9 July Wellington complained that communications with England and securing supplies from England depended on naval support along the coast of northern Spain.[37] Supplies languished at La Coruña for want of warships for escort duty and 'the blockade of the coast is merely nominal. The enemy have reinforced *by sea* the only two posts they have on the north coast of Spain'.[38] On 19 July, he complained that the naval presence off-shore was useful for communications, but provided only one frigate for blockading. This scarcely deterred the French and indeed exposed the squadron commander to French naval attack: 'Any thing in the shape of a naval force would drive off Sir G Collier'.[39] Again, on 20 July, he reported that there was 'no convoy for any thing', while 100,000 dollars of subsidy for the Gallician army lay at La Coruña for a month, 'for want of a ship to carry them'.[40] The commanding officer at La Coruña, Lieutenant Colonel Richard Bourke, reported the subsidy's arrival from Lisbon on 4 July; the money awaited conveyance to Santander by the first available warship.[41] Still without formal directions, Bourke simply forwarded everything, including the specie, with a convoy for Santander being assembled on 21 July.[42]

The third issue – deciding which troops would attack the town – did not detain Wellington long, but showed that San Sebastian's fate might well have been in Spanish rather than Anglo-Portuguese hands. Wellington wanted Spanish troops, who had initiated the blockade of San Sebastian, to conduct the siege. His own army had suffered substantial losses at Vitoria and was further depleted when thousands of troops went absent in the weeks after the battle. It was 'very desirable' to save British casualties, although some British units would 'assist occasionally to lead an assault, etc'. But he asked Graham's advice on whether he would need more British troops beyond those serving as shock troops for the assault.[43]

Within days, Wellington had decided that the Spanish could not be 'trusted alone' and were not yet ready to do more than assist Graham. Wellington, concerned at the lack of heavy artillery available in the Peninsula, especially following the loss of siege guns at Tarragona, warned of the danger of entrusting the main British siege train to Spanish forces: 'I should not like to see our ordnance exposed to the risk of their keeping. Besides they will not work, and their own officers cannot make them work'. He therefore assigned the 5th Division to the siege, backed up by one Portuguese brigade and Spanish support troops.[44] As will become obvious later, this decision, leading in fact to no Spanish participation in the siege itself, had damaging if entirely unanticipated consequences.

Even allowing for the use of battle-hardened troops in the siege, initial estimates of the numbers of troops required proved to be woefully over-optimistic. That initial assessment flowed from Wellington's belief that San Sebastian, unlike Pamplona, would readily be captured. On 4 July Wellington informed the chief engineer, Sir Richard Fletcher, that Major Smith's evaluation made him confident that 'our means are sufficient to enable us to obtain possession of that place'.[45] He assured Lieutenant General Graham that the siege train 'which was framed with a view to the siege of Burgos, is not quite sufficient for that of Pamplona' but was 'fully so for that of San Sebastian'.[46] He therefore ordered the siege train then at Bilbao to be shipped to Pasajes.[47]

Wellington remained optimistic about taking San Sebastian quickly. On 10 July, he hoped to capture the town 'in a short time after we shall have broken ground'. Two days later, he informed the secretary of state that 'I hope we shall soon have San Sebastian'. On 16 July, he told Sir Thomas Graham, who commanded the force assigned to assaulting the walls, that 'the work is comparatively trifling'. On 19 July, he suggested to Graham that the main breach in the town's defences would be made 'easily and in a very short time'. And on 20 July, in a formal despatch, he told the British commander on the east coast of Spain that he hoped to gain San Sebastian 'in a few days'.[48]

Such breezy optimism proved ill-founded. It must be seen, however, in the context of four aspects of the campaign in May–June. First, the British Light Division and cavalry, despite heavy rain and muddy roads, pursued Joseph's army closely enough to ensure that 'The enemy are much pressed . . . and prevented from breaking down the bridges' on the route ahead.[49] Although the infantry in general failed to mount the swiftest of pursuits, the cavalry, not always the most effective or plentiful branch in his army, ensured that the British advance would not be delayed by the need to construct replacement river crossings.

Secondly, Wellington's army was buoyed by the French abandonment of Burgos. The failed siege of Burgos the previous autumn badly dented British military prestige. On 9 June Lieutenant Colonel John Burgoyne, RE, wrote home to the Earl of Derby:

> We are within thirty miles of Burgos, which the French have used the greatest exertions all through the winter to strengthen. We cannot now attempt its reduction as we did last year, but must bring up a regular battering train to go through it by system, and even then the undertaking will be an arduous one, both from the great improvements that have been made in the place, and from a foolish dread that has got about our army respecting the difficulty of the enterprise, from not properly estimating the cause of our last failure.

A formal siege would take time since the battering train requested by Wellington 'several months ago' had not yet reached La Coruña. From there it would have to be shipped to San Andero and then transported 80 miles to Burgos. Five days later this major challenge disappeared. Burgoyne happily recorded the French destruction of their fortifications at Burgos and their abandonment of the town: 'This measure is very disgraceful to them; after expending so much money and labour all the winter on this work and having that time to prepare and organise a system of defence, . . . [this] shows a total want of system and unanimity of action which must be favourable to us'.[50] The prospects for rapid progress improved, since the next fortified town in the line of advance was Pamplona, far ahead of the British position in mid-June.

Thirdly, this optimism was confirmed by Vitoria. The French in retreating before Wellington's advance had persistently avoided combat in late May and for much of June. When forced to battle on 21 June, 'They showed little confidence, and seldom allowed our troops to come very near them'.[51] Such a lack of fight paired with the destruction of Burgos's defences suggested easy gains ahead. At Wellington's headquarters, Francis Larpent noted on 21 July that the French 'seem everywhere dispirited'.[52]

Fourthly, the region the British entered after Vitoria vigorously opposed French occupation. The nature and impact of the guerrilla forces which opposed the French have long been disputed. Romanticized views of politically inspired patriots energetically upholding historic rights and national honour have receded in the wake of evidence that guerrilla bands consisted of deserters and bandits, supplemented by men coerced into joining them. Guerrilla leaders sought power and plunder in their neighbourhoods rather than national restitution or renewal. But one of the most charismatic guerrilla leaders, Francisco Espoz y Mina, secured wide enough support to control many smaller towns and large swathes of the countryside in Navarre and Upper Aragon, as well as parts of the Basque country, by 1813. Opposition in Navarre was triggered by French assaults on the clergy and on local commercial and fiscal practices. It seemed strongest in north-central Navarre, led there by owners of small farms. There was also the fear that the French intended to annex it to France, following Catalonia's formal separation from Spain in 1812; Navarre was ruled by a military governor from 1810. Effective French rule by 1813 was mainly confined to the larger towns and especially to the capital, Pamplona. From early 1812, Mina's Navarre Division virtually blockaded Pamplona, forcing the French throughout the year to send substantial forces into the surrounding countryside to obtain food and firewood. The guerrillas' strength in the countryside and ability to harass French army units on the march were probably stronger in the area the British were entering than in any other region.[53]

These factors help explain the self-confidence Wellington displayed after Vitoria. But when he expressed an expectation that progress would be relatively easy, he put great pressure on his subordinates to meet their commander's wishes.

The Wider Campaign in Early July
If his optimism proved superficial, Wellington faced numerous demands. They are hinted at by the fact that he was frequently on the move. From 1 July until 16 July, he

made his headquarters at six different places before establishing himself at Lesaca until 24 July. Following an intense period of hyper-activity, he returned there from 3 August until late August.[54] That small hill village enjoyed the advantage of being near the French border while also being approximately 10 miles south of Irun and the great road to Bayonne. It provided access not only to that road and westwards to San Sebastian, but also to a range of passes into France across the Pyrenees. A position commanding multiple routes was essential where some seventy-five passes across the mountains were reportedly accessible to infantry, with seven of them accessible to carriages.[55] In addition, Lesaca enjoyed ready access to a main north–south road to Pamplona.

In early July, Wellington was busy trying to assess the situation on the French border. When Wellington gave up his pursuit of Clausel, he rested some of the force deployed in that march and moved other troops to take up duties around Pamplona. The blockade involved the 3rd, 4th and 6th divisions by 10 July. These deployments in turn had released General Hill and two British and two Portuguese brigades to push three French divisions under General Gazan from the Baztan valley during 4–7 July. This was a fertile and readily defensible salient, and 'Gazan has disputed every position in it'.[56] With the valley cleared, Wellington felt confident that 'I can hold the Pyrenees as easily as I can Portugal', unless the French significantly strengthened the army opposing him.[57]

Despite his failure to catch Clausel and despite delays in getting the siege train in place, Wellington continued, as we have seen, to paint an optimistic scenario. Such optimism was widely disseminated or shared. Lieutenant Colonel Ross of the Royal Horse Artillery noted on 10 July that San Sebastian's 'fall is not questioned in a very short time'.[58] Lieutenant Colonel Frazer of the same arm, who commanded part of the artillery being positioned for the siege, wrote home on 12 July: 'How this campaign will end, none can tell, but affairs yet look well. We shall attack St Sebastian with spirit, and surely, as I trust, take it soon.'[59]

Such optimism was dented by French movements along the Pyrenees. The French appeared to reinforce their left or eastern flank in the direction of St Jean Pied de Port, and Wellington assumed that Clausel was in contact with French units moving towards his own division much farther to the east. These shifts left the British right front looking 'ticklish'. Wellington ordered the 4th Division under Cole to march towards Roncesvalles from its blockading duties near Pamplona; Roncesvalles commanded the main route across the Pyrenees from Pamplona to St Jean Pied de Port. The 3rd Division under Picton, then blockading Pamplona, was to advance to Olague as soon as it was replaced by a Spanish force under General Henry O'Donnell, Conde de la Bisbal. Olague commanded the road due north from Pamplona to the lower Bidassoa River and Irun, near the coast. Wellington also ordered Lieutenant General Sir Henry Clinton, when he reached Lanz, to cover the roads forward of his new position. He informed Lieutenant General Hill on 14 July: 'The truth is, that having two objects in hand, viz., the siege of San Sebastian and the blockade of Pamplona, we are not strong on any point as we ought to be. These movements when effected, will render us full strong enough for any thing.'[60]

By 19 July, Wellington learned that Clausel was approaching St Jean Pied de Port.[61] But by then Wellington had more scope to manoeuvre his army. O'Donnell had arrived from the west about a week earlier with a Spanish force whose self-confidence had been boosted on 28 June by capturing a French garrison of 650 at Pancorbo, which commanded the road between Burgos and Vitoria. After a few days' rest, O'Donnell's troops took over the blockade of Pamplona on 17 July. Relatively few Anglo-Portuguese troops were needed at Pamplona once the trench works and gun emplacements had been completed.[62] Wellington's front was thus strengthened and filled in.

Clausel's withdrawal into France offered Wellington, who had been steadily reinforced over the previous three weeks, the possibility, by 20 July, of consolidating in Spain or advancing into France. His thinking turned to the situation in Aragon, to the south-east of his current position. With Clausel's departure and the movement of General Paris, with 3,000 men, in the same direction, the French, under pressure from Spanish forces, had evacuated Aragon, except for five garrisons on the border with Catalonia. Wellington was not sure whether Suchet, advancing from Catalonia, intended to retake Aragon. But on 20 July he wrote optimistically to Lord William Bentinck, commanding on the east coast: 'In the course of a few days I hope to have possession of San Sebastian, and I propose then either to move forward into France, or to make myself master of all the garrisons of Aragon, so as to connect myself more closely with you, still keeping the blockade of Pampluna.' But invading France depended on the termination of Napoleon's armistice with his Russian and Prussian opponents:

> Much will depend upon the state of affairs in the north of Europe. If the war should be renewed, I shall do most good by moving forward into France, and I shall probably be able to establish myself there. If not renewed, I should only go into France to be driven out again; and I shall do best to confine myself to secure what I have gained.[63]

To prepare for such an advance, Wellington's Quarter Master General, George Murray, asked Major General John Byng on 21 July to obtain what information he could about the roads leading to St Jean Pied de Port, about that town's defences, about the location and number of guns there, and about how the position might be turned.[64]

Wellington's situation suddenly changed during 22–4 July. Marshal Soult, whose experience of campaigning in the Peninsula rivalled Wellington's own, appeared in Wellington's letters for the first time in his new role on 24 July. Soult was not regarded as a great battlefield commander, but he repeatedly demonstrated formidable powers in managing and manoeuvring large armies. From 24 July until the final encounters at Toulouse and Bayonne in mid-April 1814, Wellington fought an intricate duel with a master of tactics and movement.

By the early morning of 22 July, intelligence reports indicated that the French were preparing a flying bridge on the Bidassoa River near the crossing to the main road to Irun. Yet to the immediate east of that position troops were being moved to the French far left flank, which was also strengthened by Clausel's arrival. Wellington responded by reinforcing the high ground between Irun and the Bidassoa, where the Spanish general Pedro Giron was in command. He ordered Graham to send Giron 'all the field artillery which is about Hernani and Oyarzun, the men of which can be spared from the heavy guns'.[65] He thus depleted his light artillery at San Sebastian.

These French troop movements intensified Wellington's concern that too many soldiers were tied down in preparing the siege trenches and artillery emplacements. Some worries about manpower were relatively minor. For example, he complained to Bathurst on 20 July that the shortage of naval personnel meant that Portuguese troops were heavily involved in unloading the ships in the harbour at Pasajes; 'I am convinced that no combined British army has ever before been employed on such duties'.[66] But other demands on his troops were more significant. Having felt on 14 July that he would be 'full strong enough for any thing' once a number of divisional moves had been completed, he was irritated a week later by the diversion of scarce manpower into sluggish siege operations at San Sebastian.[67] He let off steam to Graham on 22 July: 'Sir R. Fletcher and Col Dickson appear to be worse than usual in their demands for working parties, and unless they are forced to use the animals and cars at their disposal whenever they can be used they will work your men to death'. Fletcher headed the Royal Engineers with the army, while Dickson headed the Royal Artillery. 'I have known Col Fletcher demand hundreds of men whom he could not use'.[68] At that point, Dickson had requested 4,000 troops, to be divided into 2 nocturnal working parties of 800 each, 2 alternating daytime working parties of 400 each and 2 covering parties of 800 each.[69]

This frequently expressed frustration at the diversion of manpower was accompanied on 22 July by requests to speed up the transfer of soldiers, supplies and equipment to Santander and to improve the harbour facilities at Pasajes. Wellington wanted hospitalized British soldiers who had been successfully treated at Lisbon and 1,200 Portuguese recruits at Mafra, north-west of Lisbon and within the old lines of Torres Vedras, to be shipped as soon as possible to Santander. From that transit point they would be sent on to their regiments.[70] While pressing for extra troops, Wellington knew by the late morning of 24 July that he faced a challenge on his immediate front. He speculated that Soult had moved large numbers of soldiers to St Jean Pied de Port in order to distract the British from the lower stretches of the Bidassoa River, which the French, he supposed, would cross once British forces had been drawn off to the east.[71]

As this new and perilous phase opened, Wellington completed a general review of the year's progress for the Prime Minister's personal attention. In it he gave a new strategic significance to San Sebastian. After stressing the difficulties of holding the Pyrenees as a defensive line in the manner of the line of Torres Vedras, he emphasized the broader advantages which his control of northern Spain gave the British. He noted improvements in his allies' armies, emphasizing the size if also the limitations of the Spanish army, as well as the improvements, through regular pay, in the performance of the Portuguese army. But the key promise he held out, knowing the subject's vital importance to the government, was that the campaign of 1813 would reduce the costs of maintaining the army he commanded:

As soon as I shall get possession of San Sebastian I shall commence, and as soon as I shall have Pamplona I shall complete, the reduction of all our expenses in Portugal; not to incur others upon the northern coast of Spain; but I hope that I shall be able to have all our principal magazines in England, our hospitals in England, and that the expense of the transport of the army at least will be very much reduced.[72]

On 9 July he had suggested that the government establish a major depot at Falmouth, or at Plymouth if that were impossible, to stockpile camp, clothing, military and medical supplies for shipment to the army; money should be sent direct from England to Santander. Such direct shipments, avoiding the lengthy and costly route to Lisbon and then along the Portuguese and Spanish coasts, would lighten the burdens on his army.[73] Shortened lines of communication and supply improved military efficiency; Wellington had even advised Bentinck, 'your best magazines of all kinds will be your ships, which you should always keep close to you'.[74] Savings in time, speed and reliability for the army in the field were to be matched also by financial savings for the government at home.

San Sebastian therefore was to be taken not just to remove a French redoubt adjacent to the main road between Spain and France, or to deny the French an additional base from which to annoy, intercept and constrain British supply routes to northern Spain, or to undermine French military prestige. Instead, the town, as Larpent noted on 25 July, would support the allied army's left flank and provide a secure repository for stores and the sick and wounded. If the British had to retreat, equipment, supplies and non-effective soldiers could wait there for safe evacuation by sea, while guerrillas could take refuge there. But, more positively, it would be used by an advancing allied army as a major transport link. At present, it took six weeks for supplies from Lisbon to reach 'these wild inhospitable regions'. Removing the French from the Spanish coastal ports closest to the border would enable the British to restructure and accelerate the ways in which they sustained their land war against France.[75] At the same time, and importantly for the government, it offered the means of reducing the costs of the war. When it had been taken, the commander of the naval squadron, Sir George Collier, on 9 September described San Sebastian as 'the western key of the Pyrenees'; moreover, 'its importance as to the future operations of the Allied Army is incalculable'.[76] San Sebastian had gained an impressive importance since Wellington's fleeting mention of it in February and his brief references to it as an unchallenging tactical target in early July.

Notes

1. Jacques Vital Belmas, *Journaux des sièges faits ou soutenus par les Français dans la péninsula, de 1807 à1814*, 4 vols (Paris, 1836–7), iv, 588.
2. Thompson (ed.), *An Ensign in the Peninsular War*, 256.
3. Munro Price, *Napoleon. The End of Glory* (Oxford, 2014), 75–8, 86–8, 117.
4. Wellington to Henry Wellesley, 17 June 1813, *WD*, x, 442–3; Chandler, *The Campaigns of Napoleon*, 890–7.

5. Wellington to Henry Wellesley, 24 June 1813, *WD*, x, 456.
6. John Bew, *Castlereagh. Enlightenment, War and Tyranny* (London, 2011), 320.
7. Feltre to Clausel, 22 June 1813, SHAT C8 156.
8. Feltre to Jourdan, 25 June 1813, SHAT C8 156 .
9. Feltre to king of Spain, 28 June 1813, SHAT C8 156.
10. Wellington to Liverpool, 18 December 1811; 'Memorandum of Operations in 1811',
28 December 1811, *WD*, viii, 469, 516, 519.
11. Charles J. Esdaile, *Fighting Napoleon. Guerrillas, Bandits and Adventurers in Spain 1808–1814* (New Haven CT, 2004), 90–2.
12. Feltre to king of Spain, 2 July 1813, SHAT C8 156.
13. Feltre to Reille, 2 July 1813, SHAT C8 156.
14. Feltre to king of Spain, 5 July; to Jourdan, 6 July (1 of 2); to Rey, 6 July 1813, SHAT C8 156.
15. Feltre to Jourdan, 6 July 1813 (2 of 2), SHAT C8 156.
16. Feltre to Dalmatie, 6 July 1813, SHAT C8 156.
17. Feltre to Jourdan, 25 June; to Reille, 2 July 1813 (2 letters), SHAT C8 156.
18. Feltre to Dalmatie, 11 July 1813, SHAT C8 156.
19. Feltre to king of Spain, 5 July 1813, SHAT C8 156.
20. Feltre to Reille, 2 July 1813, SHAT C8 156.
21. Feltre to king of Spain, 5 July 1813, SHAT C8 156.
22. Feltre to Dalmatie, 11, 13 July 1813; to Reille, 13 July 1813, SHAT C8 156.
23. Feltre to Rey, 16 July 1813, SHAT C8 156.
24. Feltre to Reille, 13 July 1813, SHAT C8 156.
25. Feltre to Albufera, 24 July 1813, SHAT C8 156.
26. Feltre to king of Spain, 28 June 1813, SHAT C8 156.
27. Wellington to Graham, 3 July 1813 *WD*, x, 497.
28. Wellington to Bathurst, 3 July 1813, *WD*, x, 502.
29. Wellington to North, 15 August 1813, *WD*, xi, 4.
30. Frederick Augustus Fischer, *Travels in Spain in 1797 and 1798*, trans. from the German (London, 1802), 60; Wellington to Beresford, 15 August 1813; Wellington to Graham, 17 August 1813, *WD*, xi, 2, 8.
31. Wellington to Bathurst, 2 July 1813, 10 July 1813, *WD*, x, 495, 522–3.
32. Wellington to Bathurst, 3 July 1813 *WD*, x, 509.
33. Wellington to Collier, 4 July 1813, *WD*, x, 509.
34. Belmas, *Sièges*, iv, 599, 601.
35. John Drinkwater, *A History of the Late Siege of Gibraltar* (London, 1785), 165–6, 180, 197.
36. Board of Ordnance to Somerset, 14 July 1813, WP 9/2/2/10.
37. Wellington to Bathurst, 9 July, *WD*, x, 519.
38. Wellington to Bathurst, 10 July, *WD*, x, 522–3.
39. Wellington to Bathurst, 19 July, *WD*, x, 544–5.
40. Wellington to Bathurst, 20 July 1813, *WD*, x, 558.
41. Bourke to Somerset, 4 July 1813, WP 9/2/2/10.
42. Bourke to Somerset, 21 July 1813, WP 9/2/2/10.
43. Wellington to Graham, 4 July 1813 *WD*, x, 511.
44. Wellington to Graham, 8 July 1813, *WD*, x, 512–13.
45. Wellington to Fletcher, 4 July 1813, WP 1/373 (Folder 4).
46. Wellington to Graham, 4 July 1813, *WD*, x, 510.
47. Wellington to Graham, 4 July 1813; Wellington to Dickson, 4 July 1813 WP 1/373 (Folder 4).
48. Wellington to Bathurst, 10, 12 July 1813; Wellington to Graham, 16, 19 July 1813; Wellington to Bentinck, 20 July 1813, *WD*, x, 520, 523, 533, 541, 553.
49. Wrottesley, *Life and Correspondence*, i, 264.
50. Wrottesley, *Life and Correspondence*, i, 260–1.
51. Wrottesley, *Life and Correspondence*, i, 262.

52. Larpent (ed.), *The Private Journal*, ii, 2.
53. Tone, *The Fatal Knot*, 132–3, 146–50, 154–60, 168–70, 177–81; for a more sceptical assessment of the guerrillas' overall impact on defeating the French, see Esdaile, *Fighting Napoleon*, 157–9, 195–202.
54. His movements are detailed in *WD*, x, 459–640; he comments on this, 571.
55. Sabine (ed.), *Letters*, 167.
56. Wellington to Graham, 8 July 1813, *WD*, x, 512.
57. Wellington to Bathurst, 10 July, 12 July 1813, *WD*, x, 520–1, 523–4 (for the paragraph).
58. Ross to Sir Hew Dalrymple,10 July 1813, *Memoir*, 43.
59. Sabine (ed.), *Letters*, 193.
60. Wellington to Hill, 14 July 1813, to Clinton, 14 July 1813, *WD*, x, 526–7.
61. Wellington to Graham 19 July, *WD*, x, 541.
62. Wellington to Bathurst, 3 July, 10 July, 19 July, to Mina 19 July, *WD*, x, 503, 521, 543, 546.
63. Wellington to Bentinck, 20 July 1813, *WD*, x, 553–4.
64. Murray to Byng, 21 July 1813, WP 15/48.
65. Wellington to Graham, 22 July 1813, *WD*, x, 559.
66. Wellington to Bathurst, 20 July 1813, *WD*, x, 558.
67. Wellington to Hill, 14 July 1813, WP 1/373 (Folder 4).
68. Wellington to Graham, 22 July 1813, WP 1/373 (Folder 5).
69. 'Memorandum by A Dickson and T. Graham', 19 July 1813, Wellington (ed.), *Supplementary Despatches*, viii, 92–3.
70. Wellington to Major General Peacock, 22 July 1813; to Collier, 22 July 1813; to Captain of the Port at Passages, *WD*, x, 561–3.
71. Wellington to Graham, 24 July 1813, *WD*, x, 563.
72. Wellington to Liverpool, 25 July 1813, *WD*, x, 567–70.
73. Wellington to Bathurst, 9 July 1813, *WD*, x, 517–18.
74. Wellington to Bentinck, 20 July 1813, *WD*, x, 554.
75. Larpent (ed.), *The Private Journal*, ii, 9.
76. *The Times*, 20 September 1813, p. 2.

Chapter 5

Preparing the First Assault

British Initial Dispositions

At first glance, San Sebastian's defences seemed relatively easy to break. The town sat on an isthmus whose landward neck was 350yd across and protected by fortifications in the form of a horn-work. That front was exposed to an opponent who could secure the higher ground to its south. That plateau was occupied by the former convent of San Bartolomeo, the key to the land approach to the town.

The first obstacle for the British was that heavy guns could only be landed at the small port of Pasajes to the east of San Sebastian across the Urumea River. Defended by only 8 artillery pieces and under 150 troops, Pasajes was taken by Spanish forces at the end of June. By that time, one correspondent at the front viewed San Sebastian's fate as inescapable; 'when our heavy artillery arrives, they of necessity must surrender'.[1]

But hauling weapons and supplies from Pasajes to San Bartolomeo was a slow and cumbersome business. The French destroyed the bridge across the Urumea River below the San Bartolomeo position, thereby lengthening the route between Pasajes and the British position south of the former convent to 5 miles. The town could be bombarded from the Chofres sand-hills on the east bank of the Urumea River. That position was about 1½ miles by road from Pasajes. Opinion differed on the condition of the road, perhaps reflecting the impact on it of highly changeable weather conditions. Lieutenant Colonel John Jones of the Royal Engineers claimed it was 'an excellent road'. But Lieutenant Colonel Augustus Frazer of the Royal Horse Artillery described it as 'detestable', probably focusing on those stretches where it ran along mountain edges. However, there could be no question that it was far shorter than the route to the south and west.[2] Guns placed on the sand-hills across the river could easily fire on the town's eastern walls and were far less vulnerable to sorties from the town than artillery at San Bartolomeo would be.

On the 4 July Lieutenant Colonel Frazer rode from Deba to Tolosa and then, on the following day, to Hernani, where he attended upon Sir Thomas Graham and learned of the decision to besiege San Sebastian. He immediately proceeded with Captain Sir George Collier of the Royal Navy to take a preliminary look at the new objective. He returned to San Sebastian the next day and inspected the position with Major Charles F. Smith of the Royal Engineers, who had already offered recommendations about the siege operation. Aged 27, Smith was a relatively young man but had been involved in the capture of islands in the West Indies from 1805 and in the seizure of Fort Bourbon on Martinique in 1810. Serving in the Peninsula from that year, he was involved in the defence of Cádiz in 1811 and commanded the successful defence of Tarifa, a small port on the Straits of Gibraltar, at Spain's southern tip, from December 1811 to January 1812.[3] A former Commissary of the Siege Train, Richard Henegan, later described the situation when the French laid down their siege at Tarifa:

> the commanding officer . . . , although unimpeachable in the courageous bearing of a soldier, was wanting in the bold decision, which, in military practice, must often take the lead of science, and established rules. The quality was wanting, as shown in the opinion given by this officer on the untenable condition of the town. . . . The preservation of the fortress was therefore mainly attributable to the Engineer officer, Captain Smith, who by a more skilful and enlarged view of the application of its resources, over-ruled objections that tended to its evacuation; nor did that officer fail to place, foremost among such resources, the well-tried powers, and dauntless bayonets of the 47th and 87th regiments.[4]

Apart from stressing the importance of human assets as against scientific expertise, Henegan's assessment of Smith supports the evidence that Smith viewed the situation at the neck of the isthmus in broader terms than Frazer did. The latter wanted immediate action to seize the San Bartolomeo convent, pinning his hopes on the arrival of Lieutenant Colonel Alexander Dickson, Commander Royal Artillery in Wellington's army: 'I am so convinced of the necessity of an immediate attack of [*sic*] the convent, that I cannot with propriety conceal it, though my opinion differs from that of my seniors. However, Dickson will, I hope, be here to-day, and he is a sure card for decision'.[5] Frazer knew that heavy artillery was unnecessary for this task, which could be undertaken with light artillery brought north from the main army on the road from Hernani. A coup de main against San Bartolomeo was, however, ruled out as planning concentrated on the siege operation in its entirety.

Wellington, having received a report from Major Smith, informed Graham on 4 July that 'I feel very anxious to attack' San Sebastian. Sir Richard Fletcher of the Royal Engineers would command that specialist arm once he had completed his arrangements for the blockade of Pamplona, during which period Smith would act in his stead. Lieutenant Colonel Dickson would be sent to San Sebastian with artillery and sappers. Yet the main responsibility for the attack remained unclear, with Wellington seeking Graham's opinion on whether the siege might be undertaken mainly by Spanish troops.[6] By 8 July, that option had been ruled out, largely it seems because Wellington would not place his heavy artillery under the supervision of Spanish forces. Instead, Wellington assigned Major General John Oswald to command the siege, using the 5th Division, and Pack's or Bradford's brigades, with Spanish battalions in support if requested by Graham.[7]

Frazer was summoned to see Graham on 8 July. He and Major Smith agreed about the landing and positioning of the siege train, which had arrived by sea at Pasajes. But the disposition of the heavy artillery now available at Pasajes had to await a decision by Wellington, Fletcher and Smith. Frazer had more limited responsibility, commanding a section of the batteries.[8] The details of the attack were settled by

Wellington, Dickson and Major Smith on 12 July, when they together inspected the sand-hills on the Urumea's east bank.[9] On 13 July, the Spanish 7th Division was withdrawn from blockading San Sebastian and sent to blockade Santona instead.[10] The first step in preparing the siege had gone slowly. On 5 July, Frazer was itching for action. It was another week before the plan was formulated and all parts of it had to be in place before the outlying San Bartolomeo position would be attacked. Meanwhile, the energetic Governor of San Sebastian, Brigadier General Emanuel Louis Rey, had prepared his defence.

French Preparations
The French began planning for a siege before the British decision to launch one. On 19 June senior officials from the government and court, together with their retainers, were sent to San Sebastian from Joseph's retreating army. One estimate suggested that the town's population of 8,400 doubled in size when part of the Burgos garrison and wounded and sick soldiers arrived. Brigadier General Rey was sent to organize the town's defence, after escorting a large party of evacuees to nearby Hernani on the main road to Bayonne. Rey reached San Sebastian on 22 June, the day after Vitoria. Although he was short of money, guns and supplies, he had a company of sappers and another of pioneers, together with Lieutenant Colonel Charles Pinot, his senior engineer. On the 27th, General Maximilien Foy reinforced Rey with battalions from the 34th, 62nd and 22nd Line, as well as with 41 artillerymen and 2 captains of artillery, increasing the garrison to 2,300 troops. On the following day Foy pulled back to Irun, east of San Sebastian, and provided Rey with sixteen more artillerymen.[11] On 27 June, Pinot, who had come from Burgos, reported on the defences of San Sebastian. As might be expected, he painted a grim picture of the challenge he faced. The town was not provisioned for a siege; cash was not available; nor were the necessary barricading, shelter and communications in place. With only one company of sappers and one company of pioneers, Pinot felt himself notably short of the labour necessary to secure the town.[12]

This bleak appraisal did not deter the officers charged with holding San Sebastian from their task. They formed a team with long experience, including involvement in major sieges and service in Spain. Aged 45 in 1813, Rey had enlisted as an infantryman in 1784. After gaining a commission in 1792 and serving in the Army of the Alps, he became a brigadier general in 1796. He knew the region in which he now served, having been appointed commandant at Bayonne in 1805. He had fought in Catalonia in 1808–10, initially as chief of staff to de Gouvion Saint Cyr, and remained in the country thereafter. He had first-hand experience of the gruelling French siege of Gerona, on the Mediterranean coast of eastern Spain. His chief of staff was Colonel Jean Marie de Songeon who had joined the colonial artillery at the age of 19 in 1790 and served in the West Indies until 1793. He subsequently served in Italy, Germany and, from 1810, Spain. Command of the artillery at San Sebastian went to Lieutenant Colonel Teodoro Brion who had trained at the artillery school at Auxonne in 1786. He had served in a wide variety of postings on France's eastern borders, including at the siege of Valenciennes. In Spain, he was present at the protracted and most devastating of sieges, at Zaragoza.[13] None of these officers were high-fliers under Napoleon. But they knew their profession and some of them had first-hand experience of how besieging armies could be forced to pay a high price in casualties to achieve their objectives.

The French position worsened from the early afternoon of 28 June, when allied forces, after ascending the road from Hernani to the south, reached the plateau in front of San Bartolomeo. An estimated 7,000 to 8,000 Spanish troops, under General Gabriel Mendizabal's command, took over the heights at San Martin and the east bank of the Urumea River. That night proved busy. Rey burned the bridge across the Urumea and the suburbs of Santa Caterina and San Martin, in order to clear his lines of fire, using sappers, pioneers and 300 infantrymen, all directed by Lieutenant Colonel Pinot. The French needed an open view to counter allied fire on their hospital at San Martin, a position which Rey regarded as 'indispensable' to securing the town's outer defences. Down at San Sebastian's small harbour, two fishing boats delivered flour during the night, despite the presence of two British brigs far out at sea. This set a pattern, for the French maintained lines of supply and communications with St Jean de Luz, the nearest French port, just inside the Franco-Spanish border.[14]

The French began their defensive preparations during the evening and the night of 28 June. They evacuated the convent of San Francisco and started work on the defences for the convent of San Bartolomeo and some neighbouring houses. Trees in the area were chopped down for use in construction. Some palisades were removed to clear fields of fire. Faced with rapidly mounting pressures, Rey complained to the ministry that he needed 4,000 or 5,000 troops, but had been given only 2,300 or so by Foy, who had also pulled out the 500 gendarmes previously stationed there without replacing them. Rey further stressed that he had not received food and supplies for the artillery and engineers from Bayonne, and that the garrison had no iron-workers or carpenters. He was having the fort's cisterns filled, but they could not meet all his needs for water and they were far from the river and the defensive works. Rey employed local women to carry buckets of water from the Urumea to the cisterns in the castle and requisitioned tools, food and materials from the town's population. Munitions had to be stored in uncovered barracks or houses. Some of the construction material for the French defensive works consisted of timber taken from dismantled structures at the port's small naval depot. Rey was not short of artillery, having 76 guns available; 45 of them were distributed among the defensive works, while 13 were positioned on Mount Urgullo behind the castle defences and the remaining 18 constituted a reserve. Only very light field artillery – and not much of it – was placed at San Bartolomeo. With only 100 gunners available for the artillery, Rey transferred 50 infantrymen to that arm. Even so, his skilled manpower could operate only a portion of his artillery and then for a limited time each day. The south-facing curtain wall behind the horn-work was made ready to receive artillery guns, and munitions were distributed to supply the dispersed guns. A workshop to repair weapons and gun-carriages was established.[15]

At least some of Rey's pleas for reinforcements were answered. On 1 July, 250 chasseurs de montagne and some troops of the 119th Line arrived from Getaria, a small port to the west of San Sebastian which was hurriedly abandoned. An important addition to the defences arrived by ship from St Jean de Luz in the persons of fifty-six gunners and other artillerymen under Captain Hugon of the artillery. With his garrison now increased to nearly 3,000 men, all of whom had arrived within 8 days, Rey on 1 July informed the town authorities that they should evacuate, within 48 hours, the women, children and all who did not possess food for a long siege. On 2 July, Rey assigned 100 men of the 22nd and the 250 chasseurs de montagne to the engineers, and began work on improving the defences of the castle at the northern tip of the peninsula.[16]

The French defence initially depended on keeping coastal supply lines open. Although a British naval presence and blockade began on 3 July when a frigate, three smaller warships and about fifteen minor craft appeared off-shore, the French were confident that they would be re-supplied by sea, albeit under cover of darkness. Numerous small, flat-bottomed ships or trincadours sailed close to shore, evading the British naval blockade. The value of even small-scale blockade-running was demonstrated by the presence of a surgeon among troops and provisions arriving in early July. Flour delivered from Bayonne, along with that requisitioned from the townspeople, was made into bread only after the best means of maximizing the output had been tested.[17]

More proactively, the French predictably tried to disrupt their enemies' progress. On 3 July, they launched a reconnaissance in force across the isthmus. At 9.00 p.m. Lieutenant Colonel Dessailly led 300 men of the 22nd, accompanied by sappers and pioneers under engineer captains Saint-George and Montreal, from the convent of San Bartolomeo to probe towards the road to Hernani. He was supported by 200 reserves. To Dessailly's left, Lieutenant Colonel Blancard took 400 men of the 62nd from the small suburb of San Martin on the Urumea to press against the Spanish right. The French western flank was covered by 200 chasseurs de montagne under Lieutenant Colonel Lupe. A good deal of skirmishing ensued and prisoners captured yielded at least some information on the allies' current troop positions. The French were back in their lines by 1.00 a.m. Interestingly, Rey had committed over 1,100 men or about one-third of his garrison to this minor operation.[18]

Despite the relatively large scale of this French effort to disrupt their enemy's build-up, the British began a light artillery attack on San Bartolomeo at about 6.00 p.m. on 7 July and continued firing, without success, throughout the 8th. The defence of San Bartolomeo bought the French more time to strengthen the town's defences, thus vindicating Frazer's initial insistence that the advancing allies should have been seized the convent at the earliest opportunity. As already noted, Rey ensured that the eastern side of the horn-work was capable of taking guns with which to enfilade any storming party approaching the town's eastern wall. Rey meanwhile prepared for more serious future threats to the town itself. He required the town's population to deposit their weapons in the town offices; he also set up controls over food supplies and bread production. The allied build-up increased on 9 July when the British 5th Division, a German brigade attached to the 1st Division and a Portuguese brigade took over the siege from the Spanish with a force, according to the French, now amounting to 10,000 men.[19]

With the arrival and emplacement of British heavy artillery on the east bank of the Urumea, it was obvious by 13 July that the British would bombard the town's eastern wall. From that day, Rey ordered that the defences should be strengthened in the houses behind the targeted eastern wall, that sewers, which could be used by an assailant to enter the town, be bricked up, and that the southern curtain wall should provide enfilading fire against an assault from the east. Lest his men were forced to retreat to the castle, he built barriers 9–10ft high at cross-roads within the town, supported by trenches up to 12ft wide and 6ft deep. Nearby houses were readied to deliver flanking fire upon a pursuing enemy.[20] As late as the 16th Rey considered whether fords across the Urumea River between its mouth and the position of the destroyed Santa Catalina bridge would enable columns of troops to cross the river and attack the British batteries on the east bank. He decided, however, that any such sortie would be unacceptably risky.[21]

Clearing the Way
British tactics were shaped by the geography of the San Sebastian site and the differing strength of its defensive walls. It is unclear how much prior knowledge British officers had of the town's lay-out and defences. One source of information was available to them in the late summer of 1812, since, according to Captain Webber of the Royal Artillery, the Museo del Artilleria in Madrid contained 'models of all the fortified towns in Spain. . . . The models of the fortifications of every kind are so good that an officer of Artillery or Engineers might here make himself better acquainted with the principles of this useful branch of his profession than by a lifelong study with the assistance of books alone'.[22] Although any model of San Sebastian would not have included French additions made in June and July, it would have demonstrated the defence's basic lay-out and fortifications.

The British had two objectives. As already stressed, the high ground at San Bartolomeo was vital to controlling the neck of the isthmus. From that high ground, the defenders on town's southern wall, with its projecting horn-work, had to be suppressed for the assault to proceed. But the key to the siege was the eastern wall facing the Urumea River. This wall had modern defensive segments, but it was neither elaborate nor particularly difficult to breach. It could only be bombarded, however, from across the Urumea River. Two, quite widely separated artillery bombardments, from San Bartolomeo and from the Urumea's east bank, were therefore needed. While the east bank was by far the more important location for the allies' artillery, the main infantry attack would proceed from the parallels dug between San Bartolomeo and the town's southern wall. The neck of the isthmus containing San Bartolomeo was, according to Captain Blakiston, an engineer, about 900yd from the town.[23] The objective was to take the former convent and then construct parallels towards the town wall. Eventually the parallels came within about 200yd of the breach on the riverside wall. Each step in this process had its particular challenges.

Attacking the convent was easier said than done. On 7 July a mixed allied force (a German infantry brigade accompanied by six 9-pounders of the Portuguese artillery, an English howitzer and some Spaniards) opened fire on the convent. The acting commanding officer of Graham's artillery, Lieutenant Colonel George Julius Hartmann, may not have shared Frazer's aggressive instincts, but his attack faced severe difficulties. The allies could only bring three of their light guns into action and failed to heat the shot fired. The English howitzer could not use Portuguese shells. The aim of the serviceable guns proved to be poor.[24] The very guns with which Frazer was most familiar proved that his recommended *coup de main* using light artillery was far too ambitious. Although he no doubt envisaged deploying more of them, the practical application of light artillery failed.

The serious work of establishing artillery batteries directed against the convent began on 11 July and was completed by the 14th with the installation of four 18-pounders and two howitzers. They opened up during the 14th and suffered little interference from French artillery counter-fire. The main objective was to set the convent ablaze by landing hot shot on its roof. While the roof was hit and this effort was repeated on 15 and 16 July, the defenders prevented fire from spreading within the building. A probe by troops, described by Jones as Caçadores and by the French as English, advanced at either 1.00 or 2.00 p.m. on the 15th in three columns. One pushed upon the cemetery. The central column probed the breach at the convent, while a third threatened the houses adjoining the convent. The central position, the convent, was defended by 400 men who forced the allies to retreat pursued by the grenadiers and voltigeurs of the French 34th. The French claimed this as a 'brilliant affair', having left, they said, 150 allied dead on the open ground, at the cost of 8 killed and 59 wounded in their own force.[25]

By 9.00 a.m. on 17 July, three days of sustained fire had reduced the convent. The French defences included a reserve of 800 men at the small suburb of San Martin, on low ground by the river to the north-east of San Bartolomeo. From this position, Lieutenant Colonel Blancard watched for British movements along the Urumea River to the east. To the west, Lieutenant Colonel Dessailly watched the approaches to the convent of San Bartolomeo, particularly along the road from Hernani. In addition, the convent itself was guarded by 400 men under Lupe. According to the French, the British attacked at 12.30, though Jones has it at 10.00 a.m. Those involved consisted of the Portuguese 4th and 5th Caçadores, about 350 men from the Portuguese 13th Line, the British 9th and 3 companies of the 1st or Royal Scots.[26]

After 4 hours of fighting, with some ebbs and flows of the front, the allies took San Bartolomeo and San Martin. This preliminary action to take the convent and its own, small redoubt consumed 2,505 rounds from the 4 18-pounders and 331 shells from the 2 8in howitzers placed at 220yd and 200yd respectively from the convent. The howitzers were used mainly to suppress musket fire from the small redoubt and to prevent the defenders from organizing working parties to repair damage to their positions. Some additional fire against the redoubt was delivered from across the river on 15 July by five 9-pounders and two howitzers and on 17 July by two 6-pounders. No heavy guns were used at this stage, but the amount of ammunition spent in acquiring a vital but relatively minor position seemed considerable. This reflected French determination in defending the convent, a determination further demonstrated by the level of their casualties. Losses totalling 40 killed and 200 wounded represented a high casualty rate for approximately 1,200 troops deployed. Among the dead were the engineer captain Montreal, while the wounded included Pinot – the commander of engineers received a serious shoulder wound – and Dessailly, the commander of the reserve. The French consoled themselves with the thought that the British, long exposed on open ground, must have suffered heavy losses from French artillery fire.[27]

Despite the fact that this minor operation had taken four days, Graham seemed well satisfied with the undertaking: 'as on other occasions, Major General Oswald conducted the service in the best possible manner'. Graham's despatch singled out four officers for their 'distinguished gallantry' on the 17th: Major Kenneth Snodgrass, who led 200 men of the 13th Portuguese Line on one flank; Captain Almeyda, who led 150 men of the same regiment on another flank; Lieutenant Antonio de Quairos, who was severely wounded leading units from the 4th Caçadores; and the 20-year-old Lieutenant Colin Campbell, leading the light company of the 9th.[28] The operation proved the Portuguese battalions' effectiveness.

The French paid a relatively high price in delaying the British advance. Small-scale but quite intense actions cost them 49 killed and 154 wounded in initial fighting between 28 June and 16 July rising to 89 killed and 354 wounded by the close of fighting at the convent on 17 July. Casualties of 443 out of 3,000 troops in the San Sebastian garrison represented a considerable loss during 3 weeks which saw no formal battle. These casualties came from good units and represented a fast rate of attrition when French numbers were already low for the tasks ahead.[29] But the French destroyed British hopes of a speedy seizure of San Sebastian.

Immediately on taking San Bartolomeo, the British, during the night of 17 July, set about establishing two batteries on the site of the convent. The work 'was by no means pleasant, not so much on account of the fire of the enemy, as of the ground we had to work on, which was the burying-place of the convent. The exhumation of fat monks, whose bodies, instead of being mouldered, were turned into a kind of blubbery spermaceti, was an operation very offensive to the senses.'[30] Even further delays in using this critical position arose from difficulties in transporting 24-pounders, or indeed many guns of any calibre for siege work, up to San Bartolomeo. The best that could be done was to emplace six 18-pounders, which were not heavy enough for breaching major fortifications, and two howitzers. Four of the 18-pounders had been deployed for the attack upon the convent. On the night of the 18th the British advanced into the suburbs of San Martin, which Rey had earlier burned down and from which the French reserves had operated on the previous day. By the afternoon of the 19th the 18-pounders had been placed in the new batteries on the isthmus, thus completing a deployment which lasted nine days.[31]

Frazer had hoped that 'a few days will give us the town and works, and some more, the rock and the castle'. Once again, this proved to be seriously over-optimistic, given the sluggish pace of British preparations and the French ability on 19 July to defend the convent 'with gallantry' and direct their artillery fire accurately against the British.[32]

Wellington's optimistic expectations also went unfulfilled. His sense of urgency was revealed in three letters sent to Graham between 8.30 p.m. on 16 July and 5.30 p.m. the next day. Apart from chafing at Fletcher's and Dickson's requests for more troops for labouring duties and to guard the trenches, he responded to Smith's concern that he had too few heavy guns on the isthmus by insisting that the disposition of the guns was up to the engineer and artillery officers to decide. Wellington breezily expected that extra 24-pounders might be secured either by transfers from the east bank of the Urumea to the isthmus, or from Royal Navy warships. Very few heavy guns were available in any case.

Wellington stressed the obvious importance of digging parallels from the heights of San Bartolomeo once they were captured. He wanted all the work of consolidating and linking the positions on the isthmus – the convent, the ruined suburb and the approach trenches – to be completed before the bombardment of the town's eastern wall from across the Urumea River began. He argued that the breach should be made quickly, in 24 hours, and that the breaching bombardment should only commence when the assault could start within or at the end of those 24 hours. If the artillery needed to be engaged before all the preliminary work on the isthmus had been completed, then its best target would be the horn-work on the town's southern defences, not the intended breach on the east wall.[33] The assault therefore awaited the construction of the parallels and would depend on speed, which had hitherto eluded the besiegers.

Notes

1. *Caledonian Mercury*, 31 July 1813.
2. Jones, *Journals*, ii, 22; Sabine (ed.), *Letters*, 194.
3. *ODNB* entry.
4. Sir Richard D. Henegan, *Seven Years Campaigning in the Peninsula and the Netherlands 1808–1815*, 2 vols (Stroud, 2005, repr. of 1846 edn), I, 127–8.
5. Sabine (ed.), *Letters*, 182–3.
6. Wellington to Graham, 4 July 1813, *WD*, x, 510–11.
7. Wellington to Graham, 8 July 1813, *WD*, x, 512–13.
8. Sabine (ed.), *Letters*, 185, 189.
9. Sabine (ed.), *Letters*, 192–3.
10. Wellington Memorandum, 13 July 1813, *WD*, x, 525.
11. Belmas, *Sièges*, iv, 588, 590–1.
12. 'Rapport fait au minister de la guerre . . . Pinot', 27 juin 1813, Belmas, *Sièges*, iv, 659–60.
13. Juan Olavide, Braulio Albrellos, Juan Vigon, 'San Sebastian el Sito de 1813',16–17, 21 mss.
14. Belmas, *Sièges*, iv, 591.
15. Belmas, *Sièges*, iv, 594–9; Rey to ministre de la guerre, 29 juin 1813, Belmas, *Sièges*, iv, 660–2.
16. Belmas, *Sièges*, iv, 597–8.
17. Belmas, *Sièges*, iv, 599, 601–2.
18. Belmas, *Sièges,* iv, 599–600.
19. Belmas, *Sièges*, iv, 601–3.
20. Belmas, *Sièges*, iv, 605–6.
21. Belmas, *Sièges*, iv, 610.
22. Richard Henry Wollocombe (ed.), *With the Guns in the Peninsula* (London, 1991), 90.
23. Anon. [Blakiston], *Twelve Years' Military Adventure*, ii, 245.
24. Sabine (ed.), *Letters*, 184–5.
25. Jones, Journals, ii, 22–5; Belmas, *Sièges*, iv, 607–8.
26. Graham dispatch, 18 July 1813, *WD*, x, 547.
27. Jones, Journals, ii, 25–7; Belmas, *Sièges*, iv, 610–13.
28. Graham dispatch, 17 July 1813, *WD*, x, 547; the despatch has Lieutenant Colonel Campbell, but this was in fact the future Field Marshal Lord Clyde. John A. Hall, *A History of the Peninsular War: Volume VIII* (London, 1998), 105–6.
29. Belmas, *Sièges*, iv, 599–603, 605, 608–9, 612.
30. Anon. [Blakiston], *Twelve Years' Military Adventure*, ii, 247.
31. Jones, Journals, ii, 27–9.
32. Sabine (ed.), *Letters*, 197.
33. Wellington to Graham 16, 17 (2 letters) July 1813, *WD*, x, 533–5.

Chapter 6

The First Assault

The Artillery Bombardment

Preparations for the bombardment took far longer than Wellington initially envisaged. Even moving the guns to the east bank of the Urumea became a protracted affair. Late on 7 July, the transports whose unloading had been halted at Deba began arriving at Pasajes. The harbour at Pasajes was a long inlet surrounded by mountains which protected it from the sea and made it difficult to access and attack by land. Captain Batty described its defensive strength:

> Nothing can be more striking than the entrance of the harbour of Passages [*sic*], as seen from the Bay of Biscay. On approaching this part of the Spanish coast, no indication of a navigable inlet is at first view discernible. On closer examination, however, we discover a deep narrow cleft in the precipitous range of rocky mountains which bound the coast, and rise abruptly from it; and it is only on the vessel's approach immediately beneath the rugged steep, that those on board perceive the narrow channel between two lofty walls of solid rock. . . . Having cleared this narrow and gloomy canal, a sudden and surprising change takes place; the town or rather village of Passages is discovered skirting the little harbour, the mountains almost hanging over the houses.[1]

Although the tight entry channel provided security, it also made normal access for shipping quite difficult. The passage from the sea to the harbour was deep and about 1 mile long, but it was only 90ft wide between rocky outcrops 500ft high. Given such dimensions, movements into and out of the harbour could only be attempted with the tide. The harbour itself was described twenty-six years later as 'a salt water lake, four miles long, and two miles broad'. It could not, however, take large ships above 200–300 tons because of silting. Shipping could enter and leave only at high tide, so that landing guns and munitions was a slow process. Moreover, the town was built on a narrow belt of land against the mountains; its main street was never more than 6ft wide and in places much less.[2] Consequently, 'the houses in some places are built over this road, leaving only an archway for passengers', thus severely restricting the movement of heavy guns.[3] The limited supply of labour led to the extensive employment of women in rowing the small landing craft, in unloading the vessels and in bringing shot on shore. Frazer struggled in the first working week to provide their pay and rations. Hauling the guns, once landed, to the planned siege works also proved frustrating. On the nights of 14 and 15 July the British lost a howitzer and a 9-pounder in the Urumea River, at least temporarily.[4] Although the British had forty guns in total, a reasonable number by contemporary standards, they did not enjoy much of a margin for losses.[5]

Similarly, establishing the gun batteries was not entirely straightforward. Soldiers did not eagerly join the night-time working parties digging parallels and gun emplacements. Frazer described his frustrations on the sandy east bank of the Urumea during 15 July: 'Yesterday we had no working party of infantry, so I was obliged to run about, first here and then there, until I got a brigade of infantry placed at my disposal.' The next day, he noted that 'I have tired my fingers in writing to borrow men for a working party for to-night.' On the 19th he described how 'we tumble' in the sands and 'cry Viva twenty times before we can get a 24-pounder to budge an inch'.[6]

Some troops assigned to the east bank of the Urumea were billeted along the road from Pasajes and had to march back and forth in relays as digging parties were relieved every 6 hours, throughout the day and night, while covering parties, when needed, were changed every 12 hours.[7] The demands of marching to the lines may have got worse, for on 19 July Wellington ordered Graham to 'keep as many troops as possible assembled in your camp in front of Oyarzun'. He was worried lest the French believed that 'only one British division' occupied that point inside the Spanish frontier on the royal road. This reinforced deterrent force would back up Spanish forces under General Pedro Giron positioned between the Bidassoa River and Irun.[8] But Oyarzun was 7½ miles from San Sebastian and battalions if assigned to trench duties, even though in rotation, were unlikely to take with gusto to heavy digging once they arrived at the lines.

Bad weather added to the difficulties of assembling working parties. On the night of 20 July, urgent work on digging the parallel on the isthmus near the ruins of San Martin did not go to plan: 'A working party of 700 men had been prepared to open the parallel across the isthmus, but the night proving extremely dark, tempestuous, and rainy, the men dispersed among the ruined buildings . . . and not more than 200 could be collected together; therefore only one-third of the parallel, and the right approach to it, were opened'.[9] When the work resumed more satisfactorily the following night, the French, fully aware of British intentions, 'kept up a smart fire of musketry . . . which caused us a good many casualties'. Those badly hit received short shrift from fellow-soldiers:

> When a man was knocked down, the first thing done was to feel his pockets, the next to feel his heart; and then, with the ejaculation of 'Poor fellow! It's all up with him!' he was deposited lengthways on the parapet we were throwing up, and was soon as comfortably buried as if he had been laid six feet under ground.[10]

This 'summary mode of burial' shocked Captain Blakiston as an exceptional practice, quite unlike anything he had witnessed in India.

Hauling guns to the front proved irksome. Various mishaps meant that the main battery – number 14 – had only seven guns firing, against an intended complement of twelve, on the first day of the bombardment, and nine on the second day. Three short-barrelled guns were mounted on low carriages from warships and could not be positioned high enough above the sand to prevent some sinking when fired. Those guns' carriages were replaced overnight on 20–1 July with travelling carriages used for 24-pounders. One of the long-barrelled 24-pounders suffered from a damaged vent which was repaired by 22 July; another such heavy gun was disabled by enemy fire. Indeed, two French 14in howitzers proved especially effective in destroying the main battery's gun platforms and thus in dismounting the guns.[11]

The main bombardment of the town's eastern wall facing the Urumea began at dawn on 20 July. The cannonade could be heard 12 miles away.[12] As already stressed, this bombardment was originally intended to last 24 hours at most and be followed immediately by an assault upon the breach thus created. In fact, the assault did not occur until 25 July. Although battery 14 started firing without the expected twelve functioning guns, a breach 90ft wide was opened up by 12.00 on 22 July. Well over 30 hours later than planned, the battery, having begun firing with seven guns, at last deployed eleven 24-pounders, although one of them remained inoperative. This battery accounted for the majority of the available nineteen 24-pounders. About 5,000 shot from the 24-pounders were expended. Frazer, the battery's commander, thought that the breach should have been assaulted early on the 23rd. 'Instead, however, of storming, we were ordered to make another breach to our left of the first'. Creating a second breach allowed the French time to construct new defences at the first breach, thus forcing the British to pound the first breach a second time in an effort – a vain effort as it turned out – to ensure that it would be clear for the storming parties.[13]

On the 22nd, the third day of the bombardment, 10 24-pounders of 14 battery fired 3,500 rounds during 15½ hours of daylight, all directed at expanding the main breach to 110ft wide between 2 towers in the river-side wall. The inadequate number of guns was compensated for by their rapidity of fire. Jones proudly commented: 'Such a rate of firing probably was never equalled at any siege, great accuracy of range being at the same time observed'.[14] The effort to create a second breach to the left or south of the main breach continued 'for some hours' on the 22nd. Then a civil engineer pointed out that the wall to the north of the first breach was 'much thinner and weaker'. The batteries shifted their attention to that section of the wall and a second breach 30ft wide was made at that weaker point by the end of 23 July. Meanwhile, during the night of 22–3 July, two 24-pounders were moved from number 12 battery to number 14, thus bringing the main battery to its planned functional strength only on the fourth day of the bombardment. Cannonading to the north of the main breach was accompanied during the 23rd by a concerted effort to stop the French repairing damage to the main breach and constructing make-shift defences to the sides and rear of the main breach. This task fell to 10in mortars and 68-pounder carronades on the east bank. The carronades' shelling, from about 520m away, hit houses behind the breach and set them ablaze; 'the flames spread rapidly'.[15] The fire spread because, according to one contemporary account, the French defenders placed burning wood in a 'very wide and deep' ditch which they dug behind the breach.[16] Although it is not clear whether this wider fire was deliberately stoked by the French, it produced a great deal of smoke and had a decisive impact.

Instead of taking 24 hours at most, the bombardment had taken three days and then the assault was delayed another day while the subsidiary breach was created. The 2,000 troops assigned to the assault were at last assembled in their trenches in the early hours of 24 July. But the assault was called off, because the fire beyond the breach was judged so extensive that the attackers would not be able to enter the town once, as intended, they crossed the breaches. One artillery officer, Lieutenant Colonel Ross, reported that the commanding officer of the 5th Division, Major General John Oswald, was 'alarmed' that the heat from the fires would prove intolerable for his men.[17]

At 5.00 a.m., Graham wrote to Wellington, then at his headquarters in Lesaca, to inform him that the attack had been called off. The latter replied at 11.45 a.m. that, if the fire in the town continued into the evening, Graham should 'consider' seizing the breaches and 'entrench parties upon them, well supplied with musket ammunition, keeping a communication with them at high water by means of some of the pontoons'. He reasoned that if dense smoke prevented British troops descending from the breach into the town, then the same heavy smoke would prevent the French from firing on British soldiers inserted on the main breach. This tactical suggestion on 24 July gravely underestimated the dangers facing assault parties on the main breach. It was, unsurprisingly, ignored. Wellington also suggested that Graham might concentrate all his artillery during the evening and the following morning on creating a third breach, at the section south of the main breach initially targeted on the 22nd.[18] This third breach would provide access to the curtain wall and distract the defenders, although it was unlikely to mislead them about the direction of the main assault.

The 24th was indeed taken up with firing on the wall south of the main breach and on French artillery covering the breaches. British artillery aimed at five specific French gun positions. All were minor in weight of firepower, but all could inflict casualties on attacking troops. Two light guns placed across the ditch on the southern defences and two guns on the side of the southern, cavalier wall covered the approach to the main breach. A light gun on the horn-work and another gun behind the tower at the main breach could fire on the breach itself. Finally, if the British got to the top of the breaches and advanced upon the curtain wall, there were two light guns on the cavalier which were high enough up to rake the curtain if the British progressed that far. These five gun positions were fired on during the 24th, with disputed results. According to Jones's tart comment on the evidence available to him, 'The Artillery . . . expressed to Sir Thomas Graham full confidence of being able to keep nearly all these pieces in check, and also to keep the parapets clear of men, so as to prevent any fire being directed on the assailants during the assault of the breaches, if made during daylight'.[19] Contradicting that assessment, Ross, an artilleryman, insisted that the postponement simply gave the French the opportunity to strengthen their defences.[20]

The Assault

The assault on the morning of the 25th began before daylight. As was often the case, contemporary accounts did not agree on the precise timing. Jones, who was not present, recorded that the action began at 5.00 a.m. when it was too dark for the guns on the east bank to come into play. Frazer, however, noted the next day that 4.00 a.m. was 'a little after daybreak'. He also recorded that the attack began 'stupidly an hour before, instead of after daybreak'. Graham's despatch stated that the attack started after the ebb tide had left the defensive wall dry, 'which was soon after daylight'. The time of the morning ebb tide's low point can be determined since there is a reference elsewhere to the fact that the low tide at 4.00 p.m. on the 24th would have allowed for an afternoon assault.[21] The morning low tide would therefore have been at about 4.00 a.m. and the advance presumably began at approximately 3.00 a.m. (an hour before dawn) when the tide was well on the way out. Three weeks after the event Lieutenant Colonel Ross asserted that the signal for attack went off too early, that the tide was not low enough to offer a broad route for the infantry advance.

The storming party's advance from the trenches was covered by the blowing up of a British mine dug under the outer defences of the horn-work. That explosion created temporary confusion among the defenders so the forlorn hope 'reached the foot of the principal breach before any very heavy fire could be brought on them'. The storming party presumably needed 3 or 4 minutes to reach the breach, some 200yd from the parallel's exit. It then climbed 7m to the top of the breach. Lieutenant Harry Jones, the engineer officer, led the way forward followed by the commanding officer, Major Thomas Frazer of the 1st Foot, the Royal Scots, who had held that rank for four years. The major was killed urging his men on. The rest of the small forlorn hope stayed on the breach:

> the burning materials and the smoke, which still issued in thick volumes, caused the men to hesitate and to commence firing from the crest of the breach.
>
> After a momentary interval the garrison recovered from their surprise, and replied with a most destructive fire of musketry on the assailants, which swept away the foremost ranks, whilst the rear equally suffered from musketry and hand-grenades poured down upon them from the two towers on the flanks of the breach, and from shells thrown from the castle.[22]

Lieutenant Colonel Augustus Frazer thought that nine men of the forlorn hope remained at the top of the breach, but most of them were wounded and later taken prisoner. They were immediately isolated because few men following the forlorn hope ascended the breach. According to one who did, Lieutenant Colin Campbell, 'The breach, though quite accessible, was steep, particularly towards the top, so that all those who were struck on the upper part of it rolled down, as in my own case, to the bottom'.[23]

Three problems emerged as the assault unfolded. First, getting men out of the parallel took time. In theory the parallel was wide enough to allow four men abreast, but when fully equipped and moving quickly only two or three men abreast could be accommodated. Secondly, the approach route, a strip of wet and rocky tidal 'beach' between the river and the town wall, became a bottle-neck exposed to musket fire and grenades from the town walls and especially to French artillery at the Mirador battery in the castle grounds.

Troops at the foot of the breach tried to counter the musket fire from above their position, but they could do nothing against the Mirador battery at the castle. Contingents following the storming party became confused in the dark. One group from the 1st Foot believed that they had reached an entry to the breach when they came upon the demi-bastion at the south-east corner of the town walls. They began firing and about 200 men soon congregated in an area stretching 30–40yd back to the parallel from the demi-bastion. Lieutenant Campbell, heading a detachment of twenty men from the 9th, attempted with officers of the 1st to move men forward to support the small numbers at the main breach. Lieutenant Samuel Clarke, who had been commissioned into the regiment in 1810 and badly wounded at Salamanca, commanded the 1st's light company. He was killed while attempting to move men farther along the wall. Even though men were being hit in this crowded position, they were reluctant to advance. Only after a delay did some among them push forward around the crowded bottle-neck at the demi-bastion. As they pressed on from the demi-bastion to the main breach, many were killed or wounded by hand-grenades dropped from the wall and by fire from a round tower on the wall.[24]

According to Frazer, two companies of the 1st Foot got to the foot of the breach, where they came under infantry fire from the tower on its north and the cavalier on its south sides, as well as from shelling by the Mirador battery at the castle; 'the men, panic-struck, turned, could never be rallied, and sustained loss in running back'. Campbell, however, stated that Captain Lawrence Arguimbau explicitly ordered his company of eighty to ninety men to withdraw when he realised that they could achieve nothing in their current predicament. Arguimbau was an experienced officer, having joined the regiment as an ensign in 1801. He was hit after giving the order and had his left arm amputated. Campbell himself made two efforts to lead men up the breach. He was hit in the right hip at the first attempt and rolled back down the breach. At that time Jones was still on the breach. On his second attempt, Campbell was hit more seriously in the left thigh and withdrew with Arguimbau's company just as men of the 38th advanced along the rocky 'beach' below the town wall.

The storming party assigned to the smaller, more northerly breach marched out of the trenches to follow up the assault on the main breach. They came upon the retreating soldiers assigned to the main breach and withdrew in confusion, never approaching their objective.[25]

The third problem involved countering French fire. Along the last stretch of their route back to the trenches, British troops fired at the French on the horn-work. More usefully, batteries on the east bank fired at the town walls. But as dawn broke, Lieutenant Colonel Frazer observed 'a French officer, making sundry telegraphic signals with his sword to the English batteries'. He ordered the batteries to cease fire. At very great personal risk, the Frenchman had saved the British soldiers wounded at and below the breach from still further injury from British artillery fire. An hour's truce was arranged when it was 'fully daylight' for the wounded to be carried off, many of them as prisoners of war to the French. Only Lieutenant Jones, RE, jumped from the top of the breach into the town, but was wounded and taken prisoner.[26]

From the vague times given by Frazer and Jones, the entire action lasted a good deal less than one hour. There were four key points where significant firing occurred. At the top of the breach, the assailants simply could not hold their position. At the foot of the breach, British fire was sustained but many men were wounded. At the demi-bastion, British action served no useful purpose. From the parallel, covering fire on the horn-work may have relieved pressure on the assailants.

This failed attempt by 2,000 men of the 5th Division resulted in 44 officers and 381 other ranks being killed, wounded or taken prisoner. A significant proportion of the losses among other ranks consisted of prisoners – 118 out of 381– mostly at the foot of the breach. The British spent the rest of the day shelling the breaches to try to prevent the French from clearing and re-organizing them.[27] French losses totalled eighteen killed and forty-nine wounded.[28]

Various explanations for the failure were offered. Lieutenant Colin Campbell, who was twice wounded on the breach, argued that the breach could have been taken. He commanded twenty men of a light company of the 9th embedded with the 1st Foot and insisted that 'one main cause of failure was the narrow front and consequent length and thinness of the column in which we advanced'. This column became more 'loosened and disjointed' as it marched across broken ground and suffered from heavy French fire. As a result, 'it reached the breach in dribblets [*sic*], and never in any such body or number as to give the mind of the soldier anything like confidence of success, or such as would be in the least likely to shake the firmness of the defenders'. If 200 men of the Royals, backed up by men of the 38th, had advanced in close formation, then the breach would have fallen to such a compact body.[29] Campbell recorded this verdict in 1836, but noted that he had expressed the same view immediately after the failed assault. His was an infantryman's perspective. By the time he sent these observations to his former battalion commanding officer, very different explanations for the failure had been published.

The most prominent stressed the inadequacy of the available artillery, a view unsurprisingly pressed by artillery and engineer officers. The Anglo-Portuguese army in the Peninsula had only six 18-pounders available for this operation. These were supplemented by five 24-pounders off-loaded from a Royal Navy frigate and by twenty-eight guns, including fourteen 24-pounders, shipped from England. This artillery park of 40 guns was worked by 526 NCOs and men, 369 of them drawn from the Royal Artillery, 107 being Portuguese and 50 sailors seconded from the squadron of 5 blockading warships.[30]

The inadequacy of the artillery was implicitly, though never explicitly, recognized when Wellington prepared the second assault. While the siege artillery on 25 July consisted of 40 guns and 526 artillery NCOs and men, the second assault a month later used 50 per cent more artillery, involving 63 guns and 761 attached troops. This enhanced firepower enabled Graham to create a far wider breach, described by engineers as exceptionally wide, than had been made in July.[31]

On the other hand, an armament of forty guns was not necessarily inadequate for the relatively limited tasks required at a lightly fortified town such as San Sebastian. Lieutenant Colonel Dickson insisted after the second assault that 'the brunt of the business was in the first part'.[32] And Frazer had thought the main breach made by 22 July was wide enough to assault.

During the first siege, the 24-pounders expended 15,350 round shot. That equalled about 1,000 shot for each fully functional gun and those heavy guns were engaged in extensive action for 3 or 4 days. The total of 24-pounder shot expended approached the 18,832 total of 24-pounder round shot used at Badajoz, a more formidable fortress than San Sebastian. Granted, the British also used 13,029 18-pounder round shot at Badajoz, but only 5,034 at San Sebastian.[33] But the expenditure at San Sebastian, mostly directed to creating a breach 90–110ft wide, was certainly high.

Another tactical failing highlighted by contemporaries was the postponement on 24 July. According to Lieutenant Colonel Jones, the creation of two breaches on the town's eastern wall was part of the plan drawn up by Major Smith and approved by Wellington after they had extensively viewed San Sebastian from the hills to the east on the morning of 12 July. There were two problems with this claim. First, in the early hours of 23 July, Lieutenant Colonel Frazer was puzzled, at the very least, by the order to create a second breach, especially since he thought the main one was 'excellent'.[34] This suggests that either he was unaware of the overall plan – even though he commanded the main breaching battery – or that he ignored the plan when he argued for an immediate assault on the freshly made, main breach. After a short burst of firing on the 23rd, Frazer thought a critical opportunity was then missed; 'I fully hoped, and strongly urged, that the breach should be stormed as early on the 23rd as the light and tide would admit'.[35] Secondly, if two breaches were deemed necessary, the subsidiary one should have been created before or exactly in parallel with the main one. It was tactically essential that the main breach be assailed as soon as it was created.

The delay in effecting what was a well-known desideratum may have depressed morale and spread an impression among the infantry that the bombardment had not gone to plan. Any such demoralization was compounded by the difficulties created by the approach route. Once the surprise effects of the exploded mine wore off, the French defence was vigorous and very well directed. But two facts stood out.

First, the attack went in either before or at daybreak. Frazer insisted privately that it should have gone in, as planned, after daybreak to enable the artillery on the east bank to lay down accurate fire against French guns and infantry positions. In the poor light either side of dawn, the batteries could fire, since they knew the ranges perfectly well, but they could hardly support advancing troops. Even more curious, Frazer recorded on the following day that

When day broke we hardly thought any thing more than a false attack had taken place . . . As the day dawned, we discovered with our glasses bodies both of officers and men in the breach, and under the demi-bastion and returning wall. We then began to suspect what we soon found to be the case, that the assault had been made, and had failed.[36]

Frazer commanded not only 14 Battery, the main breaching battery, but also 15 Battery, which consisted of four 68-pounder carronades whose function was to support the assault by disrupting the defences. Given the statement cited earlier that he ceased fire at the behest of a French officer at the breach, Frazer presumably provided some supporting fire on discovering the quandary the attacking force faced. Yet this senior officer had, apparently, no forewarning of the timing of the attack.

The appropriate timing for such an attack was much debated. Organizing troops to march before dawn was standard practice. For example, Captain William Webber, RA, noted in September 1812 that marches began at 5.00 a.m. or 5.30, that is well before dawn at that time of year.[37] But attacking in the dark was controversial. An argument in favour was that darkness disguised an assailant's intentions. The British assault on Buenos Aires on 5 July 1807 was criticized for beginning at 6.30 a.m. in daylight, ensuring that 'the enemy could distinctly perceive every movement that was made' by the advancing British troops. Lieutenant Colonel Denis Pack, who commanded one of the brigades entering Buenos Aires and the 6th Division at Soarauren on 28 July 1813, unsuccessfully urged in 1807 that the advance should begin 'before day-light'.[38] Yet Colin Campbell objected in 1836 that companies became mixed up and officers could not assemble and lead their men in the darkness:

I firmly and sincerely believe that, if they had moved forward in daylight, when the officer could have seen and been seen by his men, and when the example of the former would have animated the exertions of the latter, the Royals would have gone up and over the breach . . . on the 25th July; for, as I have stated, it was perfectly feasible.[39]

Richard Henegan, the Commissary in charge of the Field Train, wrote in 1846 that the timing and the postponement were decisive:

common sense points to the error of allowing men the power of shirking danger, without being exposed to the wholesome discipline of the eye of comradeship, which alone suffices, in many instances, to make men brave. The same soldiers, who would respond to the cheering cry and bright glance of their officer, under the broad glare of daylight, by rushing to the summit of a breach, might show less enthusiasm in seeking death, if the veil of darkness were to conceal alike their deeds of valour, or the absence of them.

The day's postponement 'certainly did not add to the enthusiasm of the attack'.[40]

Secondly, the troops retreated without an order to break off the assault. Graham reported that 'it became necessary to desist from the assault' and that the troops 'only retired, when I thought that a further perseverance in the attack would have occasioned a useless sacrifice of brave men'. But he did not report that either he or Oswald had ordered the retreat. The casualty lists gave 30 officers wounded to 142 other ranks wounded, a high proportion of officers among such casualties. They included two lieutenant colonels and two majors. Such figures suggest either that officers were so rapidly cut down that the troops lost heart, or that officers tried and failed to keep their men in play.[41] Graham formally asserted that the units drawn from the 5th Division had displayed no want of commitment or courage.[42] However, the rumour-mill within the army hinted at a different conclusion and that influenced the disposition of units when a new attack was launched on 31 August. One officer wrote for publication on the eve of the second assault: 'from some accident or mischance, or mistake, the 5th division failed in effecting a lodgement in the enemy's works when that place was lately stormed: it is unfair to attach blame individually, but many reports were flying about respecting the failure, not pleasant to be heard by any British troops'.[43]

On 30 July, Lieutenant Colonel Frazer assured a family correspondent that there had been a 'want of sufficient gallantry' at the first assault. He repeated and developed the point in a letter of 4 September. The town's defences in July had not been as formidable as they became by late August. But 'our fellows took it for granted that they were all to be killed, and turned tail without looking at the reality of the danger, which, as usual, the cowardly magnified'. Such a judgement became public when the call for volunteers for the second assault went out to regiments beyond the 5th Division. The call proclaimed that 'Men were wanted to volunteer, such as knew how to show other troops the way to mount a breach'. Challenged in this blunt way, the entire 4th Division reportedly stepped forward when 400 volunteers were requested on parade just before the second assault.[44]

According to one source, the commander of the 5th Division, Major General Oswald, had argued against launching the assault. None of the accounts suggests that he participated in the key decisions about the attack, which were discussed by Wellington with senior engineers and the artillery commander plus Graham. Oswald, however, had been selected by Wellington, who wrote to Graham on 8 July, 'Upon consideration, I think you had better give General Oswald charge of the siege of San Sebastian'.[45] But when the 5th Division was assigned the task of assaulting the breach, on 24 July, Oswald reputedly objected to Graham that the attacking force could not advance in compact order to the breach if the horn-work commanding the exposed access route remained intact. He also objected that even if he secured the breach and his men descended the 20ft drop from the breach into the town, they would find themselves in a low-lying street commanded by French interior positions. Oswald repeated his objections to the commanding engineer, as well to Graham.[46] There is a strong suspicion, based however on limited hearsay evidence, that the attack was not redoubled because the divisional commander believed the assault plan was flawed.

Notes

1. Robert Batty, *Campaign of the Left Wing of the Allied Army, in the Western Pyrenees and South of France, in the Years 1813–14* (London, 1823), 15–16.
2. Alexander Somerville, *History of the British Legion, and War in Spain* (London, 1839), 48, 65.
3. Batty, *Campaign*, 16.
4. Sabine (ed.), *Letters*, 190–2, 194–5.
5. Jones, *Journals*, ii, 20.

6. Sabine (ed.), *Letters*, 195–6.

7. Wellington to Graham, 17 July 1813, *WD*, x, 534.

8. Wellington to Graham, 19 July 1813, *WD*, x, 541.

9. Jones, *Journals*, ii, 31.

10. Anon. [Blakiston], *Twelve Years' Military Adventure*, ii, 248–9.

11. Sabine (ed.), *Letters*, 197, 207; Jones, *Journals*, ii, 30–1, 34.

12. Glover (ed.), *A Gentleman Volunteer*, 107, 110, 112; 4 leagues is stated and I take a league to be equivalent to 3 miles.

13. Sabine (ed.), *Letters*, 197–8, 203; Jones, *Journals*, ii, 29; the total of rounds fired is estimated from Frazer's notes on consumption of munitions per gun.

14. Jones, *Journals*, ii, 34.

15. Jones, *Journals*, ii, 29, 35–7; Sabine (ed.), *Letters*, 203.

16. *Morning Post*, 24 August 1813.

17. Ross to Sir Hew Dalrymple, 20 August 1813, *Memoir*, 44.

18. Wellington to Graham, 24 July 1813, *WD*, x, 563.

19. Jones, *Journals*, ii, 37–9.

20. Ross to Dalrymple, 20 August 1813, *Memoir*, 45.

21. Sabine (ed.), *Letters*, 203–4.

22. Jones, *Journals*, ii, 41–2.

23. Lieutenant General Shadwell, *The Life of Colin Campbell, Lord Clyde*, 2 vols (Edinburgh, 1881), i, 25–6, 28.

24. Shadwell, *Life of Colin Campbell*, i, 25–6.

25. Jones, *Journals*, ii, 40–3; Sabine (ed.), *Letters*, 204–5; Graham to Wellington, 27 July 1813, *WD*, x, 589; Hall, A *History of the Peninsular War: VIII*, 216, 316; Shadwell, *Life of Colin Campbell*, i, 29.

26. Henegen, *Seven Years Campaigning*, ii, 32–4.

27. Jones, *Journals*, ii, 43–4.

28. Belmas, *Sièges*, iv, 626.

29. Shadwell, *Life of Colin Campbell*, i, 29–30.

30. Jones, *Journals*, ii, 20–1; *Caledonian Mercury*, 12 August 1813.

31. Jones, *Journals*, ii, 20–1, 46, 50–2, 56–8, 92.

32. Dickson to Somerset, 7 September 1813, WP 9/2/2/15.

33. Jones, *Journals*, i, 209; ii, 91.

34. Jones, *Journals*, ii, 14, 17; Sabine (ed.), *Letters*, 198.

35. Sabine (ed.), *Letters*, 203.

36. Sabine (ed.), *Letters*, 205.

37. Wollocombe (ed.), *With the Guns*, 47, 55, 56, 62, 66, 67, 70–3.

38. An Eminent English Barrister, *Buenos Ayres: the Trial of Lieut. Gen. Whitelocke* (Dublin, 1808), 164.

39. Shadwell, *Life of Colin Campbell*, i, 26, 30–1.

40. Henegan, *Seven Years Campaigning*, ii, 31.

41. Jones, *Journals*, ii, 43–5; Graham to Wellington, 27 July 1813, *WD*, x, 589.

42. Jones, *Journals*, ii, 44–5.

43. Entry dated 30 August, *Royal Military Panorama*, iii, 159 (November 1813).

44. Sabine (ed.), *Letters*, 212, 253.

45. Wellington to Graham, 8 July 1813, *WD*, x, 512.

46. *Royal Military Calendar*, iii, 53.

Chapter 7

The Consequences of Failure

Explaining Failure

Recriminations over responsibility for the failure raised questions about the competence of the engineers as well as of Major General Oswald. Lieutenant Colonel Burgoyne, an engineer, reported that many officers 'could not get the men to follow them' onto the breach. He further noted that 'Our principal loss was returning from the breach, and on the open breach and in the crowded trenches, from the heavy fire of shot, shells, and grape'.[1] Another senior engineer, Lieutenant Colonel Jones, whose son was left on the breach, concluded that 'The efforts on the breach were certainly neither very obstinate nor very persevering'. But he refrained in print from accusing the infantrymen of weak commitment, citing instead Graham's public view that continued fighting on the breach would have entailed unacceptable casualties.[2] A battalion commander, William Gomm, took a diametrically different position. Desperately won victories at Ciudad Rodrigo and Badajoz had

> checked the progress of science among our engineers, and perhaps done more; for it seems to have inspired them with a contempt for as much of it as they had attained. Our soldiers have on all occasions stood fire so well that our artillery have become as summary in their proceedings as our engineers; and provided they can make a hole in the wall by which we can claw up, they care not about destroying its defences, or facilitating in any degree what is, under the most favourable auspices, the most desperate of all military enterprises.

Some 500 men – 'the flower of the army' – had been lost in a calamitous assault.[3]

Lieutenant Colonel Ross criticized both Major General Oswald and junior Royal Engineer officers. After stories of the failed attempt circulated in Britain, he argued that Oswald lacked energy and determination. According to Ross, Lieutenant Jones and the grenadiers of the Royals mounted the breach and entered the town, only to find themselves isolated; when Jones returned to the breach to summon support he was wounded and taken prisoner. Ross believed that most of the assault party were demoralized by Oswald who had been overheard calling out to General Graham that the situation looked bad and asking whether the troops should be summoned back. Jones, when freed from captivity in September, claimed that the breach could have been seized on 25 July if enough troops had advanced in his support. Jones, of course, had every reason to feel that he had been let down by weak divisional leadership. But

Ross added an important and interesting qualification which undermined Jones's claim. Ross noted that the lead in assaulting breaches was customarily given to an engineer officer because infantry officers were uncertain about the technicalities of the construction of the defence works they were assailing. Engineer officers, however, became too eager to succeed and to make a reputation. They tended therefore to press ahead optimistically, and were encouraged to do so by their commanding officers. The engineers' heavy casualties reflected a behavioural trait which Ross felt had been carried too far.[4]

Evaluating specific criticisms requires consideration of the professional positions of those being held to account. The engineers faced considerable professional challenges. First, they did not directly command troops, and were treated as somewhat apart from cavalry and infantry officers. Secondly, they were often overworked since there were so few of them. The entire Royal Engineer establishment consisted of 73 officers in 1792 and 262 in 1813. But the number actually in service in 1813 amounted to only 201. Thirdly, their expertise was less solidly founded than many senior officers wished. The sudden increase in demand for engineer officers in the 1790s led to a loosening of the standards required, with examinations, for instance, ceasing to be public. John T. Jones, whose writings on the Peninsular sieges are frequently cited here, was commissioned in 1798 having entered the Royal Military Academy at Woolwich in the previous year at the age of 15.[5] His initial professional training was hardly extensive. Nor was the cadets' education in mathematics very rigorous. After public examinations were restored in 1811, all 29 candidates in the final year failed the mathematics examination in 1812 at their first attempt.

Fourthly, as of 1810 they did not possess much practical knowledge of warfare. Once commissioned, officers typically concentrated on the routine construction and maintenance of fortifications at, most prominently, Portsmouth, Chatham, Gibraltar and Malta, and in Ireland, the Channel Islands, Canada, the West Indies and Ceylon. As of 1809 and excluding the early days of the Peninsular War, only sixty-nine Royal Engineer officers had experience of overseas operations, as distinct from non-operational postings. Even the experience gained was narrowly based, since 28 of those officers had been in the short-lived Walcheren expedition of 1809, 11 had been in Egypt in 1801 and 9 had been at Copenhagen in 1807. Only ten RE officers on the establishment in 1809 had served in three or more overseas operations. The Peninsular War changed that pattern, with ninety-seven officers posted to the Peninsula at some point during 1809–14. But, even so, the number serving at any one time scarcely provided a large cadre of engineers. In January 1813, for example, only thirty-nine RE officers were posted to the Iberian Peninsula, which included Gibraltar. The average length of service totalled about twenty-one months. Service was curtailed by death – twenty-five of the ninety-seven sent to the Peninsula were killed or died there – and severe wounds.[6] Moreover, they competed against a French engineer corps which had been grown larger far earlier than their own. For example, there were 30 per cent more French engineer captains in 1746 than the entire complement of Royal Engineers in 1792.[7] On the credit side, engineer officers in the Peninsula had by July 1813 gained experience in a sequence of sieges even though their knowledge and skill developed from a low base.

Limited evidence makes it typically difficult to assess individual commanders' performance and John Oswald's role is impossible to determine. We can say that he had wide, long and relevant professional experience. Commissioned in 1788, he had served in Gibraltar from1790, just seven years after the end of its dramatic and much-discussed siege. During his time there, John Drinkwater, who had written the acclaimed history of the siege of 1779–83, was also serving once more in the garrison force.[8] It is highly likely that Oswald was acquainted with Drinkwater's work. Oswald went to the Caribbean in the mid-1790s to participate in the capture of a number of islands, where service included small-scale sieges. A Lieutenant Colonel in the 35th from 1797, he was badly wounded in Holland in 1799 at the head of his battalion. He went to Malta for tours of duty during 1800–5 and was present at the blockade and capture of the island. In 1806, as a Colonel, he commanded a brigade in the kingdom of Naples, at the battle of Maida and at the successful twenty-day siege of Scylla Castle. Although the castle was small and defended by only 100 or so Frenchmen, it enjoyed an excellent position. The British gradually increased the calibre of the guns deployed until they made a breach with four 24-pounders dragged with difficulty to within 160yd of the castle. According to a Royal Engineer subaltern, the French Lieutenant Colonel of Engineers was 'extremely active and clever in his defence, and gives every proof that he is determined not to surrender until breached'.[9] Oswald thus had first-hand experience of French defensive determination. Equally importantly, he worked closely at Scylla with Captain John Jones of the Royal Engineers. The latter had helped develop the defences of Gibraltar in 1798–1803, and in 1805–6 served in Malta and Naples and at Maida. Jones, by then a Lieutenant Colonel, later participated in some of the sieges of 1812 and although he missed San Sebastian while recovering from wounds, he regarded his work at Scylla as among his finest achievements. Oswald thus had close links with an engineer officer who had already won Sir John Moore's praise and was to gain Wellington's respect and became one of the pre-eminent siege and fortification experts of his generation.[10]

In 1807, Oswald was involved in the expedition to Egypt which captured Alexandria from the Turks. He was praised for his conduct as second-in-command of a force of 2,500 men sent on an abortive mission to Rosetta. Sir Henry Bunbury, who assessments of others could be acerbic, described Oswald as 'able' and a commander 'whose firmness and good judgement were conspicuous on every occasion'.[11] After being involved in operations from Sicily against the French on the Neapolitan mainland in 1808–9 and being promoted to Brigadier General, he led the expedition which took the Ionian Islands in 1809–10. Commanding about 2,000 men, he besieged and took the fortress on the island of Santa Maura, 'not without some trouble and loss', in 1810. He then organized an indigenous force, the Greek Light Infantry in 1810–11. He had plenty of experience of working effectively with locally raised troops, and a reputation for an enlightened approach to civil administration. He arrived in the Peninsula in October 1812 and assumed command of the 5th Division.[12] He had the track record of an officer whose judgement might be trusted. Service in small-scale sieges, in southern Europe, and in working with non-British troops fitted him well for this assignment. Lieutenant Colonel Gomm, commanding a battalion of the 9th within the division, described Oswald as 'a very able man and excellent officer'.[13]

Yet the assault was poorly judged. It occurred at least a day too late. In fact, it could be argued that it should have gone forward only if a far shorter bombardment, and not one lasting four days followed by a one-day pause, had been mounted. Captain John Blakiston had trained at Woolwich and served as an engineer in India. He argued that the first assault failed by 'giving the enemy too early an insight into our plans'. The main breaching batteries should not have been emplaced until after the work on the isthmus had been completed. Ideally the breaching batteries should have been established 'in one night, so as to have opened at day-light on the following morning'. In making this point, he drew upon his experience of sieges in India. Although summer nights in Spain were shorter than in India, the ground was easy to dig; he reminded his readers that the east bank consisted of sand-hills. Men preparing the batteries there were not vulnerable to sorties launched by the defenders across the Urumea River. The main breach should have been opened up 'in half the time that it really was' if the guns in San Sebastian had been silenced from the isthmus and from non-breaching artillery on the east bank. Such preparatory work should have extended to taking possession of the horn-work before assaulting the breach.[14]

One telling factor, omitted by Blakiston in this particular assessment, was that siege works in India were completed quickly because local labour was readily available. His description of the siege of Ahmednaghur in 1803, during Wellington's campaign against the Marathas, explained how the preparatory work was expedited:

> The celerity with which batteries are erected by the English in India would astonish the regular stagers of Europe, who follow the old German system of Muller. . . . Nearly three times the number of hands allowed by Muller for the construction of a battery are allotted to the work. . . . A certain portion of the party is employed in digging where the soil is loosest, and the rest are posted in chains extending thence to the battery, to pass the baskets of earth as fast as they are filled. . . . The battery is thus generally completed two or three hours before day-break.

Speed of construction, especially if everything in a main battery close to the defended walls could be finished overnight, obviously minimized the opportunities for a besieged garrison to fire upon the batteries during the preparatory phase. But the mathematical principles elaborated by John Muller, who became Professor of Mathematics and Fortification at Woolwich in 1741, depended in practice on such logistical factors as the ample supply of labour to speed up operations. Blakiston accepted that batteries in Europe took days to erect, thus enabling the defenders to disrupt them.[15]

A senior engineer, Lieutenant Colonel Burgoyne, made a similar criticism as Blakiston's, but added to it. He argued that the plan of attack was revealed far too early:

> while the enemy possessed the convent of St Bartolomeo and advanced position, and while we were forced to wait for the arrival of sufficient ammunition to commence with, *the whole* of the batteries and trenches were constructing on

the right bank of the river, which gave them immediate insight into the nature of the attack; and the breach was practicable two days before the trenches on the left attack [i.e. on the isthmus] were sufficiently forward for the reception of the storming party.

The main batteries should have been assembled only when the San Bartolomeo position had been fully established. Once the breaching batteries were in place the principal bombardment should have been unleashed, followed immediately by the assault. But Burgoyne also insisted that the direction of the assault was misguided. The discovery of a drain leading to the horn-work's ditch should have been exploited to mine the outlying structures of the horn-work. Exploding a well-placed mine would have opened the way to assaulting the horn-work. Instead, the main breach was brutally exposed to fire from muskets and a few light artillery guns on the horn-work and the curtain wall behind it.[16]

As it happened, of course, the deployment of the artillery made nonsense of Wellington's optimistic claims that San Sebastian could be taken swiftly. Moreover, the assault should not have been launched before dawn or so early in the morning that river mist made it impossible for the artillery on the east bank to support the assault. It was presumably assumed that the advance on the main breach would go smoothly, since no contingencies were drawn up to overcome the confusion which occurred when the units assigned to the minor, more northerly of the two breaches marched into the static and hesitant or even retreating troops who failed to reach the main breach. Finally, the British knew that the French had prepared a defence in depth within the town. But they appear to have planned no measures to overcome that defence except through sheer weight of attacking numbers.

Wellington did not dwell on this failure. His official despatch on the first assault was terse and offered a cursory and disingenuous explanation for the failure. He blamed lack of sufficient ammunition for the decision to lift the siege and resort to a blockade. In reporting to the secretary of state, he stated that the two breaches were prepared by 24 July, and that 'orders were given that they should be attacked on the morning of the 25th'. There was no hint of the day's enforced postponement in his brief description, which gave the impression that the assault was launched the day after the breaches were ready. He noted his visit on the 25th to consult Graham and senior engineer and artillery officers. They concluded that 'it would be necessary to increase the facilities of the attack before it should be repeated'. The only hint of inadequacy was the non-arrival of ammunition which had been requested on 26 June and 'which I had reason to believe was embarked at Portsmouth, and to expect every hour'. In fact, Wellington can scarcely have expected the arrival of such munitions within one month of his requesting them. As it happened, he received information only on 5 August that the convoy's departure had been delayed.[17]

He also claimed that the decision 'that the siege should for the moment be converted into a blockade' was taken during the afternoon of the 25th and was 'found to be the more desirable when I returned to Lesaca in the evening' when he learned that Soult had attacked the British position at Roncesvalles.[18]

This very long despatch, written on 1 August and suitable for publication, devoted only three paragraphs, two of them very short, to events at San Sebastian. The thrust of the report was to narrate the complex manoeuvres and fighting which culminated in the two battles of Sorauren. The bulk of his despatch therefore described agile and effective responses to a sudden French advance and a British victory in severe fighting against Napoleon's arguably premier marshal. San Sebastian was merely mentioned as a minor preliminary. According to Wellington, inadequate supplies of munitions, and the failure of the Ordnance and Royal Navy to deliver long-awaited replenishments, led inevitably to the decision not to renew the assault and to opt for a blockade. On 6 August, Wellington repeated this complaint about the failure of the Ordnance in England to understand his logistical requirements and especially his need for shot.[19]

Wellington's claim that he made this decision to lift the siege before learning of Soult's offensive, launched that morning, was seriously qualified, if not contradicted, by a hurried letter of 26 July from Lieutenant Colonel Frazer: 'Lord Wellington came here yesterday about 12, and remained till 4. Another attack is determined upon. We are to complete the second or half-finished breach, to throw down the demi-bastion, and to have fresh troops for another assault.' Frazer, as a senior artillery commander, would surely have been aware of the cessation of siege operations if such a decision had been reached on the afternoon of the previous day. Supplies of ammunition, as Wellington stressed, were admittedly low, but Frazer had recently ordered 6,000 round shot for 12-pounders to be cast at Santander, and he hoped to secure shot for 18-pounders from naval frigates. But such calculations about the task in hand – 'I have no fears for the success of our enterprise against St. Sebastian' – were cut short by new and frustrating orders, issued during the 26th to withdraw the guns to Pasajes. Frazer's explanation for this sudden change of course was unambiguous: 'I believe the Marquis has his fears of Soult'.[20]

That was indeed the case. Just before midday on 24 July, Wellington acknowledged Graham's letter of 5.00 a.m. informing him of the postponement of the assault. He had then during the 24th proposed practical steps to retain the initiative and seize the main breach, as has already been described. In this letter, Wellington merely noted that Soult's forces were on the move. At 10.00 p.m. on the 25th, however, he ordered Graham to evacuate the guns to Pasajes, except for four 18-pounders on the isthmus, two guns to maintain a suppressing fire on the breaches and two howitzers. Even the guns borrowed from Collier's frigate *Surveillante* were to be returned. He informed Graham that he learned on his journey to Lesaca that fighting had started in the mountains at Maya, but only after reaching his headquarters did he learn that a significant action involving the 4th Division had begun that afternoon at Roncesvalles. He conceded that 'It is impossible to judge of Soult's plan yet', and added that 'One can hardly believe that, with 30,000 men, he proposes to force himself through the passes of the mountains'. In this letter Wellington alluded to shortages of munitions, but he would have known that in the afternoon when he was at San Sebastian. The main instruction that night to Graham was that 'you should be prepared' for possible French moves in the next day or so.[21] Soult's advance lifted the siege.

The Impact of the First Assault

Although the French defenders of San Sebastian survived the first phase of the siege and were given a breathing space by Soult's advance, they faced threatening shortages of ammunition. Lieutenant Colonel Jones noted on 21 July that the French concentrated their artillery fire on the British breaching battery and pointed out: 'It was apparent from the commencement of the operation, that the garrison wished to spare their ammunition, as they scarcely ever fired at working parties bringing shot, etc, and at this time many of their shells, which having been thrown with great correctness, might have done much mischief, were not loaded with sufficient powder to burst them.'[22]

During the British preparation on the 23rd for their planned assault on 24 July, the French returned little artillery fire.[23] According to Frazer, they focused on his battery, number 14, admittedly the largest single battery in the line-up. But even those French guns which remained operational suffered from the expansion of their vents, thereby losing accuracy. Moreover, the French could not, like the British, recycle some of their own ammunition. Of the 2,500 rounds of 18-pounder shot the British fired at the convent and its redoubt, 1,000 were recovered for further use when the British captured the convent.[24]

Between 28 June and 16 August, the French garrison expended 6,135 of their 7,620 shells, 13,043 of their stock of 20,395 shot and 12,138 of their 52,934 cannon balls. They received from France only 988 cannon balls – munitions they least needed – during that entire period. More ominously, they had consumed 63 per cent of their gunpowder, again with no replenishment from France. This depletion of ammunition meant that the allies could re-instate their artillery batteries whenever they wished without serious or persistent interference from the garrison's guns. The French, however, retained the ability to inflict severe damage in close-quarter fighting. Their infantrymen used 381,514 infantry cartridges between 28 June and 16 August, but they still had 932,500 available in mid-August for a garrison of about 2,500 effectives.[25] That amounted to 363 rounds per man, or enough to resist 2 or 3 assaults on the defensive walls of the magnitude of the first assault.

The British had to decide whether the French would exact an unacceptable price if a second attack were launched. The initial operations cost the allies 1,281 casualties. In the period 7–20 July inclusive 62 men were killed and 287 wounded, while 2 went missing; of these, 42 killed and 162 wounded belonged to the Portuguese army. During 21–7 July inclusive 142 men were killed and 487 wounded, but 301 were missing, mainly taken prisoner; of these 42 killed, 179 wounded and 144 missing were in the Portuguese army.

There were significantly high losses among the officers and sergeants. The casualties during 21–7 July included 8 officers, 7 sergeants and 85 British rank and file killed, and 24 officers, 12 sergeants and 272 other ranks wounded. The distribution in the Portuguese battalions was quite different: 2 sergeants and 40 rank and file killed and 7 officers, 3 sergeants and 169 rank and file wounded.[26] British officer casualties were 8 per cent of the totals for both killed and wounded and exceeded casualties among sergeants. Such officer sacrifices were accepted without demur. For example, Lieutenant Colonel Frazer described the plight of Captain Lewis of the Royal

Engineers in laconic style: 'He has lost a leg, but is doing well'. Captain Taylor of the Royal Navy was hit by a shell and was due to have his leg amputated the next day: 'He is in my room, in excellent spirits, and will do well'. [27] The losses did not deter a second attempt.

The Wider Campaign
The first assault failed, but this failure was immediately subsumed in broader movements. Marshal Soult, having been sent to change the dynamics of the frontier struggle, arrived to take up his command on 13 July. When *The Times* learned that he had re-grouped his forces with commendable speed, it concluded that the conflict in the Pyrenees was 'hastening to another awful, but not alarming crisis'. The new French dispositions were 'twisted in' with allied positions at Irun, about a mile-and-a-half from the main bridge (destroyed by the French) across the Bidassoa, at Lesaca and at Maya. This meant that the opposing armies could hardly withdraw without coming into contact with each other. Soult, it predicted, would want to save San Sebastian while Wellington would seek to attack the marshal 'before his army, composed of so many fugitive bands, shall have acquired that perfect consistency to which it would shortly attain under his care'. But Soult was under the greater immediate pressure once the main breach at San Sebastian was opened on 23 July, which was the latest news upon which the newspaper based its assessment.[28]

Soult launched his offensive on 24–5 July. His forces based in the mountains advanced upon Roncesvalles and Maya to gain command of the routes leading to Pamplona. The action at Roncesvalles was limited, with French losses of about 530 and allied losses of about 350, but the British, outnumbered by Clausel's and Reille's divisions, retreated at night. In the more extensive fighting at the Maya pass, the British lost 1,500 casualties from about 6,000 men engaged, while French losses, higher at perhaps 2,100 troops, were hardly surprising for an attacking force.[29] As has already been noted, Wellington claimed that he had postponed further siege operations before learning of Soult's advance. But, as a result of that advance, the British hurriedly withdrew their siege guns to Pasajes, in readiness to ship them away should the need arise.

After pushing through the passes at Roncesvalles and Maya on 25–6 July, Soult marched towards Pamplona. He roused his troops with the promise of relieving Pamplona and advancing to Vitoria, to recapture the artillery lost there and to gain the emperor's forgiveness for past failure.[30] The French garrison besieged at Pamplona exceeded 4,000 men and there were 57 field guns in the town.[31]

On the 28th, Soult attacked an extremely well-defended hill in an effort to break the centre of the allies' defensive arc around Sorauren, from 3–5 miles to the north and east of Pamplona. His men had to scale about 1,000ft and then assail allied battalions in line. After heavy fighting, they failed to break through and Soult had to retreat. The allied success in a series of clashes cost them 572 killed, 3,522 wounded and 465 missing during 25–8 July. Wellington informed the Prime Minister that he 'never saw such fighting' as on 27–8 July, 'nor such determination' among his own troops.[32] The first battle was followed by an entirely different action on 30 July, when the British attacked two of the three corps in Soult's army as they marched in extended formation across the allied front. The French were pushed into headlong retreat.[33]

If the French failed in their offensive, they had thwarted the British at San Sebastian, and inflicted 7,096 casualties on the Anglo-Portuguese forces under Wellington's direct command between 25 July and 2 August.[34] Those losses exceeded the casualties the allies suffered at either of the great battles of Salamanca or Vitoria. Soult's dispositions were justly criticized by Oman for being over-ambitious and for failing to take account of real obstacles in the terrain over which his army moved. On 26 July, three French divisions were expected to march along narrow mountain-side mule tracks in order to close on their opponents. On 30 July, the line of retreat was recklessly exposed. The damage suffered was considerable. During 25 July to 2 August, French casualties amounted to at least 12,500 and probably closer to 13,000, well in excess of the allies' losses.[35] It is not unusual for an army taking the offensive to suffer higher losses than an army on the defensive, but by 3 August Soult's three corps had been defeated and forced to retreat, often in considerable disarray, back into Pyrenean France.

Yet Wellington privately conceded that he did not know what was happening on 26–7 July. He assumed that Soult's objective was San Sebastian; according to Larpent, Wellington told him on 24 August that 'I had then no notion that with an army so lately beaten he had serious thoughts, as I am now sure he had, of driving me behind the Ebro'. At 9.00 p.m. on the 26th the headquarters were ordered to move after breakfasting at 5.00 a.m. the next morning. After marching along mountain roads they were given a new destination, Lizaso on a road between Vera and Pamplona, at midday on the 27th. In the seven days from 27 July to 2 August, the headquarters shifted every day, sleeping at seven different villages, first going south and then returning eventually to Lesaca.[36]

After these hurried and sometimes frantic movements and intensive fighting from 24 July to 2 August, Wellington's campaign remained essentially static until early October, although defensive troop re-positioning within the sector was frequent and extensive. The standard explanation is that Wellington insisted that there was no point in pushing into France until he knew what was going to happen in central Europe. The armistice between France on the one side and Russia and Prussia on the other continued until mid-August.

But even the renewal of the war in Germany was beset with problems for the British. The Austrian Foreign Minister, Metternich, proposed in late June an alliance with Prussia and Russia without Britain and without including the expulsion of France from Spain as a war aim. This position was duly modified by late August, but the British continued to doubt Metternich's commitment to an extensive war, as distinct from operations in Germany. Once Wellington knew in early September that the Continental war had resumed, he could plan to renew his strategic advance. But it is arguable that the critical shift only came when Castlereagh, setting suspicions of Austria aside, decided on 18 September to seek a grand alliance of the powers opposed to France.[37] This diplomatic shift removed further hesitations about an invasion of France from Spain.

While, therefore, diplomatic manoeuvrings in central Europe were bound to shape Wellington's decision-making, he had other reasons for calling a halt. The situation on the ground in early August induced caution. On 26 July, Frazer noted that 'our ammunition draws to an end, nor do I at this moment know whence a supply is to be procured'.[38] But Wellington also recognized the effectiveness of French resilience across his theatre of operations. He made two connected points in a semi-official letter to Graham on 4 August. First, he stressed the weakening of his own forces: 'The troops are of course a good deal fatigued, and we have suffered very considerably, particularly the English troops in the 2nd division . . . which, with the existing want of shoes and of musket ammunition, induces me to delay for a day or two any forward movement, and to doubt the expediency of making one at all'.[39]

Losses among British battalions were particularly galling since Wellington wanted strong British battalions in the corps organized to include Portuguese brigades and possibly Spanish divisions. Strong British battalions would, he believed, deter desertion among non-British battalions. As he informed the secretary of state, 'Our loss is distressing . . . as having fallen a good deal on General Hill's corps: the number of British troops there has become too small in proportion to the foreigners'.[40] Such losses testified to the vigour and range of the French offensive: 'Between the 25th of last month and 2nd of this, they were engaged seriously not less than ten times; on many occasions in attacking very strong positions, in others beat from them or pursued'. Of course, he stressed, correctly, that 'The French army must have suffered terribly'.[41]

But the real set-back was that the 'Light and Quick' campaign launched in late May ground to a halt. The French resurgence after 25 July, according to one British officer present, 'greatly dampened the spirits of the army, and every thing was surprise and consternation for a day or two. No one knew what would be done, or what would become of us all if a retreat took place, which was dreaded by many'.[42]

Granted, public opinion at home could be buoyed by positive reporting. News of Sorauren dispelled the gloom, especially since heavy British losses had apparently been exceeded by French casualties and prisoners of war. Moreover, according to one report, the British assault upon San Sebastian added to 'the glory of the British soldier, whose courage on this occasion surpassed all description'. Failure was attributed to the French construction of a wide and deep ditch in the rear of the breach, into which three companies fell. One officer's published account emphasized that a shortage of ammunition and the impending arrival of more guns from England delayed the renewal of siege operations.[43]

Even so, the French for their part could draw pride and hope from their successful resistance at San Sebastian. One British officer based at Pasajes observed on 6 October that the defeat of the first assault at San Sebastian encouraged the French belief that they could hold Pamplona.[44] British losses at the first assault and their lifting of the siege were trumpeted, within the French military, as a morale-boosting example of what could be achieved by determination and courage.[45]

Overall, therefore, Wellington's operations after the battle of Vitoria on 21 June and into the first days of August were fluid and uncertain. Consider Wellington's operational objectives. He started by driving Clausel to the east, to keep the French general's division away from the main French army. But he did not want to push Clausel as far as Suchet's army in Catalonia, so an escape route into France across the

Pyrenees, via Jaca, was left open. Clausel took it, joined Soult's newly re-formed army and was back in action against the allies by late July. Secondly, Wellington hoped in late June to besiege Pamplona. Yet he was obliged to acknowledge that such a siege would tie down 15,000–20,000 'of our best troops' for perhaps 9 weeks, whereas a blockade would absorb fewer troops of lower quality and produce a surrender in 12 weeks. He therefore opted for a long blockade.[46] Even that decision did not go to plan, for in the last few days of July he was forced by Soult to fight a testing battle at Sorauren within miles of Pamplona to prevent the French from lifting the blockade.

Thirdly, between 4 and 8 July Wellington concentrated on driving the French from the off-shoots of the long, broad and fertile Baztan valley.[47] On 25–6 July, Soult's forces re-took the Pyrenean entry to the valley at the Puerto de Maya, much to Wellington's fury, and enjoyed the use of the valley as a route towards Pamplona or to the north. Fourthly, Wellington recognized in mid-July that his front was overstretched and vulnerable. He initiated troop movements which he believed secured the front. But ten days later Soult's offensive threw virtually the whole front into turmoil. Wellington misread the direction of the French advance, believing that the French build-up in the mountains around St Jean Pied de Port was a ruse to draw his forces eastwards thereby opening a way for the French to push along the coast road and relieve San Sebastian.[48] In fact, Soult's principal thrust was indeed upon Pamplona.

Finally, Wellington gave priority to San Sebastian because he believed it could be taken quickly with the guns and ammunition available or accessible to him in early July. But in his despatch of 1 August he declared that, after the failed effort early on 25 July, he had too few heavy guns and too little artillery ammunition for a renewed attack. He shifted a good deal of blame upon inadequate naval support, although he had started with the presumption of strong naval back-up which had not been defined or agreed earlier. Wellington's explanation suffered from two flaws. First, he clearly underestimated the time required to position his artillery. Even when heavy artillery was delivered at Pasajes from 7 July, those heavy guns did not begin firing until 20 July despite the fact that the distance between the harbour and the sand-hills was only about 1½ miles. The difficulties of getting the guns ashore, hauling them to their intended position, and setting them up for firing from sandy ground did not suggest that projecting British power, despite the navy's 'command of the oceans', was well planned or straightforward. Moreover, capturing the San Bartholomeo position delayed the main operation even if the logistics and transport had worked more quickly. Secondly, the decision not to renew the attack on San Sebastian resulted from Soult's advance on Roncesvalles during the morning of 25 July rather than from shortages of guns and ammunition and the more general lack of naval support. Wellington's optimistic expectations of speedy results were not matched by effective delivery and were dashed by French military resilience.

Notes

1. Wrottesley, *Life and Correspondence*, i, 269–70.
2. Jones, *Journals*, ii, 45.

3. Carr-Gomm (ed.), *Letters and Journals*, 311–12.
4. Ross to Dalrymple, 20 August, 31 October 1813, *Memoir*, 45, 50–1.
5. 'Sir John Thomas Jones' entry, *ODNB*.
6. This paragraph owes much to material in Mark Thompson, 'The Rise of the Scientific Soldier as seen through the Performance of the Corps of Royal Engineers during the early 19th Century' (PhD thesis, University of Sunderland, 2008), 47–51, 91–5, 102, Appendix B.
7. Langins, *Conserving the Enlightenment*, 86.
8. *Colburn's United Service Magazine* (1844, Part I), 439.
9. Wrottesley, *Life and Correspondence*, i, 12–13.
10. Sir John Thomas Jones' entry, *ODNB*.
11. Sir Henry Bunbury, *Narratives of Some Passages in the Great War with France (1799–1810)* (London, 1927), 203. Bunbury served in the Mediterranean in the mid-1800s and was Under-Secretary for War, 1809–16.
12. *Royal Military Calendar*, iii, 46–50; Alethea Hayter (ed.), *The Backbone: Diaries of a Military Family in the Napoleonic Wars* (Durham, 1993), 97, 231–4.
13. Carr-Gomm (ed.), *Letters and Journals*, 316.
14. Anon. [Blakiston], *Twelve Years' Military Adventure*, ii, 253–5.
15. Anon. [Blakiston], *Twelve Years' Military Adventure*, i, 135–7.
16. Wrottesley, *Life and Correspondence*, i, 270–1.
17. Wellington to Graham, 6 August 1813, *WD*, x, 604.
18. Wellington to Bathurst, 1 August 1813, *WD*, x, 576.
19. Wellington to Graham, 6 August 1813, *WD*, x, 604.
20. Sabine (ed.), *Letters*, 206–8.
21. Wellington to Graham, 24 July, 25 July 1813, *WD*, x, 563, 566.
22. Jones, *Journals*, ii, 33; see also 25.
23. Jones, *Journals*, ii, 36.
24. Sabine (ed.), *Letters,* 197, 207; Jones, *Journals*, ii, 29, 35.
25. Belmas, *Sièges*, iv, 665.
26. Official returns in *Royal Military Panorama*, iii (November 1813), 200.
27. Sabine (ed.), *Letters*, 206, 208.
28. *The Times*, 3 August 1813, p. 3.
29. Oman, *A History of the Peninsular War*, vi, 621–2, 638–9.
30. *Morning Post*, 24 August 1813.
31. Larpent (ed.), *The Private Journal*, ii, 144–5.
32. Wellington to Liverpool, 4 August 1813, *WD*, x, 597.
33. Oman, *A History of the Peninsular War*, vi, 688–9, 692, 694, 704–6.
34. Wellington to Bathurst, 4 August 1813, *WD*, x, 599.
35. Oman, *A History of the Peninsular War*, vi, 648–50, 739–40.
36. Larpent (ed.), *A Private Journal*, ii, 14–30, 72.
37. Bew, *Castlereagh*, 321–3.
38. Sabine (ed.), *Letters*, 206.
39. Wellington to Graham, 4 August 1813, *WD*, x, 591.
40. Wellington to Liverpool, 4 August; to Bathurst, 4 August 1813, *WD*, x, 597, 601.
41. Wellington to Graham, 4 August 1813, *WD*, x, 591.
42. *Morning Chronicle*, 17 August 1813.
43. *Morning Post*, 24 August 1813.
44. (Edinburgh) *Caledonian Mercury*, 23 October 1813.
45. Feltre to Albufera, 2 August; to De Caen, 2 August; to Lamarque, 3 August 1813, SHAT C8 156.
46. Wellington to Bathurst, 3 July 1813, *WD*, x, 506.
47. Wellington to Graham, 8 July 1813, *WD*, x, 512.
48. Wellington to Graham, 24 July 1813, *WD*, x, 563.

Chapter 8

Preparation for the Second Assault

Strategic and Operational Constraints in August

The balance of advantage and disadvantage was difficult to assess during the first three weeks of August. Soult failed to break the British position at Sorauren on 28 July and suffered heavy losses. But he forced the British to lift the siege of San Sebastian, if temporarily, and to focus their efforts on consolidating their lines rather than pressing beyond them. Wellington's British and Portuguese forces suffered 7,096 casualties between 25 July and 2 August.[1] Soult had halted the French headlong retreat and done the emperor's bidding in taking the fight to the enemy.

The British recognized that Soult's arrival changed the military scenario in Spain. Ensign Hennell described him as 'an able & dashing general' who was 'universally allowed to be the first general Buonaparte has'.[2] When *The Times* learned of Soult's return, it noted that he would pull together at least 60,000 troops 'dispirited, no doubt, and confounded by recent events, but yet in a degree revived by the presence, and re-organized by the skill, of Marshal Soult'.[3] As Frazer later noted, on 8 October, 'Soult is keen, thoughtful, and quite a man of business. He allows himself but one hour for dinner, and five only of the twenty-four for sleep'.[4] Harry Smith, who fought from La Coruña to Toulouse, later described Soult as 'an able officer' who in taking over 'the beaten French force' soon 'instilled its old pride of victory, and inspired all again with the ardour and vivacity of French soldiers'.[5] Reviewing the events of 1813, the *New Annual Register* described Soult as 'evincing more talents than any other of Bonaparte's generals . . . his activity and energy were accompanied and directed by more method and order; they rested on more clear and comprehensive views' than other Napoleonic generals possessed.[6]

Soult naturally boasted of his swift successes. He had driven the allies from the Baztan valley, taken many prisoners, capturing wounded men abandoned there, and severely reduced the 92nd's fighting capability. His reserves under Villatte, which contained effective battalions, had crossed the Bidassoa back into Spain.[7] He ascribed the shortcomings at Sorauren to an inability to move his artillery through the mountain passes or to deploy his cavalry, traditionally a French strength in the Peninsula. The bulk of both those two arms had been assigned to the Bidassoa front because of the difficulties of moving them from St Jean Pied de Port down through the mountain passes to Pamplona. On that claim, the marshal might be criticized for venturing so much when lacking the full spectrum of forces necessary for success. But his justifiable claim to have driven the British from their advanced positions and his assessment of the situation in early August supported his request for 30,000 reinforcements as he paused in place, evacuated his wounded, sent his field artillery to the rear and awaited the arrival of food and munitions.[8]

Soult faced an operational dilemma: Napoleon insisted that speedy movements were 'absolutely indispensable' and the minister of war had told the marshal before he left for Spain that he would receive no additional troops.[9] Soult was instructed to concentrate his forces and relieve San Sebastian, Pamplona and the small port of Santona, which, curiously, the French continued to hold, to the east of Santander. The marshal was reminded that stalemate on the frontier was unacceptable to public opinion in France. On 13 August, with campaigning resuming in Germany, the emperor wanted both a diversion to ease the pressure on San Sebastian's garrison and a plan for defending the border.[10]

Soult's moves on the border obviously denied Wellington the option, which he aired as late as 20 July, of invading France during the summer. Although Wellington entertained no such illusion in early August, such optimism had been infectious; for example, Lieutenant Colonel Hugh Gough, commanding the 2/87th, wrote home on 2 August declaring his preference for an immediate advance into France.[11] The French, however, even after their losses and hurried retreat at Sorauren, deployed six divisions and a reserve under Villatte at various points from St Jean Pied de Port to Ascain, near the royal road, and supported those forces with cavalry placed in their rear. Soult commanded enough men for a strong defence, but he repeatedly asserted that he had insufficient soldiers to move against an estimated 90,000 allied troops who were being steadily reinforced from England, Portugal and Spain.[12]

While Wellington paused and Soult pleaded for more troops, San Sebastian remained central to operational planning during August. On 17 August, as required, Soult forwarded a plan for a new offensive for the emperor's approval. Its primary purpose was to support the defence of San Sebastian by mounting a diversionary advance. He did not focus on Pamplona, which had provisions to last until the end of September, and possibly until mid-October. An offensive to relieve the pressure on San Sebastian would use selected divisions from among the 50,000 troops defending the line around St Jean Pied de Port and from among 20,000 troops near the coast.

Since he had insufficient numbers to break the allied double line of defences from the col de Maya in the upper Baztan valley area to Vera, he proposed a pincer movement. This has been heavily criticized for requiring an ambitious junction of two armies operating separately in their independent advances towards San Sebastian. About 20,000–22,000 men under Clausel and d'Erlon, from the mountain positions anchored on St Jean Pied de Port, were to cross the Bidassoa at Vera and advance north-westwards through a mountain route to Oyarzun (Oiartzun) on the Urumea River.

Meanwhile, to the north, 18,000–20,000 men under Reille would cross the Bidassoa River, seize the allied camp at San Marcial and the town of Irun, and then march west to join up with Clausel and d'Erlon. Soult acknowledged that this plan involved considerable difficulties and would entail severe fighting. But he argued that Wellington, though likely to be reinforced, would not launch an advance until the British had taken San Sebastian and Pamplona. He saw little danger of any British moves through the valleys upon Jaca, to the east of his own front, and St Jean de Pied de Port. The valleys impeded armies' mobility and occupying them offered no medium-term advantages to the British, since they would be snowed in within two months. But he insisted he needed the 30,000 reinforcements previously requested if he were to maintain '*une attitude offensive*' in this theatre. He also requested that the emperor deploy a squadron of five or six frigates to help re-victual San Sebastian and Santona, or to ensure access to those ports by smaller boats.[13] Although the naval succour never arrived, Soult's plan of 17 August provided the blueprint for his next offensive.

For the British, the first three weeks of August proved frustrating as they awaited the siege train's arrival from England. They obviously kept a close watch on Soult. For example, intelligence reports in mid-August suggested that he had been reinforced with 3,000 conscripts and was moving 1,000 men to St Jean Pied de Port.[14] But their most important decision was to renew the siege on 6 August. The artillery and supplies were once again loaded off the ships at Pasajes.[15] But the guns used in July were in poor condition. As the Commissary of the siege noted, 'The old guns . . . were found to have done their duty too efficiently to be in a condition to begin again. . . . We therefore waited for a fresh battering train from England . . . '.[16]

While the opposing armies awaited reinforcements of munitions and men, press reporting at home painted a more rosy view of events in Spain. In London, the theatres celebrated Vitoria. In early August, Astley's, known also as the Royal Amphitheatre, staged a 'loyal effusion' entitled 'Vittoria or King Joseph's Last Gun'. Sadler's Wells followed suit with a new musical piece on the same battle. To cap the military euphoria, Vauxhall, London's premier pleasure gardens, put on a Grand Illuminated Military Fete for the Prince Regent's birthday, on 16 August.[17] Before the first assault, reports from the front asserted that San Sebastian 'of necessity must surrender' on the arrival of British heavy guns.[18] The pro-government *Morning Post* of 17 August, while ignoring the failure at San Sebastian, celebrated the victory at Sorauren and the allies' success in thwarting French efforts to relieve Pamplona. It insisted that the Marquess of Wellington's fresh achievements merited a dukedom and vindicated the Duke of York's army reforms. The fact that the Prince of Orange, one of Wellington's ADCs, brought the latest despatches from Spain to London, offered yet further 'evidence' for the claim that the old order, as the young prince had allegedly demonstrated in the Peninsula, could meet modern military challenges and add new lustre to long-standing familial military reputations.[19]

The West Country newspaper, the *Royal Cornwall Gazette*, noted that 'our matchless Leader and the invincible heroes under his command' had driven a numerically superior French army back into France, inflicting 20,000 casualties, while suffering only 6,000 casualties themselves. Their victory was 'one of the most important and complete that has ever graced the military annals of England'. As an extra bonus, the Portuguese troops, inspired by 'unconquerable valour and love of freedom', had fought extremely well.[20] The outcome was obvious to the *Morning Post*. Only San Sebastian remained in French hands and it would fall to Wellington 'very shortly'. Popular resistance in the Peninsula to French domination was also inspiring uprisings throughout Continental Europe: 'Germany is now another Spain'.[21]

Such politically motivated optimism did not quite square with the situation on the ground. On 9 August an officer at the army's headquarters at Lesaca commented that the siege of San Sebastian would be resumed 'with redoubled vigour. It is a very strong place, and will, I am afraid, cost us dear'. The allies could do little about Pamplona except wait: 'nothing but hunger will subdue it: all the fortified places which I have seen are nothing to it'.[22] On 12 August, 25-year-old Captain John Aitchison wrote home from the Oyarzun valley, near San Sebastian:

> There is little going on here just now; since the defeat of Soult the Army in general has been quiet but the siege of San Sebastian has been recommenced, though it proceeds very slowly – I do not know from what cause, but somehow or other we do not manage sieges well. . . . The reduction of San Sebastian by force will now be a more serious business, as the enemy have entrenched all the streets in the town . . .[23]

On 13 August, Francis Larpent, the Judge Advocate General, attended a dinner for thirty-six senior officers to celebrate the Prince Regent's birthday. Wellington suffered from lumbago, which had left him bedridden on 6 August and still unwell on the 10th. He suffered great pain in rising from his chair and in trying to sit down again. The dinner was 'very dull'; 'all around him look pale and worn'. The build-up to a renewed assault on San Sebastian scarcely lightened the mood. Larpent feared it would prove 'hard and bloody work'.[24]

Three developments created the relative stalemate in August. One, already noted, was the resistance offered by the French. The second was the diplomatic situation in central Europe. Graham, in overall charge of the San Sebastian sector, fearing that the northern powers attached little weight to Spanish independence, suggested to Wellington that 'We shall probably be left as usual in the lurch by the allies to whom B'parte will make great concessions in order to be left free to act against Spain'.[25] Writing to the British minister at Lisbon two days later, Wellington expressed his own concern that Napoleon would indeed secure a central European peace, excluding Britain and the Peninsula from any such settlement.[26] On 27 August, just as he completed preparations for the second assault, Wellington did not know that the central European conflict had resumed. Writing to Sir William Beresford, the commander of the Portuguese army, he noted that Napoleon 'wanted either to renew the armistice after the 10th of August, or to commence hostilities with [*sic*] Russians and Prussians alone. I think he is likely to succeed in the former object'. Wellington only knew the true state of affairs, including Austria's decision to join the coalition, on 5 September.[27] This uncertainty, with its serious implications for his own position if Napoleon were able to switch forces from Germany to Spain, presumably added to Wellington's desire to rid himself of the thorn in his northern flank which San Sebastian represented.

The third, typically underplayed, was the difficulty the British had in capturing San Sebastian. The failed first assault and Soult's activism enlarged the siege operation by obliging Wellington to create a long defensive front to protect his besieging forces. On 7 and 8 August Graham reported on the progress being made by Major Charles Smith,

RE in sketching out proposed defensive lines to the east of San Sebastian. He wished to restore Fontarabia as a fortified post and to create a long line of defence to cover Irun. Any such line was, however, vulnerable to being turned along the mountain range to the south. Graham wanted defences constructed up to the heights of San Marcial and into valleys around the Peña d'Aya (Peñas de Haya), which rises to 2,400ft, to safeguard the plain below. Graham noted on 13 August that Major Smith's plans were restricted to works in the plains, whereas the valley's security 'depends entirely' on holding the heights connected with the Peña d'Aya. In addition, a second line was needed to supplement the first by protecting Oyarzun, which was Graham's headquarters. This was designed as a back-up if the allies were driven out of the first line and as a protective shield for Pasajes.[28] On 15 August, Wellington pressed Graham to complete a second line of defences behind the Bidassoa:

> You may depend upon it that, whatever we may do elsewhere, we cannot make the position between Oyarzun and the Bidasoa too strong. . . . it is desirable that no time should be lost in commencing on the works of the second line which you propose. The second line is, if possible, more important than the first, which it is not very easy to hold with an inferior body of troops without a strong second line.[29]

On 21 August, Wellington, following Graham's earlier recommendations, ordered the engineers to strengthen the defences around Irun, in the Andarra valley, on the high ground up to the convent of San Marcial, as well as the valleys around the Peña d'Aya, including an area overlooking the road from the Bidassoa to Irun and Oyarzun.[30] Defending the siege lines and siege works, the classic challenge posed by extensive siege operations, thus greatly increased the demands on Wellington's army. This inexorably expanding appetite for manpower illustrated the rationale behind Clausewitz's later scepticism about sieges as dangerously resource-hungry operations. By mid-August Wellington was confident that 'I am too strong for Soult, on the defensive', thereby vindicating the marshal's plea for reinforcements.

The need to strengthen the defensive lines protecting Irun and Oyarzun could obviously be met. But Wellington faced a number of pressures if he were to resume the offensive. Time was not on his side, since the naval blockade of San Sebastian might not last beyond mid-September, when the weather in the Bay of Biscay worsened, and he was awaiting the arrival of the new siege train. On 7 August, a further concern was raised. The Ordnance in London included in the new siege train guns initially prepared for an expedition to Cuxhaven. Lieutenant Colonel Dickson, commanding the artillery, warned Graham that they were heavier than the guns originally requested and would therefore require additional manpower – already in short supply – to operate. They were also on ships' carriages which previous experience had shown to be 'inapplicable to the service'. If the prospect of finding alternative carriages were not irksome enough, it was also suggested that insufficient shot was available for the designated weapons.[31] The news of the components in the siege train thus depressed morale, at the prospect of additional preparatory work.

In the period before the arrival of the siege train – the fleet conveying it was, at last, approaching the Spanish north coast on 15 August – Wellington was also beset by various managerial difficulties. Graham indicated that stomach complaints and continuing trouble with his right eye led him to seek to return to Britain, as he had done in 1812, in six to eight weeks' time.[32] Behind the front line, Wellington faced uncertainties about Spanish intentions and movements and growing demands for troops in non-combatant duties. Wellington's increasing frustrations with the regency government in Cádiz have been well-documented, but he also faced operational difficulties with his allies. When the allies took the small port of Guetaria, some 15 miles to the west of San Sebastian, Wellington wanted the engineers to demolish the fort at the tip of the headland upon which the town stood, on the grounds that the fort alone could not prevent a superior enemy force from retaking the town.[33] In making these arrangements, Wellington noted that he had not realized that 600 allied troops – he guessed they came from Mendizabal's army – formed a garrison there. This was in itself a curious lapse in communications since Wellington was Commander-in-Chief of the Spanish armies in the field. Somewhat airily, he ordered the Spanish force to proceed to Bilbao 'where there are a great many prisoners, and nobody to take care of them'.[34]

The continuing flow of prisoners of war created further demands on the army. Following the two actions of 25 July, 2,500 prisoners were sent to Bilbao as a first stage in their transportation to England.[35] Those numbers grew to a reported 2,800 on 11 August and 4,000 on the 21st. By 24 August the estimated grand total, including those held elsewhere on the allies' front, reached 7,000, thereby creating a mounting demand for allied troops to be assigned to guard duties.[36] Wellington hoped to relieve that pressure by using transport vessels arriving with troop reinforcements to take prisoners to England on their return voyages. On 11 August, he asked Collier to ensure that transports landing British soldiers at Pasajes should take 500/600 prisoners there to England, while transports capable of carrying 2,800 men should sail to Bilbao and then return to England with that number of prisoners.[37] When reporting that ten transport ships had arrived at Pasajes on 15 August, Collier asked that prisoners in Bilbao be moved down river to Portugalete to speed up their evacuation; some of the vessels could not pass the bar in the river to sail as far as Bilbao. Marching the prisoners to the ships would obviate delays.[38]

The sudden demand for transport and labour added further to the pressure on local resources and on the army itself. Following the first assault, Wellington ordered urgent work on repairing boats at Pasajes harbour which were damaged in 'disembarking and embarking the guns and stores for the siege'. Some boats had been lost and their owners needed to be compensated.[39] In urging the Secretary of State for War and the Colonies to press for additional naval support, he argued that any withdrawal from Pasajes would result in severe losses 'owing to the want of naval means, the harbour boats at Passages [sic] being excessively bad, and all navigated by women, who are unequal to the labor of loading and unloading them; and the greatest number of boats are already destroyed by the weights we have put in them'.[40]

The longer the siege of San Sebastian lasted, the more trying the transport position became. When the first of the great convoys arrived at Pasajes on 19 August, there were so few Royal Navy vessels present that light harbour boats, piloted by women, carried the cargoes from ships to shore. With so few sailors at Pasajes, soldiers were required to unload them.[41] Graham wanted more small boats to move equipment and materials from Pasajes along the coast and also requested 300 'country carts' for transport inland. On the first request, Wellington saw no prospect of securing extra boats from the local population. But he promised 100 artillery carts from the army and another 100 being collected at Tolosa; together they would meet Graham's needs.[42] Carrying large quantities of shot for the 24-pounders from Pasajes to the front was not straightforward.

Supplying labour proved less problematic, with officers on the ground not apparently sharing their commander-in-chief's views of the ineffectiveness of women workers. Earlier in the month the women working in the harbour had been paid a dollar a day and rations had been provided for two women per boat. These terms seem to have been acceptable because, in mid-August, they asked for further work. And there is at least fleeting evidence that the work was accomplished without complaint; one senior officer wrote of listening to the 'singing of the boat-women, whose boats surround a vessel not far from hence. One seems to give verse which the rest sing after her. The harmony is simple and beautiful: the ladies sing in parts, and with some taste.'[43] William Surtees of the Rifle Brigade observed that the local women 'do the same kind of work as the men, that is, they plough, and labour at all sorts of husbandry; but what seemed most remarkable to us, was their sole management of the ferry-boats about Passages and St Sebastian; they row as well as any men, being amazingly strong and active'. They were, according to Surtees, hard-working, 'strictly virtuous' and invariably 'cheerful and happy' in appearance, and they presumably helped raise morale among those working at the harbour.[44]

When Graham pressed the need for extensive defensive works to the east, he raised the difficulty of procuring labour. He ruled out yet further demands on his own troops and Spanish soldiers, in his view, 'do not get on with any works of their own Engineers with any energy'. He concluded therefore that they would prove even less committed to works about which their own engineers 'were not even consulted'. Yet, since the country was populous, he proposed that 'much might be done by employing the peasants at a fair rate of payment – but it would require great exertion of the authorities to oblige them to come'.[45] Wellington accepted this recommendation and instructed Lieutenant Colonel Fletcher to assign working parties of Spaniards to the defensive works around Irun and Oyarzun, hoping that they would be sufficiently well-paid and well-supervised to provide an efficient labour force.[46]

Co-ordinating the arrival of reinforcements proved less harmonious. Wellington had requested that infantry from England be sent to Pasajes and cavalry to Bilbao. But 1,200 infantrymen landed instead at Bilbao, where they had no equipment and no food for an onward march to join their regiments to the east. Wellington pressed the naval squadron commander to provide sea transport from Bilbao to Pasajes.[47] Having already complained that the resumption of his attack upon San Sebastian had been delayed by sixteen days through the chronic slowness in getting equipment and supplies from

View of San Sebastian by James Webb, 1870s. (With permission, National Maritime Museum, Greenwich)

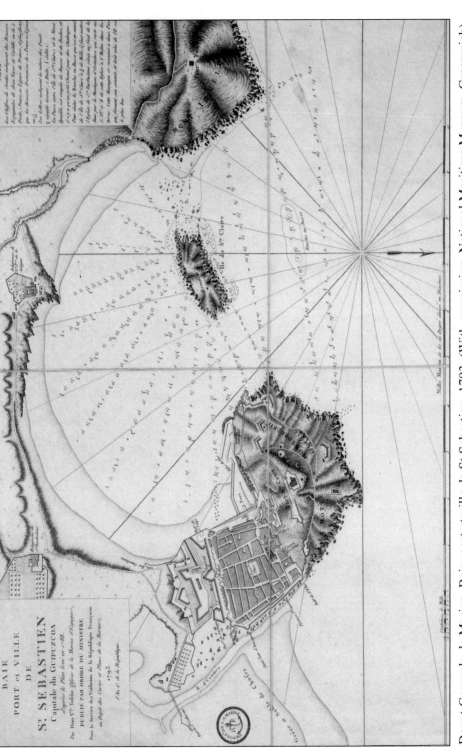

Depot Generale de Marine, Baie, port et ville de St Sebastien, 1793. (With permission, National Maritime Museum, Greenwich)

Storming of the town and castle of San Sebastian. (Copyright, The Trustees of the British Museum)

British troops advancing, San Sebastian. (Copyright, The Trustees of the British Museum)

The Storming of San Sebastian by Denis Dighton, 1817. (With permission, National Trust for Scotland)

Bridge of boats across the Adour. (Copyright, The Trustees of the British Museum)

Bayonne from St Etienne. (Copyright, The Trustees of the British Museum)

Captain Sir George Ralph Collier by William Beechey (San Sebastian is seen in the left corner). (With permission, National Maritime Museum, Greenwich)

Joseph-Désiré Court, Le Maréchal Soult. (Copyright, The Bowes Museum, Barnard Castle, County Durham)

England, Wellington thus faced further delays in assembling the materials of war when they did indeed arrive.[48]

However, the late arrival of the siege train from Britain yielded some advantages. The army gained time to reinforce and to recuperate. By 25 August, nearly 1,800 troops in new regiments – the 76th, 84th and 85th – and 800 recruits to replenish existing regiments had arrived. The hills around Pasajes, apart from being 'beautifully romantic', offered secluded camping grounds for newly arrived battalions. The 85th, for instance, had embarked on transports at Dover in late May. Adverse winds kept them at Dungeness for a week and a prolonged calm in the Bay of Biscay delayed them yet further. They did not see the Spanish coast until 13 August and even then spent nearly a day on board in Pasajes harbour awaiting the requisite orders from their divisional HQ before disembarking. Encamped about 2 miles from Pasajes, the battalion must have found welcome, if short-lived, relief in the wooded hill country with its valleys cut by mountain streams and lower hills covered by orchards.[49] Horses and mules were readily available for purchase from local people, if at inflated prices. In addition to these fresh arrivals, the army was 'gaining some men from the hospitals every day', amounting to 500 British troops in a week and 1,500 Portuguese. Although the army fell about 5,000–6,000 men short of its strength on the eve of Vitoria, it had been restored to the numerical strength it possessed at the first assault on San Sebastian; it also, according to its commanding general, enjoyed good health.[50] Moreover, two further regiments were ordered up to Santander from Cádiz and Lisbon.[51]

Apart from delays in building up his own resources, Wellington was concerned about the French ability to re-supply San Sebastian. Just as Soult pressed on 17 August for an enhanced French naval presence as part of his offensive planning, so Wellington argued on 19 August for an enlarged naval squadron on the coast. He wanted a far tighter naval blockade, complaining that the French could ship supplies as well as artillerymen, *sapeurs* and medical officers into San Sebastian at will; 'the maritime blockade of San Sebastian is not kept at all'.[52]

In fact, Wellington exaggerated the French ability to reinforce San Sebastian. Although key personnel, rations and medicines could indeed be sent into the town, the French could not ship large quantities of cargo through the blockade. The overwhelming bulk of supplies received for the military hospital to 16 August consisted of 292 kilos of Demerara sugar, 65 kilos of liquorice and 64 kilos of quinquina, the latter two used for their medicinal properties. But the garrison's stock of wine, for example, fell by 40,154 pints to 28,884 between 1 July and 16 August, leaving just over 4 weeks' supply remaining at that rate of consumption. The stock of biscuit rations had fallen by 36,557 to 29,335. No replenishments of either commodity reached the garrison. The supply of flour from France did however match consumption in those six weeks. Weapons and munitions were a different matter. The number of artillery guns of all kinds fell from 95 on 28 June to 64 by 16 August and the stock of heavy shot and shells for the artillery had fallen by 25,181 to 49,136. On 28 June, the garrison had 93,856 items of ammunition other than infantry bullets; by 16 August it held 58,824. Only 988 items of munitions arrived from France in those 6 or so weeks.[53] While some vital supplies got through the blockade, the flow of munitions was halted.

Problems over re-supply suggested two contradictory scenarios. The fact that some items were obtained, even though Wellington exaggerated the scale of what entered the port, demonstrated that a truly tight blockade was not a viable option. As Clausewitz observed, the difficulties of blockading ports made it necessary to assault them rather than attempt prolonged blockades. To be effective, a blockade of San Sebastian would have had to be accompanied by a simultaneous blockade of St Jean de Luz and the small French ports to Bayonne, to cut off coastal shipping.

But Wellington's complaints about the inadequacy of the Royal Navy's blockade raised an impending problem of great concern. The south-eastern corner of the Bay of Biscay was exceptionally challenging for larger ships, with strong onshore winds and currents. As autumn approached, conditions would become far more difficult for frigates to operate in, while winter weather would make naval blockading in those waters impossible. Small coastal craft might, however, be used by the French to navigate the short distance of about 15 miles from St Jean de Luz to San Sebastian during lulls in the weather. If the siege dragged on well into September and October, the balance would have been tipped increasingly in favour of sustained French re-supply. On 7 August, Graham warned Wellington that 'the ships will not be able to remain on the coast in this dangerous bite [*sic*] of the Bay more than five weeks longer according to Sir G. Collier's calculations'.[54] Responding to a inquiry from Wellington about the possible use of Guetaria as a winter anchorage for larger warships, Collier explained a few days later that, while he was prepared to consider keeping warships in port during the approaching winter, many high-ranking naval officers 'are decidedly opposed to ships anchoring under any circumstances upon any part of the coast'.[55] Wellington therefore had to mount his second assault before the naval squadron withdrew.

Yet Wellington worried about the risks of another failure. He tried to expand the navy's contribution to the operation beyond maintaining a more effective blockade. He wanted a naval attack on the western side of the town, across the bay. This was intended to divert French effort and attention from the main British land attacks from the south and east; it 'would probably prevent much of the loss in the assault of the breaches, if it did not tend to insure the success of the assault'.[56] He reminded Graham on 20 August that 'this attack cannot be made without great naval assistance'.[57] But Graham reminded Wellington on 28 August that the only significant diversionary attack would be a naval bombardment of the castle from the sea. Such a bombardment was improbable, since it would require extremely favourable weather in place of the customarily heavy surf and very changeable winds.[58]

The second assault was therefore planned amidst considerable uncertainty and frustration over the progress of British operations. Soult's army had stiffened San Sebastian's resistance and the Pyrenean defences. Naval support for the second assault, so strongly desired by Wellington, proved limited. When the second attack began, the political and military situation in Germany remained unclear to the combatants in Spain. Also, the British were not sure whether Suchet would withdraw his own force into south-west France or pursue Bentinck's small army in Catalonia.[59] Assailing San Sebastian was the only forward option available to Wellington, since he could not march against Soult. But San Sebastian had to be captured to enable Wellington to advance upon France if and when the war in Germany resumed. He declared his intention of assaulting San Sebastian while informing the secretary of state on the 25th that the French had been strengthening the town's defensive works but had otherwise made 'No movement of importance' since 19 August.[60] Those remarks cast harsh light on the commander's situational grasp. What he regarded as a sideshow in July had become a major objective six weeks later. And Soult was busy preparing an offensive at the precise moment when Wellington reported French inertia.

The Royal Navy's Role
The period of preparation and waiting in August highlighted Wellington's uneasy relationship with the navy. As Christopher Hall has demonstrated, Wellington's demand for more naval support clashed with pressures on the Admiralty to meet the additional demands posed by the American war in 1813. Moreover, the northern coast of Spain was particularly hazardous for ships of the line and even frigates.[61] Yet the tensions which emerged in August 1813 could have been predicted from the differences of opinion between Wellington and the naval squadron the previous year.

Once Wellington captured Ciudad Rodrigo in January 1812, he sought to shift his artillery southwards to attack Badajoz. Unfortunately, there was insufficient land transport to move the thirty 24-pounders from Ciudad Rodrigo in the time available. The sixteen 24-pounders on transports at Lisbon needed to be supplemented for the task at Badajoz. Following discussion with his senior ordnance officers, Wellington requested heavy guns from the naval squadron at Lisbon. None of his senior team realized that the ships of the squadron were not big enough to mount 24-pounder cannon. The naval commander happily offered 18-pounders and that offer was accepted. But the impact of an 18-pounder shot on a wall at 400–500yd was far less than that of a 24-pounder shot. According to Lieutenant Colonel Jones, 'No engineer should ever be satisfied with 18-pounder guns for breaching, when he can by any possibility procure 24-pounders'.[62] Further frustrations ensued when the 24-pounders transferred from the transports suffered from blown-out vents after heavy firing while the 18-pounders were less accurate and destructive than the heavier guns.[63]

Wellington's rapid advance in the summer and autumn of 1812 demonstrated further operational tensions. The squadron on the north coast – not the Lisbon squadron – was expanded in the summer of 1812 when two ships of the line, the *Venerable* and *Magnificent* (of seventy-four guns each), and an armed transport were added to the existing force of four frigates, led by *Surveillante* (thirty-eight guns), and two brigs. The new commanding officer, Sir Home Popham, arrived in early June. A dynamic and very independent-minded officer, Popham set about supplying and aiding organized guerrilla bands along the northern coast. This activity helped tie down the French Army of the North so that it would not be able to aid Marmont's army to the west. It was planned and begun before Marmont's crushing defeat at Salamanca, but its strategic value continued even after Wellington reached Madrid in August. The naval squadron co-operated with Spanish insurgents to force the French from Santander in early August 1812.

By October, however, Wellington was besieging Burgos, far in advance of his position when Popham took up his command. On 11 October 1812, Wellington complained of serious shortages of musket ammunition. He had ordered transports carrying ammunition to sail from La Coruña to Santander, a port directly north of Burgos. Although the vessels had sailed on 3 October, they had not arrived eight days later. On the 17th Wellington, assuming that he would take Burgos, pressed Popham to maintain his squadron on the Spanish north coast throughout the winter, in order to control Santander and to blockade the minor port of Santona to its east, where a French garrison was besieged. Although Santander would serve as a base for the squadron, since it could accommodate two or three line ships and six frigates, as well as numerous smaller craft, Wellington was sceptical about using Santander as a British military supply channel. Local transport resources were too limited for his army's needs and the British could not operate south of Santander unless they pushed the French east of the River Ebro or advanced beyond it. The naval squadron's implicit role was therefore to continue to harry the French farther east on the coast.[64] Yet the severe winter weather made it impossible for the squadron to operate in the extensive way Wellington envisaged, and the squadron's larger warships left their station during the winter.

The events of 1812 demonstrated the contradictory roles played by the naval squadron. Popham took a proactive role in attacking French positions along the coast, as far as the small port of Guetaria, west of San Sebastian. He supplied the Spanish locally with guns and ammunition. He conveyed Spanish insurgents along the coast. But Wellington wanted the squadron to concentrate on convoying supplies from La Coruña and to commit to remaining in full strength throughout the winter. Of course, the collapse of the Burgos campaign made such planning irrelevant, but the failure to define the naval squadron's precise role and capabilities recurred in 1813.

Wellington faced immediate and significant logistical problems once his campaign again shifted suddenly in June 1813. On 2 July, Wellington complained that ships ready to sail with provisions and military stores from the Tagus on 12 May had still not left Lisbon on 19 June. The Royal Navy, he asserted, could not protect the sea route from Lisbon to Santander.[65] One problem was the organization of the naval commands. The squadron based at Lisbon covered the seas to Cape Finisterre, while the Channel fleet covered the Bay of Biscay. Cargo ships were escorted from Lisbon to Ferrol and especially La Coruña, but had to wait at those ports for convoy protection from the Channel fleet's squadron in the bay. Problems of authority as well as naval readiness immediately arose. For example, on 15 July – still less than a month after Vitoria transformed the British position in northern Spain – the commanding officer at La Coruña, Lieutenant Colonel Richard Bourke, asked for instructions as to whether Wellington wanted all transport vessels arriving there to sail immediately for Santander. Bourke pressed the need for convoys, citing the activity of a large French privateer which had recently captured two ships east of Cape Ortegal. But he had no authority to interfere with the sailing orders of warships arriving at La Coruña. Thus thirteen victualling ships had entered the port on 14 July, but Bourke had no instructions about convoying them eastwards. Moreover, no ship from Captain Sir George Collier's squadron in the Bay of Biscay, deployed from the Channel fleet, had visited La Coruña for three weeks.[66]

Meanwhile, Bourke had 100,000 dollars in cash which had been delivered from Lisbon and awaited conveyance to Santander by the first available warship.[67] Still without formal directions, Bourke took the opportunity of a convoy for Santander being assembled on 21 July to forward everything, including the specie.[68] Even though Vitoria and its aftermath opened up a new supply route directly from England to Santander, as demonstrated by the shipment in mid-July of 3 million musket balls to the latter port, such munitions, and supplies, had still to be transported farther along the coast.[69] A pre-condition for that movement had been created with the surrender of Pasajes to the Spanish on 30 June and the French evacuation of Guetaria on 1 July.[70] Guetaria's capture removed a possible base for French gunboats and privateers, but the small port was of no value for naval operations or for British shipping.[71] Pasajes, about 2 miles to the east of San Sebastian, was an ancient and significant port which by early August teemed with ships, supplies, soldiers and muleteers.[72] Yet Collier's shortage of ships meant that he had to deploy his own frigate to protect Pasajes from possible activity by small French warships.[73]

Lord Keith, commanding the Channel fleet, explained to Wellington that he had ordered six warships to the northern Spanish coast, but that his command had been cut and was already over-stretched. His main responsibility was to watch the French squadron of six line ships and eight frigates at Brest, for which purpose he deployed there only five line and two frigates.[74] The case has been made that the Channel fleet had limited spare capacity in 1813 once it met the interlinked demands of blockading and of defending British commercial shipping in the Channel and its approaches from raiding by French frigates. The latter threat may not have been widespread, but, as late as February 1814, there were eleven French frigates at sea in the Channel fleet's area of responsibility. Lord Keith added to Wellington's frustrations by suggesting that the Field Marshal might organize his convoys more efficiently.[75]

The Royal Navy was obviously over-stretched. Although Keith commanded thiry-six warships plus cutters, his fleet had to patrol from Brest to Bordeaux. Four stations – off Brest, off the Charente and Aix roads, off Bordeaux and off Belleisle – tied down seventeen of his warships, including all ten of his line ships and four of his six frigates which were at sea in late July. He had a further three line ships and four frigates in port, essentially for repairs. Five of his thirty-six warships were currently off the northern coast of Spain, a frigate and four sloops and brigs. A further frigate was on its way, together with six cutters, which were additional to his warships. One-third of his operational frigates were thus earmarked to support Wellington. If all his frigates had been at sea, Keith could only match the eight French frigates at Brest after deducting the two frigates assigned to northern Spain. His forces also suffered from considerable wear and tear in blockading off the French Atlantic coast.

Meanwhile Vice-Admiral George Martin's Lisbon squadron of nineteen warships – of which thirteen were sloops and brigs, small ocean-going ships – covered a very wide expanse of the Atlantic Ocean. It operated southwards to Gibraltar, while cruising in the region of Cape St Vincent and Cádiz, south-westwards to Madeira, whose port of Funchal is 605 miles from Lisbon, and far westward in convoying trading vessels out into the Atlantic to 15 degrees west on their journey to Newfoundland. There was also routine cruising in the same direction to the west of Lisbon. Of the nineteen ships, six were based at Gibraltar and the Tagus, nine were convoying to the south and west, and four were convoying merchant vessels to La Coruña or Figueria, en route for Santander. Accompanying convoys northwards to La Coruña was simply one further responsibility among many obligations assigned to the Lisbon squadron.[76]

Wellington had limited leverage with Keith and Martin, both of whom were very seasoned operators who defended naval interests with calm determination. Keith had sailed to China in 1767, distinguished himself at Charleston in 1780, taken Cape Town in 1796, and, as acting and later substantive Commander-in-Chief in the Mediterranean, dealt with Nelson at his most insubordinate in 1799–1800. An austere figure from the Scottish aristocracy, he had been advanced to Rear Admiral in 1794 and, following further promotions, had long experience of commanding large fleets. Martin came from a naval family; his paternal great uncle and maternal grandfather were both Admirals of the Fleet. He had first seen action at the age of 14 in 1778, while serving on an uncle's warship. He won plaudits for skilful leadership in 1797, and fought off Cape Finisterre in 1805, when he was promoted to Rear Admiral. He commanded blockades at Malta in 1800 and Cádiz in 1807, and captured islands off the Italian coast in 1809. As a Vice Admiral, he was Commander-in-Chief at the Tagus from 1812–14.[77] Both admirals had strong career achievements and their own service's priorities determined their decisions in assigning resources. The only way Wellington could secure additional naval support was through the Cabinet in London.

In July and August, Wellington therefore repeatedly complained to Lord Bathurst, the Secretary of State for War and Colonies, about the Royal Navy's shortcomings. Locally, he objected that the naval blockade of Spain's northern coast in general and San Sebastian in particular was inadequate.[78] Even worse was the prolonged delay in assembling a convoy to deliver the siege train. By the end of July, somewhat late in the day admittedly, the need for urgency seems to have reached Portsmouth. One contemporary account reported that all seamen who could be spared from ships of war were joining the crews of vessels being loaded to haul ordnance for Wellington's army aboard transports. The newspaper added that 'Their service is considered so pressing, that the men are allowed extra wages and grog.'[79] Yet, as already noted, the convoys from Portsmouth did not arrive until 18–24 August. This tardiness did nothing to improve Wellington's limited opinion of the navy as an instrument of flexible and swift power projection. Wellington complained on 18–19 August that the delay in delivering the siege train from England had cost him eighteen days in the siege.[80]

The biggest concern from early August was the ability of the squadron to remain on station from mid-September. Collier co-operated effectively with the army, but his resources were limited. Lord Keith eventually, on 31 August, informed Wellington that his over-stretched fleet was to receive additional ships. But he insisted that he could not have helped earlier because he had received no information about Wellington's intentions. Moreover, he expressed his 'alarm' at the prospect of larger warships operating on the Biscayan coast in bad weather.[81] Yet Wellington had tried to locate a safe anchorage for warships in the autumn, ordering an examination of Guetaria's potential for that purpose. Lieutenant Colonel Fletcher, commanding the Royal Engineers, undertook to see if water could be secured to the defences on the heights dominating the peninsula on the harbour's west side. Captain Stanway, RE reported that it would take twenty-four days to set up a water supply from the port to the heights, but he added that the defences of the bastion, among other works, would also need strengthening.[82] Marshal Beresford, commanding the Anglo-Portuguese army, examined the site and concluded that Guetaria was indefensible; it 'can never answer any kind of object to us'.[83] This assessment may have been too strictly technical, since a French counter-attack so far west of San Sebastian was highly improbable. On the other hand, Collier, having surveyed the Bidassoa estuary, indicated that smaller warships could find shelter there, while *Surveillante*, of thirty-eight guns, should secure protection for a frigate of its size at Cape Figuera, perhaps modern-day Higer, a long peninsula protecting the Bidassoa estuary from westerly winds.[84]

Collier's small naval squadron played a vital supporting role but it could scarcely contribute to military offensives. It ensured that the French could not bring warships past Isla Santa Clara into the bay. The value of this was demonstrated by the British in May 1836 when they joined Spanish government forces at San Sebastian to drive off Carlist insurgents besieging the town. While about 6,000 British Legion and Spanish government troops assailed the Carlist lines at San Bartolomeo and farther west, two British warships in the bay bombarded the besiegers' positions and opened up a strategic Carlist redoubt to a British assault.[85] Given Collier's squadron's patrols off the coast in 1813, the French were unable to bring warships into the bay to disrupt British land operations. But the squadron in turn could not enter the bay because the passage between the island and the castle's outer rim could accommodate only one large ship at a time and was dominated by French guns on the island – until late August – and by artillery at the castle. The squadron could fulfil no active military role from the sea.

This episode underscored a truism about British sea power. The Royal Navy's primary roles were to prevent an invasion of the British Isles and to protect Britain's far-flung commercial activities and interests. Its control of the lines of communication at sea required persistent cruising and blockading in often demanding if not gruelling conditions. But this hard-won control of the sea lanes did not translate into control of coastal routes and coastal access unless and until the British possessed, or had access to, secure and substantial naval bases locally from which to operate. Individual commanders and their crews showed, as Hall has stressed, remarkable adaptability and initiative in contributing to land campaigns.[86] But local examples of co-operation, flexibility and learning by doing did not result from or lead to the development of any systematic planning or even clear prioritizing either in London or between senior commanders in the theatre of war. Wellington's campaign in the Peninsula provided a fine example of a venture which had become central to the army's war against Napoleon but which was peripheral to the navy's strategic missions and fleet dispositions.

Planning the Assault

On 2 August, Lieutenant Colonel Hugh Gough, commanding the 2/87th, wrote home describing how his battalion had advanced beyond Roncesvalles to a position in the Pyrenees seemingly 'one Mile above the Clouds'. From this commanding height, he speculated about the army's next moves: 'Was it left to me, I would at once move into France. It is expected that the Garrison of Pampeluna [*sic*] finding Soult's failure, surrendered the day we left it. If they have not, they shortly must for want of Provisions. St Sebastian must also very shortly follow. What they will do with us then God knows.'[87]

Gough was wrong both on the fate of the blockaded towns after the French failure to break through at Sorauren, and on the wider strategic situation. Yet he had been serving in the Peninsula since 1809 and was well versed in the vicissitudes of campaigning. His optimism showed that, despite the first assault's impact on San Sebastian, the challenges offered by the French were underestimated by even seasoned senior officers. Gough believed that the British should advance into the Pyrenees because French resistance was feeble.[88] In projecting that behaviour on to the entire front, Gough thoroughly misjudged the trend of fighting.

Planning the second assault proved more complicated than Gough allowed. Major Charles Smith, RE sought to repeat the approach used on 25 July. But there were conflicting views about the direction and nature of the artillery bombardment and the distribution of the attacking force, its size and composition. On 26 July, Lieutenant Colonel John Burgoyne, commanding the engineers on the isthmus and number two to Lieutenant Colonel Sir Richard Fletcher in overall command of the engineers in Wellington's field army, considered where the depleted besieging force should be positioned. He felt that the troops on the isthmus, excessively exposed to the castle's artillery, should be withdrawn farther south. Such a move would allow the French to retake the convent on the heights of San Bartolomeo because the French generals – like any generals, 'who always like positions in the field' – would wish to fortify the heights around the convent. Although French engineers would advise against such a step, Burgoyne believed they would be overruled. The French itch to act was demonstrated by a sortie launched at 7.00 am on 27 July against the British trenches around San Bartolomeo. In Burgoyne's scenario, the French would become over-extended and offer an open target when the British resumed hostilities, allowing the British to reduce French manpower at low risk to themselves.[89]

As for renewing the assault, Burgoyne noted on 7 August, 'I fear we can never succeed without taking the horn work, and thence breaching the main town front as extensively as we please'. If the assaulting parties captured the breach but failed to take the horn-work, they would be cut off from their base when the tide came in, and cut down when they attempted at low tide to resupply or reinforce from their trenches. Moreover the curtain wall behind the horn-work rose to a height which commanded the south–north streets in the town, making progress from the riverside breach very hazardous if such an advance became feasible. Capturing San Sebastian, in Burgoyne's eyes, depended upon securing the horn-work and gaining access to the curtain wall behind it.[90]

Doubts about the feasibility of attacking the main breach for a second time were more widely felt. On 4 August, the day before he learned that the siege was to be resumed, Lieutenant Colonel Frazer noted that the French had repaired and strengthened their defences on the main breach, and were well rehearsed in defending that section of their perimeter. Frazer wondered whether it would be possible to motivate troops to attack the same position where other soldiers had been repulsed so readily and with such heavy losses on 25 July. More generally, Frazer saw improved communications across the Urumea as a priority, arguing that a bridge should be constructed across the river and roads laid out from the bridge to the batteries.[91] No bridge was built and the roads remained difficult. This meant that there could be no direct assault upon the horn-work. At least two senior 'technical' officers thus expressed strong reservations about repeating the approach adopted on 25 July.

The refusal to assault the horn-work reflected the difficulty in hauling heavy guns to the isthmus and fears that, once at San Bartolomeo, such guns might be vulnerable to French sorties. Fears for the guns' safety also arose from the threat posed by possible French probes from across the border formed by the Bidassoa River. As was shown in late July, artillery on the east bank could be removed quickly to ships at Pasajes, but only with difficulty from the isthmus. This, of course, was the rationale for Frazer's proposal to rebuild a bridge across the Urumea. Uncertainty about Soult's troops' movements thus ensured that the French remained well placed on the horn-work and the curtain wall to pour flanking fire into the allies as they advanced from their trenches and as they crested the breach. In this detail, the fighting at San Sebastian was shaped by French movements and threats in general, as well as by Rey's actions and dispositions in particular.

For the renewed assault, a large consignment of additional ordnance had been earmarked for shipment from England, but had been diverted to the Baltic. An alternative consignment, intended for Cuxhaven, did not meet the needs for attacking San Sebastian, and so 'a fresh assortment was prepared'. This third consignment reached Pasajes on 18 August, bringing the ordnance deployed for the second assault to sixty-three guns and mortars.[92]

Meanwhile, the defenders kept up a ritual daily cannonade at 6.00 p.m. when working parties were relieved, but did little harm. They tried to protect themselves from occasional British shelling by constructing a sheltered pathway from the defensive walls back into the castle, at the town's northern extremity. The British detected small-scale French mining operations and did some counter-mining of their own. According to Burgoyne, on 12 August, 'The enemy continue to work hard', in, for example, strengthening the defences of the demi-bastions at each end of the horn-work. Burgoyne correctly deduced that they were constructing chambers from which to blow up the town wall facing the Urumea River in order to collapse the wall upon approaching British troops. With limited artillery, the British could do little but observe such activity.[93] George Gleig, a young subaltern, also suggested that the French used British prisoners of war on their defensive works, thus deterring the besiegers from bombarding them.[94]

The plan for the second assault appeared settled by 22 August, as the siege train had just arrived, in stages, from England. The initial breach was to be widened substantially. First, the towers at each side of the first breach were to be reduced. That would remove the threat of flanking fire from the breach itself. Secondly, a further breach was to be created north of the original one. Thirdly, the substantial demi-bastion supporting the horn-work would be destroyed, thus removing a source of flanking fire upon the main breach and on the access route which so perturbed Burgoyne. If Burgoyne had not won his argument, he had at least got part of the southern wall's defences on the list of principal targets. At this point, just before Graham visited the artillery at the front, Lieutenant Colonel Frazer, commanding the artillery on the east bank, privately wondered whether 'It may be necessary to reduce the town to ashes', given the ways in which the French had extended their defences deep into the town and given the experience of the first assault.[95] Thus the scale and seriousness of this second assault grew more ominous by the day.

It took until the early hours of 25 August to position the guns in their batteries. Frazer complained on 23 August of the painfully slow rate of progress:

> From want of artillerymen we cannot open until the 26th, if then. . . . I left the batteries at 2 a.m. this morning, (the 23rd,) having only got four 24-pounders, and four howitzers in battery by that time, though we began at 8 p.m. the preceding evening. Our Progress is ridiculously slow; half a dozen artillerymen were all we could get to show about 300 Portuguese infantry what was to be done. It is necessarily a work of silence, that the enemy may not hear what is going on. The bullocks are all knocked up, and the men, though willing, exhaust their strength in misapplying it.[96]

Two batteries, consisting of seven 24-pounder guns and six 18-pounders, were located at San Bartolomeo, the least accessible part of the British front. Those guns, supported by two howitzers, tasked with the 'general purposes of annoyance', were directed to demolish one of the two demi-bastions flanking the horn-work. This measure opened up the ultimate prospect of British troops, after gaining the main breach, mounting and advancing along the curtain wall behind the horn-work. While no direct assault upon the horn-work was planned, the importance of trying to suppress French flanking fire from the horn-work was more fully recognized in this plan than had been the case at the first assault.

The main breach was to be created by the 24-pounders on the east bank of the Urumea, with fifteen of them placed in battery 15 and six in battery 14. The latter also contained five howitzers and four heavy 64-pounder carronades to assist in suppressing the eastern ends of the curtain wall and the horn-work, adding to the firepower directed against those positions from San Bartolomeo. Battery 13, consisting of six mortars, directed its fire at the rear of the breach and the defences within the town and castle. Other mortars were deployed to act against both the southern isthmus front and the castle to the north of the town. The key to the attack lay with the twenty-eight 24-pounders, twenty-one of which were on the east bank. In addition to those breaching guns, there were six 18-pounders, fifteen 10in mortars and nine 8in howitzers ready to open fire at 9.00 a.m. (or 8.00 a.m. according to Frazer) on 26 August.[97]

Although the ground was by now familiar to the British, preparing the batteries was not straightforward. Just as getting men to work on emplacing the guns proved taxing, so the highly polyglot nature of the artillery forces made co-ordination difficult. Of 761 NCOs, gunners and seamen and 60 officers in the artillery force, 187 men and 12 officers belonged to the Portuguese artillery, and 80 men and 6 officers were seconded from the Royal Navy. The rest included a contingent from the King's German Artillery, with seven officers from the King's German Legion.[98] According to Lieutenant Colonel Frazer, who commanded on the east bank, the lack of artillerymen delayed the beginning of the bombardment, and that lack presumably explains the need to draft in sailors, whose presence, however, was 'much diminished after the first three days'.[99] The use of allied and naval specialists meant that twenty-five of the sixty officers present were not members of the Royal Artillery. This created inter-service difficulties even at such a relatively small-unit level. Frazer complained on 27 August: 'The batteries to-day were manned by seamen, Portuguese, Germans, and a few British artillerymen. Terrible confused work: half the number of good, well-instructed men would do twice the real service.'[100]

The preparations for the second assault once again revealed the managerial challenges posed by the siege. To suggest that success depended on deploying a larger and more effective siege train than that used in the first assault tells only part of the story. Technological capability was obviously important. But positioning and working the guns required the constant, unglamorous management of a highly diverse body of men. Nor did scientific principles solve practical questions of where guns were to be placed and in what numbers. Those choices had to be decided on the spot and argued through. To make matters worse, the preparations at every level took longer than might have been expected and further undermined Wellington's expectations of speedy progress. The slow pace of these preparations also revealed to the French the planned objectives for the renewed assault long before the date chosen for the attack. All this meant that the second attempt, despite the belief that the enlarged siege train would prove decisive, threatened to be even more challenging than the first one.

Notes

1. Wellington to Bathurst, 4 August 1813, *WD*, x, 599.
2. Glover (ed.), *A Gentleman Volunteer*, 114, 131.
3. *The Times*, 3 August 1813, p. 3.
4. Sabine (ed.), *Letters*, 294.
5. Smith, *The Autobiography*, 113.
6. *New Annual Register for 1813*, 296.
7. Oman, *A History of the Peninsular War*, vii, 38.
8. Dalmatie to minister of war, 28 July 1813, SHAT C8 149.
9. Feltre to Dalmatie, 1 August 1813, SHAT C8 156.
10. Feltre to Dalmatie, 9, 13 August 1813, SHAT C8 156.
11. Robert S. Rait, *The Life and Campaigns of Hugh First Viscount Gough Field Marshal*, 2 vols (Oxford, 1903), i, 116.
12. Dalmatie to minister of war, 17 August 1813 (1 of 2), SHAT C8 149.

13. Dalmatie to minister of war, 17 August 1813 (2 of 2), SHAT C8 149.
14. Graham to Wellington, 14 August 1813, WP 1/374 (Folder 6).
15. Wrottesley, *Life and Correspondence*, i, 271–3.
16. Henegan, *Seven Years Campaigning*, ii, 41.
17. *The Times*, 3 August 1813, p. 3; 13 August 1813, p. 3.
18. (Edinburgh) *Caledonia Mercury*, 31 July 1813.
19. *Morning Post*, 17 August 1813.
20. (Truro) *Royal Cornwall Gazette,* 21 August 1813.
21. *Morning Post*, 17 August 1813.
22. *The Times*, 24 August 1813, p. 3.
23. Thompson (ed.), *An Ensign in the Peninsular War*, 260.
24. Larpent (ed.), *The Private Journal*, ii, 39, 50–2.
25. Wellington to Stuart, 15 August 1813, *WD*, xi, 3.
26. Wellington to Stuart, 15 August 1813, *WD*, xi, 3.
27. Wellington to Beresford, 27 August 1813; to Bentinck, 5 September 1813, *WD*, xi, 47, 87.
28. Graham to Wellington, 7, 8, 13 August 1813, WP 1/374 (Folder 6).
29. Wellington to Graham, 15 August 1813, *WD*, xi, 1–2.
30. Wellington to Fletcher, 21 August 1813, *WD*, xi, 24.
31. Graham to Wellington 7, 13 August 1813, WP 1/374 (Folder 6)
32. Graham to Wellington, 15 August 1813, WP 1/374 (Folder 6).
33. Wellington to Graham, 17 August 1813, *WD*, xi, 8.
34. Wellington to Beresford, 17 August 1813, *WD*, xi, 9.
35. Pakenham to Burton, 1 August 1813, WP 9/1/1/8.
36. Wellington to Collier, 21 August 1813; Wellington to Bathurst, 24 August 1813, *WD*, xi, 28, 38.
37. Wellington to Collier, 11 August 1813, John Gurwood (ed.), *The Dispatches of Field Marshal the Duke of Wellington*, 8 vols (London, 1845; repr. Cambridge, 2010), vi, 673.
38. Collier to Wellington, 16 August 1813, WP 1/374 (Folder 2).
39. Wellington to Kennedy, 4 August 1813, *WD,* x, 592–3.
40. Wellington to Bathurst, 4 August 1813, *WD*, x, 600.
41. Wellington to Bathurst, 20 July 1813, 19 August 1813, *WD*, x, 558, xi, 18.
42. Wellington to Graham, 19 August 1813, *WD*, xi, 13.
43. Sabine (ed.), *Letters*, 216, 220.
44. Surtees, *Twenty-Five Years in the Rifle Brigade*, 268.
45. Graham to Wellington, 8 August 1813, WP 1/374 (Folder 6).
46. Wellington to Fletcher, 21 August 1813, *WD*, xi, 24
47. Wellington to Collier, 19 August 1813, *WD*, xi, 15.
48. Wellington to Bathurst, 18 August 1813, *WD*, xi, 12.
49. George Gleig, *The Subaltern: A Chronicle of the Peninsular War* (London, 1825), 1, 14–15, 21, 25–6.
50. Wellington to Bathurst, 25 August 1813, *WD*, xi, 45.
51. Wellington to Admiral Martin, 27 August 1813, *WD*, xi, 49.
52. Wellington to Bathurst, 19 August 1813, *WD*, xi, 17–18.
53. 'Situation des approvisionnements de l'hopital militaire . . . au 16 aout 1813'; 'Situation du magasin . . . a l'epoque du 15 aout 1813'; 'Etats des bouches a feu . . . du 28 juin au 16 aout 1813', Belmas, *Sièges*, iv, 664–6.
54. Graham to Wellington, 7 August 1813, WP 1/374 (Folder 6).
55. Collier to Wellington, 11 August 1813, WP 1/374 (Folder 1).
56. Wellington to Bathurst, 19 August 1813, *WD*, xi, 18.
57. Wellington to Graham, 20 August 1813, *WD*, xi, 20.
58. Graham to Wellington, 28 August 1813, WP 1/374 (Folder 6).
59. Wellington to Bentinck, 25 August 1813, *WD*, xi, 38–40.
60. Wellington to Bathurst, 25 Aug 1813, *WD*, xi, 43.

61. Hall, *Wellington's Navy*, 203, 207, 211.
62. Jones, *Journals*, i, 121, 144–5.
63. Jones, *Journals*, i, 157, 210.
64. Hall, *Wellington's Navy*, 53, 200–7; Wellington to Bathurst, 11 October 1812; to Sir Home Popham, 17 October 1812, *WD*, ix, 483, 495.
65. Wellington to Bathurst, 2 July 1813, *WD*, x, 495.
66. Bourke to Somerset, 15 July 1813, WP 9/2/2/10.
67. Bourke to Somerset, 4 July 1813, WP 9/2/2/10.
68. Bourke to Somerset, 21 July 1813, WP 9/2/2/10.
69. Board of Ordnance to Somerset, 14 July 1813, WP 9/2/2/10.
70. Wellington to Bathurst, 3 July 1813, *WD*, x, 502.
71. Wellington to Beresford, 15 August 1813; Wellington to Graham, 17 August 1813, *WD*, xi, 2, 8.
72. Wellington to North, 15 August 1813, *WD*, xi, 4.
73. Wellington to Bathurst, 9 July 1813, *WD*, x, 519.
74. Keith to Wellington, 3 July 1813 (two letters), WP 1/372 (Folder1); the dispute is fully assessed in Hall, *Wellington's Navy*, 210–22.
75. McCranie, *Admiral Lord Keith and the Naval War against Napoleon*, 158–63.
76. Melville to Wellington, 28 July 1813, Wellington (ed.), *Supplementary Despatches*, viii, 147.
77. 'George Keith Elphinstone, Viscount Keith' and 'Sir George Martin' entries in *ODNB*.
78. Wellington to Bathurst, 10 July, 11 August 1813; Wellington to Graham, 10 August 1813, *WD*, x, 522–3, 625, 633.
79. *Morning Chronicle*, 30 July 1813.
80. Wellington to Bathurst, 18, 19 August 1813, *WD*, xi, 12, 17.
81. Keith to Wellington, 31 August 1813, WP 1/374 (Folder 2).
82. Graham to Wellington, 14 August; Fletcher to Graham, 16 August 1813, WP 1/ 374 (Folder 6).
83. Beresford to Wellington, 13 August 1813, WP 1/374 (Folder 1).
84. Collier to Wellington, 16 August 1813, WP 1/374 (Folder 2).
85. Somerville, *History*, 20, 34–5.
86. Hall, *Wellington's Navy*, 233–4.
87. Rait, *Life and Campaigns*, i, 113, 116.
88. Rait, *Life and Campaigns*, i, 114–15.
89. Wrottesley, *Life and Correspondence*, i, 271–2.
90. Wrottesley, *Life and Correspondence*, i, 273–4.
91. Sabine (ed.), *Letters*, 217–18.
92. Wrottesley, *Life and Correspondence*, i, 275–8; Jones, *Journals*, ii, 57–8.
93. Wrottesley, *Life and Correspondence*, i, 274–5.
94. Gleig, *The Subaltern*, 28.
95. Sabine (ed.), *Letters*, 223.
96. Sabine (ed.), *Letters*, 225–6.
97. Sabine (ed.), *Letters*, 227.
98. Jones, *Journals*, ii, 55–9.
99. Sabine (ed.), *Letters*, 225; Jones, *Journals*, ii, 56.
100. Sabine (ed.), *Letters*, 229.

Chapter 9

The Second Assault

The Artillery Bombardment

The first day's bombardment on 26 August yielded mixed results. According to Frazer, the British benefited because French counter-fire, aiming at too many targets, inflicted little damage. By contrast, the British main effort, against the town's east wall and towers at each end of the section to be breached, went well. Bombarding the demi-bastion near the horn-work also paid dividends: 'By 3 p.m. the greater part of the face of the demi-bastion came down with a crash.'[1]

Yet the bombardment from San Bartolomeo was not especially effective and failed to reduce the eastern section of the curtain wall. Admittedly, the range was longer than that required for the main breaching battery. Maximilien Foy, who trained as an artillery officer in 1790–2 and held artillery commands in the Peninsula, criticized British artillery in the Peninsula for too often firing at such long ranges that little damage was caused to breaches.[2] Wellington visited San Sebastian on 26 August, when the artillery bombardment began. Curiously, however, he did not meet Graham, the commanding officer, even though he 'did not think that matters were going exactly right'.[3]

Graham had already, on 22 August, argued that the battery on the isthmus was 'too distant' to be effective against the bastion at the southern end of the east wall, where that bastion commanded the main breach. On the eve of the bombardment, the battery, at 800yd, was still too far from its target.[4]

In his despatch on the siege, Wellington principally criticized the positioning of the guns directed against the towers flanking the bastion on the eastern wall, the demi-bastion near the horn-work, and the eastern section of the southern curtain wall behind the horn-work.[5] He indicated to Graham on the 27th that six 24-pounders of number 6 battery on the isthmus should be moved farther to their right. They were poorly sited for their task of weakening the horn-work and the southern curtain wall. This was a significant tactical decision because there were only fifteen guns on the isthmus and eight of them were 18-pounders and howitzers, incapable of destroying heavy fortifications. Wellington was confident that the guns in their new position would significantly damage the defences. Underscoring the importance of this decision, Wellington requested detailed information on the disposition of the guns, so that he could issue the necessary orders to assign troops to the relevant tasks. In addition, he considered ways in which the assault might be staged on a broader front. He asked Graham to have staff, engineer and naval officers examine the north and west faces of the steep Monte Urgull at the peninsula's north end and upon whose southern face the castle was built. He wanted to know whether a naval attack might be viable from that unexpected direction.[6] In fact, the castle's works were too high up the hill to be vulnerable to naval gunnery and could fire down upon approaching warships. Graham apparently toyed with the idea of landing troops on the castle's defensive walls, but reconnaissance showed that the cliffs were dominated by the castle's defences.[7]

While these initiatives demonstrated the extent of Wellington's managerial interventions, they also revealed that tactics involving laborious artillery operations were still being refined on the second day of the renewed bombardment. This indicated either a failure to plan in depth or an understanding that the bombardment would necessitate improvisation. Yet significant adjustments at such a late stage defeated the objective of crippling the defences as quickly as possible.

Lieutenant Colonel Fletcher did not fully realign the guns as ordered by Wellington on the 27th. The guns were heavy to move and only four could be positioned at a height from which they might hit their target. If the guns were pushed any nearer to their objective, they would lie too low in the plain to land shot on their intended objective.[8] Instead, Fletcher sought to broaden the artillery attack from San Bartolomeo by firing on the town's western front along the bay, where small French coastal vessels continued to access the harbour. This minor deployment became irrelevant during the night of 26–7 August in a rare instance of Wellington's use of conjoint operations. Conveyed by a Royal Navy squadron, a party of 200 men from the 9th seized Isla Santa Clara. The island, defended only by a small French contingent, commanded the entrance to the bay and therefore San Sebastian's harbour. Only one ship at a time could pass between the island and the mainland.[9] Since its seizure severely reduced French seaborne access to San Sebastian, a matter about which Wellington complained frequently, Christopher Hall reasonably queries why plans for the first siege failed to include such an important objective.[10] The British, over the next few days, positioned five 24-pounders on the island to fire upon the castle from the west.[11] Applying such pressure involved a significant commitment from the total stock of twenty-eight 24-pounders.

Thus the scale of the bombardment expanded on 26–7 August. The timing, however, indicated once again the difficulties of acting promptly. The new siege train began arriving from England on 22 August, but, despite Wellington's repeated complaints about the siege train's slow appearance, his forces were not prepared when the transports sailed into view. Only half a dozen artillerymen were available on the night of 22–3 August to direct 300 Portuguese infantrymen in setting up the main artillery battery. Such work had to be completed at night in silence, and the level of supervision fell woefully short of requirements. Adequate manpower arrived only by 26 August. Once the bombardment began, however, Frazer found the Portuguese infantry to be 'good-humoured' and extremely hard-working in serving the batteries with ammunition.[12]

While the bombardment proceeded, measures to weaken the defences behind the main breach were discussed. One important decision concerned the use of mortar or vertical fire. The main purpose of the bombardment on 26–30 August was to destroy sections of wall and wreck French gun emplacements. Only with the assault on

31 August did some sixteen mortars join the bombardment.[13] This usage resulted from a positive tactical choice. On 23 August, Wellington authorized Graham to use howitzers and mortars as he saw fit. He criticized one officer for inaccurately determining distances and failing to grasp the value of British howitzer and mortar fire from the left of the east bank in degrading the main breach. However, he warned that mortar fire needed to be used carefully and sparingly:

> the use of mortars and howitzers in a siege, for the purpose of . . . *general annoyance,* answers no purpose whatever against a place occupied by French troops, excepting against the inhabitants of the place; and eventually when we shall get the place against ourselves, and the convenience we should derive from having the houses of the place in a perfect state of repair.

Wellington doubted the effectiveness of mortars and howitzers against specified targets. Citing French mortar fire's lack of impact on British entrenchments at Ciudad Rodrigo, he questioned whether even precisely directed fire would inflict much damage. British experience of the first assault further intensified this scepticism:

> I hope he will not forget the opinions entertained at the time the breach was first practicable at San Sebastian, of the increased difficulties of storming it, in consequence of the fire in the neighbourhood. If the general bombardment should set fire to the town, as it probably will, then the attack of the enemy's entrenchment will become impracticable.

Overall, an extensive bombardment would be 'materially injurious in the attack, and will be very inconvenient to our friends the inhabitants, and eventually to ourselves'. Yet Wellington then left the decision to the specialist officers and Graham, with the caveat that the bombardment should be launched from the left of the sand-hills, in order to 'save much transport and labor'.[14]

On the 27th 'good progress' continued against the main breach, but the demi-bastion and high curtain wall remained powerful obstacles. During the night of 27–8 August, an effort was made to move 24-pounders forward to the right of the British front on the isthmus, as ordered by Wellington on the 26th. Difficult conditions, made worse by a French sortie against the British right, meant that the work was not completed on time. On the following night three of the intended four 24-pounders (pared down from the six initially desired by Wellington) were positioned as ordered and ready to fire on the morning of the 29th.

By then, most of the main breach had been broken down, but the French still kept a gun on the parapet of the severely damaged tower B, commanding a flank of the main breach. The demi-bastion retained its key revetments and the high curtain wall was still in place. Much British effort had been devoted on the isthmus to creating parapets for musketry. But work had been held back by the lack of transport for the fascines, which were necessary to protect the parapets and were being constructed in the woods to the rear. Three-quarters of the 400 Portuguese troops assigned to this work were engaged instead in hauling the finished fascines to the front. Again, essential preparatory work had not been completed in anticipation of the siege train's arrival seven days earlier. Wellington had therefore to press his subordinates hard, visiting the front on the 28th to give further orders.[15]

On the 29th, British artillery destroyed two French defensive positions among the ruins at the main breach. A French gun in the remains of tower B was taken out, as was another gun in the rubble of tower A. Continued efforts were made against the demi-bastion and high curtain wall, but an attempt to collapse part of the horn-work into French mines dug at the left and west of that fortification failed. By 6.00 p.m., Lieutenant Colonel Frazer noted that 'The enemy's fire is now comparatively trifling: it is hardly worth regarding'. It was difficult for the British to know whether the French were conserving their ammunition or suffered widespread damage to their guns. The British completed the trenches on their right on the isthmus, giving good protection for covering infantry fire. They made a second effort to neutralize the French mines near the horn-work during the night of 29–30 August, failing with a feigned attack on the French defences to panic the defenders into blowing the mines.[16]

Wellington visited the east bank of the Urumea at noon on 29 August, chalking up his third inspection in four days. He viewed his own presence on such occasions as a vital morale-booster because it signified to the troops that the task they had been assigned was important; 'they will do for me what perhaps no one else can make them do'.[17] According to Frazer, he spent 'some time' there discussing the next move with four senior officers: Sir Thomas Graham, Sir James Leith, who resumed command of the 5th Division from Major General Oswald, having just recuperated from wounds, and the engineer and artillery commanders, Alexander Dickson and Sir Richard Fletcher. Only those officers were present, and they agreed that the attack would occur at or before 1.00 p.m. on 31 August.[18]

During the morning of 30 August, the main breach was further softened up. Sustained fire was then directed against the castle's defences and the Mirador battery at the castle; the main breach lay within the range and ready view of the Mirador guns. This firing damaged non-military targets. For example, a British shell blew up five mines near the hospital in the town, and a former hospital near the Mirador battery was in flames by the late afternoon. On the isthmus, the breaching battery having at last been assembled as ordered on the 26th, six 24-pounders in two batteries reduced the demi-bastion and the high curtain to a breachable state. Altogether, some 460ft of the walls were open to assault. About 130ft of wall had been breached in July, so that 330ft of wall had been broken down since the bombardment launched on 26 August. Wellington visited the batteries at 3.00 p.m. on the 30th and decided that the breaches were satisfactory for storming at 11.00 the next day. Timing was critical since the tide had to be out, to enable troops on the isthmus to move along the shoreline to get to the breach. Another minor obstacle was part of a wall projecting from the horn-work, which was mined and blown up at 2.00 a.m. on the 31st.

What seemed like the steady pace of operations was rudely interrupted on the 30th when news spread that Soult had advanced the previous evening upon Irun. The 4th Division left for Oyarzun. Artillery was rushed eastwards, with all horse artillery and heavier guns not being used in the siege being despatched.[19] Before learning of this advance, Frazer had recorded, at 7.00 a.m. on the 30th, his aversion to 'delay, as breaking the spirit of the troops'. By 9.00 p.m. that night, he noted

> All the troops of horse artillery are ordered to march: an attack by Soult is expected. Much is at stake at present: more than generally occurs. The consequences of to-morrow may have a great effect on the campaign. Should Soult be successful, our siege is over: should our assault fail, we shall be awkwardly off. The stake is serious.[20]

The second bombardment took longer to complete than had been expected, hampered by delays in getting the heavy guns into place, soldiers' reluctance to act as labourers in digging trenches and gun positions and in hauling ordnance, and inefficiencies resulting from a shortage of artillerymen and the use of multi-national artillery teams.

Eventually, however, twenty-eight 24-pounders went into action. For the entire period of the siege to 8 September, these guns expended an average of just over 1,000 shot and grape each. The data available does not provide daily figures, but Frazer estimated on 1 September that the artillery had been expending about 8,000 rounds per day. He noted that until 31 August only three to four mortars had been used.[21] The 24-pounders thus bore the brunt of the work. The most sustained firing from those heavy guns occurred during 26–30 August inclusive but they were essentially in play for six days, with some activity on 31 August, occasional activity on 1 September, and a 2-hour burst on 8 September; mortar fire dominated the artillery attack on the castle from 1–7 September. The heavy guns could fire 20 rounds an hour, so each gun, if used at full capacity, would have needed to fire for at least 50 hours to expend 1,000 rounds.[22]

The second bombardment of San Sebastian was by far the biggest artillery assault launched by the allies in the Peninsular War. One ensign excitedly reported that the castle had 'more shells burst over it than any other place in the world it is supposed'.[23] About 50 per cent more shot was discharged than at Badajoz, and well over four times more was used than at Ciudad Rodrigo. The two bombardments of San Sebastian together consumed 59,000 shot (18,000 and 41,000 respectively) whereas only 26,500 rounds were fired at Badajoz. One explanation was that wider breaches were made at San Sebastian, the total from the two bombardments being 460ft compared with 320ft at Badajoz.[24] At Badajoz success eventually came through escalading the castle wall, while no attempt at escalading was made at San Sebastian. The breaches provided the only route to victory.

A heavy, sustained bombardment was also necessary since the French devoted weeks to repairing and extending their defences. Some breaching work in late August repeated work undertaken earlier. This activity lay behind Frazer's impatience to start the assault; extra days taken up by the bombardment in part resulted from simply re-doing destructive work previously undertaken. But there is another explanation. Jones observed that the cement used in building walls in Spain, and elsewhere in southern

Europe, hardened to a consistency greater than that of the stones which it bound together. A wall made of small, rough-hewn stones and large amounts of mortar became very difficult to fragment into large slabs. Such walls 'can only be brought down from distant batteries by being pounded into small particles'. Jones estimated that breaching might take about twice as much effort as breaching brick defences in France or Flanders.[25] But one officer recorded that such pummelling did not occur. The wall facing the river appeared to him like a rock-face of masonry which broke into large masses rather than into small pieces. Rolling down the breach like 'crags from the face of a precipice', these blocks of rock were very difficult to climb.[26] Even when scaled, the breach offered extremely limited footholds. Fletcher, commanding the Royal Engineers, pointed out on the eve of the assault that the defensive wall consisted entirely of masonry. The wall was narrow and there was no soil on the breach. The assailants would have the tedious work of hauling sandbags to the top of the breach in order to stabilize it. Graham therefore expanded the range of the assault upon the ramparts by bombarding the curtain wall and cavalier.[27]

San Sebastian thus provided the final reminder, which should already have been clear at Badajoz, that the light and quick approach to campaigning which Wellington brought from India did not work against well-defended European towns, even when their fortifications had not been re-configured on Vaubanian principles. The defensive walls of traditionally fortified Indian towns were easier to breach because the materials from which they had been constructed fragmented and shattered more readily than did the walls Wellington tried to destroy in Spain.

After all this protracted preparatory work, one nagging question remained and exercized the army. Did the troops have the determination to carry this assault to a successful conclusion? Morale could be undermined for various reasons. For example, on 5 August, Major General Frederick Robinson, commanding a brigade in the 5th Division, reported from the camp in front of San Sebastian that the 59th had joined his division earlier in the year after marching from Lisbon and had not had time to rest, recuperate and re-order. The men, who had not been paid since 24 May, suffered from shortages not only of comforts, but also of necessities.[28]

The waiting period before an attack left plenty of opportunity for gossip, some of it likely to corrode morale. As one soldier wrote home on 25 August, 'The tittle-tattle of an army is similar to a county town'. He reported that the engineers were quarrelling, with pressure for a division other than the 5th to be assigned to the renewed assault, because the 5th had allegedly been 'cowed' by their experience of the first assault. The writer noted that anyone would approach the task of assailing the breaches in a sober frame of mind. But the failure on 25 July was widely attributed to the 5th Division's lack of drive and determination. One reaction to such criticism of the infantry was the counter-claim that engineers led men to disaster in the breach by taking wrong directions or by supplying ladders which proved inadequate for tasks which the engineers declared practicable.[29] We have seen (in Chapter 7) that opinions differed sharply in attributing responsibility for the unsuccessful first assault. Given the experiences of 1812 and of 25 July, worries remained that this might prove a siege too far. On 22 August, Graham reported to

Wellington that 'all the officers' of the 5th Division agreed that an attack in one column would be 'extremely doubtful' in the adverse conditions facing the assailants. He added that 'I much fear that the effect of this general opinion may increase the risk of its failing'.[30]

Wellington responded to these rumours by effectively siding with the engineers and bluntly challenging the 5th Division. At 11.00 a.m. on 27 August he requested that named battalions raise volunteers ready to undertake the assault. Larpent, at headquarters, described this as 'a cut at the fifth', which had been in 'a sort of panic' at the first assault. He felt that 'The fifth division ought now to volunteer, trying first alone' at the second attempt.[31] As late as the morning of 30 August, however, Frazer noted that 'New Troops are requisite: those who failed last time will not do again'.[32]

Wellington's initiative in the morning of the 27th was preceded by a letter to Graham, to which the latter was unable to reply until 9.00 a.m. on the 28th. Graham consulted Major Generals Oswald, Hay and Robertson (presumably Robinson) before responding. Graham assured Wellington that 'the best spirit prevails' in the 5th Division and that 'the troops would feel great mortification, if relieved by others so as to have no share in the termination of their labour'. He reported Oswald's view that the men were 'greatly exhausted by the severity of the duties of the trenches and of the fatigue and working parties'. Oswald was therefore anxious that other troops join the attack. Although the attack would occur in more favourable conditions than the first assault encountered, it would still be launched 'from one narrow debouche' essentially in one column, exposed to enfilading fire, and vulnerable to mines whose location had not been detected but which might include the horn-work's angles, the left bastion and the sea wall. Graham agreed with Oswald that, at the very least, it would be desirable to have troops from other divisions in reserve.[33]

By 2.30 p.m. on the 28th Wellington had directed 300 volunteers from the 4th and Light Divisions to proceed during the morning of 29 August to Oyarzun, where they were to join another 400 volunteers from the 1st Division. Strengthened by unspecified numbers from Lord Aylmer's brigade, these volunteers would lead the assault if the breaches were suitably prepared.[34] The 200 volunteers from the 4th Division had to march 20 miles from their camp at Lesaca to San Sebastian.[35] Volunteering became a point of honour. There was confusion among the Light and 4th Divisions as officers sought to volunteer. A specified number of volunteers by rank was requested from the battalions in those selected divisions. In the 52nd, ten subalterns volunteered for the two slots required. The senior officer in each rank had first preference in volunteering. The commanding officer, Lieutenant Colonel John Hunt, insisted on his right to go. Although his rank precluded him from gaining promotion by such service, he refused to allow Major George Napier the place Napier wanted on the grounds that the latter had already led a storming party; he lost an arm at Ciudad Rodrigo. In the 43rd, those who volunteered did so 'without any bombast; they look serious and pale'. Sergeants and men argued about their right to go. The sense of honour was such that even those who participated in earlier assaults refused to concede that prior service should debar them from joining yet another assault.[36]

Graham left the selection of the units leading the assault to Lieutenant General Sir James Leith. The large assault force included companies from the 5th Division's battalions. Leith, the division's commanding officer who was wounded at Salamanca, returned to duty the day before the attack. He was well known for his energy and a desire that his division should lead.[37] He had shown initiative and drive at Badajoz, where the 5th was in reserve but launched diversionary attacks on outlying positions.[38] His self-possession and outstanding indifference to enemy fire were exemplary at Salamanca.[39] Leith refused to allow the volunteer units specially raised from other divisions to lead the assault, instead assigning that extremely dangerous task to Robinson's brigade from the 5th Division. Leith put the rest of the 5th Division and the volunteers in reserve.[40] His presence, together no doubt with resentment at the accusations of weak commitment in July, galvanized the 5th Division, whose men allegedly threatened to bayonet troops belonging to any other unit who tried to climb the breach before they did.[41]

The elements were now in place for the denouement of the most demanding of Wellington's four principal Peninsular War sieges. Yet, paradoxically in view of the scale and length of the preparations, it remains impossible to attribute responsibility for the final decisions to individual officers. An accurate account of Wellington's decisions on the last days before the assault cannot be given, since his correspondence contains only one letter for 29 and 30 August. He was constantly on the move, returning to headquarters at 9.00 p.m. on the 29th and leaving again at 8.00 a.m. the next morning.[42] Nor indeed are there any letters for the day of the attack, the 31st, or the day after the attack, 1 September. An eloquent testimony to the enormous and divergent pressures on the commanding general, the one letter from those four days was dated 30 August. Some 3,000 words long, it concerned complex issues of civil-military and Anglo-Spanish relations and the management of the Spanish army, and responded to a letter dated 20 August from the Spanish minister of war at Cádiz.[43]

While all this preparation proceeded, how did the French assess the effects of the bombardment? Rey reported to Soult on 29 August that the British had subjected the town to a prolonged hail of shells, shot and bullets on the 28th and the 29th. The fortifications were smashed on the bastion's front and flank; the far eastern section of the curtain wall was opened to assault; and the whole space between the earlier first and second breaches had been broken. Rey noted that he might have to withdraw from the town into the castle under pressure from an assault, partly because he had so few troops – only enough, he claimed, to form 2 reserves of 125 soldiers each. The brigadier general therefore requested that Soult advance as soon as possible in order to relieve San Sebastian. He added to the sense of urgency by noting that, at 4.00 p.m., his men had observed five generals visiting the British batteries, among whom they believed they spotted Wellington.[44] As already noted, it was indeed the Field Marshal, making his final assessment with Graham, Leith and Lieutenant Colonels Dickson of the artillery and Fletcher of the engineers.[45] Whatever differences of opinion over tactics, dispositions and force-levels may have been expressed earlier, the evidence suggests that the final decisions were collectively taken by that group.

The Assault

Detonating a British mine at 2.00 a.m. on 31 August announced the impending attack. According to Belmas, the well-armed defenders, responding to their officers' call 'They will not enter', competed to take the most exposed positions from which to inflict the gravest casualties on the attackers.[46]

Dense fog delayed the start of the British artillery assault on the 31st, with the guns opening up only at about 8.00 a.m. Some of the firing was extremely closely directed. For example, at one point between 10.15 and 10.55, Sir Richard Fletcher on the isthmus sent a message to the main battery, number 15, on the sand-hills. Carried by a soldier who swam the Urumea River, the message requested that seven guns fire upon French working parties re-organizing defences in the battered northern round tower at the main breach. Those working parties could not be seen from the east bank. The battery then laid down a precise barrage which foreshadowed the celebrated and more dramatic firing over the heads of British troops later in the assault. As Frazer remarked of this earlier episode, 'We are firing delicately, since we are directing our fire over points which our troops are now passing'. Sir Thomas Graham, who later ordered the general bombardment over the British forces in the main breach, was present with 15 battery which delivered this closely targeted bombardment.[47]

Once the tide had gone out far enough and long enough for the foreshore to be exposed, the advance along the east side of the isthmus began, at about 10.55 a.m. (Rey gave the time as 10.30.[48]) One danger spot was the stretch of the defensive perimeter which the French had mined and which the British had failed to trick them into exploding the night before. Marching was impeded by very wet surfaces. Even those not washed by the high tide were presumably wet, since there had been 'violent rain with thunder and lightening' overnight and the fog had only recently lifted.[49]

Despite earlier and widely expressed doubts about its fitness for the attack, the 2nd Brigade from the maligned 5th Division led the storming party. The brigade's three battalions – the 4th, 47th and 59th – each supplied two companies. Lieutenant Colonel Brooke took over command of the brigade when Major General Robinson was wounded in the trenches before the assault began. These men from the 2nd Brigade of the 5th Division were to be followed, and not led as had been mooted a few days earlier, by 750 volunteers. Some 400 volunteers were from the 1st Division, consisting of 200 Guards under Lieutenant Colonel Cooke, 100 men of the light battalion and 100 men from battalions of the King's German Legion, under Major Robertson. The 4th Division supplied 200 volunteers under Major Rose of the 20th, and the Light Division provided 150 under Major Hunt. The reserves consisted of the two remaining brigades of the 5th Division – the 1st Brigade under Major General Hay, and the Portuguese brigade under Major General Sprye – as well as the 5th Battalion of Caçadores, commanded by Major Hill, from Major General Bradford's brigade, not of the 5th Division. The forlorn hope at the fore of the breaching party consisted of Lieutenant Francis Maguire of the 4th and thirty men.[50] Frazer correctly viewed the initial allocation of about 1,200 men – the 6 companies from the 5th Division plus 750 volunteers – as 'too few; it may fail'.[51] The force was distributed thus:

Forlorn hope: Lieutenant Francis Maguire of the 4th + 30 men
Breaching Force:
2nd Brigade of 5th Division: Lieutenant Colonel Francis Brooke + 2
    companies from each of the 4th, 47th and 59th = about 600 men
1st Division: Lieutenant Colonel Cooke + 200 Guards; Major Robertson +
    100 Light Battalion + 100 King's German Legion
4th Division: Major Alexander Rose of 20th + 200 men
Light Division: Major John Hunt + 150 men
Reserve:
5th Division: Major General Andrew Hay + 1st Brigade of the 1st, 9th and
    38th; Major General Sprye + Portuguese brigade
Major General Bradford's brigade: Lieutenant Colonel Snodgrass + 250 1st
    Portuguese Line; Lieutenant Colonel M'Bean + 250 24th Portuguese Line
Lieutenant Colonel Thomas Hill + 5th Caçadores

The storming party first had to cross the 200yd between the parallel and the breach. The British knew that the French had dug mines from which to blow up part of the town wall across this route. As the forlorn hope pressed forward, a party consisting of a sergeant and twelve soldiers tried to neutralize the French mine. The French blew it up prematurely, so that the collapsing town wall killed or wounded about thirty to forty advancing troops, rather than the much larger number who would have perished had the detonation occurred slightly later.

Having reached the main breach, the assault party had to survive at the breach and then climb it. Both tasks proved extremely difficult. The position below the town wall and breach was exposed to musket fire from above and from heavy artillery fire from the more distant Mirador battery and the St Elme bastion at the castle. At one point on the mountain side a parapet normally supporting one 24-pounder had been extended into the rock-face to accommodate three such heavy guns. They 'had a full view of the breach'.[52] Lieutenant General Leith, accompanied by Major General John Oswald who had commanded the 5th Division in Leith's long absence, took position some 30yd from the demi-bastion. From there he could summon, inspire and direct reinforcements. He had commanded a brigade at La Coruña in 1809 and won admiration at Salamanca for his indifference to enemy fire and his leadership of the 5th Division from the front.[53] Gomm reported from Salamanca that Leith 'addressed the troops with the eloquence of a Caesar, before they advanced; and he led them, like something that had descended for a time to favour the righteous side; . . . the enthusiasm excited could hardly have been greater'. Nine days after the battle, he wrote further of Leith's impact:

At headquarters they are full of his praises; . . . he threw a truly chivalrous spirit into all who were about him. The wits say that while he was advancing he looked like the presiding spirit of this tempest; his division the thunder-cloud that he rolled after him; and his staff were flashes of lightning that he scattered about him.[54]

If Oswald's leadership had been at fault on 25 July, that defect had been repaired for the second assault. There were no apparent hesitations as battalions marched to the breach.

If reaching the breach was hazardous, the assailants faced French grenadiers and voltigeurs firing from above when they attempted to ascend it. A 12-pounder placed on the nearby cavalier and an 8-pounder in the cavalier's casement commanded the flanks of the main breach and, according to Rey, inflicted heavy casualties on the attackers. The length of the breach was also exposed to a 16-pounder firing from the bastion at St Elme, at the far northern end of the town's east wall. The British decision not to assault the demi-bastion at the south-eastern corner of the horn-work allowed the defenders to reinforce that position. Captain Gorse of the French artillery transferred a 4-pounder from the horn-work's west bastion to its east bastion, 100m from the main breach; he could fire upon the attackers from a position which Burgoyne had warned would pose a threat. This initiative was strengthened by infantry from the horn-work, led by a captain in the French 62nd, who also moved to the same east bastion, from which they inflicted heavy casualties on the British. Four weeks *after* the assault, Captain John Aitchison visited the site and noted, 'The breach is I think as strong as any part of the defences – it is still so difficult that I could hardly get at it even now'.[55]

Of the forlorn hope of thirty men, none reached the top of the breach. Lieutenant Maguire, whose father served in the same regiment and died from yellow fever in 1806, used his 'old cocked hat with its white plumes' to wave on his depleted followers. He was killed high on the breach on his 21st birthday. Troops supporting the forlorn hope took heavy casualties and retreated to its foot. According to Burgoyne, no troops at this stage climbed to the top of the breach.[56]

The direction of the assault was logical. The thrust at the river wall was designed, as the French understood, to enable troops from the breach to enter the town by flanking two layers of defence inside the town wall. One layer, visible in general but not in its detailed arrangements by the British, had been created around the main breach from the masonry of buildings and defensive structures already ruined by the British bombardment. The second layer, which the British knew had been created, consisted of defences across the north–south streets within the town. If the British had entered the town from behind the horn-work they would have come directly into the line of fire from those defensive lines. In this assessment, assailing the breach offered the best way of dealing with the town's internal defences. But by not reducing the horn-work, the British allowed the French to free up men and a gun to add extra firepower against the troops assailing the breach.[57]

In concentrating on the main breach, the British limited themselves to one route into the town, but they could not move off the breach into the town. The defensive wall dropped by 20ft at its rear. In the ground below the breach, the defenders had embedded rows of sword blades. The only other route was a single-file gap to the south side of the breach well covered by the defenders.[58] This lapse was particularly damning in the light of the elaborate and lethal defences which the French had prepared at Badajoz. British surprise at not being able to move off the breach was curious given the ample time which the French had enjoyed to fine-tune their defences and given the French reputation for ingenuity in making such preparations.

A critical point had been reached. In describing the construction of the lines of Torres Vedras in 1810, Lieutenant Colonel Jones stressed the importance of inserting obstacles to an attacker's progress in assaulting the defences, an issue 'seldom sufficiently attended to':

> The great object of defence should be to contrive some expedient to check the assailants, and cause them to halt, if only for two or three minutes, under a close fire of musketry from the parapet. Such an advanced obstacle has ten times the effect of one of equal difficulty opposed to an assailant, when he has closed with the defenders of a work.

Instead of closing with the enemy in the knowledge that they had 'but to overcome one difficulty to obtain complete success', soldiers assaulting defences would 'exhaust their ardour and lose their formation on a mere preliminary effort' if they encountered obstacles before reaching their objective. Once troops were pinned down, it was 'extremely difficult . . . to revive confident boldness, and restore order for a second effort after a check'.[59] Such a situation tested leadership and required new initiatives.

Following this hesitation, Lieutenant General Leith ordered three British columns in turn to attack the main breach. Exposed to French gunfire from the Mirador as they approached the breach and as they positioned themselves at its foot, each one added to the piles of dead.[60] According to Frazer, reinforcements marched from the parallels to the breach at 11.45, 12.00 and 12.25.[61] While directing these reinforcements, Leith suffered contusions after being hit in the chest by half a cannon shot which hit a rock, broke up and ricocheted. He was next bruised by 'a spent grape-shot', and later had to leave the field when his left arm was broken by shot.[62]

A third challenge was therefore to create a diversion and add extra weight to the attack. To take pressure off the main breach and to take out at least some French artillery, a further advance was launched by about 500 Portuguese, who crossed the Urumea at low tide to assail the small breach made farther north between the Hornos tower and the St Elme bastion. The crossing occurred at 11.35–11.45 in broad daylight and in an open river with no cover, resulting in 'great loss '. Frazer said the men were up their knees in water.[63] Aitchison noted that the water was waist high, while the troops were 'literally showered' with shot, shell and grape.[64]

This Portuguese contingent came from two formations. The 10th Portuguese Brigade, commanded from June 1813 by newly promoted Major General Thomas Bradford, provided 9 officers and 250 men for the audacious crossing. This force was commanded by Major Kenneth Snodgrass of the 13th Line, who was one of four officers mentioned in Graham's despatch on the first assault. Promoted on the day of the second assault to brevet Lieutenant Colonel, he was enterprising as well as brave. At 10.30 on the night of the 30th, he crossed the Urumea to determine that the river was passable, with water just above waist height, at a point opposite the smaller of the two breaches. He climbed the breach under cover of darkness to reconnoitre. About

12 or so hours later he led his 258 officers and men, advancing 30–40 paces ahead of them, across the river to that lesser breach. Exposed to enemy gunfire in broad daylight, Snodgrass's men, who volunteered for this service, suffered seventy-three casualties, or 28 per cent.[65] Ensign Hennell noted that 'It is impossible for troops to have behaved better than the Portuguese did. . . . they did not hurry or spread, but marched regularly to the breach . . . to the admiration of all the spectators', despite being up to the waist in water and under fire from 'grape, cannon & musketry'.[66] The second formation, led by Lieutenant Colonel William M'Bean, was of equal strength and drawn from the Portuguese 24th Line, which he had commanded since 1810.[67] This supplementary advance succeeded with experienced and determined leadership.

The willingness to cross the river in broad daylight against a strong artillery defence had been built into the planning. It resembled the attack, in which Wellington had participated, against Seringapatam in 1799. On that occasion, the city's fortifications were bombarded from two directions, creating confusion as to the intended point of attack. Only after a great deal of preparatory trench digging and artillery fire did the Indo-British army concentrate on creating its selected breach on one section of the walls. As soon as the breach was ready, the assault parties crossed the river, admittedly shallow at that time of year, at 1.30 p.m. under covering artillery fire. The artillery preparation had been extremely thorough, with initial work on placing the guns and establishing batteries beginning on 17 April and the attack occurring on 4 May.[68] At San Sebastian, the river crossing was a secondary, daring diversion against a far more vigorous and tactically adroit defence.

The fourth challenge remained: how were the attackers to advance from the top of the breach? The French position at the main breach was far stronger than the Mysoreans' defence had been at the breach at Seringapatam. Graham described the difficulty in his report to Wellington the next day. 'There never was any thing so fallacious as the external appearance of the breach', because the defensive wall being breached ended in 'a perpendicular scarp of at least 20 feet to the level of the streets'.[69] The only way down into the town from the breach was across a narrow ridge formed by rubble from the bombardment at the southern corner of the river wall and the higher curtain wall behind the horn-work and at a right angle to the river wall. Entry into this south-east corner of the defensive system was effectively by a single-file gap.

Graham's assessment of the crisis which confronted him revealed serious miscalculations in planning the assault. Much effort had been put into widening the original breach. That widening of the main breach did nothing, however, to make entry into the town easier. Troops ascending the breach could fan out across a broader front than was possible at the first assault, but they were still cruelly exposed to French fire if they could not move quickly off the breach and descend into the town. The rubble created by the British cannonade did not provide materials from which the engineers could create defences on the breach. Those rare parts of the breach which gave shelter from French musket fire from above were also exposed to artillery fire from the castle's guns.[70] The mistake of supposing a wider breach would assist the attack flowed from the fundamental failure to detect the key strength in the defences – the sheer and steep drop behind the river wall. The handful of soldiers who reached the top of the breach in the first assault could not report this problem because they were killed or taken prisoner. Even so, persistent and long drawn-out observation of the breached wall did not reveal this fact to the British on the east bank of the Urumea River. Frazer admitted privately on 1 September that the breaches were 'more difficult (as I now believe) than I had apprehended'.[71] French guns at the castle maintained grape fire on the breach and exit from the parallels throughout the attack. The wider breach offered no protection against that fire or the musketry from the demi-bastion on the horn-work, the curtain wall and the ruins behind the breach. The only relief offered the men on the breach was that they were not fired on from the tower to the breach's north side, which was unoccupied.[72] The French failure to use the tower could not have been predicted when the breach was created.

By 12.00, the attack was stalled, with the assailants unable to advance from the breach. Time was not on their side. As the tide flowed, access to the breach would become more difficult. Moreover, it is possible that the storm which broke later in the afternoon was already threatening. One account at least stated that low clouds remained all morning, creating a 'close and oppressive heat'. Rain began as the troops marched into the trenches and by noon a black cloud hung over the city.[73] An incoming tide and a breaking storm would have made the assault even more challenging. It is highly likely that these factors added to the intense pressure on Graham to regain momentum.

Graham ordered the bulk of the artillery on the east bank of the river to fire over the heads of the British force, in order to take out the guns dominating the breach and to suppress the French musket fire. The particular targets of this bombardment were the French positions on the high curtain wall abutting the far south end of the breach. If those defences could be reduced, allied troops on the breach would be able, with difficulty and very slowly, to squeeze into the narrow gap between the breach and the curtain wall and then enter the town. The curtain wall was 10–12ft above the demi-bastion, which in turn was higher than the breach.[74] This action was recommended to Graham by Lieutenant Colonel Dickson, commanding the artillery, and reflected his 'knowledge of the precision exercised by his gunners'.[75] Success depended on the artillerymen's understanding of the heights and ranges involved. This barrage has been regarded as highly significant for its accuracy – essential to avoid casualties from friendly fire – and daring. This claim requires some qualification. According to Belmas, the French curtain wall, one target of the bombardment, was high above the men at the foot of the breach, making the artillery bombardment of the curtain wall less risky to the assailants than other targeting.

The bombardment failed to achieve the desired breakthrough. The decisive turning point on the breaches occurred instead between 12.15 and 12.35 p.m., about 20 minutes *after* the British bombardment over the heads of their assailants began. French munitions had been placed forward on the ramparts, for ready use by the defenders. A sudden explosion ignited a firestorm, stunning the defenders and killing many of them on the high curtain: 'In every direction these hapless beings fell by the force of the explosion; legs and arms, heads, and headless bodies, showered over the ramparts among our men, who, shouting with exultation, rushed with frenzied enthusiasm to every crevice that offered admittance, proving how much the occurrence had contributed to renew the ardour of the attack.'[76] Smoke from the explosion in the French munitions may have helped by forcing a pause in French artillery fire from the castle.

Two battalions from the 5th Division's 1st Brigade, the reserve for the assault, reached the breach as the French munitions on the curtain wall's rampart exploded. Men from the 2nd Brigade of the 5th Division, under Colonel Charles Greville, reinforced by those two battalions – the 1st Royal Scots' third battalion, under Lieutenant Colonel James Barnes, and the 38th under Lieutenant Colonel Edward Miles – pressed onto the curtain wall, where they gained support from an attack upon the horn-work by other troops sent in from the 2nd Brigade. Given the critical importance of the south-east corner of the town's defences, Frazer afterwards wondered why the French, so expert in defence, had not mined the demi-bastion at that point; if they had done so, the British attack would have failed.[77]

There was intense fighting as British troops crossed the breach made in the curtain wall, defended themselves against counter-attacks, and entered the town. Lieutenant Colonel Miles of the 38th was said to have been one of the first to enter the town.[78] The French had converted houses behind the main breach into strong defensive positions. Success on the curtain wall allowed for renewed efforts at the main breach, since the British from the curtain wall breach pushed into the town behind the main breach. Frazer, on inspecting the main breach on 3 September, noted 'Many of our poor fellows lay dead on the roofs of the adjoining houses; the roofs seemed almost to have fallen in with the number of the dead.'[79] Since the assault had become an exercise in competitive bravery, involving the 5th Division's honour, it was not surprising that so many fell on and just beyond the main breach. Frazer, in contemplating the corpses on the breach, unconsciously invoked the language of emulation which Wellington used on 28 August in calling for volunteers: 'as the really brave always fall in a day of open assault, our late loss is in truth a severe one. It is impossible to look at the dead in the breach without admiration of the brave men who had fallen. Their wounds all in front . . .'[80]

The British entered the town first from the curtain wall breach and then from the old breach, by about 12.40 p.m. By 12.45 p.m. the French pulled out of the horn-work and British troops were able to fire from a position to the right of the main breach's northern tower. Further British reinforcements were sent from the parallels at 12.40, 1.00 and 1.35 p.m., following the explosion. By 1.15 p.m. some French soldiers remained on the curtain wall, but within 10 minutes there were relatively few men still on the breaches. Faced with significant losses, depleted reserves, wear and tear on his few remaining guns, and the prospect of further British reinforcements, Rey ordered a withdrawal.[81]

Once the allies crossed the curtain wall, fighting spilled over into the town itself. The streets were laid out in a grid pattern. Jones noted that 'the principal square and every street presented a succession of retrenchments', but the French fell back in the path of a wide-ranging and vigorous British advance.[82] Gomm noted that the enemy 'made some obstinate stands in the town, which was barricaded with great attention, and might have been more obstinately contested than it was; but they were exhausted by the long stand they had made at the breach'.[83] The French, unsurprisingly, described their withdrawal as steady, but they had far too few reserves, a problem which Rey had previously highlighted to Soult. Presumably the destruction of large areas of houses also deprived them of cover. There is some disagreement about when fighting ended. At 1.20 p.m., Frazer reported 'Very heavy fire of musketry in the town'. At 1.45 p.m. he noted 'Heavy musketry in the town. Our bugles sound the advance in all parts of the town.' Widespread fighting began falling off by 1.55 p.m. By then the French were retreating into the Mirador bastion at the castle. But fighting at a lower intensity continued in the town at 2.15 p.m., and the British used mules to bring ammunition from the parallels into the town at 3.00 p.m. The heavy batteries ceased fire at 2.15 p.m., although the carronades, howitzers and mortars continued their fire on the Mirador. Troops started carrying gabions into the town, to defend their positions in the streets. By then the sky had become very dark and the temperature had fallen to 'really cold'. Rain added to the discomfort.[84]

The standard French account states that the French had not pulled the vast majority of their force into the castle grounds until 5.00 p.m. They also continued to hold the large convent of Santa Teresa, in the north-west corner of the town's walls opposite the castle, until 4 September. The French claimed that the British lost many casualties within the town, and notably near the castle at the barricades at the church of Santa Maria. Such losses occurred, it was asserted, because the British advanced in large numbers – presumably offering easy targets – and in disorder. Confirming the extent of fighting within the town, Frazer later described seeing 'Heaps of dead in every corner'.[85] One contemporary report noted that 'Every street in the town was traversed; and in several there were guns, as also at the end of the street nearest the castle'. It claimed that the British took control of the three roads leading to the castle and then the town itself within an hour.[86] But that conclusion is incompatible with recorded incidents of scattered firing later than about 2.00 p.m. Major General Andrew Hay, on entering the town from the curtain wall, encountered a 'great deal of musketry fire' and 'some firing' of cannon in the streets. Once he had taken command of the 5th Division, when Leith was carried from the breach with multiple wounds at about 2.30 p.m., his first priority was to secure the streets leading to the castle from the San Elmo position on the right to a large white house overlooking the harbour on the left. But reaching the northern bounds of the town did not mean that fighting had ended, for he despatched patrols into the streets, many of which were very narrow.[87]

As fighting spread within the town, so did a major fire. At 2.00 p.m. there was a fire at the northern, lesser breach. At 2.48 p.m., Frazer reported 'Great fire and smoke in centre of town near the square'. Mines exploded while the French held a church and enclaves in the western part of the town. By 3.30 p.m. the fire was intense; 'Nothing of the town to be seen from excessive smoke'. Conditions were made worse by high winds, reported at 1.35 p.m., and rain starting about an hour later, both whipping up by 8.00 p.m. into a night of thunder and rain.[88]

Opinions differ as to the decisive action in achieving a breakthrough. Major General Hay acknowledged in his summary report of the 5th Division's actions, among other commendations, the valuable services of the Portuguese infantry in the attack on the right. The Portuguese entered the town from the small breach to the north of the main one. But he attributed the crucial breakthrough to the Royal Scots when they cleared the demi-bastion and drove the French from the curtain wall: 'I conceive our ultimate success depended upon the repeated attacks made by the Royal Scots'.[89] This focus on the 1st apparently down-graded the contribution of the 38th which seems also to have played a prominent role on the curtain wall.

For some participants, the timing of the second assault made a crucial difference. Launching the first assault before dawn on 25 July was criticized for creating great difficulties for small-group leadership. The second attempt avoided that mistake. According to Gomm, 'The attack of a breach by daylight is something new in the annals of modern warfare, and spectators say that the *coup d'oeil* answered their expectations'.[90] In fact, as we have indicated, Wellington participated in a similar day-time operation at Seringapatam. But the co-ordination of the attack from three directions – the isthmus, the sand-hills and the river crossing – as well as the clear sight of each step in the assault on the main breach allowed for a far more extensive and prolonged operation than had been possible in July.

Rey took a different view of what decided the assault, isolating two factors in particular. Despite mounting a determined resistance which forced the British, extraordinarily, to attack the main breach four times before they broke through, Rey bemoaned his lack of reserves to reinforce the breaches. But the more important factor was the accidental explosion among the munitions on the curtain wall. The explosion inflicted heavy casualties especially upon the French elite forces, the grenadiers, voltigeurs and the chasseurs de montagne, while it also spread confusion. Rey repeatedly insisted that without the destruction of the munitions, the British attack would have been held.[91] Lieutenant Colonel Burgoyne, RE, agreed: 'The difficulties of storming this breach were undoubtedly very great, and the enemy were sensible of it, and had proportionate confidence. Nor do I conceive we should have gained it, but for their premature explosion behind it.'[92]

The assault on 31 August gave the allies the town, but the garrison held fast to the castle. Rey initially hoped for rescue by Soult, but the marshal's bold plan for relieving San Sebastian failed at the battle at San Marcial on the very day of the second assault. Rey naturally tried to buoy up his own and his men's spirits by stressing the 'immense' casualties his men had inflicted on the British.[93] He had no intention of capitulating after the assault.

Notes

1. Sabine (ed.), *Letters*, 227.
2. Foy, *History of the War*, i, 209.
3. Wellington to Beresford, 27 August 1813, *WD*, xi, 47.
4. Graham to Wellington, 22, 25 August 1813, WP 1/374 (Folder 6).
5. Wellington to Bathurst, 2 September 1813, *WD*, xi, 61.
6. Wellington to Graham, 27 August 1813, *WD*, xi, 45–6; Jones, *Journals*, ii, 57–8, 60–1.
7. Gleig, *The Subaltern*, 17, 40.
8. Graham to Wellington, 26, 27 August 1813, WP 1/374 (Folder 6).

9. Gleig, *The Subaltern*, 17.
10. Hall, *Wellington's Navy*, 218.
11. Jones, *Journals*, ii, 59–62, 67; Sabine (ed.), *Letters*, 227.
12. Sabine (ed.), *Letters*, 223, 225–6, 234.
13. Sabine (ed.), *Letters*, 242.
14. Wellington to Graham, 23 August 1813, *WD*, xi, 31–3.
15. Jones, *Journals*, ii, 63–7.
16. Jones, *Journals*, ii, 67–70; Sabine (ed.), *Letters*, 230.
17. Larpent (ed.), *The Private Journal*, ii, 49.
18. Sabine (ed.), *Letters*, 230.
19. Jones, *Journals*, ii, 70–2, 332; Sabine (ed.), *Letters*, 232–3.
20. Sabine (ed.), *Letters*, 231.
21. Sabine (ed.), *Letters*, 242.
22. Jones, *Journals*, ii, 84–7, 91; Sabine (ed.), *Letters*, 261.
23. Glover (ed.), *A Gentleman Volunteer*, 129.
24. Jones, *Journals*, ii, 332.
25. Jones, *Journals*, ii, 333.
26. Gleig, *The Subaltern*, 30.
27. Graham to Wellington, 30 August 1813, WP 1/374 (Folder 6).
28. Robinson to Oswald, 5 August 1813, Wellington Papers 9/2/2/12.
29. Letters in *Royal Military Panorama*, ii (1813–14), 64, 159.
30. Graham to Wellington, 22 August 1813, WP 1/374 (Folder 6).
31. Larpent, *The Private Journal*, ii, 78–80.
32. Sabine (ed.), *Letters*, 230.
33. Graham to Wellington, 28 August 1813, WP 1/374 (Folder 6).
34. Wellington to Graham, 28 August 1813, *WD*, xi, 50.
35. Major B. Smyth, *A History of the Lancashire Fusiliers*, 2 vols (Dublin, 1903), i, 259.
36. Larpent (ed.), *The Private Journal*, ii, 80–1; Glover, *A Gentleman Volunteer*, 123–4; Hall, *A History of the Peninsular War*, viii, 429.
37. Carr-Gomm (ed.), *Letters and Journals*, 248, 250, 287.
38. Wellington to Liverpool, 7 April 1809, *WD*, ix, 37.
39. Rory Muir, *Salamanca 1812* (New Haven CT, 2001), 107–8, 110.
40. Cowper (ed.), *The King's Own* , i, 419.
41. M.S. Moorsom, *History of the 52nd Regiment 1755–1816* (Felling, 1996, repr. 1860 edn), 199.
42. Larpent (ed.), *The Private Journal*, ii, 82.
43. Wellington to the minister of war, 30 August 1813, *WD*, xi, 51–9.
44. Rey to Soult, 29 aout 1813, Belmas, *Sièges*, iv, 715–18.
45. Sabine (ed.), *Letters*, 230.
46. Belmas, *Sièges,* iv, 638.
47. Sabine (ed.), *Letters*, 233–4; Jones, *Journals*, ii, 72–3; Frazer confusingly describes being with number 5 battery, which has to be an error for number 15.
48. Rey to Soult, 31 aout 1813, Belmas, *Sièges*, iv, 718.
49. Sabine (ed.), *Letters*, 232.
50. Volunteer numbers are in *Royal Military Panorama*, iii (February 1814), 445.
51. Sabine (ed.), *Letters*, 233, 236–8.
52. Glover, *An Eloquent Soldier*, 178.
53. Carola Oman, *Sir John Moore* (London, 1953), 604–5; Muir, *Salamanca 1812*, 41.
54. Carr-Gomm (ed.), *Letters and journals*, 278, 280.
55. Thompson (ed.), *An Ensign in the Peninsular War*, 267.
56. Wrottesley, *Life and Correspondence*, i, 279.
57. Belmas, *Sièges*, iv, 639–41.
58. Cowper (ed.), *The King's Own*, i, 419–22; Wellington to Graham, 28 August 1813, *WD*, xi, 50.

59. Jones, *Journals*, iii, 84.
60. Henegan, *Seven Years Campaigning*, ii, 43.
61. Sabine (ed.), *Letters*, 236–8.
62. *Royal Military Panorama*, iii, 447 (February 1814).
63. Sabine (ed.), *Letters*, 236.
64. Thompson (ed.), *An Ensign in the Peninsular War*, 264.
65. *Royal Military Calendar*, v, 137; Moorsom, *History of the 52nd Regiment*, 201; Oman, *A History of the Peninsular War*, vii, 530.
66. Glover (ed.), *A Gentleman Volunteer*, 127.
67. Entered under Macbean, *Royal Military Calendar*, iv, 345–6.
68. Beatson, *A View of the Origin and Conduct of the War*, 99–106, 125–7.
69. Graham to Wellington, 1 September 1813, *WD*, xi, 62.
70. Graham to Wellington, 1 September, 1813, *WD*, xi, 62.
71. Sabine (ed.), *Letters*, 241.
72. Wrottesley, *Life and Correspondence*, i, 279–80.
73. Gleig, *The Subaltern*, 32.
74. Sabine (ed.), *Letters*, 241.
75. Henegan, *Seven Years Campaigning*, ii, 43.
76. Henegan, *Seven Years Campaigning*, ii, 45.
77. Graham to Wellington, 1 September 1813, *WD*, xi, 63; Sabine (ed.), *Letters*, 241; *New Annual Register for 1813*, 304–5.
78. *Royal Military Calendar*, iv, 396.
79. Sabine (ed.), *Letters*, 245.
80. Sabine (ed.), *Letters*, 253.
81. Jones, *Journals*, ii, 73–8; Sabine (ed.), *Letters*, 236–8; Belmas, *Sièges*, ii, 641–2.
82. Jones, *Journals*, ii, 79.
83. Carr-Gomm (ed.), *Letters and Journals*, 319.
84. Sabine (ed.), *Letters*, 237–9.
85. Sabine (ed.), *Letters*, 24–4, 252; Belmas, *Sièges*, iv, 642–3.
86. *Royal Military Panorama*, iii, 448–9 (February 1814).
87. Hay to Wellington, 18 October 1813, WP 12/1/8.
88. Sabine (ed.), *Letters*, 237–9.
89. *Royal Military Panorama*, iii, 448 (February 1814).
90. Carr-Gomm (ed.), *Letters and Journals*, 319.
91. Rey to Soult 31, aout 1813 (two despatches), Belmas, *Sièges*, iv, 718–23.
92. Wrottesley, *Life and Correspondence*, i, 280.
93. Rey to Soult, 31 aout 1813 (two despatches), Belmas, *Sièges*, iv, 721–2.

Chapter 10

The Impact of the Assault

Critiques of British Performance

As we have seen, the British conduct of the siege was severely criticized. Lieutenant Colonel Gomm, commanding the 9th in the 5th Division, immediately accused both 'those Philistines, the Engineers' and artillery officers of failing to apply scientific methods at the first assault. Victory at Ciudad Rodrigo and Badajos, 'owing to the almost miraculous efforts of our troops', stunted their professional development during the campaign.[1] Captain John Blakiston, an engineer in the Anglo-Portuguese army, published his wartime memoirs in 1829 when he was on half-pay. He concluded that the heavy loss of manpower, substantial expenditure of ammunition and 'the destruction of a fine town belonging to our allies' were 'unnecessary'. A classic siege conducted by a brigade combined with an effective naval blockade by a brig or two would have forced an eventual French surrender.[2] For Major Hay, the assault confirmed the British troops' fighting prowess; no other troops in Europe, in his view, would have taken San Sebastian in such circumstances. But success was dearly bought. He asserted that whereas the tardy and slow-witted often fell to the enemy in battle, it was the bravest, keenest and most dedicated officers who were killed and wounded in sieges.[3] Predictably, John Jones also insisted that a steadier, more scientific approach would have been more effective than assaults causing heavy casualties in an intensive effort 'not to be expected from ordinary troops'.[4] In 1930, Charles Oman noted that the siege had been of 'little credit to British engineering science' and insisted that 'there is little to commend in the whole conduct of the siege save the desperate courage of the regimental officers and the rank and file'.[5]

Two senior technical officers later offered public critiques of the British performance at San Sebastian. A wide-ranging assessment by a Royal Engineer appeared in Sir John Jones' journals. These were initially published in the 1810s to draw 'general attention to the very inefficient composition and inadequate strength of the siege establishments of the empire, which certainly at that period had the effect of rendering our attacks of fortified places far less certain and less powerful than our natural advantages, great resources, and liberal military expenditure, entitled the nation to expect'.[6]

The extensive journals were republished in 1846, with additional material, by the author's brother, Lieutenant Colonel Harry Jones. Sir John was an ambitious and influential commander. He had been commissioned into the Royal Engineers in 1798 and served with distinction at Badajoz.[7] As late as 1841, he was sent to review Gibraltar's fortifications and the government accepted 'his irrefragable opinion' that extensive remodelling was needed.[8] On his death, a statue was erected in St Paul's Cathedral. He was 'known to civilians as well as military men by his work on the *Sieges in Spain*'.[9] Admittedly, he assessed operations at San Sebastian from the official records rather than personal experience, since he was absent from that particular siege.[10] His judgement may also have been shaped by the fact that his son led the forlorn hope at the first assault, where he was wounded and taken prisoner.

Jones argued that insufficient artillery had been applied in the first attack. If enough artillery had been deployed, the horn-work could have been taken with little loss to the assailants. Heavy artillery fire should have been directed from the Chofre sand-hills on the east bank to enfilade the horn-work, supported by strong British firepower from the San Bartolomeo position and the parallels in front of it. With the French artillery and infantry on the horn-work suppressed in hours rather than days, the British would have been able to push their trenches forward and gain access to the horn-work. Their batteries on the east bank would then have smashed a breach in the river wall, while the isthmus artillery created a breach on the curtain wall behind the horn-work. With covering fire from British troops positioned on the captured horn-work, the breaches would have been taken without severe loss.[11] In Jones's view, the critical step, denying the French defenders the use of the main breach's flanks, could have been achieved only by securing the horn-work first. Casualties would also have been cut by suppressing French artillery fire upon the main breach from the castle. Neither deployment nor bombardment was speedy at San Sebastian, where, according to Jones, the British failed to mount 'a scientific attack'.[12]

Jones's assessment depended on hindsight. But the decision not to take the horn-work first was strongly questioned at the time, especially when planning for the second assault. Wellington and his senior engineer, Sir Richard Fletcher, rejected the argument of the second in command of the Royal Engineers, John Burgoyne, that the main objective should be the eastern end of the horn-work and the curtain wall behind it.[13] Fletcher argued that the works across the isthmus were 'very formidable' and would have to be battered in front by a large train for 30 to 35 days. The second assault, therefore, had to retrace the original line of attack, but with more 24-pounders placed in the batteries on the Urumea River's east bank than were available in July.[14]

A different criticism was that the assault could have thwarted French firepower in the horn-work without seizing the horn-work. Colin Campbell, who was a 21-year-old subaltern at San Sebastian, argued privately twenty years later that the first assault failed because the British advance from the trenches to the main breach was too dispersed and too staggered. It should have been undertaken by dense columns to counter the effects of heavy French fire. It should also have occurred in daylight. Officers simply could not lead their men effectively in the confused conditions which prevailed in the dark at the breach. Properly organized, more troops could have been marched into the breach and seized it.[15]

An important topic for discussion was the quality of the artillery available for siege operations. Sir John May published a succinct set of reflections in 1819. Commissioned into the Royal Artillery in 1795, May became a brevet Lieutenant Colonel in 1812 and participated in many of the important engagements from Badajoz to Toulouse, including San Sebastian, to the spring of 1814. He also served, as Assistant Adjutant General, at Waterloo, receiving a KCB at the end of the long wars.

May stressed that the reliability as well as the number and size of guns determined the artillery's impact. A comparison of the time it took for the British and French to suppress walled towns led May, from his experience at San Sebastian in July, to conclude that British iron guns were superior to French brass guns. Iron guns suffered from the expansion of the entry into the vent after heavy use; the vent was the narrow tube through which the fuse reached the gunpowder. The repeated lighting of fuses at the vent entry caused melting and the enlargement of the hole. But that did not affect the accuracy or frequency of fire. May noted that an iron 24-pounder could fire 300–50 rounds in 15 hours at 500–700yd without damaging the bore, or main barrel of the gun. It could keep on doing that for 3,000 rounds. Brass guns, however, were limited to 100–20 rounds in 24 hours and suffered expanding bores, and therefore diminished accuracy, if pushed harder. The British artillery's ability to fire over the heads of their advancing troops at the breach on 31 August depended upon the high accuracy of iron guns even after heavy previous use. If the British had preferred iron because it was substantially cheaper than brass, they soon found that iron guns were also far superior in firepower.[16]

Although the iron guns withstood the demands of the first siege, they did wear out. Commissary Henegan pointed out that 'The unceasing vomiting of destructive missiles at the first attack . . . had not only caused the metal to droop at the muzzle, but had so enlarged the vents of the guns, that few of them were at all serviceable.'[17] Alert to the need for technical modifications, Lieutenant Colonel Frazer of the Royal Horse Artillery wrote 'long letters home on the subject of the vents of our guns, and recommended their being bushed with fine copper'. After the lengthy bombardment of late August, the vents in some guns had become distorted with use. Frazer thought this was because the iron had been made soft, in order to prevent the vents bursting. He suggested that the vents' durability would be enhanced by adding fine copper. That had been done at Elvas in 1811 after the Portuguese guns suffered severe deterioration at Badajoz. Another complaint was that many 8in howitzer shells burst immediately on being discharged.[18]

Possessing effective guns achieved little if they were poorly used. The besiegers' artillery should have completed three distinctive tasks. First, the defenders' guns needed to be taken out of action and fire from the infantry on the walls and in the flanking towers suppressed. Secondly, heavy guns would create a breach with an intensive bombardment using shot. Thirdly, vertical fire from mortars would prevent the defenders repairing their defences or erecting new defences behind the crumbling breaches.

May argued that the heavy breaching guns should not have opened fire until what he called the ricochet guns had taken out enemy guns commanding the breach. Instead, French guns at the castle continued to play upon the breach during the British assault. May claimed that if the castle guns had been suppressed, the British breaching guns would have created the breach within one day. The breaching guns' efforts should also have been more fully supported by mortars and howitzers to prevent the French erecting defences behind the breach. If the defenders' artillery had not been suppressed within two days at most, May argued that a formal, gradualist and time-consuming siege should have been mounted, avoiding a direct infantry assault upon a breach still exposed to the defenders' guns.[19] This was a serious judgement on the heavy casualties suffered by attempting a speedy breakthrough at San Sebastian unsupported by rigorous artillery tactics.

A more technical, but still significant, tactical criticism offered by Blakiston was noted in Chapter 7. He argued that the British should have positioned their artillery batteries only at the last feasible moment, so as to disguise their intentions from the enemy. Final assaults in British sieges in India generally depended on bringing up artillery at night and then unleashing brief bombardments, quickly followed by storming breaches thus speedily made.[20] At San Sebastian difficult access to the isthmus from Pasajes and the lack of readily available and large supplies of labour made the rapid deployment of heavy guns impossible.

These criticisms reinforced the argument that the siege took too long. May tried to determine how much heavy artillery might be required to seize a defended town. On the one hand, Ciudad Rodrigo, Badajoz and San Sebastian possessed traditional, pre-Vauban fortifications offering relatively simple targets to the attacker. On the other hand, assaulting walled towns required the transportation of heavy guns long distances across difficult terrain or by sea. After analysing the three great sieges of 1812–13, May estimated the time it might take to open and seize a breach before the defenders could repair it. He found that the desired results could be attained by using fifty guns of 24-pounds calibre. At San Sebastian, he argued that the main breach attacked on 25 July had been created in two-and-a-half days of firing by twenty 24-pounders. With daylight lasting from 4.30 a.m. to just after 8.00 p.m. the British had 15½ hours available each day for their bombardment. If fifty guns had been deployed, the breach of 100ft in width would have been created within a day. This would have left no time for the defenders to repair the breach. The assault could, therefore, have been immediate. There would have been no need for a subsidiary breach, which took up a fourth day of firing, on 23 July. May insisted that at San Sebastian, as at Ciudad Rodrigo and Badajoz, an assault on the evening of the bombardment would have been feasible if fifty powerful guns had been at work all day.[21]

Jones made a different point, based on the artillery resources actually available. He distinguished between the active siege, when the trenches were open, and the time taken for the full operation, including the preparation of the gun sites, the installation of the gun batteries and the long pause between the first assault and the arrival of the siege train. The active siege, including the attack on the castle during 1–8 September, had lasted thirty days, not he stressed, particularly long in comparison with French sieges in the Peninsula. But the costs had been high, with 3,500 casualties suffered and 70,000 rounds of artillery ammunition consumed in taking a very small town with limited fortifications. He argued that the entire operation could have taken sixteen days instead of thirty at the cost of far fewer casualties.[22]

This argument raises an obvious question: did the French conduct Peninsular sieges more efficiently? At Ciudad Rodrigo in 1810, the town was thoroughly reconnoitred on 30–1 May. Poor roads and delays in obtaining enough transport wagons and horses to pull them meant that work on digging trenches began only on 15 June. The artillery opened the bombardment on 25 June and the breach was assaulted on 10 July. The active siege lasted twenty-six days. But the Spanish surrendered once French troops reached the breach; there was no phase of fighting to capture defensive positions within the town, as was required to secure the castle at San Sebastian. The French needed 1 assault rather than 2 and lost 1,225 casualties compared with the allies' 3,500 at San Sebastian. But the French bombardment destroyed many houses and killed many civilians.[23] In surrendering when the breach was taken, the Spanish garrison commander may have been more sensitive to the consequences for those remaining in the town if the French had to fight to gain it than Rey was at San Sebastian.

The French record in Peninsular sieges did not suggest that easy victories were likely. But it is possible that Wellington's Indian experience made him over-optimistic in assessing the challenges posed by sieges. The defences at Seringapatam and Gawilgarh were breached by artillery of lesser calibre than the guns needed in Europe. The besieging army at Seringapatam was well-equipped, but its most powerful guns were only 18-pounders. Yet these created the necessary breach, while less powerful guns ensured that the Mysoreans' defensive artillery was neutralized before the assault went in. In Spain, Wellington began his bombardments, optimistically, with relatively few 24-pounder guns. Despite the fact that seizing Spanish fortified towns had cost him dear in 1812, his dispositions suggest that he repeatedly underestimated the depth and intensity of French resistance. Perhaps the ease of *entry* into Seringapatam served as a misleading precedent. One British officer there described Tipu Sultan's army as poorly led and poorly paid. Tipu had created a top-heavy, ill-educated officer corps based on favouritism and discrimination against non-Muslims. He had expected that the invading army would eventually run short of food and would not be capable of attacking the city's walls before the Cauvery's waters rose to make the river impossible to ford. But when the breach was made prior to those eventualities, he appeared to become withdrawn, incapable of action and fatalistic.[24] Obviously, Tipu's reactions were *sui generis*, but Wellington may have over-estimated the impact a successful breach made on defenders' morale. It is possible also that the French army's collapse at Vitoria and its hurried retreat from the second clash at Sorauren led him to under-estimate French resolve at San Sebastian, where they had not been hard-pressed at the first assault. Wellington possessed a broad enough experience to understand that no tactical blueprint would resolve any given siege, but he may still have failed fully to balance the lessons of Ciudad Rodrigo and Badajoz against those of Seringapatam and Gawilgarh.

On one important factor, however, Jones agreed entirely with Wellington. The first assault did not fail, as some claimed, because of inadequate manpower. Adding extra troops to the assault on 25 July would have resulted, he insisted, simply in higher losses. The problem was insufficient artillery in the first assault, and lack of concentration on the horn-work throughout. System had been sacrificed to speed in planning and preparing the first assault, but the failure on 25 July ensured that the siege became far more protracted than it should have been:

> the operations against St Sebastian afford a most impressive lesson on the advantages of proceeding step by step, and with due attention to science and rule in the attack on fortified places; for the effort there made (though necessary) to overcome or trample on such restrictions, caused an easy and certain operation of eighteen or twenty days to extend through a space of sixty days, and to cost the besiegers 3,500 officers and men killed, wounded, or made prisoners . . .

Success had depended upon a military effort 'not to be expected from ordinary troops'.[25]

The Cost of British Victory
If Vitoria reduced the French army to a broken rabble, the siege of San Sebastian restored the French reputation for tenacity and courage. For example, Captain Blakiston, with long experience of warfare in India, remarked that the initial plan for taking San Bartolomeo 'would probably have succeeded with an ordinary enemy' but 'the French showed that they were not to be bullied out of the place in this manner'.[26] Continuing in similar vein and admittedly with hindsight, he described the first assault as: 'a kind of half-and-half business, which might succeed against a timid enemy; but which was most likely to fail against such troops as the French, who, by the laws of Napoleon, were bound to stand at least one assault before they surrendered'.[27]

The surrender of Pamplona in October reinforced that reputation. The city boasted such elaborate, strong fortifications that blockade proved the only option, being conducted by the Spanish army, supplemented by British Royal Engineers.[28] The widespread assumption that Pamplona's food stocks would last a few months proved accurate.[29] It was so effectively blockaded that 'sheer starvation', according to Surtees, forced its larger garrison of 4,000 troops to surrender.[30] When, in November 1813 Private William Wheeler recorded its classic capitulation, he admired the French soldiers' dedication to duty:

> Pampaluna [*sic*] held out until the 31st October. A considerable time before they surrendered the Garrison was reduced to the greatest privation, not an animal of any description escaped the butcher save the Governor's horse. Dogs, cats and rats were all devoured, and when they marched out with the honors of war, so gastly [*sic*] were the appearance of the men that one would have supposed they had all risen from their graves. I was told, by some who witnessed the sight that the men could scarcely stand, they held out until completely starved. What more could be expected from them. They are an honor to the Imperial Army and to their country.[31]

For the British, the losses sustained at the second assault demonstrated the importance of restoring reputation after the failure of 25 July. Oman gave a grand total of killed, wounded and missing on 31 August as 2,376. The core of the attacking force consisted of six British and six Portuguese infantry battalions. Nine of those battalions constituted the 5th Division and three battalions constituted Bradford's Portuguese Brigade. In addition some 750 volunteers were drawn from 3 other divisions and their specialist forces as well. The forces committed to the whole operation, though not necessarily involved in the fighting, amounted to about 9,000 officers and men.

One party, commanded by Lieutenant Colonel John Hunt, consisted of volunteers from the Light Division. The 52nd supplied a contingent of two officers, eight sergeants and corporals, and thirty men. Lieutenant Augustus Harvest was killed and six of the officers, sergeants, and corporals were wounded. Of the thirty privates, two were killed and eleven wounded. Half the men of the storming party were casualties, a very high proportion. These men came from seven different companies, so their cohesion under fire owed something to a sense of identity beyond the immediate peer group or indeed company.[32] It is often argued, from research initially done on troops' experience during the Second World War, that fighting spirit is forged from platoon and company loyalty and commitment. Yet the willingness to volunteer at San Sebastian revealed the importance of both small-group and broader military identities, with many men fighting in unfamiliar formations and motivated in part by a desire to uphold the military reputations of their division and of the army as a whole.

From the 43rd, Lieutenant John O'Connell, who had participated in the assaults at Ciudad Rodrigo and Badajoz, two sergeants and 30 men (including three sergeants who joined the ranks for the occasion) volunteered. O'Connell was wounded by grape and musket fire and both sergeants were badly wounded. Of the thirty men, five were killed and fourteen wounded.[33] Among the 200 volunteers from the 4th Division, who had marched from Lesaca the previous day, the 23 officers and men of the 20th suffered 4 killed and all the others wounded. Those killed included the commander of the 200 divisional volunteers, Brevet Major Alexander Rose of the 20th. These men, of both the Light Division and the 4th Division, were not in the first waves of attack on the main breach. The 1st Battalion of the 4th Regiment, as part of the 5th Division, was. It lost 122 killed and 176 wounded during the entire siege of San Sebastian.[34]

The 500 or so Portuguese rank and file from Bradford's brigade lost heavily in crossing the Urumea River. The 250 men of the 13th Portuguese Line, under Snodgrass, lost 26 officers and men killed and 47 wounded, while the similar number of rank and file of the 24th Line, under Lieutenant Colonel M'Bean, suffered 47 killed and 35 wounded. The other small volunteer contingents lost heavily. The King's German Legion volunteers from the 1st Division lost 53 of 100 men; the 300 men from the Guards brigades of that division suffered 122 casualties.[35]

The 5th Division more than vindicated itself. The division suffered 1,783 casualties at the second assault and 2,503 casualties for the whole period 28 July to 31 August. This heavy attrition afflicted all the battalions, as well as Bradford's Portuguese brigade which fought beside it in the assault. (See the table below.)[36]

Casualties in the 5th Division at San Sebastian, 28 July–31 August 1813

	Officers K/W		Sergeants K/W		Other Ranks K/W (Incl. Drummers)	
Battalions of the 5th Division engaged in the assault						
1st Brigade under Hay, then Greville						
3/1st	1	5	3	9	43	133
1/9th	4	7	5	2	42	106
1/38th	3	10	–	2	32	87
2nd Brigade under Robinson, then Brooke						
1/4th	5	6	7	10	107	146
2/47th	7	10	9	8	19*	119
2/59th	8	14	4	8	106	214
Portuguese brigade under Sprye						
	8	19	incl. under men		119	182
Separate from 5th Division						
From Bradford's Portuguese brigade						
	4	8	incl. under men		90	82

* Interpolating from Oman's figures, this must be 79.

Lieutenant Colonel Gomm of the 9th wrote after the attack that 'All circumstances considered, it is very gratifying to us all (of the Division I mean) to have been forced at length to carry the town by assault'. The six weeks following the first assault had subjected the 5th Division to wholly unfounded doubts about the men's 'patience and endurance of hard labour' and 'their intrepidity in the hour of assault'. Success at the second attempt served to vindicate the Division's efforts in the first.[37] He wrote home on 9 October, 'I am glad you are all pleased with us at San Sebastian, for we were obliged to put up with many insults here during its progress'.[38]

It is worth emphasizing that the 5th Division, so publicly dismissed for its lack of commitment after the first assault, suffered heavy losses during the campaign. Its strength on 25 May, when the campaign began, stood at 6,725 men. This total included Sprye's large Portuguese brigade of 2,372. At Vitoria on 21 June, the heaviest casualties were taken by the 2nd and 3rd Divisions. Among the seven divisions deployed in that battle, those two divisions accounted for 2,082 of the 3,475 casualties suffered by the British and King's German Legion, and 433 of 921 Portuguese casualties. Even so, the 5th suffered the third highest divisional total, at 496 casualties for the British brigades and 81 among the Portuguese. At the final storming of San Sebastian, the 5th lost 1,783 casualties. Of those, 675 men were killed. At Vitoria, 12.5 per cent of the division's British casualties were killed; at San Sebastian the proportion killed was an enormous 37.8 per cent.

The heaviest losses – 865 of 1,783 – were in the brigade commanded by Major General Frederick Robinson. That brigade's battalions, the 2/59th, the 1/4th and the 2/47th suffered 352, 281 and 232 casualties respectively, following losses of 149, 91 and 112 at Vitoria. The brigade's total strength on 25 May had been 2,061 officers and men, including a company (say 100 soldiers) of Brunswickers. By early September the three battalions had taken 1,217 casualties. Of course, some of those wounded received light injuries or wounds which healed within weeks. Some were wounded in both Vitoria and San Sebastian. But collectively these men took a terrible pounding between 21 June and 31 August.

Taking comparisons back to Salamanca in July 1812 is difficult because there had been changes in the division's composition since then. Robinson's brigade contained only one battalion, the 1/4th, which fought at Salamanca. But three battalions served in the 1st Brigade throughout the period July 1812– September 1813.[39] Their losses are given in the table below.

Battle Casualties of the 5th Division's 1st Brigade, 1812–13

	Salamanca	Vitoria	San Sebastian	(Strength at Salamanca)
3/1st	160	111	194	761
1/9th	46	25	166	666
1/38th	143	8	134	800

While not as intense as Robinson's brigade's experience, these men had faced severe fighting in two or three spasms in little over a year.

Despite suffering such losses, the six British battalions in the division continued to be operational, if relatively weak. On 25 May those battalions amounted to about 3,950 officers and men. At the battle of the Nivelle on 10 November those six battalions numbered 2,788 officers and men or an average of 465 officers and men each. The 2/47th fielded only 345 officers and men, the second lowest complement in the army involved at the Nivelle. Not surprisingly, these six, numerically weak battalions took little part in the sharpest fighting. Altogether they suffered 136 casualties at the crossing of the Bidassoa, with the 3 battalions of Robinson's brigade accounting for only 14 of them. At the Nivelle the 6 battalions' 2,788 officers and men suffered fewer than 20 of the 2,526 Anglo-Portuguese casualties on that day. At the Nive, however, from 9–11 December, the 6 battalions lost 414 casualties on 10 December and, together with the 2/84th, suffered a further 506 casualties on 9 and 11 December. These were significant, since the Anglo-Portuguese army lost approximately 5,000 casualties from extensive fighting.

Obviously, the battalions received replacements during those months, and some men recovered quickly from their wounds, while some may been casualties more than once between June and December. After suffering so severely in less than six months, they were not heavily engaged from mid-December. But the winter brought its own miseries; rains were heavy, with roads reportedly 'knee-deep in mud', and sickness was rampant. After the weather improved somewhat, the Division was engaged from 26 February in the siege of Bayonne, initially headquartered at Anglet. Much work had to be done in establishing defences across roads and in the farmhouses and villages, but the Division was deployed to the quieter stretches of the siege lines.[40] For example, the 3/1st, 1/9th, 2/47th together suffered only seveny-eight casualties when they ended their war at the siege of Bayonne.

It should be noted that the 6 Portuguese battalions involved at the assault on San Sebastian fielded 4,674 officers and men on 25 May but saw their strength by 10 November fall to 3,379. Thus Portuguese as well as British battalions committed to the second assault lost heavily during this phase of the long campaign.[41]

In addition to depleting particular battalions, the assault resulted in heavy losses among officers. This was a common consequence of battle. Officers took up exposed positions in leading their men and opposing forces often targeted their opponents' officers; moreover, private soldiers 'were much more likely than officers to slip away to the rear'.[42] Oman criticized the lack of science in the final assault. More might be said of the desperate pressure which an assault of this nature placed upon those managing it in detail. *The Times* reflected that while Wellington's army received a steady stream of reinforcements, it was losing too many officers who were 'too prone to court danger for its own sake': 'the talents of many of the officers, both among the killed and wounded, were of a superior class; their experience was great, and the value of their services could only be appreciated justly by those who had long been in the habit of relying on their counsel or assistance'.[43] The criticism that officers took excessive risks ignored the fact that assaulting breaches was highly dangerous and required close management at the front.

Officers' Professional Experience

The collective effort also indicated the strength of officers' professional networks and *esprit de corps*. The sense of commitment was well demonstrated by the 5th Division's commander, Lieutenant General Sir James Leith, who left his forward position only after his left arm was broken. Hoping he would not lose the arm, Gomm noted that 'General Leith, behaving as usual, was struck several times, at last very severely'.[44]

The 5th Division's 2nd Brigade followed the forlorn hope on to the breach. Its commander, Major General Robinson, was badly wounded in the face and had to return to base. Companies from the 2nd Brigade's three battalions participated. The officers in command of two – Major Kelly of the 47th and Captain (acting Major) Scott of the 59th – were killed, and their replacements – Captains Livesay and Pilkington respectively – were wounded and in turn replaced. Of the 38 officers killed on the 31st no fewer than 20 belonged to those 3 regiments, as were 28 of the 69 officers wounded; significantly 20 of those 28 wounded suffered severe wounds, a high proportion. The

Royal Engineers lost their commanding officer, Lieutenant Colonel Sir Richard Fletcher, killed by musket-fire from the horn-work; his successor, Burgoyne, though not severely wounded, retired with heavy bleeding from a head wound.[45]

The senior officers engaged understood the challenges and dangers they faced in assaulting the breaches. Indeed, the extent of officers' acquaintance with sieges, given historians' general disregard for siege warfare in this period, was striking. At the grassroots level, the Royal Artillery officers at the second siege certainly had the opportunity to learn from the first siege; of the twenty-five such officers at the first siege, eighteen served in the second, reinforced by fifteen others.[46] Senior commanders, from their service over the years, were very likely to have acquired detailed information about siege warfare. Graham, in overall command, had visited Gibraltar in 1793 and, as a Brigadier General, led the siege of Valetta on Malta in 1797–9. Leith had been commissioned in 1780. He was posted to Gibraltar in 1784 and it would be inconceivable that he did not hear a great deal about the four-year siege which had ended only the previous year. He was involved in operations against fortifications as an ADC at Toulon in 1793. His later career landed him in campaigns which resulted in difficult fighting or heavy casualties. Becoming a Lieutenant Colonel in 1794, he raised fencibles in Aberdeenshire and led them in Ireland during the rising of 1798. As a Major General, he commanded a brigade under Moore in 1808–9 up to and including the battle at La Coruña. After going to Walcheren, he led what became the 5th Division in the Peninsula from 1810 and commanded it at Badajoz and Salamanca.[47] Oswald had been posted to Gibraltar in 1790, while Fletcher worked on fortifications there in 1798–1803. Major General Andrew Hay, who replaced Robinson, served in Gibraltar, among other postings, in 1798–1802.[48] Lieutenant Colonel Rodolphus Bodecker, who commanded a battalion of the King's German Legion at San Sebastian, had served as an ensign throughout the siege of Gibraltar in 1779–83 and was Town Major of the fortifications at Copenhagen after it was taken in 1807.[49]

Again, the breakthrough at the crest of the breach was made by Lieutenant Colonel James Barnes of the 1st Royal Scots and Lieutenant Colonel Edward Miles of the 38th. Barnes became an ensign in the Royals in 1792, saw action at Toulon in 1793, in Corsica, and with Abercromby in Holland in 1799 and in Egypt in 1801. He had served variously in the West Indies and in the Mediterranean, including at Gibraltar and Malta. After promotion to Lieutenant Colonel, he served in the Walcheren campaign of 1809, and then from March 1810 in the Peninsula, being wounded at Salamanca. Miles similarly entered the regiment he commanded at San Sebastian as an ensign, in 1794. He too saw early action, that same year, at Lincelles in Holland. He served in the West Indies in 1796–1801, participating in a number of minor sieges. He went with the 38th to Portugal in 1808 and evacuated from La Coruña. Like Barnes, he joined the Walcheren expedition, as a major. He returned to the Peninsula in 1812 and commanded the 38th at Salamanca, where he also was wounded. He recovered in time to go to Burgos, to fight at Vitoria and to be severely wounded at San Sebastian. But the latter occurred only after he entered the town, as one of the first to do so. In 1817, his coat of arms was augmented to include the depiction of a bastion captioned San

Sebastian and the battlements of a ruined fortification containing a grenadier of the 38th carrying that regiment's colours.[50]

The officers who led the Portuguese troops had equally extensive track records. Major General Bradford had begun his military career as a volunteer ensign in October 1793, and had served as a major in the Nottingham Fencibles during the Irish rebellion of 1798. He joined a line regiment, as a major in the 87th, only in 1805 and then went to Hanover before participating in the siege of Monte Video and the street fighting in Buenos Aires. He fought at Vimiero and La Coruña in 1808–9 before becoming a brevet Colonel in 1810 and Assistant Adjutant General in the Peninsula.[51] Lieutenant Colonel William M'Bean (later Macbean) had served in Holland in 1794, the Irish rebellion of 1798 (including at Vinegar Hill), and in the Peninsula from 1808. From 1809 he trained the Portuguese 19th Line and led it in a charge at Bussaco. He was badly wounded at Benevente, and fought at Salamanca.[52] Brevet Lieutenant Colonel Kenneth Snodgrass became an ensign when war resumed in October 1803. Now aged 29, he had attracted the attention of Sir John Moore in 1805, had gone to Sicily as adjutant of the 52nd in 1806, then in 1808 to Sweden in Moore's expedition and later in that year to Portugal. From the battle of La Coruña in January 1809 to July 1813, he fought in at least nine actions, including the assault on Ciudad Rodrigo, an action in the retreat from Burgos, and at Vitoria. He was wounded while commanding an assault party in his tenth engagement, at San Sebastian on 25 July, and severely wounded at Orthes in 1814.[53]

The commanding officers of the main contingents of volunteers were Majors Rose and Hunt. Alexander Rose, who was killed, had been commissioned in 1794 and joined the 20th in 1796, becoming a Brevet Major in 1812. Rose served in Holland, Menorca and Egypt (at the attack on Alexandria). He fought at Maida and in the retreat to La Coruña. After going to Walcheren, he led light troops at Vitoria. A very popular officer, he was described as 'high-spirited, brave . . . of an excellent temper'.[54] John Hunt, commissioned in 1799, had served at Ferrol and Cádiz and in Portugal in 1800–1. He was an ADC to Sir John Moore in Sicily, Sweden and Portugal in 1807—8. He fought in the campaign which ended at La Coruña, and then participated in the Walcheren expedition. Returning to the Peninsula in 1811, he commanded the 1/52nd at Badajoz and at Salamanca, and temporarily took charge of a brigade at Badajoz. Having been badly wounded at San Sebastian, where his 'ringing voice' was heard above the clamour as he urged on volunteers from the Light Division, he was promoted to Lieutenant Colonel and appointed to a post at Horse Guards.[55]

Although it is clear that many middle-ranking and senior officers at San Sebastian had extensive experience of siege warfare, it is exceptionally difficult to determine how far officers informally discussed and evaluated their previous professional experiences. They did not write reflective letters on past campaigns. Before the 1820s very few wrote memoirs or semi-historical accounts. But the occasional major court martial, notably for this study Whitelocke's following the failure at Buenos Aires, showed that senior officers could review past operations in considerable detail. At the very top, Wellington presumably had no objections to the daring river crossing launched across the Urumea by the Portuguese brigade at a critical point in the second assault. It replicated the main attack across the Cauvery (or Kaveri) River at Seringapatam. We have no evidence that the precedent was ever discussed, but officers with memories stretching back fourteen years would have been aware of that fundamental aspect of that celebrated attack.

But, even for officers of such lengthy and varied experience as Wellington commanded, the main breach at San Sebastian was a cruel challenge: a tiny, exposed place, treacherous to climb, immensely difficult to find level footing on, seemingly impassable as a route into the town, and riddled by French firepower. Infantry officers and men had perfected battle tactics based on long, line formations of two men deep; they fired by volley, aiming only at concentrated bodies of enemy soldiers; and they charged in line to bayonet their opponents. In assaulting breaches, this training was of limited relevance. With little more than skill in improvisation and their courage, determination and professional pride to rely on, the assailants acted with impressive commitment in the knowledge of what faced them.

Not surprisingly, the main British reaction to the assault was not analysis or assessment or regret but pride in the troops' bravery. John Atchison reported to his father on 31 August:

> Whatever may have been the discredit which the British Army suffered by the defeat at San Sebastian [i.e. on 25 July], it has been most fully compensated by the success there today – in no instance since the commencement of the Peninsular War has it had more obstacles to encounter and in no instance – not even the capture of Badajoz – have they been more gloriously overcome. The conduct of every man engaged was so truly admirable, that no words in our language can do them justice – it required to be seen to be conceived; and when history should give to future ages the simple narrative of this day's deeds – they will excite admiration rather than belief.[56]

In his celebrated account of twenty-five years in the Rifle Brigade, published in 1833, William Surtees records visiting the town a few days after San Sebastian's surrender. He went up to the castle to inspect the works, incidentally getting a panoramic view. It was 'a melancholy spectacle' where 'the houses were still on fire', with only 'half-dozen in the whole town that remained habitable'. Yet what impressed him was the 'glorious exhibition of British valour and prowess' at the assault. Volunteers from his own division participated in it, 'sustained their full share of the casualties' and demonstrated through necessary sacrifices their courage and commitment.[57]

Other Factors Influencing the Outcome

The quest for group vindication and honour and the commitment of officers fully aware of the challenges which assaults posed were key factors in the operation to end the siege. But other contingent factors came into play.

First, the river, the bay and the sea played an important role in determining the character of this operation. Sea power did not, of course, play a direct part in the assault itself, even though Wellington had perhaps hoped for some form of naval attack from the sea, meeting Collier on the 29th to seek such assistance.[58] Yet one of the most dramatic moments was when the Portuguese brigade waded across the Urumea River to attack the small, northern breach. It is not clear whether those troops entered the town before the men on the main breach. On the opposite side of the isthmus, the British deployed a small force on Isla Santa Clara to inflict an irritating fire upon the western walls of the castle and thus upon that part of the town where the French held out longest. Finally, the sea enabled the British to stage a demonstration of power; just after midday on 31 August, twenty-nine boats, most of them small craft, were visible a mile and more off the coast, perhaps adding psychological pressure on the French, although there was never any intention of attempting a landing.[59]

The naval presence was more imposing than at any other time in the campaign. The squadron normally consisted of one frigate, the *Surveillante* of thirty-eight guns, and smaller warships of eighteen guns or fewer. It was briefly reinforced with the presence of *Ajax*, a ship of the line of 74 guns, 5 more frigates each of 36 or 38 guns, 3 brigs of 18 or 12 guns, and 5 smaller craft.[60] These warships were deployed on various tasks to support the attack on the castle. Some were based at Isla Santa Clara, opposite the castle headland and commanding the entrance to the bay to the town's west. The island had been seized by the British only days earlier. The three brigs and a cutter were stationed in the Bidassoa River or patrolling off its estuary, presumably to watch for and possibly help limit French movements across that river. Four of the frigates anchored off San Sebastian. The firepower available from the Royal navy vastly exceeded the capability of the artillery on land. But little of it was usable in the attacks on town or castle. In his despatch of 9 September, Captain Collier reported that 'gales now blow home, and the sea is prodigious', so virtually all his ships had to go out to sea in order to avoid being driven ashore.[61] Private Wheeler does record that 'A heavy fire from our ships of war was kept up' on the castle during the assault on 31 August, but this was not described as having any significant impact.[62] Frazer noted at 8.00 a.m., hours before the assault, that 'There is to be a demonstration by sea, but no troops are to attempt to land; it is judged too difficult. The tide is fast receding.'[63] Since the assault had to be launched at low tide, close naval involvement was impossible. The worst the squadron could do was to make conditions more trying at the castle. Significantly, Wellington mentioned the naval squadron's 'cordial assistance' in one paragraph of his despatch, and focused there specifically on seamen's work in the land batteries. Graham noted Captain Sir George Collier's 'zealous co-operation' in three lines of his lengthy official report to Wellington.[64] Collier tried to tighten control after San Sebastian fell. Facing a continuing threat from local French raiding at sea, he secured Wellington's agreement that he should act against all vessels 'hovering about the coast' between Pasajes and the Bidassoa River and ban fishing between Pasajes and Figueras, while allowing it off the Bidassoa estuary.[65]

Various challenges arose in managing Pasajes's harbour, where overcrowding by 5 September made entry difficult and dangerous. Other disruptions followed. A few days later, high seas dispersed small ships outside Pasajes and ensured that 'no vessel can get out of the harbour'. There was an incident of arson, with Royal Navy sailors tackling the fire in the harbour with spades and tarpaulins from their ships.[66]

Following the siege, the evacuation of wounded soldiers by sea once again showed the limitations of British naval domination. The wounded from the first assault were taken by transport ship to Bilbao. The ship, described as a 'living charnel-house', conveyed the injured 'crowded together on a close deck, at the hottest season of the year, in a wretched state of helplessness, groaning, and dying, and calling for water'. No medical supplies or cooking materials were available. Many wounded men died, some at least for want of basic care.[67] One solution was to require soldiers of the Chasseurs Britanniques who were being conveyed to England at the end of their term of service to act as orderlies for the wounded on hospital ships from Pasajes to Bilbao.[68] Of course, lapses in the performance of routine duties were not confined to the navy. The lieutenant commanding the *Gleaner*, a cutter, reported that the military messenger he brought to Pasajes 'showed such symptoms of being deranged that he placed him under charge of a sentry the greater part of the voyage'. But the ship had to await the messenger's return before sailing back.[69]

Worse still, the navy was criticized for failing to furnish strong supporting firepower in operations against the French garrison. Once the town had been seized, but before the castle surrendered, Sir Thomas Graham argued that the attack on San Sebastian would have been aided by the presence of 'a large naval force'. Such a force would have ensured the earlier capture of Isla Santa Clara, thereby strengthening the blockade and opening the possibility of bringing heavy guns on gunboats into play against the castle. A more credible threat from the bay would have drawn off a significant portion of the garrison, whereas only 300 'of the most infirm' among the garrison of 2,000 men had been detached to defending the castle during the siege of the town. The delay in taking both town and castle created a further problem in that the weather worsened in September, making it far too risky to deploy larger warships along the coast.[70]

A second important factor was the weather. The 26th was 'a nice day, cool and without sun till just before sunset', whereas the 27th proved to be 'very hot with a broiling sun' followed by a cold night. By 9.00 p.m. on the eve of the attack, 30 August, the weather had turned 'very stormy: violent rain with thunder and lightning'. This left a morning of dense fog which did not clear until 8.00 a.m. on the 31st. The assault took place in good conditions, but by 1.35 p.m. the wind was reported as being 'very high; sand blows and destroys the view'. By 2.48 p.m. it was cold, rain had begun to fall and the sky was 'very lowering'. By 3.00 p.m. it was 'very dark', and the late evening brought heavy thunder and rain.[71] The attack occurred during a short break in the weather between the storm of the night of the 30th followed by the foggy morning of the 31st and the next storm beginning between 1.30 and 3.00 p.m. on the afternoon of the 31st. It is highly unlikely that the impending change in the weather was unforeseen by 12.30 p.m., for high winds struck within an hour. An assault depending upon artillery support had to succeed by early afternoon, for by then high winds and low visibility would have negated the impact of artillery support. The artillery barrage over the heads of the troops on the breach was the last opportunity to push for victory before the weather intervened. It may have been a bold, imaginative and professionally impressive move, but it was also a desperate expedient to try to find a breakthrough before the impending storm forced a British withdrawal.

A related and obvious point often overlooked was that the attack occurred during daylight. Such timing ran against the accepted practice of storming a defended town at night or at dawn. It is difficult to see how the river crossing could have been achieved at night, as co-ordinating it with the attack on the main breach would have been impossible. More significantly, the decisive bombardment of the main breach over the heads of the stalled assault columns would have been out of the question at night. As we have noted, Colin Campbell later argued that the first assault had failed largely through lack of co-ordination in the darkness; officers simply could not re-organize their formations in the chaotic conditions approaching and at the main breach.[72] Lieutenant Colonel Ross concluded that San Sebastian 'never could have been carried in the night' and that daytime assaults were in fact preferable to nocturnal ones.[73] Wellington had participated in the successful attack on Seringapatam at midday and was ready to see what might work rather than intent on following preconceived models.

The third factor was Soult's rapid advance. Frazer recorded that news of Soult's movements had been revealed by a deserter at Wellington's headquarters at Lesaca at 5.00 a.m. on the 30th. By the end of the day all the horse artillery was despatched to counter an expected attack by Soult, who aimed, it was said, to raise the siege of San Sebastian. At 10.00 a.m. on the 31st news arrived at the San Sebastian front that 8,000 French soldiers had crossed the Bidassoa. At 11.15, Wellington asked Graham if he could release some units from Bradford's Portuguese brigade to reinforce the front against Soult. While the threat from Soult did not weaken the attack itself, Soult's advance spurred the British to finish the job at San Sebastian. As soon as the town was taken, Graham left San Sebastian for the main front late on the 31st and did not return until about midday on 1 September.[74] His actions showed how the wider threat from Soult suddenly added to the pressure on the allies.

Notes

1. Carr-Gomm (ed.), *Letters and Journals*, 311–12, 314.
2. Anon. [Blakiston], *Twelve Years' Military Adventure*, ii, 273.
3. Major Leith Hay, *A Narrative of the Peninsular War*, 2 vols (Edinburgh, 1931), ii, 247, 254–5, 266–7.
4. Jones, *Journals*, ii, 93.
5. Oman, *A History of the Peninsular War*, vii, 61–2.
6. Jones, *Journals*, i, v.
7. *Royal Military Calendar*, iv, 423.
8. *The Times*, 24 December 1841, p. 5.
9. *Critic*, 6.149 (6 November 1847), 299.
10. Charles J. Esdaile and Philip Freeman, *Burgos in the Peninsular war, 1808–1814* (Houndsmill, 2015).
11. Jones, *Journals*, ii, 94–5.
12. Jones, *Journals*, ii, 93.
13. Oman, *A History of the Peninsular War,* vii, 8–9.
14. Fletcher to Wellington, 29 July 1813, Wellington (ed.), *Supplementary Despatches*, viii, 148–9.
15. Shadwell, *Life of Colin Campbell*, i, 29–31.
16. May, *Observations*, 2, 10, 13, 30–4.

17. Henegan, *Seven Years Campaigning*, ii, 41.
18. Sabine (ed.), *Letters*, 254, 263.
19. May, *Observations*, 39–42.
20. Anon. [Blakiston], *Twelve Years' Military Adventure*, ii, 252–5, 273.
21. May, *Observations*, 26–9.
22. Jones, *Journals*, ii, 93, 95.
23. Horward, *Napoleon and Iberia*, 81, 83, 101, 120, 136–7, 141, 171–3, 177, 180–2.
24. Revd G.R. Gleig, *The Life of Major-General Sir Thomas Munro, Bart*, 3 vols (London, 1830), i, 215, 217–18, 221.
25. Jones, *Journals*, ii, 92–6.
26. Anon. [Blakiston], *Twelve Years' Military Adventure*, ii, 246.
27. Anon. [Blakiston], *Twelve Years' Military Adventure*, ii, 251.
28. Hay, *A Narrative*, ii, 216.
29. (Edinburgh) *Caledonian Mercury*, 12 August 1813.
30. Oman, *A History of the Peninsular War*, vii, 155–6; Surtees, *Twenty-Five Years in the Rifle Brigade*, 245.
31. B.H. Liddell Hart (ed.), *The Letters of Private Wheeler 1809–1828* (Moreton-in-Marsh, 1993 repr.), 135.
32. Moorsom, *History of the 52nd Regiment*, 202–3.
33. Glover (ed.), *A Gentleman Volunteer*, 125.
34. Smyth, *A History of the Lancashire Fusiliers*, i, 259, 261–2; Cowper (ed.), *The King's Own*, i, 421, 423.
35. Oman, *A History of the Peninsular War*, vii, 530.
36. *Royal Military Panorama*, iii, 305–8 (December 1813).
37. Carr-Gomm (ed.), *Letters and Journals*, 318.
38. Carr-Gomm (ed.), *Letters and Journals*, 325.
39. Figures for Salamanca are from Muir, *Salamanca 1812*, 246.
40. Cowper (ed.), *The King's Own*, i, 433–5.
41. The figures in this and preceding paragraphs are from Oman, *A History of the Peninsular War*, vi, 751, 757–60, 769–71; vii, 35–6, 529, 534, 538, 542, 545–7, 562; some figures in Oman are given by brigade rather by battalion.
42. Muir, *Tactics and the Experience of Battle*, 190–1.
43. *The Times*, 16 September 1813, p. 3.
44. Carr-Gomm (ed.), *Letters and Journals*, 318.
45. Graham to Wellington, 1 September 1813, *WD*, xi, 62–5; *Royal Military Panorama*, iii, 305–6 (December 1813), 449 (February 1814).
46. Duncan, *History of the Royal Regiment of Artillery*, ii, 361–2.
47. *ODNB* entry.
48. Entries in *ODNB* and in *Royal Military Calendar*.
49. *Royal Military Calendar*, iv, 327–8.
50. *Royal Military Calendar*, iv, 158–60, 394–7.
51. *Royal Military Calendar*, iii, 295.
52. *Royal Military Panorama*, iii, 450–1 (February 1814); *Royal Military Calendar*, iv, 345–6.
53. *Royal Military Calendar*, v, 137.
54. Smyth, *A History of the Lancashire Fusiliers*, i, 261–2.
55. Henegan, *Seven Years Campaigning*, ii, 45; *Royal Military Calendar*, iv, 412–13.
56. Thompson (ed.), *An Ensign in the Peninsular War*, 264.
57. Surtees, *Twenty-Five Years in the Rifle Brigade*, 237–8.
58. Wellington to Graham, 28 August 1813, *WD*, xi, 50.
59. Sabine (ed.), *Letters*, 233, 237.
60. William Laird Clowes, *The Royal Navy*, 6 vols (London 1997, repr. 1900 edn), v, 529–30.
61. *The Times*, 20 September 1813, p. 2.

62. Liddell Hart (ed.), *Letters of Private Wheeler*, 128.

63. Sabine (ed.), *Letters*, 233.

64. Wellington to Bathurst, 2 September 1813 (with enclosure Graham to Wellington, 1 September 1813), *WD*, xi, 65, 69.

65. Collier to Somerset, 19 September 1813, WP 9/2/2/15; Somerset to Collier, 21 September 1813, WP 9/2/2/17.

66. Collier to Somerset, 5, 8 September 1813, WP 9/2/2/15.

67. Anon. [Blakiston], *Twelve Years' Military Adventure*, ii, 258–61.

68. Pakenham to Aitchison, commandant at Pasajes, 14 September 1813, WP 9/1/1/8, p. 308.

69. Aitchison to Somerset, 1 September 1813, WP 9/2/2/15.

70. Graham to Somerset, 5 September 1813, WP 9/2/2/15.

71. Sabine (ed.), *Letters*, 228, 232, 238–9.

72. Shadwell, *Life of Colin Campbell*, i, 30–1.

73. Ross to Sir Hew Dalrymple, 10 September 1813, *Memoir*, 47.

74. Sabine (ed.), *Letters*, 232–4, 237, 240, 242.

Chapter 11

The End of the Siege

The Attack on the Castle

Having retreated from the town into the castle, the French prepared a further defence. Although the French suffered far fewer casualties than the British, they started with a relatively small garrison. British and Portuguese losses for the 31st August were 2,376. The French lost 250 killed and 270 prisoners, most of whom were wounded and were left in their temporary hospital at the San Vicente church. Among those killed were Lieutenant Colonel Gillet, who commanded the engineers, and Captain Saint Georges of that branch. Two battalion commanding officers were killed. Captain Gorse of the artillery, who played a key role in defending the breach, was badly wounded. Rey, two of his senior staff officers, another battalion commander and the commander of the artillery were all wounded, though none seriously. The French were left with 1,280 effectives, but had to look after or guard 366 wounded and 400 prisoners with very limited accommodation in the castle. They were short of water and cooking utensils, and had to find shelter and cover as best they could on the rocky hillside of Mount Orgullo.[1] On 31 August Rey pleaded for assistance from Soult. He was bereft of effective artillery and he was short of bayonets and cartridges.[2]

The plan for assaulting the castle was approved by Wellington on the morning of 1 September. It involved a thorough re-organization of the artillery which would take some days. Mortars were fired regularly on the castle while that work proceeded and up to the final bombardment by breaching guns. The French returned very limited fire. On 3 September two batteries were prepared for three 18-pounders placed near the circular redoubt and for seventeen 24-pounders along the horn-work, facing into the town rather than out towards the isthmus. The heavy guns, drawn from the north of the line on the east bank of the Urumea, were to be hauled across the river during the night of 3–4 September. But the wind was high, making for a rough crossing.[3] At 5.00 a.m. on the 4th Lieutenant Colonel Frazer noted different impediments: 'I sit down more dirty, and as wet as ever I was in my life, having for the last two hours been wading through the Urumea. What with lazy folks and sleepy ones, tired working parties, and worn-out bullocks, we have got over only two carriages and one gun.'

The fear of being shelled by the French led to the suspension of further work as soon as it was light. Yet, during 4 September, soldiers crossed the Urumea to plunder the burning town without attracting French fire. The Royal Artillery therefore decided to take the guns across at low tide and did so without being fired on; according to Frazer, 'Our men have worked famously'. If the French had fired, 'a confused multitude of six or seven hundred men, and seventy or eighty pairs of bullocks, pulling heavy loads, might have suffered severely'. Further effort was devoted late on 5 September to determining the route by which to haul the guns to their designated batteries from their temporary parking places under ruined buildings near the shoreline. Finding an appropriate position for the battery on the horn-work was not straightforward. The curtain wall to the north of the horn-work had been the initial preference but was too narrow, and so the batteries were placed temporarily in the curtain wall's ditch, with fascines installed to protect the guns. Work continued on preparing the batteries during the 5th and on the following night the seventeen heavy guns were moved into position on the horn-work, a task completed by 11.00 p.m. By midday on the 7th the artillery was appropriately manned and ready for the planned bombardment on the following day.[4]

The resources available to the defenders were limited in two key respects. Supplies of infantry ammunition remained plentiful. There were 785,000 musket cartridges in stock, compared with 1,314,000 on 28 June and 932,500 on 16 August, after the first siege. Ammunition for the artillery was less plentiful, with shortages varying between different weapons. Although round shot for the 16-pounders was amply available, the stores held only 1,220 rounds for 12-pounders, 2,776 rounds for 8-pounders and 4,640 for 4-pounders, and those lower calibre guns were the weapons suitable for close-contact, fluid fighting. The main handicap was the lack of artillery. Lieutenant Colonel A. Dickson later described the French guns as mostly 'in a very bad state, from excessive use, or being damaged by the besieging fire'.[5]

On 4 September, Lieutenant Colonel Brion, who commanded the artillery, formally reported to Rey that his inspection of the castle's extensive defences on the previous day showed that the guns had effectively been destroyed. Brion noted that by 1 September the French had only seven guns on the landward side of the castle and Mount Orgullo, and those included only one 16-pounder, plus two 4-pounders, which were defective, and three mortars. That battery faced formidable British artillery on the east bank of the Urumea and what Brion believed to be a battery of eight heavy guns being established on the curtain wall; the latter would destroy links between the French positions on Mount Orgullo. On the seaward side, the French had only three 24-pounders and one 18-pounder, and those guns could be hit in their flanks by the five-gun battery the British had established on Isla Santa Clara to the west. Moreover, the British had additional firepower available offshore: one ship of the line, two frigates and large numbers of barges.[6]

The second problem was the lack of manpower. When the eight most senior officers met Rey and reviewed their position on 5 September, their garrison had shrunk from 3,000 men on 1 July to 1,200 effectives; their hospitals and the wounded were in a 'deplorable' condition; their infantry had no shelter, little relief from active duty and were constantly bombarded by the British. To add even further to the troops' demoralization, they were very short of brandy. Facing an overwhelming build-up of British artillery for a final assault, all present recommended that Rey seek a capitulation.[7] The brigadier decided instead to await the impending British bombardment.

One can suggest various reasons for this preference. Rey knew that considerable symbolic importance had been attached to defending the town, especially as he resisted for far longer than Napoleon required of his garrison commanders. Secondly, Rey may have thought that the British would take longer than they did to transfer a battery to the captured horn-work. On 9 September, after the French capitulation, the French artillery commander, Colonel Brion, told Frazer of his 'surprise at the facility with which we had thrown up the battery'.[8] Linked to this consideration, Rey was under pressure to buy time as well as maintain French prestige. In military terms, an extra week might well have had a wider operational significance.

So, the French waited for the final stage of the assault. It proved very brief, lasting from 10.00 to 12.00 a.m. on 8 September. On the right of the attack five batteries shared thirty-three guns, mortars and howitzers. Of these only ten were heavy guns, including four 68-pounder carronades and six 24-pounder guns. There were sixteen mortars. The objective was to suppress the Mirador battery and to bombard the castle generally. The left of the attack, sited on the isthmus, consisted of twenty-five guns, including twenty-two 24-pounders and one howitzer. These were tasked with destroying the Mirador and the de la Reyna batteries, with minor fire directed at the castle defences and rear more generally. The depleted French batteries made no significant response to a rapid and intense bombardment which severely damaged the walls of the Mirador and the battery of de la Reyna.[9]

Rey justified the capitulation by stressing the overwhelming allied advantage in artillery. In his report to Soult on 7 September, Rey emphasized the impact of the sustained 4-hour assault on the 31st, followed by four days of shelling and mortar fire, which continued on 5 and 6 September while the British re-positioned most of their heavy guns. By the 7th Rey reported on the advanced state of British preparations and the complete lack of any artillery with which to reply. Moreover, the castle keep had been destroyed. Continuing his despatch into the morning of the 8th, he reported that the British had opened fire with sixty-two guns and destroyed the batteries of Mirador and de la Reyna and the fort's defensive walls. Nearly half the gunners fell at their guns, and only 19 of the original cohort of 110 sappers were among the effectives at the surrender, while 32 were wounded or sick. As a consequence, the French fired only a small amount of grapeshot on the morning of 8 September. In concluding that he had no option but to accept terms, Rey sought Soult's and the emperor's recognition that the garrison had heroically withstood far superior odds until it could continue no longer.[10]

At 12.00 on 8 September, General Rey asked for terms which were agreed that afternoon. The terms were honourable enough, despite Wellington's anger in early September that British prisoners in the castle were exposed to incoming artillery fire.[11] Colonel St Ouary, the French commandant of the castle, conceded on 9 September that British prisoners were killed by British shelling because the castle lacked enough protected places in which to house them.[12]

The formal surrender occurred at 12.00 on 9 September in fine weather. Portuguese troops lined the streets and some of their regimental bands provided music. British troops were placed on the ramparts. A formal salute was given in the Plaza Vieja, near the town's main gate. Frazer noted that 'Many of the French soldiers wept bitterly: all looked sorrowful'; they 'laid down their arms in silence' and were then held in a convent, which had survived in the town, pending transhipment to England from Passajes. As the Spanish flag was raised over the castle, the British artillery fired a twenty-one-gun salute.[13]

This was a fitting last act, since the artillery had delivered the critical final blow. During these proceedings, the commander of the French artillery, Colonel Brion, asked to see the battery which the British had positioned in the captured horn-work a few days earlier. According to Frazer, Brion 'repeatedly said that the fire of the artillery during the siege had been admirable'. Admittedly, Frazer also stressed that Brion had 'very pleasing manners', unlike some of his senior colleagues, and in commending a fellow artillery commander, the Frenchman may simply have indulged in professional politeness.[14]

Nevertheless, Brion's observation accurately acknowledged that the sheer weight of British firepower carried the day. The British prevailed because the French eventually faced the prospect of being massacred by artillery fire to which they could make no response. Of course, the garrison had been increasingly isolated once the town had been seized. Before 31 August, the French had received supplies and munitions at night by means of small boats running into the bay and harbour on the western side of the town. This became more difficult after the harbour was largely cut off during the night of 26–7 August. Once the town was taken, the small harbour or mole was inaccessible to even the smallest French cargo-carrying vessels. The best they could do was run messages in and out of the castle. Since the French were essentially devoid of artillery power after 31 August, the British might have starved the besieged into surrender without a further heavy bombardment. Their capture of Isla Santa Clara not only closed the French re-supply route; it also enabled the British to install a battery which could destroy the castle's water supply, though heavy rainfall presumably counteracted that in part.[15] Starving the garrison, however, would have taken time since the defenders' physical condition seems to have been good; Aitchison, on supervising the prisoners of war's embarkation for England days after the surrender, described them as 'the finest men I have ever seen of their numbers from the French army'.[16]

From a garrison which at its maximum during the siege numbered 3,200 men, the French were left with 1,858 soldiers, of whom 481 were wounded. The French losses can be demonstrated by comparing the strength of the initial garrison with the numbers who remained at the point of surrender.

Attrition of the French Garrison			
	Main Units' Strength, Beginning of Siege[17]	**At Capitulation**	**Of Whom Wounded/Sick**
1st Line	219	279	59
22nd	464	294	86
34th	434	307	83
62nd	812	424	116
119th	195	122	26
Chasseurs de Montagne	255	116	42
Artillery	166	89	21
Engineers	248	110	44
Grand total of army	3,185	1,858	481

While the garrison included units not separately listed in the table, the specialist units – the artillery, the engineers and the chasseurs – suffered most heavily. From the initial contingent of 414 artillerymen and engineers, only 134 were fit for duty on 8 September. Only 74 of the original body of 255 chasseurs were available by the end of the siege. The management of the siege took its toll among officers. Of the eight officers on the army staff, five were wounded, including Rey and his two most senior subordinates, the chevalier de Songeon, who was the adjutant and chief of staff, and Colonel de Sentuary, who was the town commandant. Of the eight artillery officers originally assigned to the operation, five were wounded. Of the nine engineer officers, three were killed and two were wounded. The heads of both the artillery and engineers, Lieutenant Colonels Brion and Pinot respectively, were wounded.[18]

Consequences for the British Command

When *The Times* reflected on the state of the war on 21 September, it concentrated on two weeks of campaigning in central Germany around Dresden, which inflicted an estimated 60,000 losses on the French army. All credit went to Field Marshal Blucher and the Prussians. San Sebastian merited far less space, but its capture remained of 'incalculable value'. Dominating the area through which the royal road passed, the town had been Napoleon's first conquest when he invaded Spain. The French government had made 'desperate efforts' to hold the town in July–September 1813 and had used its retention as one argument for conscripting an extra 30,000 troops. Its fall demonstrated to the French how vulnerable Napoleon's position had become. Moreover, General Graham, in offering honourable terms of surrender to the garrison had acknowledged the defenders' bravery while also reinforcing the status of those who could defeat such a foe.[19] Given such a context, Cribb and Sons of High Holborn believed that public interest would justify their publication, at 6s. a copy, of a print of the town and castle showing 'the trenches, Breaching-battery, etc from a Drawing made by an Officer on the spot, during the late Siege'.[20] This commercial commemoration of victory was underway within three weeks of the final outcome.

Yet the siege had mixed consequences for the officers involved in it. The defenders' determination won official recognition when most surviving French officers were promoted by the French government while British prisoners of war.[21] On the British side, Snodgrass, who led the river crossing by the Portuguese, became Lieutenant Colonel of the 1st Caçadores, commanding them at the Nivelle (10 November), the Nive (9–11 December), where he was wounded, and Orthes (27 February, 1814), where he was too seriously wounded to continue on active duty. He became CB in 1814, at the age of 30.[22]

On the other hand, the surrender of San Sebastian yielded no laurels for the British senior commanders. Within three weeks of the siege's end, Graham returned home and was replaced by Sir John Hope. The 48-year-old Hope held responsible posts in the West Indies, Holland and Egypt during 1796–1801 under Abercromby, and had been Sir John Moore's number two in Sweden and the Peninsula in 1808–9, supervising the withdrawal at La Coruña. He had thus impressed the ablest generals of the previous generation. Graham, though born in 1748 and thus much older than Hope, had followed an unconventional career, and been junior in rank to the younger man at La Coruña (where he was on Moore's staff) and in the Walcheren expedition, where Hope commanded a division whereas Graham led a brigade.[23] In the summer of 1813, before the second assault, Graham had requested to leave Spain. He had returned to Britain in the summer of 1812, suffering from an eye problem and had been greatly missed by both by Wellington and more widely in the army.[24] It is difficult to offer any assessment of his generalship. He had been innovative in training his battalion in light infantry tactics in the 1790s and he enjoyed Moore's professional respect.[25] Following his return to Britain in 1813, he led a small expeditionary force against Antwerp and co-operated effectively with the Prussian army invading the Low Countries.[26] In his study of that expedition, Andrew Bamford concluded that Graham was a busy commander who created a good deal of confusion by making hurried and contradictory decisions, but his record was not discreditable and he remained popular with most of the officer corps.[27]

From a modern perspective, it seems striking that a full Lieutenant General needed as much supervision as Wellington exerted over Graham in a relatively limited, if very demanding, operation. But, of course, roles and rank differed in their importance in the early nineteenth century. More significantly, the decision to bombard across the breach at the climax of the second assault smacked of desperation; the assault at the main breach was stuck and the weather, which turned increasingly bad from about 1.20 p.m., may already have begun to look threatening an hour or so earlier. Equally significantly, Commissary Henegan later claimed that the action was urged 'in my presence' upon Graham by Lieutenant Colonel Dickson 'whose experienced eye, and knowledge of the precision exercised by his gunners, made him foresee the advantages to be derived from it'.[28] On a personal level, Graham attracted little criticism and some praise. Gomm wrote of him in 1812 after the siege of Ciudad Rodrigo:

he had several narrow escapes at this siege. All the world would say that he exposes himself too much on all occasions if he did not make such good use of his time while he was exposing himself. He is one of those men who set us in good humour with ourselves and with the times we live in as often as we approach them; and, while we honour them for their own merits, we feel a secret pride at the recollection that we belong to the same order of being with themselves, and are glad to witness the elevation of which our nature is susceptible. . . . Such men do more good among us than they ever calculate upon.[29]

Eighteen months later, Frazer, who appreciated the general's liveliness and good-will, stressed that he 'is no longer young, and the fatigues of the siege pressed somewhat upon him'. Sir John Hope, as Graham's replacement, impressed Frazer as being very experienced and battle-tested; significantly, Frazer added, 'No man is more looked up to, and with just reason'.[30]

In his formal despatch on the second assault, Graham went to some lengths to praise Major General Oswald, who commanded the disparaged 5th Division at the first assault and until 30 August. Oswald had been blamed for making demoralizing comments about the impossibility of taking the breach on 25 July. Yet Graham specifically mentioned and commended Oswald's readiness to accompany Leith on the 31st, demonstrating 'a liberality and zeal for the service in the highest degree praiseworthy'. Oswald was in the thick of the action, talking to Sir Richard Fletcher when the latter was fatally shot in the neck. Graham pointedly added: 'I have infinite satisfaction is assuring your Lordship of my perfect approbation of Major General Oswald's conduct, ever since the 5th division formed a part of the left column of the army'.[31] Such a comment in a despatch which would be published might be somewhat formulaic. But this made at least public amends for earlier doubts about the 5th Division. Moreover, Gomm mentioned the despatch to his sister on 27 September, stressing that, 'I am glad to find General Oswald so handsomely mentioned; it is no panegyric, I assure you'.[32] It is noteworthy that Oswald took the salute of the French officers as the garrison marched out of the castle on 9 September into captivity.[33] He commanded the 5th Division in operations to and beyond St Jean de Luz. But in December, Oswald, apparently disappointedly, also returned to Britain, on personal grounds following a meeting with his wife in Bilbao.[34] The memory of his role in the siege lingered. Oswald died in 1840, agreeably bedecked with both a GCB and a GCMG, the highest orders of chivalry available to public servants other than extremely senior politicians and commanders-in-chief. By then he had become a full general, through seniority rather through any further active service. His obituary in the *Edinburgh Observer* was copied in *The Times*. He was, so the paper claimed, 'one of the bravest soldiers of modern times'.[35]

One award was unusual. The volunteers from the 52nd were allowed to wear a distinctive badge on their uniforms. The commanding officer ordered that the men's names be inscribed in the regimental records both to commemorate 'their exemplary conduct' and 'to point out their meritorious service at some future period, when they may find it necessary to appeal to the regiment for a character, either in the event of their return home or of their soliciting promotion or pension'. He also promised that the battalion's officers would write to magistrates in the men's home parishes to lodge a record of individuals' 'important service'.[36]

Two further reflections on the siege's impact on the British command are in order. On 26 February 1814, Lieutenant Colonel Frazer received news that Wellington had ordered an initial reconnaissance of Bayonne 'with a view to a siege'. Frazer was a humane observer of the campaign and had been appalled by British troops' excesses in, and the destruction of, San Sebastian. Yet, exhausted at the work involved in preparing for a blockade of Bayonne, his response to the news of Wellington's instructions remained strictly professional: 'I like the idea of a siege, as offering employment'.[37]

Such buoyancy needs to be set against a more sobering lesson from San Sebastian. The renewed assault upon San Sebastian was feasible after the French counter-stroke had been repelled at Sorauren on 30 July. Yet the French still posed a threat and Soult tried to lift the siege when he attacked the allies along a wide front hinged on San Marcial on 31 August. They were repulsed with losses exceeding 4,000 men. Significantly, much of the defensive fighting at San Marcial was sustained by the Spanish, whose casualties accounted for 1,679 of the 2,524 stricken allies. Throughout August Wellington had remained cautious in his plans for advancing against Soult's army. He had no intention of pursuing it into France, partly, as already noted, because he did not know until 3 September that the war had resumed in Germany. But he also remained uncertain about the reliability of his Spanish allies and the condition of his own army. Desertions increased as Spain was cleared of the French and the nearer his forces approached the French border.[38] Taking San Sebastian thus became a priority as a useful acquisition to make, as a far less risky initiative than invading France, and as a prominent item of unfinished business to resolve. Victory at San Sebastian destroyed a symbol of French resistance. But it served as a warning of the determined opposition the British would encounter as they pushed forward into France.

Notes

1. Belmas, *Sièges*, iv, 644–5.
2. Rey to Soult, 31 aout 1813, Belmas, *Sièges*, iv, 722.
3. Jones, *Journals*, ii, 83–6.
4. Sabine (ed.), *Letters*, 245, 251–2, 255, 258–9, 271.
5. Official returns in *Royal Military Panorama*, iii (January 1814), 379; Belmas, *Sièges*, iv, 665.
6. 'Rapport fait au general Rey . . . par le chef de bataillon Brion', 4 septembre 1813, Belmas, *Sieges*, iv, 734–6, 646.
7. 'Proces-verbal de la deliberation du conseil de defense . . . 5 septembre 1813', Belmas, *Sièges*, iv, 737–9.
8. Sabine (ed.), *Letters*, 265.
9. Jones, *Journals*, ii, 88.
10. Rey to Soult, 7 septembre 1813, Belmas, *Sièges*, iv, 739–41; Sabine (ed.), *Letters*, 261.
11. Wellington to Graham, 5 September 1813, *WD*, xi, 79–80.

12. Sabine (ed.), *Letters*, 268.
13. Sabine (ed.), *Letters,* 264–6.
14. Sabine (ed.), *Letters*, 265–6.
15. Sabine (ed.), *Letters*, 242.
16. Thompson (ed.), *An Ensign in the Peninsular War*, 265.
17. Belmas, *Sièges,* iv, 654–6, 746.
18. Belmas, *Sièges,* iv, 654–6.
19. *The Times,* 21 September 1813, p. 3.
20. *The Times*, 28 September 1813, p. 1.
21. Belmas, *Sièges*, iv, 652–3.
22. *Royal Military Calendar*, v, 138.
23. *ODNB* entries.
24. Wellington to Graham, 3 July 1812; to Bathurst 7, 9 July 1812, *WD*, ix, 267, 273, 277; Muir, *Salamanca 1812*, 40.
25. Oman, *Sir John Moore*, 241, 503, 508, 531.
26. Leggiere, *The Fall of Napoleon*, 406, 418, 440.
27. Bamford, *A Bold and Ambitious Enterprise*, 35–6, 260–1.
28. Henegan, *Seven Years Campaigning*, ii, 43.
29. Carr-Gomm (ed.), *Letters and Journals*, 251.
30. Sabine (ed.), *Letters*, 276, 309.
31. Graham to Wellington, 1 September 1813, *WD*, xi, 65; Sabine (ed.), *Letters*, 240.
32. Carr-Gomm (ed.), *Letters and Journals*, 323.
33. Sabine (ed.), *Letters*, 264.
34. *Royal Military Calendar*, iii, 55; Carr-Gomm (ed.), *Letters and Journals*, 329.
35. *The Times*, 12 June 1840, p. 7.
36. Moorsom, *History of the 52nd Regiment*, 202.
37. Sabine (ed.), *Letters*, 418.
38. Oman, *A History of the Peninsular War*, vii, 1–3, 57.

Chapter 12

British Actions in San Sebastian

The Dispute over the Destruction of San Sebastian

On 9 October Wellington was at Lesaca, known today for its pleasant location in a small valley in the mountains and for its flowers. This side valley gave easy access to the far broader and fertile valley of the Bidassoa River, and the main road south to Pamplona. The river as it flowed northwards to the sea formed the Franco-Spanish frontier. Its upper reaches ran through the Baztan valley, whose rich pasturelands supported cattle and sheep, as well as a reported population of about 7,000 people.[1] Having maintained his headquarters there for two months, he was preparing to move to Vera, a short distance away and about 22 miles east and south of San Sebastian. Vera had better access to the royal road leading to France. The move had been delayed until 10 October because the town was congested with wounded men after the crossing of the Bidassoa into France on the 7th and 8th cost the Anglo-Portuguese armies 814 casualties.[2] But Wellington had little time for celebration. One of many causes of anxiety sprang from his tense relations with the Spanish Regency.

At first sight, this was surprising since the allies' entry into France reflected an enlarged Spanish role in Wellington's operations. The battle of San Marcial on 31 August and the Bidassoa crossing on 7 October involved substantial and warmly praised Spanish contributions. Of their performance at the Bidassoa, Wellington reported that 'The Spanish troops . . . behaved admirably, and turned and carried the enemy's entrenchments on the hills with great dexterity and gallantry . . .'. In an action on 8 October at the mountain of La Rhune, against a very strong position, Spanish planning, operational command and fighting prowess won similar approval: 'The attack . . . was made in as good order and with as much spirit as any I have seen made by any troops'. Wellington emphasized that 'I cannot applaud too highly the execution of the arrangements for these attacks'.[3] Such acknowledgement of Spanish fighting effectiveness appears not to have been formulaic. William Surtees commented on the fighting around San Marcial that 'This was the only time I ever knew the Spaniards act in a body like good soldiers'.[4] Lieutenant Colonel Ross of the artillery noted that the Spanish division under Lieutenant General Don Manuel Freyre had won the respect of the British army on 31 August by thwarting repeated French attacks, notably at bayonet point 'several times'. Ross similarly commented on Spanish courage and fighting ability at the crossing of the Bidassoa.[5] Both engagements vindicated Wellington's long-running effort to bring Spanish regular forces and embodied militia into integrated operations with his own armies.

Yet the relationship between the Field Marshal and the Council of Regency suffered from two immediate difficulties. The first concerned authority and process. On 30 August Wellington resigned the command of the Spanish armies after a year in that post. He objected that the Regency's military instructions had not been channelled through him as commander-in-chief and its appointments and promotions had been made without consulting him. He insisted not on the authority to make all appointments and promotions, but on the right to recommend them and to be consulted if his recommendations were to be rejected. As part of the background, he also complained privately to his brother, Sir Henry Wellesley, of the lack of support he had received from any political group in the Cortes. He wanted Henry, as British diplomatic minister to the government in Cádiz, to ensure that the reasons for his resignation were publicly available to the Cortes.[6] He was still waiting in October for the new Cortes to convene and to accept his resignation.

On 9 October, however, Wellington clashed with Spanish politicians over a second issue. The Spanish minister of war wrote to Wellington on 28 September enclosing a letter of 5 September from the Xefe Politico of Guipuzcoa province, the Conde de Villa Fuentes, criticizing British and Portuguese troops' conduct in San Sebastian. Such criticism was then embellished in a report of 27 September in *El Duende* newspaper. (The name meant 'sprite' or 'hobgoblin', a figure from popular folklore.) The newspaper article made more explicit charges than those outlined in the count's letter to the minister of war. Wellington particularly deplored the accusation that Sir Thomas Graham deliberately ordered the burning of San Sebastian to punish San Sebastian for trading with French ports. He categorically denied that senior officers ordered the destruction of a commercial rival, arguing that if he had wanted the town destroyed he would have systematically bombarded it, but refused to do so, following the same policy as had been adopted at Ciudad Rodrigo and Badajoz.[7]

It is difficult to determine how widely these charges circulated within Spain. The first mention of Spanish criticism of British behaviour in Lieutenant Colonel Frazer's normally informative letters was on 22 October, when he noted that the Cádiz newspaper's article of 27 September accused the British of gross misconduct and of intentionally destroying the town because of its commercial links with France.[8] Frazer had already commented on the town's destruction, and had noted the suffering and traumatization of the town's civilian inhabitants, but he never assessed San Sebastian's significance in other than strictly military terms.

El Duende's charges were printed in *The Times* of London on 30 October. They alleged that allied troops, intent on pillaging, failed to capture the castle at around 4.00 p.m. on the 31st. The soldiers allegedly plundered churches and on the following day started raping, murdering and deliberately burning the town, beginning with a corner of the main street during the morning of 1 September and proceeding that evening and during the 2nd to neighbouring streets, ending with Juan de Bilboa street and the new square.[9] The paper accused the British of deliberately bombarding the town, destroying it by setting it on fire and allowing its soldiers to murder, rape and plunder with impunity. Each of these accusations merits review.

The Bombardment

The charge that San Sebastian was deliberately burned when the allies marched into the town flatly contradicted British accounts which described the town as being ablaze before their soldiers entered it. In detailing his rebuttal to Sir Henry, Wellington stressed that the damage started with the first assault:

> To set the town on fire was part of the enemy's defence. It was set on fire by the enemy on 22nd of July, before the final attempt was made to take it by storm; and it is a fact that the fire was so violent on the 24th of July that the storm . . . was necessarily deferred till the 25th. . . . I was at the siege . . . on the 30th of August, and I aver that the town was then on fire. . . . It is well known that the enemy had prepared for a serious resistance, not only on the ramparts, but in the streets of the town; that traverses were established in the streets, formed of combustibles, with the intention of setting fire to and exploding them during the contest with the assailants.[10]

Unfortunately for Wellington, a rather different version of events, written on 6 September, was already in circulation in *The Times* by 9 October. This claimed that when the British took the town, the French bombarded it from the castle, with the result that 'in a few moments this beautiful city was in flames. A few days later, it was a heap of ruins, and there is nothing now remaining of one of the most handsomest towns in Spain'.[11] Although this account omitted to mention the fires raging well before French troops reached the castle, it raised the possibility that legitimate defensive artillery fire from the castle further fuelled the blazes already destroying the town. Whether French shelling occurred at that point remains unclear, but Wellington insisted that there was 'a most severe contest in the streets of the town' and that the French action on the 31st in detonating many traverses cost 'many lives on both sides' and 'set fire to many of the houses'. Those fires, far from being desired by the British, gravely handicapped the British troops' progress. Moreover, officers would not deliberately and without tactical justification destroy what they had struggled so long to secure.[12]

Accounts of the first assault written before the public dispute erupted in October indicated that much destruction occurred during the first attack. Fires were started from a combination of some British shelling of positions behind the breach, either intentionally or through misdirected aim, and the French decision to defend the town in depth and set off fires in buildings to assist that defence.

On 26 July, following the first British assault, the French governor reported that half the town was 'totally destroyed by fire' and the majority of the remaining houses were heavily damaged. He saw little prospect of putting out the fire; 'if the wind rises, the remainder of the town will be lost'.[13] The next day he noted that the wind had indeed strengthened so that the fire continued, 'despite all our efforts'.[14] In early August, after the first bombardment, Lieutenant Colonel Frazer observed some civilians returning 'to take a wistful look at their houses, or rather the ruins of them. There will be more ruin yet in that town before we shall get possession of it'.[15]

A tipping point occurred on 23 July when the British used four 10in mortars and four 68-pounder carronades to stop the French entrenching the breach and establishing defences behind the breach. Lieutenant Colonel Jones of the Royal Engineers described how the houses near the breach were on fire by the late morning 'and the flames spread rapidly'.[16] On 23 July, Frazer noted: 'Great part of the town is ruined by our fire. The crashing of houses, and the roaring of guns on all sides, make a horrible din.' He added in a letter dated 24 July at 3.00 a.m. that 'The town was on fire when I lay down at eleven last night. . . . Poor inhabitants, how many women and children are at this moment in the agonies of despair!!' The burning of some houses behind the intended breach then delayed the planned assault because smoke obstructed further artillery firing in support of an attack.[17] A letter from a Spaniard in Bilbao to a 'reputable mercantile house' in the city of London described the 'tremendous' cannonade from both sides on 23–5 July. Artillery fire damaged the old town especially badly, with Atocha and San Juan streets being 'reduced to ashes'. According to this report, the inhabitants were not allowed to leave, with the result that many tried to escape by water and drowned.[18]

It is difficult to determine how far British artillery targeted defensive positions within the town or simply aimed inaccurately, hitting streets beyond the breaches. At Wellington's headquarters, the fires on the 24th were attributed either to British shells hitting a house from which the French encouraged the fire to spread, or to deliberate French action in setting fire to that part of the town.[19] It is possible that some artillery fire was directed against defences within the town. British accounts did not describe the town's inner defences in detail, but we know that such defences were constructed, and were indeed extended after the failed first assault. On 26 July, after repelling the first British assault, General Rey reported that work continued on barricading the town's streets so that he could resist step by step if he had to withdraw from the town walls.[20] Burgoyne observed on 7 August that the ground level seemed to fall off behind the main breach and that the houses there were 'in flames . . ., apparently intentionally, by the enemy'.[21] Captain John Aitchison, who was Military Commandant at Passajes from August to November, noted on 25 August that 'The town probably will be destroyed, as the enemy have intersected the streets so with different defences that this measure will be indispensable to communication.'[22]

A further possibility was that buildings were hit because artillery targeting proved so unreliable. The gun batteries were positioned on sand-hills and keeping the guns stable during prolonged firing was not easy. Moreover, the weapons deployed against the town were highly inaccurate at most ranges involved at the first siege. In tests carried out as late as 1846, shot from 10in and 8in mortars hit a target 40ft by 80ft at 600–700yd only once in every nine attempts. In 1821, howitzers, used to dismantle opponents' guns, were accurate two-thirds of the time at 400yd, but only half the time at 600yd.[23] These were the weapons used to fire at the tops of the defensive walls and over them, and the distances involved were in the order of 400–600yd.

The second assault on 31 August was more challenging than the first because the French had strengthened their defences. Frazer, from his command position on the east bank of the Urumea River noted on 22 August how this strengthening increased British difficulties and added, as we have seen, that 'It may be necessary to reduce the town to ashes', after allowing the women and children to leave.[24] The preliminary bombardment for the second assault predictably caused further destruction. According to Frazer on 27 August, 'You never heard such a row as is going on. Walls and houses falling, guns and mortars firing'.[25] On 30 August, Frazer recorded that 'Five little mines have this moment blown up near the hospital in the town; one of our shells found them out'. A little later, he noted that 'Another great building under the Mirador has just burst out in flames; it was formerly a hospital; all this is very dreadful'.[26] While acknowledging the destructiveness of British artillery fire, Frazer highlighted the contradictory nature of the approach adopted: 'It is settled that we are to do the town as little damage as possible, but that little will, I dare say, extend to the destruction of half of it'.[27]

If such a dismissive conclusion seems callous, senior officers regarded random destructiveness as a regrettable but unavoidable consequence of bombarding cities. Frazer, for example, was acutely aware of the human tragedy of war and repeatedly regretted the damage inflicted on San Sebastian. Described as 'an officer as brave as gentle, and so truly a Christian, that no man had ever heard an oath from his lips', he rescued a wounded French officer after Vitoria from the path of advancing British guns, saving the Frenchman's life at great risk to himself.[28] Both privately and publically, British officers deplored the consequences of the attack. Sir Richard Henegan referred in 1846 to 'the ravages of man' leaving 'the town in flames, the wretched inhabitants houseless and beggared'.[29] Lieutenant Colonel Gomm wrote privately at the time of the 'melancholy' fate of this 'very handsome' town; 'Never surely was there a more complete picture of devastation than this place presents'.[30]

Wellington's stated desire to limit the destruction of civilian property in attacking Spanish towns appears to have been sincere. One means of limiting damage was to use vertical fire as little as possible. As a general principle, the British avoided aiming vertical howitzer fire into besieged Spanish towns, on the grounds that such fire destroyed allies' houses. The bulk of artillery fire against San Sebastian was aimed at breaching. However, the French converted buildings immediately behind the walls to provide a second line of defence. Moreover, the French heavy guns firing from the castle, at about 350yd from the main breach, attracted British counter-fire which swept across most of the east side of the town. The town itself was only about 470yd east–west and about 350yd north–south, and some inaccurate firing into the town beyond the defensive walls inevitably occurred, causing collateral damage. But Graham, in noting his discussions with Dickson, commanding the artillery, stressed that vertical fire was to be directed against the castle and the defences immediately behind the town walls and not the town itself.[31]

The build-up to the second assault involved shot used against the walls. The bulk of the munitions used by the artillery in the second siege consisted of 32,286 obstacle-busting round shot. During the entire course of the second siege, the British fired 8,282 shells, which had explosive power. These were used by 10in mortars and 8in howitzers. Most of the shells were fired during the artillery attack on the castle after the allies took the town. All accounts indicate that the French guns in the castle were totally incapacitated by British artillery fire, and the expenditure of shells was likely to have come during the brisk and frequent fire from mortars and howitzers noted daily during 2–8 September. Some twenty-four howitzers and mortars were assigned to this bombardment of the castle.[32] The British mortar fire – sometimes heavy – continued on every day until the French capitulation on the morning of 8 September. The destruction of buildings still standing when the British entered the town could scarcely have been avoided in such a limited battle-space. Moreover, the town's layout made it necessary and straightforward to clear lines of fire. As one British officer observed, 'The streets are parallel, and at right angles. We could not discover a lane or alley anywhere'.[33] The 24 howitzers and mortars would each have had to fire merely 50 rounds per day – not a large number – to expend the 8,000 shells which they collectively discharged. This pattern of firing makes it probable that limited shell-fire was directed against the town before the assault. The fires which broke out within the town before it was stormed may have resulted from British shelling. But there is no evidence that the shelling arose from a deliberate decision to destroy the town.

The Fire

What happened on the afternoon of 31 August once allied troops entered the town is impossible to determine in detail. As we have seen, there were extensive fires in the town during the French withdrawal to the castle in the early afternoon of 31 August. British soldiers entered the town from about 12.40 p.m. and heavy fighting continued until at least 1.45 p.m. As early as 1.20 p.m. the wind was described as 'very high'. The British maintained artillery fire on the outer defences of the castle, about 350yd from the main breach, until 2.15 p.m. At 2.45 p.m., when the French still held a church and part of the town, there was a major fire in the centre of the town near the square. By 3.30 p.m. San Sebastian was engulfed: 'Great fire in the town; as dark as it is generally at half-past six'.[34] While any artillery shelling at this point would have simply added to the conflagration, fighting continued in parts of the town, thereby fanning the fires. One contemporary account suggested that the fire started in a French tumbril exploded by a British shell and spread to combustibles liberally distributed about the town by the French.[35]

Troops entering the town were fully aware of the threat from urban fires. Gomm had described the entry into Ciudad Rodrigo in January 1812:

> Surely there never was a place, and all that it contained, so exposed to utter ruin as this was, for several days after we entered it. The French had left magazines of powder and loaded shells in every part of the ramparts uncovered. But the town also was full of powder; and many houses, some from negligence, others from wantonness, were set on fire in the course of the first night, and continued burning for several days. One of the magazines blew up during the assault, and another the following morning . . . both accidentally. We lost many valuable lives on both these occasions . . .[36]

As Lieutenant Colonel Burgoyne noted of San Sebastian, 'An extensive fire broke out in the centre of the town soon after the assault, and our people say they found fires made on the floors in several houses . . .'. On the next day, 1 September, 'the fire in the town spreads to an alarming extent; the streets are narrow, and the houses high and very combustible'.[37] Gomm believed the French on the 31st deliberately started the fires, which reached such intensity as to drive the assailants back 'almost to the ramparts'. They erected barricades and 'made some obstinate stands' on the 31st, but were too exhausted by hours at the breach to prolong their resistance within the town. Even so, the fires impeded further British operations because 'The houses were so lofty that every street has been completely choked up with the ruins' as the buildings collapsed.[38]

At 7.00 a.m. on 1 September, Frazer noted that the enemy 'fires with angry animation from his upper defences', despite having lost the town; 'He also rolls shells into the unhappy town, already on fire in several places'.[39] By 6.00 p.m., Graham reported that plundering was occurring – in his view mainly by Portuguese troops – and that drunkenness was common among British soldiers. Without enough functional officers to keep order, he was trying to bring Lord Aylmer's brigade into the town, but could not do so immediately. He feared a counter-attack by the French from the castle. The fires spread and by 3 September threatened communications between British troops below the castle walls and the main body of men at the town's southern boundary, where the artillery was being re-deployed. On that day, Graham urged Lieutenant Colonel Burgoyne to take steps to control the fires, and suggested opening up the town wall near San Elmo, to secure river water and to provide a communications route at low tide along the town wall's river bank back to the British lines on the isthmus.[40] With the fires continuing, British troops evacuated a church, which had served as a hospital, on the 4th and retired to the ramparts. Frazer concluded that the town could not be saved 'even if the experiment were made' as parts of the town remained ablaze on 5 September.[41] At the same time, Wellington urged that Major General Hay should retain few troops on his front line, hold a second line anchored on the Plaza, but keep his greatest force at the southern wall or its adjoining streets. Such dispositions would mean that, if the French turned his exposed left flank, Hay would lose few men and would be strong enough to counter-attack.[42]

There was some discussion about the possibility of saving the town. On the evening of 3 September, Wellington advised Sir Thomas Graham that British forces should prevent the further spread of the fire into 'the unburnt parts of the town' by pulling down 'a house or two'. He hoped that the fire would soon be extinguished. But Wellington's humanitarian concerns centred on the French misuse of allied prisoners as shields to deter British shelling; they placed prisoners in the yard of the castle's magazine, which was a key target for the Royal Artillery.[43]

For his part, Graham insisted on the 4th that he could not prevent the town from being 'totally destroyed'. He pointed out that 'no effort of cutting down houses could be made so violent and rapid was the extension of the flames during the gale of yesterday'.[44] The British continued shelling the castle with the objective of destroying the French artillery; in fact there was little or no response from the latter. By mid-day on the 5th a small section of the town, exposed to French fire, remained standing, but elsewhere 'the occasional crash of falling houses alone disturbs the silence'.[45] Surtees visited a 'few days' after its surrender only to find that 'the houses were still on fire, and not I believe half-a-dozen in the whole town that remained habitable'.[46]

The final phase in the town's destruction followed from its position as a virtual no man's land between the British guns on the horn-work and curtain wall and French musket fire from the castle. As Lieutenant Colonel Jones, a Royal Engineer who fought at various Peninsular sieges if not this one, explained, 'from the indiscipline which follows such hard-fought actions, and the castle continually firing on all who showed themselves in the streets, little or no exertion could be made to extinguish the flames'.[47] Given that houses were often if not typically four storeys high and built together, it was difficult enough to pull down individual burning buildings. But French fire from the castle only a few hundreds of yards away made organized clearing dangerous as well as uncongenial.

British Soldiers' Behaviour in the Town

A further charge published in *El Duende* was that British and Portuguese soldiers systematically sacked the town. Indeed, their eagerness to plunder allegedly led them to give up pursuing the retreating French at around 4.00 p.m. on 31 August. One British officer deplored the extent of destruction, describing it as unprecedented in the history of war. He felt that a town taken by storm should not be handed over to disciplined and well-led troops because such an 'incentive' as the right to sack and plunder was more appropriate to mercenaries.[48] But such reservations were outweighed by the more prevalent tendency to accept soldiers' misbehaviour as unavoidable. Burgoyne laconically noted that the breakdown of discipline was 'as great as usual on such occasions'.[49]

The quest for plunder undoubtedly spurred soldiers during sieges. A veteran of Wellington's Maratha campaign and San Sebastian recollected the siege of Gawilgarh (Gwalighur) in 1803: 'During the siege of Gwalighur we were all buoyed up with the hope of making our fortunes, as immense treasures were reported to be deposited in the fort. But in this expectation we were grievously disappointed, not much booty having been found.'[50] Gomm described what happened when Ciudad Rodrigo was seized: 'John Bull, though heartily fond of fighting, is not a man of blood, but he is a greedy fellow, and he plundered this time with all the rapacity of one to whom such liberty was new'. But by comparison with the drunkenness and looting which occurred at Badajos three months later, 'The ceremonies at Rodrigo were but the rehearsal of all that took place here'.[51] Interestingly, a midshipman serving offshore wrote home on 29 August 1813 recounting a rumour that San Sebastian contained much treasure, gathered in when the French evacuated the coastal towns between Bilbao and San Sebastian.[52] Ensign Hennell noted that San Sebastian 'was suffered to burn for none of our soldiers showed the least inclination to put out the fire but suffered it to burn, keeping steady to their only object, plunder'.[53] This assertion probably underestimated soldiers' fear of being fired on from houses, a fear which may explain why British soldiers allegedly shot at civilians leaning from their windows to cheer. Houses destroyed by artillery fire or by soldiers within the town were 'filled with dead bodies', particularly of those who took refuge in their cellars only to have their houses burned above them.[54] Women were wounded leaping from burning houses.[55] But a Hanoverian commissary with the army noted in 1827 that civilians were killed because they had sided with and assisted the French.[56]

Wellington conceded that some excesses had occurred. He summarized his thinking in a long and important letter to his brother on 9 October:

> In regard to the plunder of the town by the soldiers, I am the last man who will deny it. . . . It has fallen to my lot to take many towns by storm; and I am concerned to add that I never saw or heard of one so taken, by any troops, that it was not plundered. It is one of the evil consequences attending the necessity of storming a town, which every officer laments, not only on account of the evil thereby inflicted on the unfortunate inhabitants, but on account of the injury it does to discipline, and the risk which is incurred of the loss of all the advantages of victory, at the very moment they are gained.[57]

As Gomm noted of the 31st, 'The day closed as it always has done since the first town was taken, in riot and tumult'.[58] Wellington strenuously denied condoning such excesses, and mentioned efforts to constrain looting; for example, soldiers were posted at house doorways, though some inhabitants had objected to that measure. Efforts were made to curtail plundering by stationing sentries at all exits from the town and obliging plunderers to give up their booty.[59] But much plunder got through by being hidden and presumably through collusion between sentries and looters. A thriving trade in loot immediately arose. As Frazer observed on the 3rd, 'The people of San Sebastian are robbed and plundered; those of Ernani and Passages [*sic*] come with smiling faces, and purchase their neighbours' goods'.[60] Some soldiers were summarily punished and there were two incidents of individual failings or misconduct being examined on 7 September, but no widespread disciplinary action was reported centrally since the summary punishments were imposed at battalion level.[61]

Control, however, also broke down for two managerial reasons. Wellington pointed out, first, that 170 out of 250 officers and non-commissioned officers organizing the assault had been killed or wounded in storming the breach. If casualties had not been so high, especially among more senior officers 'the plunder would have been in a great measure, though not entirely, prevented'. Second, the troops involved in the assault were not replaced until 2 September, leaving men who had survived the assault free to drink and loot. The failure to pull men out more quickly was partly explained by the involvement of so much of Wellington's army in the battle of San Marcial on 31 August. The only way, Wellington claimed, that he could have relieved the troops in San Sebastian earlier would have been by taking troops from the south, to the detriment of the blockade of Pamplona.[62]

But the continued presence of those troops in the town was an organizational failure. With the exception of the 15th Portuguese Line, the heaviest casualties at the assault on 31 August were sustained by battalions in the 5th Division, as follows:[63]

1st Brigade	3/1st Foot	194
	1/9th Foot	166
	1/38th Foot	135
2nd Brigade	1/4th Foot	281
	2/47th Foot	232
	2/59th Foot	352

Four of those six battalions, excluding the 9th and the 4th, provided the infantry troops for the operation against the castle, together with the 1st Line Battalion of the King's German Legion.[64] These consisted of men who had suffered the worst of the horrors and tensions of the assault. They then witnessed not just the heaps of bodies of fallen comrades but also the continued suffering of the wounded. According to Frazer on 3 September, the makeshift hospitals where wounded soldiers were neglected 'present a shocking sight'.[65]

The problem of indiscipline raised acute concerns. Frazer was horrified by the savagery with which the town had been 'sacked'; 'Women have been shot whilst opening their doors to admit our merciless soldiery' who were drunk beyond military capability on the night of 31 August.[66] Graham was worried enough to write to Wellington at 6.00 p.m. on 1 September about the composition of his force within the town. Irritated at the delay with which this letter reached him, Wellington replied as soon as he had received it, at 6.40 a.m. on 2 September. He vetoed the despatch of units recently arrived from England into the town. Such men, 'quite unfit for active service . . . may do very well to restore order to the town' but would not be fit to 'carry on the siege'. He wanted two brigades from the 1st Division to relieve the 5th, which was to march to the 1st Division's camp. The brigades commanded by Pack and Bradford would also be assigned to the town. He did not want Spanish troops involved, despite his glowing official opinion of their behaviour in battle two days earlier; 'Spaniards', he told Graham, 'would do you no good'. He then added his views on tightening discipline: 'You had better send a provost into the town, and have a gallows erected; and the gates kept shut, and *nobody* to be allowed to go in excepting on duty'.[67]

The breakdown of discipline raised difficult questions about the nature of military cohesion and individual responsibility. Edward Coss has reviewed accounts of soldiers' behaviour following assaults on besieged towns in 1812–13. There were relatively few references to murder and rape. Coss argues that, while there was certainly widespread looting and drunkenness, vicious attacks upon civilians may have been the work of a hard core of violent soldiers who form an element in any army. He is less inclined to attribute savage assaults and murder to the strains of fighting than to see acts of rape and murder as the doings of a small minority of maladjusted men – one contemporary suggested about fifty men per regiment – habitually causing trouble within the ranks.[68]

While this seems a fair assessment, it remains true that soldiers' experience of the second assault was particularly violent. The British pinned down on the breach took exceptionally heavy losses from French soldiers firing from the rubble and especially from the buildings behind the breach. About one-third of the British casualties were killed outright, a very high proportion; by way of comparison, in the battle at San

Marcial on 31 August/ 1 September, fewer than one in seven of the casualties were killed.

George Gleig of the 85th was at Irun but visited San Sebastian to witness the second assault. He described the scene on the afternoon of 31 August as 'truly shocking' as the troops became madly drunk. The few women remaining in the town suffered a terrible fate. More drink was found the following day as further cellars were raided and within hours of dawn the men were again drunk.[69] Despite his disgust and moral outrage – he later became a clergyman – Gleig conceded some mitigation. He understood how ordinary soldiers came to hate those resisting them at San Sebastian:

> There is no species of duty in which a soldier is liable to be employed, so galling or so disagreeable as a siege. . . . It ties him so completely down to one spot, and breaks in so repeatedly upon his hours of rest, and exposes him so constantly to danger, and that too at times and in places where no honour is to be gained . . .

In visiting the brigades before the assault, he found 'little mention made of *quarter*' in reference to the impending attack: 'They could not forgive the French garrison, which had now kept them during six weeks at bay, and they burned with anxiety to wipe off the disgrace of a former repulse.'[70] Gleig had felt the intensity of anticipation as men awaited the signal for the assault and the overwhelming ferocity of the explosion on the curtain wall behind the breach. If he was shocked by the drunken criminality which followed, he attributed officers' loss of control over their men to the cumulative horrors of siege warfare.[71]

Heavy casualties, the pressures of the assault, the loss of officers and NCOs and the continuation of artillery shelling, though not of infantry fighting, cumulatively undermined discipline. Misconduct was too sudden, intense and widespread to be punished. Yet the soldiers involved in the assault were certainly aware of the army's disciplinary reach. There were, after all, instances during the campaign when soldiers' misconduct was thoroughly investigated. For instance, a peasant farming in an exposed stretch of the frontier with France was relieved of a dozen pigs around 17 July. The army wanted him to remain active in a location where he could be useful to them – presumably to garner military intelligence. The Adjutant General for the army in the Peninsula insisted that a full inquiry be held. If it proved necessary in order to ascertain the culprits, the whole Portuguese brigade involved in the affair would be kept under arms for several hours.[72] In a different context, British officers at Bilbao, where the army maintained a hospital, were forbidden to ride their horses along the public rope walk and were reminded of the need to respect the local citizens; one senior officer was removed from the town as a result of complaints about officers' behaviour.[73] On the more serious crime of rape, severe sentences were certainly handed down. At the time of the first assault, a soldier was sentenced to death for rape, which he 'justified' by claiming that it had been perpetrated on the border and he believed he was then in France. He escaped two weeks later just before his execution was due.[74]

The extent of civilian casualties remains impossible to define. Contemporary estimates suggest a population of about 8,400, but how many civilians were in the town at the time of the final assault is unknown.[75] Just before the first British siege, the French governor advised the municipal authorities on 1 July to evacuate women, children and all those who did not have the means to feed themselves during a long siege.[76] How many took this advice was not recorded. According to a report from the French ministry of the imperial treasury, the receiver of the province of Guipazcoa stated on 30 June that the civil administration had left for France; 'la majeure partie des habitants étant aussi retirés en France ou dans l'intérieur de l'Espagne'.[77] Given the fact that, after lifting their first siege on 26–7 July, the British maintained a blockade and resumed serious siege preparations within ten days, it seems unlikely that many inhabitants returned to the town. According to French accounts, half the population died during the siege, which in total lasted two months if the period of blockade is included. Although 1,500 families were left without homes or food, no specific information on civilian casualties was offered, and many presumably died of hunger and inadequate treatment in makeshift hospitals.[78] The article in *El Duende* cited many civilian casualties but named only eight victims, including two priests and four shopkeepers.[79]

If British officers knew that assaulting the town would destroy much of it, they insisted that the town was a necessary military objective. Lieutenant Colonel Frazer was an interesting commentator on the campaign. His letters home were detached, wry, alive to natural beauty and quite frequently conscious of the tension between his own witness to the horrors of war and his wish to see an end to those horrors. For example, during a quiet interlude at Deba on 30 June, he wrote home, 'If I am long detained here amid these scenes of repose, I shall lose all relish for more active employment; in truth, no one can return to those I am about to revisit without at least repugnance, if not disgust'.[80] Again, on dining at a 'comfortable' farmhouse after being present at an artillery engagement at the convent of San Bartolomeo on 8 July, he noted: 'It is impossible to return from ruined walls and smoking houses, on the embers of which are hundreds of human beings ready to destroy their fellows, without feeling a relief in even looking at the peaceful occupations of husbandry'.[81] After three days of bombarding San Sebastian's walls, he pondered on 23 July the suffering being inflicted on the inhabitants: 'We who witness these horrid scenes do not feel them as we ought: the habit of continually seeing shocking sights takes away every finer feeling; 'tis well that it does'.[82] Yet on 26 July, following the failure of the first assault, he insisted that the task had to be completed: 'I have no fears for the success of our enterprise against San Sebastian. It must be taken: the honour of our country requires it'.[83]

The Political Dispute

As we have seen, on 9 October Wellington outlined his rebuttal to his brother, the British diplomatic representative in Cádiz. Insisting on Graham's integrity, he dismissed the allegation that Graham had refused to seek Spanish assistance in putting out the fires and acerbically claimed that the Spanish had proffered little help during the siege. Since the published charges seriously undermined relations between Britain and Spain, he wanted Henry to pursue legal redress against libellous accusations.[84]

Wellington declined to discuss the issue with the Regency's minister of war, but treated it as an inter-governmental matter to be dealt through the diplomatic channel provided by his brother. Wellington snubbed the minister of war by reminding him that his official dealings with the Spanish authorities concerned military matters and were addressed to the captains general of the provinces, who had military powers delegated from the Crown.[85] On 11 October he urged that Henry should 'hint occasionally to some of our friends at Cádiz that all this will tend to put people in England very much out of humor with the Spanish alliance; and that if the people should once become disgusted with it, they will not find the Government, or any of the leading men, very warm'. He added that 'I was never so much disgusted with any thing as with this libel'.[86]

By 16 October Wellington claimed that he had only become involved in the deepening dispute because the minister of war had sent him the original newspaper article. He suggested that the minister himself might have been helped to spread the accusations. But even British accounts of the siege proved difficult to reconcile. For example, Wellington objected to one British officer's published statement because it omitted to mention the fire in the town before the assault and erroneously described the French as shelling the town from the castle after the town had been taken. Adding further to Wellington's discomfort, Don Miguel Alava, the regional captain general, reported that a letter was circulating in Vitoria from a British officer present at the assault who was 'boasting of the outrages committed there in revenge, as the officer says, for the inhabitants having fired upon our troops in the first storm'. Wellington acknowledged that if that letter was genuine it discredited his assertion, made on 9 October, that officers followed his orders not to mistreat civilians. But he noted the account's major flaw; the only British troops vulnerable to enemy fire within the town in the first assault were those taken prisoner, because no other troops entered the town and could not have been fired on by its inhabitants.[87]

Given these differences in describing events, Wellington ordered Major General Andrew Hay, who assumed command of the 5th Division on the afternoon of the assault and thereafter commanded in the town after its capture, to report on the assault. In his response on 18 October, Hay noted that the French began the fires on 23–4 July and cited Lieutenant Jones's statement that French soldiers set fire to houses with long torches, so that they could plunder them. He insisted that British officers warned their men on 25 July that discipline had to be maintained because the French would probably hold out in the castle; taking the town would not end the engagement. Officers also made every effort to 'prevent outrages' during and after the second assault. But it was difficult to control troops when parties dispersed, including to some 'narrow streets and barricades where only one man could pass at a time'. He repeated the point that loose powder and ammunition were ubiquitous in the town and were easily ignited during the second assault. He suggested that 700 male inhabitants were on the French ration lists and some at least of them fired on the British from house windows. The most interesting claims he advanced concerned interactions with the inhabitants. When the alcalde and others were asked for engines, buckets and other implements to use in fire-fighting, they insisted that the French had removed such equipment and tools to the castle. Hay claimed that he provided escorts and carriages to convey inhabitants' possessions from the town when asked to do so, or stored possessions, and plunder seized from troops, at the Old Guard room in the Plaza Vieja, which was 'generally full of the property brought by the inhabitants till it could be successfully carried out by them'. Admittedly, removal did not guarantee safety, for he indicated that, during the first two or three days after the second assault, inhabitants on the roads with their possessions were plundered by Spanish and British troops and by local peasants. Hay stressed that courts martial were held in the Plaza Vieja, where Deputy Provost Marshal Williams erected a gallows. Williams reported flogging 'every man I found plundering or committing excesses'. About thirty soldiers were thus punished on each of 1 and 2 September, but there were few floggings on the 3rd. Assistant Provost Marshal Johnstone of the 5th Division, working at various times at the breaches and the town's gate, tried to prevent people removing plunder from the town. Like Williams, he was 'very active' in dealing with soldiers' misconduct. While battalion commanders repeatedly denied that their men set fire to houses, the extent of other misconduct noted by Williams points to wrong-doing by perhaps a hundred or so men.[88]

Senior commanders stressed three things in providing information for Hay. First, Major Halford, who took over command of the 59th on the morning of 1 September, sent 'frequent patrols' into the town to 'take' any men found there and to assist the inhabitants. Second, Colonel Greville, commanding the 1st Brigade (which did not include the 59th), emphasized that his force, deployed to the north end of the town and stretched from San Elmo church on the left to the artillery arsenal on the right, had limited capacity to send out patrols and gave up trying to extinguish the fires, having made considerable efforts to do so on 31 August. He emphasized instead the continuing impact on the front line of 'the galling fire of grape' from the French defenders' 'commanding situation' in the castle just above them. Third, Lieutenant Colonel Cameron, commanding the 9th in Greville's brigade, claimed that he 'never' refused the requests he received from 'Many Spaniards' to assist them in taking property from the town, even though he could not guarantee that the individuals approaching him were the rightful owners of such property. These reports depict the confusion within the town as houses and streets burned, patrols sought to prevent or punish misconduct, civilians treated with troops to protect their possessions and some battalions took refuge from French fire.[89]

The official conclusion Wellington drew from Hay's returns was unambiguous: 'the officers and troops did everything in their power to stop the progress of the fire, which was set to the town by the enemy; and many lost their lives in the attempt, owing to the fire of musketry kept up upon the roofs of the houses, by the enemy in [the] castle'. Interestingly, General Rey's official report also noted that six areas of the town were on fire when the assault began. Wellington emphasized that Hay's conclusion that some inhabitants worked with the French and 'actually fired upon the allies' was confirmed by Chevalier de Songeon and other French officers. In conceding that plundering had occurred, he provided evidence that at least some looting had been punished. He added that he had not heard of any allegations about the British setting fire to the town until the minister's letter of 28 September, even though his headquarters were near San Sebastian and he visited the town four times from 1 to 8 September.[90]

Adhering to his brother's wishes, Sir Henry Wellesley took legal action against *El Duende*. When the case was dismissed, Wellington angrily pointed out that, even though the owner of *El Duende* was a government official, his newspaper's accusations were not deemed harmful to the state. When a subsequent article called upon the Spanish to avenge San Sebastian by attacking British officers, Wellington informed his brother that he would recommend to the British Cabinet a withdrawal from Spain unless the libel and the threat against British officers were punished.[91] He also raised the possibility of appealing against the decision by the Junta de Censura by concentrating on *El Duende*'s call for revenge against the British.[92]

One critical paragraph in the accusatory letter published in *El Duende* fuelled suspicions that it was politically inspired. That paragraph warned the populations of Pamplona, Tortosa and Barcelona to beware the approach of British forces and to resist their overtures as liberators.[93] To counter this anti-British propaganda, the Regency therefore re-affirmed its confidence in its ally. On 4 November, it published Wellington's refutation of the charges, including many of the detailed points the Field Marshal had made to Henry Wellesley on 9 October. The rebuttal asserted that the fire had begun before the first assault, that there was no intention to destroy the town, that the British deplored the sacking of the town, which could not have been avoided in the circumstances, and that civilian casualties resulted from accident rather than from deliberate acts. The *Madrid Gazette* quoted General Rey's statement that there were fires in six different parts of the town when the assault began.[94]

The British government had sufficient information available to repudiate the accusations when they appeared in London on 30 October. Parliament had been in recess since 22 July and the new session opened only on 4 November.[95] Lord Bathurst, the responsible secretary of state, made a statement to the House of Lords on 8 November. Citing the heavy losses sustained by the allies, he denied the charge that troops stopped to plunder San Sebastian instead of pushing on to attack the castle. He dismissed the charge that the British had set fire to the town; it was in the French defenders' interests to do so, not in the interests of the British seeking to capture and use the town. He added that only four of the sixteen mortars deployed had fired on the defensive works during the assault phase and officers were instructed not to direct their fire into the town. Although he conceded that 'some excesses might be committed in a town taken by storm, after a most obstinate defence', he denied that any 'deliberate cruelties' had been perpetrated. He devoted a disproportionately long time refuting relatively minor charges which could readily be discredited. For example, accusations that British troops plundered church treasures were dismissed on the practical grounds that the French had converted most churches into barracks and hospitals. He attributed what he deemed libels in the Spanish press to 'French partizans in Spain', pointing out that Graham remained at San Sebastian for a month after the second assault, but received no complaints. Instead Bathurst moved that the House formally thank Sir Thomas Graham for his distinguished services in the Peninsula and particularly for his taking of San Sebastian.[96] No sustained objections ensued and accusations of British misconduct gained little traction at home.

In fact, the capture of San Sebastian was celebrated the day following Bathurst's statement during the swearing-in of the new Lord Mayor of London. After processing through the city, with his carriage pulled by the crowd, the Lord Mayor presided over the customary banquet in the Guildhall, where the Council Chamber was dominated by Copley's vast painting of the siege of Gibraltar in the early 1780s. On the Lord Mayor's side of the banqueting hall 'St. Sebastian' was blazing in letters of fire. Above it there was 'an excellent representation of a fortress, with ramparts, bastions, and trenches'. Relegated to a place beneath 'St. Sebastian' were the words 'Leipzic' (the greatest battle fought before 1914) and 'England by her firmness has saved herself, and her example has saved the rest of Europe'. In the presence of the Spanish ambassador, the Prime Minister, Lord Liverpool, spoke of the city of London's perseverance in the struggle against France. Perseverance had been the key to Britain's 'salvation' and that in turn would lead to the 'safety, happiness, and security of Europe'.[97]

Wellington reviewed the controversy in writing to Graham, who by then had resigned his command, on 18 November. Although he had learnt of Spanish charges before Graham left for England, he 'did not wish to annoy you immediately on your departure, with a matter really not worth your attention'. Accusations of atrocities had been widely repeated in the press and when Henry took his case before the Junta de Censura, it was rejected. Wellington complained that his use of the word plunder was misrepresented in Spanish publications by being translated as *saquear* or sack.[98]

Some form of modified rebuttal appears to have been published in the Regency's official Gazette on 20 October. But Wellington, who by November was focusing on *El Duende*'s call for revenge against the British rather than the initial charges, began to see the polemical attacks as part of a political effort to discredit him: 'The fact is, that the libels in the *Duende* were published by an officer of the War department, who is the editor of that paper; and they were part of a scheme to reconcile the Spanish public to my removal from the command'.[99]

On 27 November he wrote a long private letter to Lord Bathurst. It began on a sombre note: 'Matters are becoming so bad between us and the Spaniards, that I think it necessary to draw your attention seriously to the subject'. The newspaper articles condemning the British over San Sebastian were not simply attributed to an official in the War Department but were instigated, so Wellington now alleged, by the war minister, Don Juan O'Donoju, earlier described as 'that greatest of all blackguards'.[100] They formed part of a broad propaganda campaign against the British. Accounts of British excesses in the retreat to La Coruña in 1808–9 were revived. Commercial rivalries in South America were stressed. The motives behind the presence of British garrisons in Cádiz, Cartagena and Ceuta were queried. The Regency government did not reject such allegations and criticisms and thereby signalled to senior Spanish officers that 'we are odious to the Government, and they treat us accordingly'. Co-operation between the British and Spanish officials had broken down in key areas. Plundering by Spanish troops was not being punished and the authorities locally made it very difficult for the British to secure supplies. Wellington urged Bathurst to press the Spanish government to back down. He advised that the British minister to Cádiz be withdrawn and the level of representation there reduced to that of a chargé d'affaires.

He wanted the Spanish government to be reminded that the British had garrisoned Cádiz, Cartagena and Ceuta at the request of the Spanish government; he argued that Ceuta would have been taken by 'the Moors' if a British force had not been sent there. He pressed for a British garrison to be allowed by the Spanish in San Sebastian. But he reasoned that if the British had to evacuate Spain, they could do so very easily through Pasajes and San Sebastian. They would not have to march across the country to the west coast further inflaming public opinion which was being stirred against them. His final recommendation therefore was that the British government should withdraw its army from Spain if its demands were not met.[101]

Here, then, was a further curious twist in Wellington's thinking about San Sebastian's role. Capturing the port had started in July as an incidental acquisition to be scooped up in a fast moving thrust to the French border and possibly beyond. By mid-July, it became apparent that a more serious effort would be required. Napoleon made San Sebastian into a symbol of French resolve and a means of delaying Wellington's advance and draining his resources. This decision in turn converted the seizure of the town from a minor action into a major demonstration of British determination and military ability. Once taken, it enabled the British, as we shall see, to re-align their supply routes. But British behaviour in bombarding and taking the town provoked an acrimonious argument between the British and a significant faction in the Spanish government and parliament in Cádiz. By late November, Wellington, entangled in this dispute, used the possession of San Sebastian as a means of asserting that his army could, if he wished, easily disengage from its alliance with the Spanish and make a speedy exit from Spain. If the capture of San Sebastian triggered this 'diplomatic' crisis, the port's availability to the British offered a convenient means to end both the crisis and the relationship with Spain.

Notes

1. Batty, *Campaign* (London, 1823), 39.
2. Wellington to Graham, 8 October; to Bathurst, 9 October 1813, *WD*, xi, 168, 179.
3. Wellington to Bathurst, 9 October 1813, *WD*, xi, 176–8.
4. Surtees, *Twenty-Five Years in the Rifle Brigade*, 236.
5. Ross to Sir Hew Dalrymple, 10 September, 9 October 1813, Ross, *Memoir*, 47–9.
6. Wellington to the minister of war, Cádiz, 5 October; to Henry Wellesley, 6 October 1813, *WD*, xi, 163–4, 167.
7. Wellington to Henry Wellesley, 9 October 1813 *WD*, xi, 170–3.
8. Sabine (ed.), *Letters*, 320.
9. *The Times*, 30 October 1813, p. 2.
10. Wellington to Henry Wellesley, 9 October 1813, *WD*, xi, 172–3.
11. *The Times*, 17 September 1813, p. 2.
12. Wellington to Henry Wellesley 9 October 1813, *WD*, xi, 171–3.
13. Rey to minister of war, 26 July 1813, Belmas, *Sièges*, iv, 674.
14. Rey to minister of war, 27 July 1813, Belmas, *Sièges*, iv, 677.
15. Sabine (ed.), *Letters*, 217.
16. Jones, *Journals*, ii, 37.
17. Sabine (ed.), *Letters*, 198, 204.

18. *Morning Post*, 17 August 1813.
19. Larpent (ed.), *The Private Journal*, ii, 8.
20. Belmas, *Sièges*, iv, 675.
21. Wrottesley, *Life and Correspondence*, 273.
22. Thompson (ed.), *An Ensign in the Peninsular War*, 263.
23. Strachan, *From Waterloo to Balaclava*, 129.
24. Sabine (ed.), *Letters*, 223.
25. Sabine (ed.), *Letters*, 228.
26. Sabine (ed.), *Letters*, 232.
27. Sabine (ed.), *Letters*, 229.
28. Henegan, *Seven Years Campaigning*, ii, 14.
29. Henegan, *Seven Years Campaigning*, ii, 46.
30. Carr-Gomm (ed.), *Letters and Journals*, 319–20.
31. Graham to Wellington, 24, 25 August 1813 WP 1/374 (Folder 6).
32. Jones, *Journals*, ii, 84–91.
33. Glover, *An Eloquent Soldier*, 177.
34. Sabine (ed.), *Letters*, 238–9.
35. Anon. [Blakiston], *Twelve Years' Military Adventure*, ii, 269–70.
36. Carr-Gomm (ed.), *Letters and Journals*, 247–8.
37. Wrottesley, *Life and Correspondence*, i, 280–1.
38. Carr-Gomm (ed.), *Letters and Journals*, 319–20.
39. Sabine (ed.), *Letters*, 240–1.
40. Graham to Wellington, 1, 3 September 1813, WP 1/376 (Folder 6).
41. Sabine (ed.), *Letters*, 239, 248, 251–2, 255–7; Thompson (ed.), *An Ensign in the Peninsular War*, 264.
42. Wellington to Graham, 5 September 1813, *WD,* xi, 80.
43. Wellington to Graham, 3, 5 September 1813, *WD*, xi, 71, 79–80; Jones, *Journals*, ii, 84–7.
44. Graham to Somerset, 4 September 1813, WP 9/2/2/15.
45. Sabine (ed.), *Letters*, 257.
46. Surtees, *Twenty-Five Years in the Rifle Brigade*, 238.
47. Jones, *Journals*, ii, 80–1, 86.
48. Hay, *A Narrative*, ii, 256–7, 260.
49. Wrottesley, *Life and Correspondence*, i, 281.
50. Anon. [Blakiston], *Twelve Years' Military Adventure*, i, 234–5.
51. Carr-Gomm (ed.), *Letters and Journals*, 247, 262.
52. *Liverpool Mercury*, 15 October 1813.
53. Glover (ed.), *A Gentleman Volunteer*, 130.
54. *The Times*, 30 October 1813, p. 2.
55. Glover (ed.), *A Gentleman Volunteer*, 130.
56. A.L.F. Schaumann, *On the Road with Wellington: Diary of a War Commissary in the Peninsular War* (London, 1999), 389.
57. Wellington to Henry Wellesley, 9 October 1813, *WD*, xi, 173.
58. Carr-Gomm (ed.), *Letters and Journals*, 319.
59. Wellington to Henry Wellesley, 9 October 1813, *WD*, xi, 174.
60. Sabine (ed.), *Letters*, 248–9.
61. Letter books of Adjutant General's Department of the army in the Peninsula, 23 March 1813–14 October 1813, 288–90, WP 9/1/1/8.
62. Wellington to Henry Wellesley, 9 October 1813, *WD*, xi, 173–4.
63. Oman, *A History of the Peninsular War*, vii, 529.
64. *Royal Military Panorama*, iii, 379 (January 1814).
65. Sabine (ed.), *Letters*, 244.
66. Sabine (ed.), *Letters*, 244.

67. Wellington to Graham, 2 September 1813, *WD*, xi, 59.
68. Edward J. Coss, *All for the King's Shilling. The British Soldier under Wellington, 1808–1814* (Norman OK, 2010), 226–34.
69. Gleig, *The Subaltern*, 37–8, 41.
70. Gleig, *The Subaltern*, 27.
71. Gleig, *The Subaltern*, 34, 36, 38.
72. Pakenham to Dalhousie, 22 July 1813, WP 9/1/1/8.
73. Wellington to QMG and for Adjutant General, 28 August 1813, WP 9/1/1/8.
74. Larpent (ed.), *The Private Journal*, ii, 5, 43.
75. Belmas, *Sièges*, iv, 588.
76. Belmas, *Sièges*, iv, 598.
77. 14 July 1813, SHAT C8 142.
78. Belmas, *Sièges*, iv, 650–1.
79. *The Times*, 30 October 1813, p. 2.
80. Sabine (ed.), *Letters*, 176–7.
81. Sabine (ed.), *Letters*, 185.
82. Sabine (ed.), *Letters*, 198.
83. Sabine (ed.), *Letters*, 208.
84. Wellington to Henry Wellesley, 9 October 1813, *WD*, xi, 175.
85. Wellington to minister of war, 9 October; to Conde de Villa Fuentes, 10 October 1813, *WD*, xi, 170–1, 182.
86. Wellington to Henry Wellesley, 11 October 1813 *WD*, xi, 185–6.
87. Wellington to Henry Wellesley, 16 October 1813, *WD*, xi, 199–200.
88. Hay to Wellington, 18 October 1813; 'Undated statement by Edward Williams' enclosed with Hay's report, WP12/1/8 (Folder 5).
89. Colonel G. Greville to Hay; Lieutenant Colonel J. Cameron to Greville; Major J. Halford to Hay, 18 October 1813, WP 12/1/8 (Folder 5).
90. Wellington to Henry Wellesley, 23 October 1813, *WD*, xi, 214–15.
91. Wellington to Henry Wellesley, 30 October 1813, *WD*, xi, 232–3.
92. Wellington to Henry Wellesley, 2 November 1813, *WD*, xi, 246–7.
93. *The Times*, 30 October 1813, p. 2.
94. *The Times*, 27 November 1813, p. 3; far briefer notes of the Regency's endorsement of Wellington's rebuttal appeared in the *Morning Chronicle*, 27 November 1813 and the (London) *Examiner*, 28 November 1813.
95. Thorne, *The House of Commons*, i, 388.
96. House of Lords *Debates*, 8 November 1813, Vol. 27, cc 45–9.
97. *The Times*, 10 November 1813, p. 3.
98. Wellington to Graham, 18 November 1813, *WD*, xi, 297–8.
99. Wellington to Bathurst, 22 November 1813, *WD*, xi, 313.
100. Wellington to Henry Wellesley, 19 November 1813, *WD*, xi, 301.
101. Wellington to Bathurst, 27 November 1813, *WD*, xi, 325–7.

Chapter 13

The Alliance Maintained

Political Contexts

Managing an army is subject to political requirements and expectations. The operations against San Sebastian were no exception in having political consequences. To satisfy politicians, generals need to manage both armies and the political expectations of what can be achieved by those armies, while delivering results to match or exceed those expectations.

By late 1813 four governments were involved in the Peninsular War, and Wellington worked with three of them. The independent Spanish Regency Council held limited direct territory but sought to shape events from Cádiz, where the council worked alongside a representative body, the Cortes. This fragile government tried to control all groups, scattered across Spain, who opposed the Bonapartist monarchy in Madrid. In reality, the armies raised in the name of the Regency depended on support from within their several provinces, drawing upon venerable traditions of provincial autonomy. Wellington found the relationship between the Regency and Cortes on the one side and the scattered Spanish armies very difficult to master, despite serving, with increasing frustration, as commander-in-chief of the Spanish armies in the field from late 1812 to late 1813.[1] The decision to appoint Wellington arose from political manoeuvrings in the Cortes where the *liberales* tried to gain British backing against their opponents by conferring what they regarded as a mainly honorific title. If anything, they hoped the appointment might increase their leverage over the Anglo-Portuguese forces under Wellington's command. They were certainly not bent on creating a more purposeful military command structure. Apart from confronting deeply polarized groupings within the Cortes, the British also faced underlying Spanish suspicions about their motives for intervening in the Peninsula. Initially, in 1808–10, many influential Spaniards believed that the British wanted to take over Cádiz as a valuable commercial port. It would have complemented their control of Gibraltar, the strategic sentinel at the entry into the Mediterranean, and given them a preponderant role in Spanish colonial trade. If those suspicions receded after 1810, Spanish politicians faced a new challenge as rebellions against colonial rule broke out throughout Latin America in that year. Having failed to secure British assistance in crushing insurgency, they not unreasonably suspected that at least some senior British politicians wanted to open up Latin America to British trade and were less than enthusiastic about the continued existence of Spain's New World empire.[2] It is easy to see how the destruction of San Sebastian could be woven into existing narratives about the commercial ambitions which apparently underpinned Britain's involvement in the Peninsula.

Wellington also had to deal with the Portuguese authorities in Lisbon. To solve the problem of controlling troops, the British had created a Portuguese army, recruited from among the Portuguese but with a number of British officers in senior commands and on the staff. Although this army performed well in 1813, Portuguese arrangements concerning logistics remained periodically contentious. Further tensions arose from Portuguese officials' delays in paying troops, despite the fact that the British government provided a subsidy which readily exceeded the costs of the Portuguese army. During the four years between 1810 and 1813, Portugal was the leading recipient of British wartime subsidies, benefiting from an average of over £2 million annually. The largest number of Portuguese troops with Wellington's field army in 1813 was about 30,000. The subsidy more than covered the soldiers' costs. In 1804 and 1814 the British calculated the subsidies offered to continental coalition partners on the basis of an annual cost of £12 10*s*. in wages for each soldier provided. Over time the administrative chain for making payments to the Portuguese was shortened. In 1813 and 1814, Wellington or the Portuguese commissaries and paymasters with the army were directly responsible for spending about 70 per cent of the subsidy.[3] By the end of 1812, Wellington viewed the relationship with the Portuguese as infinitely preferable to any which might be established with northern European allies if his army were to be transferred to that sector. As he informed Lord Bathurst: 'it must not be expected that any of the Powers of the North of Europe would give us the direction and management of their concerns, as we now have of those of the Portuguese, at least, if not of the Spaniards'.[4] The performance of the Portuguese brigades at San Sebastian cemented the military relationship so carefully created in the previous four years.

Although Wellington occasionally faced larger questions from London, the third government with which Wellington worked, that of Britain itself, generally backed its commanding general. Wellington served in 1807–9 as a minister alongside many of those still in office in 1813.[5] One difficulty concerned the strained relationship between Wellington's eldest brother, the Marquess Wellesley, and the new Prime Minister appointed in May–June 1812, the Earl of Liverpool. Wellesley, who had been Foreign Secretary in 1809–12, refused to support the new ministry. Another brother, William Wellesley-Pole, backed Lord Wellesley, at least initially, and also declined to continue in political office. Curiously, however, both of them pressed in the first half of 1813 for a measure which did Wellington's standing among well-informed Spaniards no harm. They worked for legislation to relax legal restrictions on Roman Catholics' civil rights.[6] Their efforts failed in the teeth of the government's opposition, but Wellington's prestige stood so high that his influence with ministers was not diminished. His outstanding ability to work with the British governing establishment, of which he was a member, did not, of course, preclude frequent disagreements about resources and the prompt delivery of required munitions and supplies. His conduct of the campaign as such in the second half of 1813 was not marred by strategic disagreements with ministers in London. But, as we have seen, the campaign against San Sebastian led to a heated confrontation between Wellington and the Admiralty over naval support.

Meanwhile, the fourth government with an interest in the Peninsula, the imperial regime in Paris, essentially treated Spain as a pawn in the emperor's larger European game after displacing Joseph as King of Spain in July 1813. The key decision to defend San Sebastian came from Paris, rather from the French authorities in Spain. Wellington's dilemma, of course, was that the collapse of French rule in Spain strengthened the command of the French army opposing him and encouraged greater assertiveness among his Spanish liberal opponents in Cádiz. San Sebastian became a contentious factor in that new relationship.

The Anglo-Spanish Alliance in Practice
As we have stressed, allegations about British intentions in San Sebastian added to tensions between Wellington and the Spanish Regency and Cortes. The Field Marshal had long found the *liberales* especially tiresome. News of his resignation of the command-in-chief of the Spanish armies reinforced the clash over San Sebastian to give a public impression of a dysfunctional alliance. How far did this and other disputes threaten to undermine military collaboration between the allies?

It was hardly surprising that the British presence provoked numerous disputes. New ones arose when the campaign shifted to the north. For example, the government of Biscay, based at Bilbao, proposed that local customs officials had the right to inspect the mass of goods being brought into northern Spain by British ships. On 14 October Wellington outlined his practical objections to the provincial captain general. He accepted that Spain had the right in principle to regulate, constrict and levy duties upon goods imported for the British army's use. He conceded that inspecting cargoes would not be problematic at four of the six ports used by the British. La Coruña and Santander were mainly used as rendezvous ports, with the goods landed at La Coruña being intended for the Spanish and those at Santander being mainly for hospitals. Bilbao was also used. San Sebastian took cargoes for the town's garrison and for the Spanish army. But two small, more easterly ports were used for military cargoes which needed to be unloaded quickly, leaving no time for customs inspections. Fuenterrabia was very little utilized. Pasajes, however, proved exceptional because of its physical configuration and its vital importance to the campaign. The harbour was so tight and so crowded that up to twelve ships at a time were unloaded, immediately filled with ballast and sent on their way. The pressures on the port meant that delays in unloading might well endanger Wellington's ability to maintain his army on the French frontier. The Field Marshal also asked that the provincial government of Biscay be reminded that Wellington's official co-operation would be essential to the smooth execution of customs officials' duties.[7]

This particular Spanish claim seems to have lapsed, but a different intervention – this time over quarantine – occurred in mid-January. With heavy demands upon shipping and difficult winter navigation in the Bay of Biscay, all freight ships bringing supplies for the army called first at Santander and waited there for the opportunity to sail to the more easterly ports. On the grounds that there were instances of yellow fever at Santander, the Xefe Politico of Guipuzcoa, without warning to the British, quarantined British ships and refused to allow them to sail eastwards. Wellington insisted that no contagion afflicted the hospital at Santander in mid-January and cited the quarantine decision as yet further proof that 'Duties of the highest description . . . are made to depend upon the caprice of a few ignorant individuals . . . '.[8]

Friction was intensified by the destruction of San Sebastian. For example, the house in San Sebastian occupied by the British and Portuguese artillery was burned down in December. The Spanish government objected to this continued and in their view provocative presence and the artillerymen were withdrawn in early January. No British forces remained in the town.[9] On 16 January 1814, the junta of San Sebastian published a formal complaint against the destructiveness of the British assault. Although it did not mention mass slaughter or suggest how many civilians died, it complained of killings, savage rapes and extensive looting. It noted that plundered items were openly sold under the eyes of the British military authorities. Only 36 of the town's 600 or so houses in the town were allegedly intact by the end, and 1,500 families were left without food or shelter.[10]

This concerted protest may have been stimulated by a quest for compensation. Precedents had been set at Zaragoza and Gerona. In April 1809 representatives of the Spanish royal government publically promised wide-ranging financial recognition for the suffering inflicted upon Zaragoza. Once restored to power, they pledged that all public buildings in the city would be rebuilt, that there would be a ten-year exemption from taxation, that soldiers involved in defending the city would be promoted, with consequent increases in pensions, and that all inhabitants who survived the siege would be accorded higher civil status. During the siege of Gerona, Spanish local officials promised that the Catalonian authorities would meet the costs of rebuilding all houses destroyed.[11] But since the British inflicted the damage in 1813 and since the Cortes had little love for Wellington, there was no impetus for the Spanish parliament to suggest, let alone offer, compensation for the destruction of San Sebastian.

In February 1814, Frazer visited Usnibil, where some of those displaced from San Sebastian lived. He found that the people of San Sebastian were about to protest formally about their treatment in September. In early March he noted that attacks on a British employee and a British lieutenant had occurred. It was reported that 'the minds of the people near St Sebastian are much inflamed by the late manifesto on the subject of our burning the town'.[12] Frazer chose not to dwell on any of these matters or to consider, however fleetingly, the merits or otherwise of the charges made or the sentiments they stirred.

Wellington's frustrations arose partly from the pressures of managing a Spanish army, in addition to the Anglo-Portuguese army, in the invasion of France. But those pressures went back to the days after the battle of San Marcial, where, arguably, the Spanish for the first time fought effectively within an integrated allied operation. Operational success was undermined by logistical shortcomings. On 3 September 1813, Wellington complained to the Spanish minister of war that the Spanish troops who had fought so well at San Marcial were starving. On the 5th, he strongly criticized, again to the minister, the entire Spanish plan for organizing military corn supplies and complained to the British war minister about the *liberales*' anti-British political machinations in the Cortes at Cádiz.[13] The system's defects had been pointed out since January and left the Spanish forces dependent on British supplies. Wellington, in a dig against his local protagonist, stressed to the Spanish minister of war 'I doubt not that the *Xefes Politicos* have taken care to inform the Government of the misery inflicted on the people by this military system'.[14] With Wellington fulminating about Spanish failures in supplying their troops, some officials at Cádiz may have been tempted to make political capital out of San Sebastian's destruction.

While the siege of San Sebastian exacerbated disputes between the British and the Spanish, the rebuilding of the town's defences and the use of Pasajes as a depot fostered military co-operation. One practical need was the use of San Sebastian as a working port. On 9 September, an officer pointed out that the British artillery currently held its supplies at Bilbao, which was convenient enough for landing and re-embarking by sea, but which depended for its security on British control of the neighbouring countryside. San Sebastian, by contrast, offered a more secure depot for military stores.[15]

Detailed plans to repair San Sebastian's defences were drawn up as soon as the castle had been taken. The estimates were approved on 20 September. Solid masonry could not be used until the weather improved in the spring. But this difficulty was resolved when, on Burgoyne's recommendation, work proceeded with dry masonry. Wellington, though preferring that solid masonry should be used 'whenever it is possible', agreed that using dry masonry was preferable to delaying the work.[16] The Spanish garrison was well treated, with the British supplying full kits of clothing and accoutrements for its 4,000 Spanish soldiers.[17] Reconstruction created employment. Spanish troops provided working parties, receiving British rates of pay for 5 to 6 hours per day, with each working party being paid on completion of their assigned tasks.[18] More skilled artisans would be drawn from the allied army, preferably from the Portuguese contingents. Burgoyne noted that much of the old wall remained, so that the principal work in rebuilding would consist of cutting out those damaged sections of wall which had not been battered down in order to establish 'a solid bed for the permanent repairs'.[19] The engineers' report indicated that the damage inflicted by the British bombardment had been neither extensive nor irreparable. The town wall on the Urumea River had been rebuilt and the main breach cleared by early October.[20]

Trade began to return to San Sebastian. By late October sixteen British transport ships were in the port, although this total fell far short of the forty-eight transports at Pasajes, despite the difficulties of entering the latter compared with San Sebastian's ease of access to the open sea.[21] On 18 September, Ensign Hennell noted that, although in ruins, the town 'is repairing fast'.[22] It began to return to normality early in 1814. For example, Wellington visited it at the beginning of February in order to greet the Duc d'Angoulême, the nephew and ultimate heir to the Bourbon claimant to the French throne. In March he commandeered small boats from San Sebastian to be used for transports, and activity in the harbour was further evidenced when boats there were wrecked in storms in early March.[23]

Again, co-operation at Pasajes and in the countryside was generally effective. On 13 September, Captain John Atchison, the British Military Commandant at Pasajes, noted that the Spanish local commander and the civil magistrates met his requests promptly and willingly. He attributed this response to his honesty in requisitioning and to his avoiding 'all interference' in the 'internal government' of the district.[24] On

31 September, 15 transports arrived with 700 Foot Guards and later unloaded the troops and supplies into the small town square. The square became 'a scene of indescribable bustle and noise, of endless variety of costume and confusion of languages' as allied soldiers sought out goods newly shipped from England while the 'peasantry from the surrounding mountains brought their vegetables to market here'.[25] In October, 'supplies of all kinds' were transported to the army along the road following the Bidassoa River. The river's valley was entered by 'long trains of muleteers, winding along the mountain paths, and singing their wild national airs, while conveying their loads of provisions to the camp'.[26] Five months later, when the allies spread out into southern France, 'large convoys of Spanish muleteers' delivered food supplies stockpiled at Socoa, on St Jean de Luz's expansive bay, to the dispersed divisions.[27] Despite the destruction of San Sebastian and the periodic recurrence of plundering, the campaign stimulated economic exchange and positive human interactions between the British and their Spanish allies.

As the allied armies advanced into France, Wellington's hostility to the Spanish authorities eased. By 1 December, he recommended that his brother remain in ambassadorial rank, whereas he had earlier advised Sir Henry's withdrawal from his diplomatic post at Cádiz. He saw no need to demand full access to San Sebastian unless the British government felt that the Spanish were failing to co-operate effectively with the British. He awaited formal permission to withdraw the British garrison from Cádiz, so that the withdrawal would symbolize British goodwill and be accompanied by a public statement that the Spanish government had pressed the British to provide garrisons for Cádiz and Cartagena in the first place. This sudden moderation resulted from advice from Henry Wellesley in Cádiz that sentiment in the Cortes was shifting against the Spanish government 'principally on account of their conduct towards us'. Channels of communication were being re-opened with 'the anti-democratic party' in the Cortes and Sir Henry was being listened to once more.[28] Days later Wellington went further and ordered the withdrawal of British troops from both Cádiz and Carthagena to scotch newspaper rumours that the British had sinister political designs upon Spain's strategic ports, or the country's political future.[29]

The prospect of better relations did not, predictably, extend to Wellington's approach to the minister of war. On 7 December he complained of the failure to give the captains general sufficient authority to supply the Spanish armies in the field. He asserted that 'the Intendants of the provinces and the Xefes Politicos are unable or unwilling to perform their duty; all authority has been annihilated in Spain; and at the moment the greatest exertions are required to form and maintain armies to save the State . . .'.[30]

Yet greater stress was placed on Anglo-Spanish co-operation as the allies pushed into France. Accusations that San Sebastian had been deliberately and systematically sacked and then destroyed infuriated a commander who wanted to conciliate, not antagonize, the French as he invaded their country. Such accusations, however, receded in importance once the allied army secured an expanding foothold in south-west France. In retrospect, Wellington's irritation over this dispute proved transitory. It is significant that when, in 1823, Wellington enumerated for George Canning, the Foreign Secretary, examples from his own experience of why the Spanish authorities could not be trusted, he did not include their behaviour over San Sebastian in his long list of complaints.[31]

The Problem of Civilian Casualties

The controversy over the destruction of San Sebastian concerned loss of property rather than loss of life. But the general absence of sustained reflection on the siege's impact on civilians indicated an important contradiction. Enlightened policy-makers in the eighteenth century tried to protect civilians from the severity of modern war. They made two types of distinction. One differentiated between soldiers and civilians during war, treating the latter as separate from the fighting and not responsible for the hardship and bloodshed produced by war.[32] Russell Weigley argued that 'up to 1815, military professionalism had helped restrain rather than escalate the violence of war, and particularly had helped to restrict that violence to enemy combatants while protecting civilian lives and property'.[33] Another approach argued that military opponents were not mortal enemies. Wars might be fought hard, but they should not be inspired by hatred of an 'enemy'. Emmerich Vattel, in his pioneering reflections on the conduct of war, published in 1758, claimed that 'At the present day, the Nations of Europe almost always carry on war with great forbearance and generosity'. Rousseau, in *The Social Contract* (1762), asserted 'War, then, is not a relationship between man and man, but between State and State, in which private persons are only enemies accidentally, not as men, nor even as citizens, but simply as soldiers. . .'.[34] It therefore followed that wartime propaganda should not inflame popular passions against the inhabitants of another country. Even Napoleon claimed that harm, even if sanctioned by custom, inflicted on an enemy was 'excusable only so far as it is absolutely necessary; everything beyond that is criminal'.[35]

Such intellectual distinctions broke down in practice for two compelling reasons. Armies take what they want and need no ideological invocations to handle enemy civilians roughly. The allied invasion of France in 1793 resulted in widespread plunder, destruction and the mistreatment of civilians. For example, the six-week siege of Valenciennes in 1793 destroyed a third of the town's houses. The department of Alpes-Maritimes witnessed rampant pillaging and the destruction of houses in the same year.[36] The French in 'liberating' neighbouring peoples were no less energetic in their depredations. French armies after storming cities occasionally put the defenders to the sword, and certainly plundered with a purpose, as at Pavia in 1796.[37] More generally, the French soon found that, as their armies grew in size and became continuing rather than temporary drains on their finances, those armies had to live off the lands they invaded and generate funds for government coffers in Paris. Plunder and state-enforced cash levies became endemic during 1793–6, setting the pattern for future French conduct.[38]

Secondly, laudable efforts to professionalize fighting came under severe strain in 1793–5 with the French revolutionaries' recourse to the *levée en masse* and their insistence that all citizens had a duty to defend the republic against invasion. The willingness to bear arms became a positive attribute of citizenship when the very existence of the republic was threatened. The distinction between soldier and civilian had already been blurred during the American War of Independence when militiamen took up arms if their localities were threatened by British forces. But the guerrilla warfare which followed was directed principally against soldiers and those assisting them. The distinction between the two roles was becoming blurred by the 1790s and became more so when Spanish guerrilla warfare acquired both its name and widespread acceptance as a response to invasion from 1808.

Growing violence in the Peninsula resulted in part from the prolonged and indecisive nature of the conflict. Russell Weigley saw French soldiers' plundering and savagery in Spain and British troops' excesses as a reaction to tensions created by the guerrilla war and a protracted, frustrating and indecisive military campaign. Shortages of food and grim conditions also helped stoke resentments against the civilian population. According to Weigley, soldiers felt accumulating resentment at the apparent futility of the struggle in the Peninsula. In an age when armies' objective was to seek out battle and win a decisive victory, the Peninsular War seemed to offer the antithesis of military fulfilment.[39]

In the eighteenth century, there was open debate as to whether civilians should be permitted to leave a besieged town. Since the purpose of most sieges was to starve the besieged into surrender, the larger the number of people being confined within a besieged town, the more rapidly food stocks would be exhausted. There was also the problem of how acceptable it was to bombard civilians within besieged towns. Guidelines were developed about how far a besieged garrison which resisted could ask for and secure reasonable terms for a capitulation. It was customary to allow reasonable terms up to the point where a breach had been made but before the breach was assaulted. A capitulation was not only honourable but might also involve the retention of side-arms and possessions.[40] As we have seen, the French capitulation at San Sebastian occurred with strict military proprietary.

British behaviour in San Sebastian fell between two stools. Attempts were made to limit civilian casualties. As has been noted earlier, Wellington stressed that an extensive bombardment would be 'materially injurious in the attack, and will be very inconvenient to our friends the inhabitants, and eventually to ourselves'. Yet Wellington then left decisions about the nature of the bombardment to the specialist officers and Graham.[41] The artillery attack had concentrated on military targets, but fires could easily spill over from the defences behind the walls themselves. Moreover, the town was far too small to allow the attackers, once they entered the town, to confine their assault to strictly designated military zones within its walls. Lapses, crimes and atrocities occurred during the storming of the breaches and in the day or so after, probably fuelled by heavy drinking.

Such behaviour was deplorable in eighteenth-century terms, but had a precedent in the charivari of the seventeenth and eighteenth centuries. For set periods it was acceptable during urban festivities for social hierarchies to be overturned and a species of popular or perhaps even mob rule to run its course. Some charivari went beyond customary bounds and ballooned into rioting. Senior officers basically regarded soldiers' plundering in assaulted towns as similar to urban charivari. There were even parallels in the ways in which soldiers dressed, sometimes outrageously, in stolen clothing. Officers regarded soldiers' misconduct beyond 'normal' plundering with grim resignation.

In the case of San Sebastian, the contrast between dealing with general indiscipline and addressing individual injustices was demonstrated by Lieutenant Colonel Frazer's reactions to two distinctive cases. We have shown that he expressed mortification and regret in briefly describing the sacking of San Sebastian. But he recorded no action in response to that horror. In contrast, he was extremely exercized during the siege by Wellington's disciplining of Captain Norman Ramsay of the Royal Horse Artillery, Frazer's own unit. This occurred on 23 June. Believing that an injustice had been done, he pressed Ramsay's case with Wellington's military secretary, Lord Fitzroy Somerset, as well as with Sir Thomas Graham. Ramsay was restored to active command by September.[42] This same concern about the appropriate treatment of a wronged officer preoccupied Frazer's son over thirty years later. Planning to publish his father's letters, Captain Augustus Frazer (also of the Royal Horse Artillery) wrote to Sir Thomas Graham's family asking if they had any of Lieutenant Colonel Frazer's letters to the general concerning Wellington's arrest of Ramsay.[43] It was understandable that a matter of honour involving a fellow officer in the same regiment should excite interest and indeed anxiety. But the incident illustrated senior officers' implicit recognition of the limits of their authority. While Frazer could make representations about Wellington's disciplining of a fellow officer, he felt no such scope for taking action against or making any representations about soldiers' conduct during the sacking of San Sebastian. He simply accepted that under certain conditions normal discipline broke down.

The charge that the British deliberately destroyed San Sebastian created further difficulties for Wellington because he naturally wished to reassure French public opinion about the allied armies' behaviour once they invaded France.

After the allies' first incursion into France, he reported that the British and Portuguese troops had behaved well. Although 'The Spaniards plundered a good deal . . . even this misfortune has been of service to us. Some were executed, and many punished; and I sent all the Spanish troops back into Spain to be cantoned, which has convinced the French of our desire not to injure individuals'. The successful invasion of France depended upon peeling the population away from Napoleon and securing their co-operation; all therefore depended on 'our moderation and justice, and upon the good conduct and discipline of our troops'.[44] The problem, however, continued, with a particularly striking case in December when General Morillo and his officers failed to constrain their men's plundering and Wellington ordered that the troops be kept under arms all day. This provoked the response that the Spanish were being discriminated against, an accusation which Wellington vigorously sought to discredit.[45]

The British perfectly well understood the Spanish resentment against French depredations and the desire to avenge them. The French had a record of destroying the villages through which they retreated. Lieutenant Colonel Frazer, for example, noted after two days pursuing the retreating French from Vitoria towards Pamplona that 'Every village we have passed through since we left Vitoria has been on fire, houses all gutted; the inhabitants have generally fled; some of those who remained have been murdered'. The houses remaining had been saved by heavy rains.[46] Five days later Frazer was told by Sir George Collier that the French at Castro Urdiales, east of Santander, had 'murdered every person in the town whom they could find, and committed every indignity'. This retribution occurred after the French blamed the inhabitants for failing to warn them that a bridge had been destroyed by Collier, as a result of which some French soldiers fell to their deaths down a ravine.[47]

The Legacy of the Siege

Although the destruction of San Sebastian provoked recriminations in 1813–14, it did not leave a permanent legacy of British guilt or local hostility to Britain. There were, however, two occasions in the 1820s and 1830s when further British intervention was considered or occurred. In 1823 the restored Bourbon government of France sent an army into Spain to uphold the absolutist claims of the restored Borbón of Spain, Fernando VII. It was led by the same Duc d'Angoulême who Wellington had met in 1814. In advancing into Spain, the main French army marched down the royal road through Tolosa on its way to Madrid. But subsidiary forces were detached to Pamplona and San Sebastian, with 5,000 troops assigned to the latter. San Sebastian's defences were well capable of mounting 24-pounders and the French did not possess siege guns to overwhelm those defences. The small suburb of San Martin, which had been cleared by the defenders in 1813 to provide an open field of fire and to deny its use to the attackers, was the site ten years later of a powerful bastion covering the southern approach to the town. The French, however, deployed 'a strong naval force' to blockade by sea.[48]

The Whig opposition naturally denounced the intervention, insisting that Britain should oppose French support for authoritarianism in Spain. To embarrass the government, led still by Lord Liverpool as it had been in 1813, Lord John Russell, a prominent Whig, reminded the House of Commons in March 1824 that Britain had lost many excellent men in fighting for Spanish freedom from French occupation, yet the French flag was now flying over Cádiz, Badajoz and San Sebastian. Lord John's selection of towns was pointed. Cádiz had remained a centre of resistance to Napoleon's forces throughout the Peninsular War, while Badajoz and San Sebastian had cost the largest number of British lives lost in Wellington's sieges. The following year, another leading Whig, Henry Brougham, asked how long the French army would remain, noting that it had fortified Cádiz and held San Sebastian, among other places.[49] The use of such symbols to remind ministers of previous victories now turned to defeat was clearly deliberate and it indicated no sense of regret or guilt at the impact of the British assault in 1813.

Britain became involved in the region more actively during the civil war of the 1830s. On 5 May 1836, members of a specially formed British Auxiliary Legion sailed into San Sebastian from Santander. This force consisted of volunteers permitted to fight in Spain through the Whig government's decision to suspend the Foreign Enlistment Act, which forbade British subjects from fighting for foreign powers. They were there to back the cause of Queen Isabella II, Fernando VII's baby daughter and heir, as represented by her mother, Fernando's widow, Queen Cristina, who acted as Regent and pursued constitutionalist policies. The queens were opposed by Fernando's brother, the conservative Don Carlos, who claimed that the crown could pass only through the male line and that Fernando had illegitimately changed the law to enable his daughter to succeed him. The Carlists intensified their armed struggle for power in 1835 and were blockading San Sebastian. Over a period of about five months, they had constructed a double line of fortifications 2 miles long from the Urumea in the east to a deep ravine running to the sea. This line was well-entrenched; it linked villages along high ground; and it commanded the road south to Hernani. The first fortified part of the position lay about half a mile south of San Sebastian. About 4,500 troops of the British Legion and 1,500 Spanish soldiers attacked this line on 5 May from the town, supported by gunfire from two British warships in the bay west of the town. One of the steam ships, at 1,600yd, destroyed an angle in one of the key Carlist fortifications, Fort Lugariz, and opened the way for an assault by the British Legion. The British lost 823 casualties in the intense fighting, consisting of 10 officers, 5 sergeants and 116 other ranks killed, and 65 officers, 33 sergeants and 594 other ranks wounded. The victory was celebrated by gifts of clothing from the town of San Sebastian to the soldiers and, later, with a commemorative memorial.[50]

This was followed by the capture of Pasajes from the Carlists on 28 May. British support for the Queen Regent continued after the British Legion disengaged and was dissolved by 1838. Cristina had accepted in 1836 the liberal constitution of 1812, much despised by Wellington during the Peninsular War. In the following year, she won the endorsement of Lord Palmerston, the Foreign Secretary, as an exemplar of those challenging 'arbitrary government' in contemporary Europe. But from 1837 at the latest, relations with the Spanish government became entangled with a shift in French policy, which had initially promoted co-operation with Britain. Britain thereafter sought to counter the efforts of the French ministry headed by Marshal Soult to shape Spanish politics.[51] In those circumstances, British influence in San Sebastian provided a symbol of British commitment directly across the French border. British forces specializing in fortifications and seaborne operations remained at San Sebastian until August 1840, despite their prominent role in the town's destruction twenty-seven years earlier. Only then were 700 officers and men of the Royal Artillery, Sappers and Miners, Royal Marine Artillery and, especially, the Marine Battalion evacuated in a combination of merchant and Royal Navy ships, with a squadron of the latter patrolling off the coast.[52] Any legacy of the controversies of 1813–14 had thus receded by the late 1830s.

This role reversal, with British troops becoming the honoured defenders of the town, was interesting enough. Equally notable was the stress placed by Alexander Somerville in his voluminous account of the campaign on the friendly reception given to the British in San Sebastian. Although he recognized that the British had committed atrocities against civilians during the Peninsular War, he saw the seizure of the Carlist lines as a moment of reconciliation with the town's inhabitants. In considering the capture in 1837 of Irun, he emphasized British restraint on taking a town, which refused to surrender on being summoned. Moreover, in looking back to the Peninsular War for instances of British ill-discipline and excess, he freely cited the examples of gross misconduct at Badajoz, omitting all reference to San Sebastian in 1813.[53]

In general, Badajoz dwarfed San Sebastian in Victorians' remembrance of the great sieges of the Peninsular War. It figured in celebrated theatrical re-enactments. Astley's in 1840 produced 'The Wars of Wellington' centred on Seringapatam, La Coruña, Badajoz and Waterloo. The storming of Badajoz won the *Theatrical Journal*'s praise as 'superior to any thing [*sic*] of the kind ever seen before'.[54] In the summer of 1849, the Surrey Zoological Gardens staged the storming of Badajoz climaxing in a fireworks display described as 'one of the most brilliant that has ever been exhibited'.[55] It also stood out as a fearsome case-study of the horror of siege fighting. In the midst of the savage suppression of the Mutiny-Rebellion in India, the *Saturday Review* reminded its readers that atrocities inevitably resulted when besieged towns fell: 'The license of all armies at captured towns, from Magdeburg to Badajoz, never admitted of a moment's doubt'.[56] Magdeburg suffered a terrible fate during the Thirty Years War, but the modern exemplar was notable. The ferocity of the fighting and sacking was not being condemned, but instead cast as the natural outcome of an assault upon a keenly defended town. Thus when Sir William Napier died in 1860, the *Saturday Review* singled out Badajoz as the engagement memorialized in his multi-volume *History of the Peninsular War* which most graphically confirmed the British soldiers' reputation for valour and determination.[57] A semi-official history of the Royal Artillery published in 1873 concluded that 'The story of the storming of Badajoz is one which will thrill the heart of every Briton for all time', but, in addition, it 'will impress on all who study it, the truth of Napier's words that "a British army bears with it an awful power"'.[58]

If Spanish anger at the fate of San Sebastian had no significant impact on Victorians' recollection or assessment of the siege, the immediate legacy of the destruction of San Sebastian meant different things to different parties. For the French, the capitulation was an honourable defeat. The defence of the town and castle had lasted two months and had been conducted with vigour, determination, skill and courage. Soult praised the commander, Brigadier General Rey, and his staff. Holding out for so long and inflicting heavy losses on the enemy offered an example of careful planning and purposefulness so signally lacking at Vitoria. In combination with other measures, and the political-military truce in Germany, the defence of San Sebastian helped halt Wellington's progress and wrecked the plan he outlined in early July for the rapid seizure of Pamplona and San Sebastian. The defence gave the French a lodestar for their own operations, an outpost which they sought, if unsuccessfully, to relieve. If somewhat desperately used by Napoleon as a rallying point, the isolated garrison provided senior commanders with an exemplar in galvanizing their forces after seven weeks spent retreating in May–July.

For the Spanish, San Sebastian had both political and military significance. The town's destruction was used by those politicians in Cádiz who sought to discredit the British alliance. Tensions between Wellington and O'Donoju, the minister of war, were already acute by early September. Wellington came to believe that the minister was behind a systematic campaign to demonize the British now that the French had been expelled from most of Spain. The fall of San Sebastian made the politics of the alliance with liberal Spain more rather than less difficult. On the other hand, the two-month defence of the town and the frontier region in general encouraged and eased military co-operation between the British and some Spanish generals. The largely Spanish success at San Marcial, in preventing the French from relieving San Sebastian, seems genuinely to have boosted Spanish military standing among the British. This signified effective co-ordination in battle, rather than simply co-operation in assigning separate armies to dispersed operations. Close collaboration continued and there is no British evidence that senior Spanish officers in the frontier theatre blamed Wellington or his subordinates for the destruction of San Sebastian. Wellington's own correspondence on the dispute focused entirely on relations with Cádiz.

For the British, San Sebastian was a success, however flawed and long-delayed. A siege had not been part of any plan until early July. Losses were heavy, and embarrassing. Victory required the delivery from England of a more substantial siege-train than had initially been allowed for. The fall of San Sebastian did not put a spring into many British officers' steps. It came as more of a relief than a triumph. In terms of Spanish public relations, it marked a set-back. At home, on the other hand, it was used to stir national pride. *The Times* drew a firm lesson from the second assault: 'Never did British soldiers act with more spirit and gallantry, overcoming obstacles which, perhaps, to any other troops would have appeared insurmountable'.[59]

Yet in preparing for the invasion of France the gains were real. The destruction of a sizeable, and very well defended, outpost of French resistance indicated the strength of British intentions and a commitment to crushing resistance wherever it might be offered. The French had been removed from the northern coast of Spain, so reducing possible interference with allied coastal shipping. The delivery of the siege train supported preparations for the invasion of France. It was obvious that the French had begun strengthening their defences at Bayonne from early July, and Bayonne commanded the road to Bordeaux. That road northwards was the most accessible route for the British from the coast. But above all else, San Sebastian had to be taken in order to secure the use of the harbour at Pasajes without tying down large numbers of troops. When the invasion proceeded, this superbly protected harbour became the forward maritime base for British operations in the south-west corner of France. Although this had not figured in the original plan, the possession of Pasajes enabled Wellington to re-align his supply lines from Britain. Santander remained as a major transhipment centre from England, while Pasajes became the key to supplying the invading army with arms, munitions and clothing. The strategic gain was palpable and immediately felt as the allies invaded France.

Notes

1. Charles Esdaile, *The Duke of Wellington and the Command of the Spanish Army* (London, 1990).
2. Charles Esdaile, *Napoleon's Wars: An International History 1803–1815* (London, 2007), 370–6.
3. John M. Sherwig, *Guineas and Gunpowder* (Cambridge MA, 1969), 204–5, 263–4, 322, 367.
4. Wellington to Bathurst, 7 November 1812, *WD*, ix, 542.
5. This is one theme of two exceptional studies: Muir, *Britain and the Defeat of Napoleon*; Knight, *Britain Against Napoleon*.
6. The issue of Catholic relief was complex and 'party' differences on it were blurred. But the Wellesleys in Parliament favoured relief in 1813. Thorne, *The House of Commons*, i, 205–6, 208–25; v, 509, 514.
7. Wellington to Don Miguel Alava, 14 October 1813, *WD*, xi, 191–4.
8. Wellington to Henry Wellesley, 19 January 1814, *WD*, xi, 465–6.
9. Sabine (ed.), *Letters*, 378, 389.
10. Belmas, *Sièges*, iv, 731–3.
11. *The Times*, 15 April 1809, p. 4; 11 August 1809, p. 2 – both articles used translated Spanish sources.
12. Sabine (ed.), *Letters*, 394, 425.

13. Wellington to Minister of War, 3, 5 September 1813; to Bathurst, 5 September 1813, *WD*, xi, 73–4, 81–3, 90–1.
14. Wellington to minister of war, 8 November 1813, *WD*, xi, 262.
15. *The Times*, 25 September 1813, p. 3.
16. Somerset to Burgoyne, 10, 20 September 1813, WP 9/2/2/17.
17. Somerset to Kennedy, 26 September 1813, WP 9/2/2/17.
18. Somerset to Burgoyne, 21 September 1813 WP 9/2/2/17.
19. Burgoyne to Somerset, 22 September 1813, WP 9/2/2/15.
20. Glover, *An Eloquent Soldier*, 177.
21. Hall, *Wellington's Navy*, 220.
22. Glover (ed.), *A Gentleman Volunteer*, 130.
23. Sabine (ed.), *Letters*, 399, 425; Wellington to Hope, 18 March 1814, *WD,* xi, 591.
24. Thompson (ed.), *An Ensign in the Peninsular War*, 266.
25. Batty, *Campaign*, 15–16.
26. Batty, *Campaign*, 31–2.
27. Batty, *Campaign*, 80.
28. Wellington to Bathurst, 1 December 1813, *WD*, xi, 338–40.
29. Wellington to Henry Wellesley, 7 December 1813 *WD*, xi, 351–3.
30. Wellington to minister of war, 7 December 1813, *WD*, xi, 349.
31. 'Memorandum from . . . Wellington to George Canning . . .', 2 March 1823, WP 1/759/1.
32. Geoffrey Best, *Humanity in Warfare* (London, 1983 edn), 60–5.
33. Weigley, *The Age of Battles*, 542.
34. Best, *Humanity in Warfare*, 36, 56.
35. Best, *Humanity in Warfare*, 49.
36. Marie-Cecile Thoral, *From Valmy to Waterloo: France at War, 1792–1815* (Houndsmill, 2011), 203–4.
37. T.C.W. Blanning, *The French Revolutionary Wars 1787–1802* (London, 1996), 166; David A. Bell, *The First Total War: Napoleon's Europe and the Birth of Modern Warfare* (London, 2008 edn), 213–14, 280, 290–1.
38. Blanning, *The French Revolutionary Wars*, 158–63.
39. Weigley, The *Age of Battles*, 543.
40. Best, *Humanity in Warfare*, 61, 67.
41. Wellington to Graham, 23 August 1813, *WD*, xi, 31–3.
42. Sabine (ed.), *Letters*, 186–8, 193, 276, 291.
43. Captain Augustus Frazer to Robert Graham, 11 April 1845, Papers of Maxton Graham Family of Cullquhey, Perthshire GD155/1102, National Records of Scotland.
44. Wellington to Bathurst, 21 November 1813, *WD*, xi, 303–6.
45. Wellington to General Don Manuel Freyre, 25 December 1813, *WD*, xi, 399–400.
46. Sabine (ed.), *Letters*, 164.
47. Sabine (ed.), *Letters*, 177.
48. *Gentleman's Magazine* (April 1823), 362; *Monthly Magazine, or British Register* (December 1831), 652.
49. House of Commons *Debates*, 18 March 1824, Vol. 10, c 1233; 1 July 1825, Vol. 13, c 1472.
50. Somerville, *History*, 14–15, 20, 34–5, 37–8.
51. Kenneth Bourne, *Palmerston: the Early Years 1784–1841* (London, 1982), 553–5; David Brown, *Palmerston: A Biography (*New Haven CT, 2010), 200–6.
52. *The Times*, 25 August 1840, p. 5.
53. Somerville, *History*, 39, 571–7.
54. *Theatrical Journal* (1840).
55. (London) *Examiner*, 11 August 1849, 507; *London Journal*, 23 June 1849, 249–50.
56. *Saturday Review*, 17 April 1858.
57. *Saturday Review*, 18 February 1860, 207–8.
58. Duncan, *A History of the Royal Regiment of Artillery*, ii, 317.
59. *The Times*, 17 September 1813, p. 2.

Chapter 14

To Bayonne

The Impact of San Sebastian on the Army
If Napoleon had not been forced to abdicate in April 1814, Wellington's forces would have attempted to take Bayonne. The siege of this important garrison town had begun when the French empire collapsed, thus ending the campaigns begun in 1809. At least one senior member of Wellington's headquarters staff was intensely relieved that the operation against Bayonne did not proceed to the next stage.[1] An obvious question is whether the British had learned and applied lessons after two years of conducting hard-fought sieges.

The advance to Bayonne was a necessary step in any invasion of France from the western Pyrenees. But the timing of the advance was more uncertain than its direction. The two phases of the siege of San Sebastian occurred during two months when the military and international diplomatic situations were in flux. Despite the advantages which Wellington had in intelligence-gathering, he did not know when, where, whether or in what strength the French might regroup and counter-attack. Soult's advance in July caught him unprepared for its scale and speed. On the larger scene, it was not clear how the war would progress in central Europe and therefore how feasible it would be for Wellington to invade France. Only when news arrived that Austria had joined Russia and Prussia, followed days later by the final surrender at San Sebastian, did a realistic opportunity to invade France re-appear.

This uncertainty at the front from July to September was compounded by the rapid and recurrent re-positioning of Wellington's forces as more Spanish divisions marched to the Pyrenean borderlands. Battalions and divisions were in continual motion in the imposing but isolated mountain passes and valley plains which criss-crossed the region. The frequent movement of large forces absorbed both time and energy. As Blakiston, an engineer officer, pointed out, although the royal roads were very good with 'their sides walled in, and the intermediate space filled with small stones and earth, which soon makes a hard and compact substratum, not to be injured by rain', progress on interconnecting roads was quite a different matter: 'The cross-roads hereabouts, as usual in Spain, are execrable'.[2]

The high level of movement and uncertainty in July–September and then the pressures of the advance into France from October militated against taking stock or formulating closely argued lessons from any particular engagement. Most soldiers reacted to the siege by suppressing memories of the horrific casualties and the mayhem of the assault and its aftermath. This reaction to trauma and heavy casualties was the reverse of the psychologist's or historian's desire to pause, ponder and, perhaps, pontificate. Whatever the horrors they experienced, or indeed inflicted, the battalions had to re-group and march on to the next challenge with determination, self-confidence and, if possible given the condition of many of the roads, a spring in their steps.

Letters from the front suggested both the desire and need to advance into France. Late in September, an officer in the 7th Hussars expected that the invasion of France would begin soon. Although the allied forces were constructing batteries and strong defences from Fuenterrabia, at the estuary of the Bidassoa River, to Pamplona, he argued that an advance would lead to the swifter surrender of Pamplona, where hope for relief would be destroyed by an allied invasion of France. A medical man serving with the army also expected an advance. The troops enjoyed good health, with food plentiful and work on the defences keeping them exercised. Remaining in position, he concluded, would be undesirable, for 'the Pyrenees are not a tenable stage for an army in winter; the rains, and fogs, and mists, would be more destructive to the troops than the worst battles'. On 29 September, an officer at Pasajes noted that defensive works were being built at Irun, the last Spanish town on the great road before the Bidassoa River, some 1½ miles to the east. But rain and snow in about one month's time would make movement impossible for either army in the Pyrenees. The only scope for military activity would be along the narrow strip created by the road; 'we must, therefore, go forward or go back'.[3] If San Sebastian left some battalions physically depleted, the army as a whole was, as one officer wrote from Pasajes on 6 October, eager to advance.[4]

The invasion of France, however, involved severe fighting. Even the initial steps in any allied advance were challenging. The French position covering St Jean de Luz and running eastwards into the Pyrenees from that port 'was intrenched [*sic*] and defended by a series of remarkably strong redoubts, one behind the other'.[5] One contemporaneous review of the war's progress argued that the battle for the Pyrenees was more significant than the much-celebrated triumph at Vitoria had been. Three reasons supported this claim. Soult was a more challenging opponent than King Joseph and Marshal Jourdan had been at Vitoria. Secondly, the British destroyed the myth of superior French fighting acumen within sight of France itself. Thirdly, the contest in the mountain region gave the British control of strong positions and vital mountain passes which provided more tangible strategic assets than those secured by the earlier battle.[6]

The last phase of the war for Wellington's army witnessed repeated engagements with the retreating but still resilient French. Fighting between 31 August 1813 and the end of the war in the third week of April 1814 inflicted heavy casualties, particularly at the Nivelle on 10 November, the Nive on 9–13 December and at Toulouse on 10 April. The casualties suffered by the Anglo-Portuguese army, together with the Spanish contingents assigned to it, in their principal encounters demonstrated the point.

Battle Casualties Suffered by Wellington's Forces, June 1813–April 1814[7]

Battle	Killed	Wounded	Missing
Vitoria, 21 June	740	4,174	266
San Sebastian, 7–27 July	204	774	300
Sorauren, 25 July–2 Aug.	881	5,510	705
San Sebastian, 28 July–31 Aug.	761	1,697	45
San Marcial, 31 Aug.–1 Sept	400	2,067	156
Bidassoa, 7–8 Oct.	127	674	3
Nivelle, 10 Nov.	343	2,278	73
Nive, 9–13 Dec.	650	3,907	504
Orthez, 27 Feb.	277	1,923	70
Toulouse, 10 April	595	4,046	18
Bayonne, 14 April	150	457	236

The ability of Wellington's army to maintain fighting momentum in October-December 1813 was the more striking because it followed ten weeks of heavy losses. Between 21 June and 1 September the allied armies lost 2,985 men killed and 14,222 men wounded. Such casualties were comparable to the 3,500 killed and 10,200 wounded in Wellington's army at Waterloo, a notoriously bloody battle.[8]

Maintaining the advance was probably helped by additional Spanish contingents now serving directly under Wellington. At San Marcial the Spanish suffered 1,679 killed and wounded to 527 Portuguese and 417 British. At Toulouse, in April, the Spanish killed and wounded totalled 1,927, compared with 2,107 British and 602 Portuguese. Whatever Spanish resentments arose against British behaviour at San Sebastian, they did not reduce Spanish military participation or sap Spanish fighting efforts. Wellington in fact described an improving Spanish military effort.

Some problems did not, however, disappear. The usual undertow of ill-discipline continued. Well before the invasion of France, Wellington tried to reassure French opponents of Napoleon that he would restrain and punish the predicted abuses which Spanish and Portuguese troops might commit on entering France.[9] Once well-established in France, however, Spanish troops conducted themselves in 'terrible' style. He found it difficult to intervene since 'every question is taken up as one of national honor [*sic*]. The truth is, the officers will not discipline their troops, and the Generals will not give themselves any trouble about the matter, and rather encourage indiscipline'.[10] But Wellington's own forces did not behave any better. In early 1814, some units were reportedly 'kept under arms for days at a time to prevent the men from roaming about the country-side'. Privates of the 4th, whose effectives numbered only 343 in January, were punished in February for burning window shutters and stealing clothes and table linen from the houses where they were billeted.[11] On 18 March, an officer in the Inniskillings noted: 'Our men, in true Irish spirit, have commemorated St Patrick to excess and committed many misdemeanours. The natives attended our mornings muster with so many complaints that the triangle was pitched, and a drum's head court martial summoned. Two or three offenders were tied up and received their deserts on the spot.'[12]

On 23 March, Wellington admonished a brigade commander, Colonel Lord Charles Manners, for his troops' behaviour at Galan. They had 'plundered nearly every house they were in of linen, fowls, and every thing the people had'. The colonel was ordered to search all the baggage belonging to his NCOs, soldiers and all women 'following the regiments' and to remove everything except 'regimental necessaries'. An account of what had been plundered would be sent to Manners, who would meet the resulting costs. As in the past, Wellington blamed the officers for weak supervision of their men.[13]

Supply was not straightforward. One officer later claimed that the fighting in the Pyrenees 'was certainly the most arduous and enterprising duty that British troops ever performed', compared with which the Waterloo campaign, apart from the three days of battle, was 'a mere party of pleasure'. The weather and terrain were far more testing, but the main difference was the lack of ready support from the Commissariat.[14] At one level, supply should have been assisted by the ready availability of local labour and by the close connections between Biscayan Spain and south-west France. Bayonne's external trade in the late 1790s was mainly with Spain; the town was described by a German traveller as having a distinctly Spanish air; Basque was the language heard in St Esprit, Bayonne's northern outlier; the Biscayan coastal populations of both countries shared a long and impressive tradition of seamanship; and when formal trade was disrupted in the 1790s by war, French privateers from Bayonne smuggled their prizes into Bilboa.[15]

Yet practical difficulties created friction. Local distribution relied on thousands of muleteers who were supposed to be paid one dollar a day for each animal plus rations, but whose pay was substantially in arrears by late 1813. The area around Lesaca was stripped of wheat and Indian corn by August 1813. Soldiers and muleteers fed their horses and mules with it, while British soldiers roasted the heads of Indian corn. These actions created food shortages for the local population during the winter.[16] Some muleteers, short of payment, simply took what they regarded as their due share from the food supplies they were conveying. Well-armed and described by Ensign Wheatley as 'notorious thieves and murderers', they had every opportunity to trade in plundered goods with British soldiers eager for the brandy with which they seem to have been well stocked.[17]

Transporting men and goods in the Bay of Biscay proved far from straightforward. Maintaining re-supply proved challenging because St Jean de Luz, just inside France, was an inadequate working harbour. The bay where the port was sited was nearly a mile wide. Piers from each side of the bay had been planned originally to protect shipping in the harbour, but were far too short to serve that purpose. Transatlantic trade had declined after the Treaty of Paris in 1763 confirmed the loss of the colony of Quebec, so that commerce by the 1810s was essentially confined to coastal activity. Boats trading from St Jean de Luz were well suited to breaking the Royal Navy's blockade of San Sebastian, but the harbour was far too exposed to gale-force winds to host sustainable traffic involving larger, ocean-going merchant ships.[18] Even in the small, but well protected, harbour of Guetaria, ships could wait for many days, in June, before a 'fair wind' enabled them to sail.[19]

The support system therefore depended on Pasajes, although Wellington had his headquarters at St Jean de Luz from 18 November to 20 February.[20] The harbour at Pasajes was deeper and more secure, providing the main base for supplies from September until well into March, particularly for supplies forwarded from La Coruña, and for transport back to England.[21] Pasajes was used as a staging point for the accumulation of the ordnance intended for future siege operations in south-west France. The ships holding the battering train remained there.[22] By late February, the battering train at Pasajes harbour consisted of 145 guns, including 52 guns of 24-pounder calibre and 22 carronades of 68-pounder weight. There were 193,500 rounds of artillery ammunition available.[23] When a rising in favour of the Bourbons seemed likely in Bordeaux, Wellington was able to supply 2,000–3,000 captured French muskets from Pasajes immediately, while awaiting the arrival of 30,000 more muskets from Lisbon.[24] This accumulation of heavy guns and munitions was unprecedented for the campaign and demonstrated the value of the secure harbour in itself and the geographical position which San Sebastian commanded.

Pasajes' value in the face of frequently changing and often stormy weather in the Bay of Biscay was demonstrated on 2–4 March. Two days of 'dreadful' storms left seventeen transport and small gun-ships wrecked in the exposed harbour of St Jean de Luz. Lieutenant Colonel Frazer described the scene on the morning of 4 March:

> Casks, chests, logs of wood, and bodies, floating in all directions. I never saw a grander or more terrific scene: the clouds of fowl hovering over their prey, seemed almost to dispute the bodies with those who were rescuing them from the waves; the beach itself is more altered than I should have imagined possible in so short a time . . . [25]

The storms also wrecked four ships at San Sebastian, but no losses were reported from Pasajes.

Pasajes remained vital to the siege of Bayonne. Local vessels designed for coastal trading could be rented for military purposes. For example, Wellington obtained forty boats of 15–30 tons and extensive cabling from Pasajes to support his operation against Bayonne.[26] Some 2 million musket cartridges were to be sent forward from Pasajes for the besieging forces, with half the number going by sea to St Sever.[27] The strategic importance of capturing San Sebastian in order to control Pasajes as the principal holding base for the invasion of southern France had become overwhelming.

Bayonne as an Objective
Following a pause in fighting after the crossing of the River Nive by 13 December, Wellington resumed campaigning within south-west France on 12 February. By then the worst of the winter weather had relented. Soult initially tried to lure Wellington

back south-eastwards towards the Pyrenees but eventually struck out eastwards to Toulouse, which was the main regional arsenal and supply base for the French army. The marshal reached his objective on 24 March and Wellington arrived a few days later. The last formal battle of the war occurred at the outer rim of defensive lines at Toulouse on 10 April. Wellington's army did enough to force Soult to withdraw the next day and on 12 April Wellington made a triumphant entry into the city, which welcomed the end of the Napoleonic regime with apparent enthusiasm.[28] Fighting continued, however, at Bayonne. The town remained in French hands and Brigadier Pierre Thouvenot, its military commander, refused to accept that Napoleon had abdicated until he received official notification of any such action. His orders from Soult to end the conflict did not arrive until 26 April.

Bayonne's strategic importance was a commonplace. Commanding the only bridge across the Adour for many miles, the town controlled the direct road from St Jean de Luz to Bordeaux. The main road south-eastwards to the strategically important Pyrenean town of St Jean Pied de Port started at Bayonne. The Romans had first fortified it. In 1680, Vauban initiated a programme of works which by 1694 ensured its status as the main military stronghold in south-west France.[29] When Napoleon began his preparations to take over Spain, he assembled in August 1807 a so-called Corps of Observation of 25,000 soldiers at Bayonne. As French involvement deepened, Bayonne became an active base for heavy artillery as well as a transit point for troops. But it also acquired an impressive symbolic significance for contemporaries. In 1808, Napoleon summoned the newly installed Fernando VII and his father Carlos IV to Bayonne and forced them to resign their rights to the Spanish throne and acknowledge his brother, Joseph, as king in their place. A selection of leading Spaniards, including some of the most prominent aristocrats, was then gathered to ratify a new constitution for their country.[30] Bayonne was where the new French regime was organized and proclaimed and where many of Spain's ruling elite made their obeisance to it.

The strategic importance of Pamplona and Bayonne had been stressed in 1809 when *The Times* indicated their role as the key staging points on the Spanish route into France.[31] In mid-September 1813, the *Morning Chronicle*, in reviewing the strategic situation in the Pyrenees, emphasized that 'an invading army from Spain must consider the possession of Bayonne as indispensable to their further operations, for that town only presents a strong and tenable post, in which to form an establishment in that part of France'.[32] Captain Blakiston, who served in the campaign, later noted:

As a frontier fortress nothing can surpass the position of Bayonne. Situated at the conflux of two rivers, no invading army can attempt to pass it to the eastward without either abandoning its communications, or leaving a force of at least three times the strength of the garrison to blockade it; because, as the blockading force must necessarily be divided into three parts by the rivers Adour and Nive, and spread over a large circumference, the garrison have it in their power to bring their whole force to bear on any one part, without risk of being cut off. But when occupied, as the place was, by a whole army, it was impossible to penetrate into France.[33]

The heavily fortified town lay on both sides of the River Nive where it flowed into the River Adour. Across the river, on the Adour's north bank, Vauban had built a star-shaped citadel, Castelnau, on the hill above the village of St Esprit.[34] He thus created the three fortified sections mentioned by Blakiston. The main road from St Jean de Luz entered the south-east corner of Bayonne, crossed the Nive within the town and then crossed the more important bridge over the Adour to St Esprit and St Etienne.

A new commandant, Brigadier Thouvenot, who had commanded earlier in the year at Burgos, took charge on 9 August 1813 to review the town's works, magazines and general serviceability. He sent detailed plans to Soult following the fall of San Sebastian. By 21 September, two urgent projects headed Thouvenet's priorities. The first was to build a redoubt to the right of St Esprit church, on the north bank of the Adour River, to cover the main road bridge crossing the river from the centre of town. The second, ordered by Soult, involved entrenching defensive works in front of the camp being established at Mousserolles, an open space just outside the town's eastern fortified wall. Timber for palisades and other defences had been delivered and gun embrasures and platforms were being installed.[35] One contemporary criticism was that, if Wellington had capitalized more vigorously on Vitoria and advanced to near Bayonne, his army's presence would have 'prevented the enemy from throwing up those formidable works in our front'.[36]

Other extensions and repairs to the existing defences had to be made. For example, protection against flooding had to be provided at the horn-work and at the arsenal. The magazines at the St Esprit bastion and at the old castle needed attention. Guns had to be positioned and cannon balls and powder had to be distributed to the scattered defensive positions. By 3–4 October, work was being perfected at Mousserolles while most necessary work had been accomplished at the large citadel on the north bank. The effort involved was considerable. For example, during the fifteen days between 20 September and 4 October, Thouvenot noted the number of men at work each day on eight occasions. On 1 day only 1,193 men were at work; on 2 1,614 and 1,720 were; but on the other 5 between 1,813 and 1,942 were engaged.[37]

As the threat of a British invasion increased, so French reinforcements arrived and more accommodation had to be provided. In addition to organizing a large labour force, the commandant had to accommodate a steady inflow of wounded men from the front and fresh troops from the interior. Thus 556 conscripts and reinforcements arrived on 3 October, bringing the total received since early August to 2,000, exceeding the 1,300 soldiers Thouvenot had expected. Barracks for this inflow were far from complete.[38] The demands far exceeded those of the designated garrison of 6,098 officers and men.[39] By early October, there were 700 wounded in camp. The 34th Leger moved out to two villages, making barrack space available to the wounded. The 31st Leger was mainly housed at Biarritz, not then as fashionably significant as it was to become. Simply taking into account the soldiers concentrated at Bayonne, Thouvenot estimated that he needed accommodation for 8,300 men. Most were allocated to military installations; 2,300 were at the Citadelle across the river Adour from the town itself; 1,600 were in the old castle, the new castle and the redoubt at the river port's harbour entrance; about 1,000 were at the camp at Mousserolles, and 540 were stuck in the defensive trenches being built at the old and new castles. But temporary arrangements had to be made for others; 1,000 were in position by the river at the foot of the Citadelle; 900 were lodged in a former church and 3 merchant warehouses at the place d'armes; 500 went to the customs warehouse and a further 360 were in 2 other warehouses.[40] The citadel itself commanded any hostile approaches from the west and north. One visitor described it being on 'a mountain'.[41] Boats in the Adour were armed with artillery to cover (improbable) river access from the south. More importantly, those boats' guns also covered approaches to the citadel from an arcing movement around the north aimed at attacking the fortress from the east.[42] Overall, the French went to considerable lengths from September to prepare for a British advance.

The critical south-eastern side of the town was defended by entrenchments well on the way to completion by 9 December. This strong line was placed up to 1,000yd from the town wall and stretched 3 miles from the Adour to the north and west in a wide arc down to the Nive. From the Adour, 2 miles of the entrenchments faced 'a wide marshy valley . . . almost impracticable'. More elaborate works defended the open ground for the last mile to the Nive.[43] By December, Bayonne allowed the French to operate against advancing allied forces from a secure base. Its position astride the Nive and in an area where the east–west roads were of poor quality meant that any attacking army would have to concentrate its numbers on a single approach route. If it advanced by dividing its corps, individual corps could be assailed from Bayonne. Captain Robert Batty described Bayonne as 'the centre of a circle, in the circumference of which the Allies were posted, having their communications divided by the Nive, and the worst possible cross roads to march on, in case of support being required'.[44] After extensive fighting during 9–13 December, the armies went into winter quarters until the weather lifted and campaigning resumed in mid-February.[45]

For the British, Bayonne had to be neutralized. Wellington believed the garrison's provisions would last six months, so that a prolonged blockade was out of the question. The British were less certain about its military capability, estimating its core strength at 5,000–6,000 troops, but speculating that the presence of a further division, under General Abbé, raised its strength to about 10,000 men. They believed that many battalions were 'very weak' and that many troops were recent conscripts, including 'refractory conscripts' with limited enthusiasm for working on the defences.[46] Rory Muir suggests that the British wished to avoid a siege, after the experience of San Sebastian, both because high casualties were likely and because the siege would alienate the French from the invading army. He notes, however, that maintaining a blockade tied down 20,000 allied troops.[47]

The operation against Bayonne was entrusted to Sir John Hope, commanding 13,000 troops by 20 March. These consisted of the 1st Division, the 5th Division, a brigade under Lord Aylmer, a brigade of cavalry under Vandeleur and two Portuguese brigades under Major Generals Bradford and Wilson.[48] This Anglo-Portuguese army was supplemented by 4,000 troops of the Spanish Division commanded by a very experienced general, Don Carlos de España. The Spanish contingent appears to have been expanded, for returns on 14 April indicate that Spanish troops at Bayonne totalled about 8,300, drawn from 3 divisions, including Don Carlos's, all in Manuel Freire's

'Fourth Army'.[49] Freire's army had participated in the battle of San Marcial, shielding San Sebastian from Soult's attempted relief, on 31 August. Although Hope had only arrived in the Peninsula in October, to replace Graham, his force included the 5th Division and Bradford's Portuguese brigade which had played the leading role in the assault on San Sebastian.

The Blockade and Siege

In moving upon Bayonne, the allies had to cross the Adour River and blockade the citadel and St Etienne on the river's northern bank. Bayonne's historically strong fortifications were deemed to be capable of withstanding twenty-five to thirty days' attack. Soult had added to the challenge facing an attacker by constructing the line of defensive trenches in front of the fortifications. Wellington therefore decided that any attack should be on the smaller and more vulnerable citadel. He would have to blockade St Etienne anyway to prevent troops, ammunition and supplies entering Bayonne from St Etienne across the bridge which joined the two towns. Since there were no bridges along the river's 4-mile stretch between Bayonne and the sea, the British had to construct a crossing to reach St Etienne. Transporting siege guns and munitions to the Adour and then across the river would test the army's logistical and engineering skills and capabilities. Lieutenant Colonel Howard Elphinstone, RE was tasked on 7 February with preparing a bridge.

Elphinstone was yet another senior officer with extensive overseas experience. Having been commissioned in 1793, he had served in the taking of Cape Town in 1795, in India from 1796 to 1801, and in Egypt in 1801 with a contingent from the Madras presidency under Major General David Baird, who had led the assault in 1799 upon Seringapatam. He first visited Lisbon in 1806 to advise on the city's defences and returned as commanding Royal Engineer under Sir Arthur Wellesley in 1808. Severely injured, he resumed his duties in 1812, being based in Portugal until September 1813. Wellington treated him dismissively and assigned him to Bayonne partly because he wanted Lieutenant Colonel Burgoyne to take charge of the engineers with the main army as it marched upon Toulouse.[50] But Burgoyne fully assessed the problems involved in bridging the Adour on 9 December and revisited them on 12 February. By the 19th detailed preparations were in place. Wellington left on the 21st to pursue Soult's main army.[51] By then, many doubted whether the bridging operation would succeed.[52]

Much of the material for the siege and forty-eight coasting craft or chasses marées were accumulated at Socoa, the small harbour on the west side of St Jean de Luz's bay. These preparations were complete by the 19th. The shallow coasting vessels were hired from Pasajes and St Jean de Luz, as well as Socoa itself. They sailed on the evening of the 22nd, with the Royal Navy providing an escort of a frigate, a brig and five gunboats. The time for the journey to the Adour was planned at 16–18 hours. Part of Sir John Hope's forces marched at 1.00 a.m. on the 23rd, with those assigned to meet the flotilla arriving at the Adour by dawn. The troops also carried equipment and small boats. However, half the required pontoons failed to arrive on time from Bidart, on the coast between St Jean de Luz and Bayonne.

By 11.00 a.m. on the 23rd the operation stalled, since the flotilla for constructing the bridge had not arrived. The British had to secure a toe-hold on the north bank of the Adour before they could build the bridge across the river. The only defended position on this stretch of the north bank was the tiny hamlet of Boucau. Without a full complement of pontoons, fifty light infantrymen crossed the river in four small 'jolly' boats. Their arrival put the French picket to flight. Then 2 rafts were formed from 5 pontoons so that, by dusk, 6 companies of Guards – perhaps 600 men in total – had crossed. But the strong tide made rowing extremely difficult and the troops in place fell far short of the 2,400 planned for. The advance party, assisted from the south bank by artillery fire and the innovative discharge of Congreve rockets, defended itself against 1,200 French troops sent out to disperse them. Another two companies of the 60th Rifles, as part of this advanced guard, were on the north bank by the morning. Following long delays, pontoons from Bidart began arriving at night on the 23rd. On the morning of the 24th there were far too few troops on the north bank and the materials for constructing the bridge had still not arrived. Hope decided to row the entire division across the Adour, deploying some 300 soldiers capable of rowing to jolly boats and pontoons. They were rewarded for their labours against strong tides with half rations of rum on starting their journey and on returning from it. The round-trips lasted an hour and could only occur during 4 hours of each 6 as the tides went through their daily rhythms. But by 8.00 p.m. the 1st Division of 6,000 had deployed to the north bank.[53] This risky operation was supported by feints against the defences of Bayonne itself which were designed to deceive the French as to the main direction of the allies' advance.

Meanwhile, the chasses marées and their escort had sailed on the evening of the 22nd, but they reached the entry to the Adour only by daylight on the 24th, taking far longer than the 16–18 hours allocated for their journey. The flotilla of sixty mainly small boats then met high onshore winds and a rough sea. The sailors on the chasses marées were reluctant to attempt a crossing of the bar to the Adour estuary. The bar of shifting sands and westerly and southerly winds made entry into the Adour notoriously problematic. Vessels trying to get out to sea could be held in the river for six days, and indeed far longer, by onshore or southerly winds. It was said five or six ships were wrecked on the bar in most years. Under pressure, the naval agent at Socoa tried to enter the river but his craft hit the bar. The crew eventually dragged the boat across the sands into the river. The officer commanding the flotilla, Captain Dowell O'Reilly, RN, decided to lead the flotilla into the river. He had commanded the naval battery of six 24-pounders at the first assault at San Sebastian, where he and his men displayed notable energy and commitment, and where he suffered bad concussion from shelling. He now enjoyed another narrow escape when 'the giant surf' carried his cutter to 'a fearful height' and smashed it to the shore. 'O'Reilly was thrown senseless on the sands, and before the rushing surge could reclaim its victim, the soldiers had linked their hands in one strong line, and running into the turbulent waves, had borne him from his perilous position'.[54] With some sailors swimming ashore, the landing left 'all her crew bruised dreadfully', and drowned four men. Faced with further delays, Rear Admiral Penrose offered a reward for the first locally hired chasses marées that crossed the bar. The incentive worked and at 2.00 p.m. the flotilla began moving forward.[55] Lieutenant Colonel Frazer described the result:

> As the tide rose, the vessels attempted the bar. I have never seen any scene so awful; in crossing the bar they were agitated in a most extraordinary manner, sails flapping, and all steerage-way lost; as each passed it seemed inevitably lost, as indeed several were. . . . I believe two vessels went down entirely; a gun-boat and two other vessels and a boat were driven on shore. We had several poor fellows struggling for life in the surf literally within ten yards of us, without being able to save them, though we had men on the beach tied with ropes, and apparently, as the waves receded, close to them. [56]

He believed that about fifty sailors had been drowned on 24 February; Burgoyne guessed at thirty to forty navy sailors, with two small Royal Navy vessels lost. Two of the chasses marées were beached on the bar or onshore and twelve returned to port. But thirty-four entered the estuary.[57]

The Royal Navy's sailors worked hard and bravely to deliver to plan, but the failure to do so added a further example of the acute challenges raised by sea-based support for land operations. Of course, weather and geographical conditions led to this failure, but local conditions were either well known or could readily be ascertained. The experience underscored once more the shortcomings in land–sea operations revealed earlier in July–August 1813.

Entering the river and constructing a temporary bridge across it remained essential to besieging Bayonne. Although the 1st Division crossed the Adour by boat, the siege train could not be transported to the north bank by similar means. Much of it would have to come by land and cross the river by more stable means than could be provided by small craft. Assembling a bridge depended, yet again, on improvisation. The site selected for the bridge was 1½ miles from the sea, thus providing enough space between the bridge and the estuary bar to anchor 200–300 small transport boats along the estuary. The bridge was positioned west of a long bend in the river so that it could not be observed from Bayonne. The bridge had to span 270yd.[58] The river, however, had been artificially narrowed for miles in the late 1780s by high, thick stone embankments designed to channel spring floods, when mountain snows melted, so that they flushed away parts of the large sandy bar at the estuary. The strong embankments meant that the river rose and fell 14ft between high tide and low tide at the season's peak tidal changes.[59] The bridge therefore had to be supple enough to rise and fall with the tides and yet robust enough to remain intact. It also had to withstand occasional strong winds and the resulting estuarine swell from the open sea.

The construction of the bridge required considerable ingenuity. Wellington decided that pontoons would prove too flimsy and preferred instead the low draft, decked chasses marées of 30–50 tons. These varied from 53ft to 40ft in length and from over 15ft to over 10ft in width. Twenty-five of the thirty-four which entered the estuary were anchored across the river, each one parallel to the river's banks to provide the floating 'pillars' for the bridge. Engineer officers were assigned to groups of seven or eight boats.

Each boat, numbered on the bow in yellow paint, got two sappers. Once the boats were in position the artillery's gun platforms were stretched across them to create the walkway supported by the boats. New platforms had to be made for the artillery guns. Five 13in cables supplied by the navy held the chasses marées together while giving them the flexibility to bob up and down with the shifting tides. The cables were each secured at one end of the bridge by an 18-pounder iron gun thrown into the marshy soil and at the other by a large timber frame linked to sleepers and stabilized by 60 tons of sand bags. The navy also supplied masts of 50–100ft in length and other materials to create a boom shielding the bridge on its Bayonne side.[60] The boom would block any boats or objects which the French might send down river to burn or wreck the bridge. At Badajoz, for example, a British pontoon bridge had been broken up by trees deliberately floated down-river for that purpose. The boom, in turn, was covered by 18-pounders on the river bank. Thus protected, the bridge was operational by 11.00 a.m. on the 26th.

The tactical situation promised well. On the 25th, Wellington suggested that the engineers should assess the best means of attacking the citadel, indicating the key points from which to enforce a close investment of it. An attack could be planned with the assurance that Soult could not march to relieve Bayonne.[61] This was because Wellington had enough troops to pursue Soult while also deploying a separate force for the siege. He had not enjoyed comparable advantages at San Sebastian where his dispersed divisions, organized into informal corps, operated in contact with each other along a single if attenuated front. In moving the 1st Division to the north bank west of Bayonne, Hope had used the 5th Division to demonstrate against the eastern approaches to Bayonne on the south bank. That pressure neutralized the garrison which failed on 25–6 February to attack the 1st Division when it was isolated with limited artillery support on the north bank. On the 27th, with the bridge and its protective boom in functional order, the 1st Division completed the investment, closing to within 700–1,000yd of the French outer defences 400yd in front of the citadel south-west of St Etienne. The allies occupied a lane protected by 'banks, walls, and large country houses'.[62] The fighting to clear these positions at St Etienne 'was dreadfully hot'. Brigades from the King's German Legion led the action, losing 371 casualties on 27 February.[63] Meanwhile, the road south had seen the departure of civilians who could not provide six months of provisions for themselves. Allied soldiers and Basque men and women carrying baskets of bread and biscuit on their heads pushed northwards against this flow of refugees ordered from the city.[64]

Once the city's northern approaches had been sealed off, Wellington had to decide two obvious issues: the amount of artillery required for siege operations and the size of the force being committed to the siege. On 2 March, Wellington promised reinforcements when they were available. At that point, however, he did not know the whereabouts of the engineers' stores needed for a siege. He had thought they were at Pasajes, on board ship, but in fact they were either still at Santander, or en route from Santander.[65] The siege train, amounting to 145 guns of all calibres, including an imposing complement of 52 24-pounders, together with plentiful ammunition, was available at Pasajes as of 27 February. But operations were disrupted by atrocious weather during 2–4 March.[66]

Moving guns, ammunition and supplies to the improvised bridge in large quantities was difficult. Coastal shipping faced the severe hazards of tempestuous weather and the Adour estuary's bar. But the land route was slow. Most of the area west of Bayonne and south of the Adour consisted of 'a sandy tract' stabilized by the Bois de Bayonne. The local road to the west of Bayonne which led north to the Adour was a 'deep, sandy road'. It was clearly not intended for through traffic or heavy use since it ended at the river bank. On 23 February, four 18-pounders were hauled along this track, to support the river crossing and bridge building. That task involved 'great labour . . . across soft sandy ground'.[67] On the 24th, the carts carrying pontoons sank into the sand and thirty horses could not move them. Elphinstone was 'quite in despair'. Each pontoon was carried by thirty soldiers.[68]

On 6 March Wellington sent Hope his plans for supplying the siege. Large quantities of ammunition for the guns were to be conveyed by boats of 30–40 tons from Pasajes to St Jean de Luz, and were then to be forwarded to the Adour River 'as soon as the weather and the state of the bar will admit'. Some ordnance at Pasajes was to be forwarded by land, using horses from Hope's corps, as well as by sea. Given the uncertainties bedevilling coastal transport beyond St Jean and at the bar to the Adour, substantial amounts of munitions were conveyed by land from St Jean de Luz. The Commissariat provided 200 carts to haul the ammunition from St Jean to Bas Anglet; mules would carry it to the base camp for the siege. Wellington thought eighteen days would suffice for these movements. The stores for the engineers were also to be brought by boat from Pasajes to St Jean de Luz, with half being landed there and half being kept on board for possible shipment to the Adour if needed. Although fifty-two guns of 24-pounder calibre were available at Pasajes, Wellington planned for the use of only twenty of those, with six being held in reserve, but these were added later to the batteries. He also believed that the siege would last only 4 days, for he supplied only 4 days' shot at 160 rounds per day for his heavy guns.[69] Presumably Wellington wanted a reserve of heavy guns available at Pasajes for other purposes at short notice as his campaign evolved. San Sebastian had not impressed upon Wellington any urgent need to apply concentrated and overwhelming artillery power.

The appropriate level of manpower proved contentious. On 5 March, Wellington sternly rejected the request that 15,000 troops be assigned to the siege: 'I carried on the siege of Badajoz with 11,000 men, and we constructed, I believe, the heaviest works that ever were seen. The garrison was near 6,000, and all applicable to the point of attack.' He rejected the need for working parties of 3,000 men per day. He indicated instead that each working party would consist of 700–800 men engaged on the first parallel and that 2 rather than 3 working parties, each labouring for 6 hours, would suffice each day. He also insisted that the covering parties, each on duty for 12 hours, were too large for the proposed first parallel of 1,500yd. The trenches would simply become overcrowded with troops. He therefore ordered Hope to review the numbers, stressing that Hope's request for so large a force as 15,000 men made it highly unlikely that an attack on Bayonne would be viable.[70]

When he returned again to detailed planning, Wellington noted that the commanding engineer 'like other engineers, has called for more men than he wants, or can employ; . . . the loss would be enormous if so many men were placed in such a small space'. He wanted necessary stores landed before the siege work began, to save labour later. But providing back-up for the siege of the citadel required much additional preparation. It was estimated on 8 March that 200 men would be needed for 20 days to furnish 4,500 fascines (bundles of wood to line trenches for the batteries) of varying lengths, 17,000 gabions (baskets of earth to protect the approaches to entrenchments), and 30,000 fascine pickets.[71] So, too, he urged that 600 men be assigned for 15 days to making fascines and gabions. Troops marching to the trenches could carry those items with them, saving labour and shielding them en route against enemy fire.

He agreed that the siege would require three parallels. The first would be undertaken by 1,597 men on the first night, including 700 men working on 700yd of approach lines. The men at work would require protection against sallies from the citadel and that would be supplied by 2,000 infantrymen. Because very large working parties offered a massed target to the French, those parties had to be halved during daytime. In all, Wellington cut 1,300 men from the engineers' request for 2,897 to be assigned to the first parallel and its supporting approaches. Clearing the second parallel and its approaches, amounting in all to 3,000yd, would absorb 1,500 men for 3 nights. If the gabions and fascines were constructed before the works on the lines began, far fewer troops than the number requested by the engineers would be needed for additional tasks. Wellington estimated a grand total for the second line and its approaches at 1,801 men instead of 3,629. The third and final line would be a 'flying sap' of a length which 200–300 soldiers could dig in a day. He agreed that 386 specialists including sappers, miners and carpenters would be needed for that work. The last stage of siege works would require fewer men: 'The quantity of work to be performed is but small, and its danger and difficulty considerably increased; and it is desirable to have as few men as possible at one time in the trenches.' More men might be needed in short, unpredictable bursts to complete specific tasks. Overall, however, only 1,200 men would be needed at this final stage.[72]

Wellington's scrutiny and questioning at this level of detail indicated that, even at this late stage in his army's conduct of sieges, there was no agreed blueprint or set of guidelines from which to organize operations. The senior engineers were still putting forward what the Field Marshal regarded as grossly inflated manpower requests and he felt impelled to spell out specific manpower allocations for each main stage of the preparatory work for the siege. Of course, the senior engineers, in bidding for maximum manpower, may have been engaging in a stock bureaucratic manoeuvre with Sir John Hope, their immediate commander who was new to the campaign. But they would have been curiously naïve not to understand that Hope would have to secure Wellington's approval for the allocation of so many troops to these duties. Whatever the particular circumstances may have been, planning parameters did not exist or were not agreed and laid down. Wellington had to manage in detail the manpower planning for what should have been a standard operation. Nor could it be said in mitigation that the town and its fortifications were unknown to the British. Bayonne could be seen plainly from the Pyrenean peaks on the Franco-Spanish border.[73] The truth was that an operational framework for siege warfare had not been established even after the Anglo-Portuguese army had undertaken four major sieges.

By 18 March, Wellington's plans for forwarding the stores and guns had still not been implemented. He told Hope that he had 'ordered all the small vessels in San Sebastian to be pressed, which will give the Commissaries the means of moving the stores from Pasages [*sic*]'. Until the stores were moved, there was no point in Hope trying to bring up his guns. Wellington also insisted that his intelligence on the garrison's food stocks was better than Hope's; he believed the defenders could survive for six months. Civilians might not be so well provided for, but they could leave the town because the blockade was not particularly tight. He did, however, recommend that Hope seize the citadel on the north bank of the Adour River, in order to strengthen the blockade. He held out the possibility that the citadel if taken might be garrisoned by Spanish troops.[74] Meanwhile, the mayor of St Jean de Luz was asked to supply carpenters to repair the bridge which would be used to convey the heavy guns across the Adour.[75] It was not until 6 April that the siege guns were ready for transfer directly to their batteries.[76]

The slowness in preparing for the bombardment resulted not just from transport difficulties but also in part from dramatic shifts in the overall campaign. On 12 March Beresford entered Bordeaux, where the British had to deal with local calls for a Bourbon restoration, while not knowing whether the UK government might negotiate a peace settlement with Napoleon. Bordeaux's disaffection from the regime now opened the Garonne River as the likely route by which military supplies might be fed into the campaign.[77]

The French under Soult continued meanwhile to withdraw eastwards at a rapid pace, reaching Toulouse on 24 March. With Soult's army about 95 miles east of Bayonne and given the speed of British advances, the strategic need to take Bayonne became far less urgent. Wellington was close to Toulouse by 26 March, when he sent Hope what appears to have been his first letter to his subordinate for eight days. He intended to strengthen the siege forces with extra sappers and engineers marching immediately, to be followed by 'some volunteer engineers from the line'. Yet Hope's operations scarcely dominated the commanding general's thoughts; his letter finished with the observation that 'I shall be glad to hear how you are going on'.[78] Wellington sent the briefest of letters tersely up-dating Hope on 1 and 12 April, concluding the latter with the more pressing remark 'I am anxious to hear how you are getting on'.[79] A longer letter of 16 April described Wellington's own entry into Toulouse on 12 April and the French political situation, noting Napoleon's abdication and the formation of a provisional government. Hope was authorized to suspend hostilities at Bayonne if the governor there recognized the provisional government.[80]

Events at Bayonne ran their separate course. The critical front line north of the river formed an arc centred on St Etienne and was held by 1,500 troops with others encamped to their rear. The French artillery occasionally fired on the British position. To the west, the 5th Division blockaded from the Adour's south bank to the left bank of the Nive while Carlos de España's Division took up the eastern front from the Nive's right bank to the Adour.

At least one subaltern resented the tedium of what felt more like a blockade than an active siege. On 10 April he noted his frustration with conditions on the St Etienne front: 'We have now been piquetting for two months before this infernal fortress endeavouring to starve them out, while we are in want of food ourselves. For nothing but herrings and brandy are come-attable. Our tents are pitched by a large swamp and the French pour in cannon shot and shells every ten minutes among us.'[81] Yet, by 13 April, Hope had a formidable siege train available at Bayonne. His 26 24-pounders and 44 mortars and howitzers were supported by 670 gunners, 400 sappers and miners and 66,500 rounds for his artillery.[82] He intended to open a bombardment on 27 April.

The stalemate was broken, however, not by a British attack but by bold French action. At 2.00–3.00 a.m. on 14 April some 6,000 French troops sallied forth to attack the British lines at various points. Under cover of darkness, they achieved surprise and deployed superior numbers at the moment of contact. 'The air filled with stars and shells like a Vauxhall exhibition; and the very earth appeared like a mirror reflecting the lights of the atmosphere, for every bush and hedge was spangled with flashing stars from the musketry . . .'.[83] Launching their main effort from the citadel north of the Adour, the French took the village of St Etienne and pushed the British outer piquets back across the line to the west of its church. Two Guards battalions, the 2nd Infantry Battalion of the King's German Legion and the 24th Portuguese Battalion counter-attacked and regained the village by 4.00 a.m. Repeated attempts by tirailleurs and other French troops failed to dislodge the allies and fighting ended by 6.00.

The sally has been described as a futile and irresponsible gesture by Thouvenal, perhaps made possible by a failure on the British side to take earlier warnings of an impending attack sufficiently seriously. The criticism of the British response needs to be assessed against three factors. First, as Oman pointed out, Hope believed that the objective of any sortie would be the bridge of boats and he therefore maintained his forces at the western end of his siege lines. The most dramatic French thrusts actually aimed at the centre and St Etienne. Secondly, some stretches of the front were indeed reinforced. But reinforcements served little purpose against the sheer weight of the French attack, by perhaps 6,000 troops. Those sections of the siege lines which were strengthened simply added to the number of prisoners. Thirdly, the defending units at St Etienne belonged to Major General Andrew Hay's brigade from the 5th Division. The division had been assigned to the east of Bayonne and Hay's brigade moved to St Etienne on the day before the sortie. Under attack, the men of the brigade abandoned the church at St Etienne. Hay, the duty general officer, tried to rally his troop, but was killed as he told them he would show them how to defend the church.[84] Some present blamed Hay for failing to respond to information received earlier about French intentions, and for his professional incompetence.[85]

A more fundamental criticism was that Hope had pushed his final parallel close to the French defences, making the line vulnerable to a sortie. The British had to fight hard to recover possession of that line, because if the French had held it the British would have had to storm it or resort to a blockade. The last parallel was therefore a legitimate military objective. But Hope's 'eager courage' may have been at fault.[86] Hope's approach was not exactly out of character. Four months earlier Wellington had informed Horse Guards of his concern that Hope – about whom he had 'the highest opinion' – went too far forward and exposed himself too readily to enemy fire;

Wellington had asked one officer to have a word with Hope, as he would try to do so himself, 'but it is a delicate subject'.[87]

The commanding officer's attempt to resolve the crisis was similarly misdirected. Summoned from his bed, Lieutenant General Hope and his staff rode to the cross-road just west of St Etienne. Advancing along 'a narrow road, with high embankments on either side', they heard troops ahead of them. Hope thought they were Portuguese, but was immediately hit by French musket fire. His horse was shot and he was trapped under it and taken prisoner. He was shot a second time by British troops counter-attacking the French in a vain effort to rescue him.[88]

Lieutenant Colonel H.D. Jones later argued that the besieging troops should not have remained in the sunken road connecting the citadel with St Etienne at night; they should have camped at night beyond the road turning it into a defensive ditch. As it was, they were trapped in the lower ground, suffering heavy losses there.[89]

Hope's forces suffered 838 casualties on 14 April. The 5th Division, which had been moved from the eastern defences of Bayonne to cover the south bank, accounted for only ninety-seven of them, in Hay's detached brigade. Three battalions in that Division – the 3/1st, 1/9th, 2/47th – had fought at San Sebastian and suffered only seventy-eight casualties to add to their heavy campaign losses. The 1st Battalion of the Coldstream Guards and the 3rd Guards, belonging to the 1st Division, suffered the worst casualties, at 245 and 204 respectively. Their brigade's commanding officer, Major General the Hon. Edward Stopford, was wounded. The 2nd Light Battalion, King's German Legion, came next with 90 casualties, half the 181 casualties sustained by the KGL in this episode.[90] Those losses reflected the severity of the fighting at the exposed siege lines.

Thouvenot's decision to launch the attack has often been dismissed as the outcome of frustrated pique; Wellington was furious about it and Oman believed that it 'had no military justification'.[91] But the sortie occurred on the day after the siege train of twenty-six 24-pounders, twenty-two mortars and twelve howitzers, together with ample ammunition, reached the British siege lines on the north bank.[92] It severely disrupted any plans the British entertained to end their campaign by bombarding Bayonne's citadel. This was achieved not only through the casualties inflicted but also by destroying essential siege equipment. As soon as the siege lines were established, in late February, Captain Batty reported that 'the making of gabions, fascines, and platforms for the guns, was rapidly going forward'. Fascines, made by tying bundles of wood, supported the earthen walls of trenches and gun batteries, while gabions, consisting of baskets filled with soil, protected soldiers at work on the trench line. According to Batty, 'An enormous quantity of fascines and gabions had been prepared, and deposited in the ravines close behind the advancing picquets'. As the night attack unfolded, French artillery shot fireballs to assist their gunners' targeting. 'Some of these fireballs and shells fell in the midst of the depot of fascines, which naturally caught fire and burnt with great fierceness; so as to require constant exertions before they could be extinguished'.[93] Even at this late stage, insufficient care had been taken to protect vital support material.

The final act of the Peninsular War saw high-profile British losses in one of the timeless vulnerabilities of siege warfare, the sudden, unexpected sally launched by the besieged against the extended and momentarily undermanned lines of the besiegers. This inglorious contest ended the fighting as news of Napoleon's abdication circulated. The siege itself formally ended only on 26 April when Thouvenot at last accepted that reality.[94] This act had added symbolism, for Thouvenot had been responsible in 1808 for gathering French troops into San Sebastian and seizing it by subterfuge from the Spanish.[95]

This final reversal outside Bayonne was significant also because the British had assembled a substantial siege train. Reflecting on the armaments available at Pasajes by February 1814, Lieutenant Colonel John T. Jones insisted that 'Never before had the army possessed similar means for a siege, and in a few days an attack of the citadel, so utterly irresistible from force and combination, would have commenced, as to insure a bloodless triumph, when intelligence of the capture of Paris damped [*sic*] their hopes and checked their ardour'.[96]

In fact, Bayonne did not witness such a culminating point in the British provision of siege weaponry, for the ordnance deployed at Bayonne included fewer heavy guns than had been engaged at San Sebastian. There were twenty-six 24-pounders, compared with twenty-eight at San Sebastian, and twelve 10in mortars, as against fifteen at San Sebastian. There were no 18-pounders or heavy carronades at Bayonne. The only advantage was in smaller, non-breaching artillery, with twelve 8in howitzers at Bayonne as against nine at San Sebastian and twenty smaller (4.4in) mortars at Bayonne, whereas by 26 August there had been none at San Sebastian. The amount of ammunition provided for the latter (4,000 shells compared with over 5,000 shells each for the 10in mortars and the howitzers, and 29,440 round shot for the 24-pounders) indicated that they would play a limited role.[97]

Nevertheless, the siege of Bayonne was later used to create an illusion that an opportunity to excel had been lost. In the 1840s, John Jones's brother, Harry, also a Lieutenant Colonel in the Royal Engineers, revised and expanded Sir John's standard account of the Peninsular sieges. He argued that, at last, the British had assembled adequate ordnance, expert and experienced artillerymen, capable engineers and effective sappers and miners. These assets at Bayonne contrasted with the British experience at their sieges in 1811–13. The earlier sieges demonstrated skilful tactical preparation, decisiveness, initiative and courage 'scarcely to be paralleled in other similar operations'. But, according to Harry Jones, they also posed four problems for the British. First, the allies' siege forces were small and had 'inadequate ordnance'. Secondly, the country in which the sieges occurred had such depleted resources that transport facilities were defective. Thirdly, the French defended their positions with 'the most veteran and most confident troops in the world'. Finally, the sieges occurred when the French had 'powerful armies' capable of advancing, or threatening to advance, upon besieging armies and force them to lift their sieges. Given this context, British actions at Badajos, Ciudad Rodrigo and San Sebastian were 'daring efforts of firmness and talent . . . brilliant instances of courage triumphing over art . . . and proud deeds of arms, alike honourable to the army and to the national character'. But they could not be commended as models which exemplified 'skilful combinations of science, labour, and force'. The situation facing the British at Bayonne differed in all those four particulars. Harry Jones therefore regretted that the siege of Bayonne did not run to its proper military conclusion because it 'would have given an example of a sure and almost bloodless triumph over a fortress, by combinations of labour and art, which would have served as a guide and authority for the future'.[98]

The verdict was curiously mixed. San Sebastian, the scene of a military victory won by sustained, vigorous fighting, was carried by the determination and self-sacrifice of the infantry which in this judgement would have been unnecessary if proper, scientific methods had been followed. At Bayonne, the infantry suffered a minor reversal resulting from elementary tactical inefficiency. Their incompetence had disguised the fact that the siege could have been resolved by the skill and resources of properly planned operations. This assessment, made long after the war in revisions to John Jones' earlier book, was probably inspired in part by a desire to maintain government spending on weapons, ammunition and the specialist arms of the army. But the conclusions were significant. The book continued to be studied closely at the Royal Military Academy, Woolwich, the training school for Royal Artillery and Royal Engineer cadets, at the very least until 1853.[99] The most authoritative professional account of British siege operations in the Peninsular War claimed that the final episode, at Bayonne, was incomplete and would have provided a ringing climax to an extended and demanding exercise in that scientific species of warfare.

Notes

1. Larpent (ed), *The Private Journal*, iii, 203.
2. Anon. [Blakiston], *Twelve Years' Military Adventure*, ii, 235.
3. *The Times*, 16 October 1813, p. 3.
4. (Edinburgh) *Caledonian Mercury*, 23 October 1813.
5. Batty, *Campaign*, 29.
6. *New Annual Register for 1813*, 303.
7. *WD*, x, 453, 590, 599, xi, 66, 71, 179, 285, 371, 540, 638, 664.
8. Barbaro, *The Battle*, 419.
9. Wellington to General Dumouriez, 18 July 1813, *WD*, x, 538.
10. Wellington to Beresford, 7 February 1814, *WD*, xi, 502.
11. Cowper (ed.), *The King's Own*, i, 433–4.
12. Glover, *An Eloquent Soldier*, 245.
13. Wellington to Manners, 23 March 1813, *WD*, xi, 603.
14. Muir, *Tactics and the Experience of Battle*, 273.
15. Fischer, *Travels in Spain*, 41, 44–5.
16. Larpent (ed.), *The Private Journal*, ii, 57, 68.
17. Hibbert (ed.), *The Wheatley Diary*, 22–3, 35.
18. Batty, *Campaign*, 61–5.
19. Fischer, *Travels in Spain*, 63.
20. *WD*, xi, 297, 524.
21. Wellington to Penrose, 25 February, to Sir John Hope, 26 February, to Bathurst, 1 March, memorandum, 6 March, to Commissioners of the Transport Board, 7 March, to Bathurst, 16 March 1814, *WD*, xi, 528, 530, 534, 554, 560, 587, 591.
22. Wellington to Rear Admiral Penrose, 6 February 1814, *WD*, xi, 501.

23. Sabine (ed.), *Letters*, 422.
24. Wellington to Bathurst, 7 March 1814, *WD*, xi, 562.
25. Sabine (ed.), *Letters*, 423–4.
26. Wellington to Penrose, 7, 9 February 1814, *WD*, xi, 505, 509.
27. Sabine (ed.), *Letters*, 425–6.
28. Rory Muir, *Wellington: The Path to Victory, 1769–1814* (New Haven CT and London, 2013), 532–3, 570, 573, 576, 582–3.
29. Jean-Denis G.G. Lepage, *Vauban and the French Military under Louis XIV* (Jefferson NC, 2010), 230–1.
30. Foy, *History of the War*, i, 3, 266, 303–7.
31. *The Times*, 24 March 1809, p. 4.
32. *Morning Chronicle*, 16 September 1813.
33. Anon. [Blakiston], *Twelve Years' Military Adventure,* ii, 306.
34. Lepage, *Vauban*, 231–2.
35. Thouvenet to Dalmatie, 9 August, 20, 21 September 1813, SHAT C8 221.
36. Anon. [Blakiston], *Twelve Years' Military Adventure*, ii, 305.
37. Thouvenot to Feltre, 20 September; to Dalmatie, 24, 26, 28, 29 September, 1 (1 of 2), 3, 4 October 1813, SHAT C8 221.
38. Thouvenot to Dalmatie, 3, 4 October (2 of 2) 1813, SHAT C8 221.
39. 'Situation des Troupes . . . I Octobre 1813', SHAT C8 372.
40. Thouvenot to Dalmatie, 1 October 1813 (2 of 2), SHAT C8 221.
41. Fischer, *Travels in Spain*, 42.
42. Batty, *Campaign*, 141.
43. Wrottesley, *Life and Correspondence*, i, 288.
44. Batty, *Campaign*, 89.
45. Batty, *Campaign*, 110–11.
46. Wellington to Hope, 2, 8 March 1814, *WD*, xi, 542, 564; one estimate places the garrison at 11,800, including many unfit for duty, Ian C. Robertson, *Wellington Invades France* (London, 2003), 249.
47. Muir, *Wellington. The Path to Victory*, 570.
48. Wellington to Bathurst, 20 March 1814, *WD*, xi, 593.
49. Oman, *A History of the Peninsular War,* vii, 563.
50. Larpent (ed.), *The Private Journal*, ii, 141; 'Sir Howard Elphinstone' entry in *ODNB*.
51. Wrottesley, *Life and Correspondence*, i, 288–9, 291–2.
52. Larpent (ed.), *The Private Journal*, iii, 7.
53. For the previous paragraph and this one: Jones, *Journals*, ii, 108–10, 115–20; Wrottesley, *Life and Correspondence*, i, 293–4.
54. Fischer, *Travels in Spain*, 52–6; Henegan, *Seven Years Campaigning*, ii, 26–7, 29, 111.
55. Wrottesley, *Life and Correspondence*, i, 294–5; Sabine (ed.), *Letters*, 416.
56. Sabine (ed.), *Letters*, 417.
57. Jones, *Journals*, ii, 120–1; Wrottesley, *Life and Correspondence*, i, 294–5.
58. Batty, *Campaign*, 126.
59. Jones, *Journals*, ii, 108–9.
60. Jones, *Journals*, ii, 106–15; Wrottesley, *Life and Correspondence*, i, 291–2, 295–6; Sabine (ed.), *Letters*, 418–19.
61. Wellington to Hope, 25, 26 February 1814, *WD*, xi, 528–30.
62. Sabine (ed.), *Letters*, 422.
63. Hibbert (ed.), *The Wheatley Diary*, 41, 44.
64. Larpent (ed.), *The Private Journal*, iii, 17, 19–20.
65. Wellington to Hope, 2 March 1814, *WD*, xi, 541–2.
66. Sabine (ed.), *Letters*, 422–4.
67. Jones, *Journals*, ii, 117–18; Batty, *Campaign,* 116, 168.

68. Larpent (ed.), *The Private Journal*, iii, 9.
69. Wellington to Hope (& memorandum enclosed), 6 March 1814, *WD*, xi, 554–5.
70. Wellington to Hope, 5 March 1814, *WD*, xi, 550–1.
71. Wrottesley, *Life and Correspondence,* i, 296.
72. Wellington to Hope, 8 March 1814, *WD*, xi, 563–5.
73. Glover (ed.), *A Gentleman Volunteer*, 117, 130.
74. Wellington to Hope, 18 March 1814, *WD*, xi, 591.
75. Sabine (ed.), *Letters*, 431.
76. Henegan, *Seven Years Campaigning*, ii, 113.
77. Wellington to Beresford, 14 March; to Dalhousie, 16 March 1814, *WD*, xi, 578, 583.
78. Wellington to Bathurst, 25 March; to Hope, 26 March 1814, *WD*, xi, 604, 606–7.
79. Wellington to Hope, 1, 12 April 1814, Gurwood *Dispatches*, xi, 615, 629.
80. Wellington to Hope, 16 April 1814, *WD*, xi, 648–9.
81. Hibbert (ed.), *The Wheatley Diary*, 45.
82. Jones, *Journals*, ii, 127–8.
83. Hibbert (ed.), *The Wheatley Diary*, 47.
84. Oman, *A History of the Peninsular War*, vii, 508–11; Robertson, *Wellington Invades France*, 246–9; Larpent (ed.), *The Private Journal*, iii, 200–1, 203.
85. Robertson, *Wellington Invades France*, 247. Hay was born in 1762 and had been a Lieutenant Colonel since 1798; he had commanded a column at the storming of San Sebastian and was dismissed as a coward by his fellow column commander there, Major General Frederick Robinson. Hall, *A History of the Peninsular War: VIII*, 268–9, 498. C.T. Atkinson, 'A Peninsular Brigadier', *Journal of the Society of Army Historical Research*, XXXIV (1956).
86. Larpent (ed.), *The Private Journal*, iii, 201, 203.
87. Wellington to Torrens, 15 December 1813, *WD*, xi, 371–2.
88. Major General K.A. Howard to Major General C. Colville, 15 April 1814, *WD*, xi, 662–4; Robertson, *Wellington Invades France*, 246–8; Henegan, *Seven Years Campaigning*, 117; Beamish, *History*, 302–4.
89. Jones, *Journals*, ii, 130–1.
90. Oman, *A History of the Peninsular War*, vii, 561–2.
91. Robertson, *Wellington Invades France*, 246; Oman, *A History of the Peninsular War*, vii, 506–8, 512.
92. Jones, *Journals*, ii, 127–8.
93. Batty, *Campaign*, 134, 150, 164.
94. Robertson, *Wellington Invades France*, 249.
95. Foy, *History of the War*, ii, 121.
96. Jones, *Journals*, ii, 127–8.
97. Jones, *Journals*, ii, 57–8, 127.
98. Jones, *Journals*, ii, 349—50.
99. *The Times*, 19 December 1849, p. 5; 21 December 1853, p. 10.

Chapter 15

Urban Warfare: Comparisons

Although it was not the most deadly or destructive of the numerous sieges in Spain between 1808 and 1814, the siege of San Sebastian was the most challenging and controversial of the sieges conducted by Wellington's army. The town's destruction and the horrors resulting from the soldiers' drunkenness and quest for plunder fuelled Spanish liberal politicians' antipathy to Wellington. For the British, these events were quickly subsumed in the intensive fighting which flowed from the invasion of France. Yet, before concluding this study, it is worth considering how the siege should be placed in the broader context of urban warfare in this period. What happened in San Sebastian partly reflected the psychological and physical conditions in which urban fighting occurred. Yet, despite being a recurrent feature of the Peninsular War, urban warfare has not been analysed as a distinctive phenomenon in these years. What happened in San Sebastian is better understood in the context of British and French experiences of urban warfare in the early nineteenth century.

Of course, the plundering and destruction of Spanish towns went far beyond siege operations. Captain Webber noted in 1812 the extensive destruction wrought by the French at Medellin and he later estimated that the war had left two-thirds of the houses at Talavera uninhabitable. When the British abandoned Madrid in October 1812, he wrote, 'I never recollect on any occasion (where my family were not concerned), being more melancholy and depressed than in . . . giving up Madrid to the plunder and wanton cruelty of the enemy. I would willingly have lost a limb in a battle to save it, and I know every man felt the same sentiments'. Webber later deplored French behaviour on re-capturing Salamanca in 1812, when they 'levied contributions without mercy. The troops were allowed to plunder and commit every kind of outrage for two days after their arrival and the distress of the people is said to have been inconceivable'.[1]

Although warring countries inevitably blame their enemies for extreme misconduct, the British in admitting their own excesses pointed to French misbehaviour. Spanish denunciations of the allegedly deliberate destruction of San Sebastian simply provoked British denials. Even though the impact of siege warfare on civilians troubled some British officers and even though the fate of besieged towns merited more extended scrutiny than contemporaries' fervent accusations and heated refutations allowed for, the politicization of Spanish reactions contributed to a lack of any British assessment of the challenges of urban warfare. Two other obstacles to such reflection were the argument that misbehaviour was limited to a disruptive few and the acceptance of some, recurrent ill-discipline as a necessary if regrettable part of how an army operated on campaign.

Some senior officers later recognized that soldiers' behaviour needed improving. They tried to curb soldiers' excessive drinking, which Wellington in the 1830s viewed as the main cause of ill-discipline. Various measures aimed at reducing the frequency and attractiveness of alcohol consumption included the introduction of evening meals, libraries, competitive sports and, in the 1840s, savings banks to encourage soldiers to save rather than spend all their ready cash on drink.[2] Even so, dramatic cases of misconduct recurred. The assault on Delhi in September 1857, following a long siege, resulted in a familiar collapse of order and discipline among British troops and widespread drunkenness and savage violence against civilians.[3] But efforts to address drunkenness, although shaped by those remembering the Peninsular War, did not gain traction during the 1810s.

The more glaring failure was the lack of attention paid in the mid-1810s to the distinctive challenges and horrors of urban warfare in general. For the French, with all the much-touted Napoleonic legacy of administrative and legal reform, this was a significant derogation from Enlightenment concerns about the impact of war upon civilians. For the British, the absence of such thinking was less ideologically striking, since no one has claimed that British law-makers in this period set out to give Europe a reformed legal code. But in empirical terms, the failure to consider urban warfare as a distinctive challenge remains an interesting lapse.

In describing the descent into drunkenness and 'an immense amount of unlicensed pillage and wanton destruction of property' at Ciudad Rodrigo in 1812, Oman noted 'This was the first time on which the Peninsular Army had taken a place by assault, and the consequent confusion does not seem to been foreseen by any one'.[4] Oman's conclusion seems curiously innocent in overlooking precedents for soldiers' misconduct. For example, John Drinkwater's well-known account of the siege of Gibraltar noted that artificers and a soldier were executed for marauding and that soldiers were searched for loot when they returned to quarters from duties within the British garrison town.[5] One officer's wife publically reported that 'many of the men were shamefully intoxicated. The Town-Major, and a party of soldiers, were busily employed in staving all the casks of liquor they could find in the town.'[6]

Oman also omitted to mention that Wellington had first-hand experience of such events in India, while his senior officers had ample opportunity to learn from French attacks upon Spanish cities in 1809–11. Wellington was wholly accustomed to the problems created by soldiers' excesses in captured towns. At Seringapatam in 1799, he was given the responsibility of bringing order to the chaos which followed the town's capture on 4 May. He famously reported to his brother, the Governor General:

> It was impossible to expect that after the labour which the troops had undergone in working up to the place . . . they should not have looked to the plunder of this place. Nothing therefore can have exceeded what was done on the night of the 4th. Scarcely a house in the town was left unplundered. . . . I came in to take command on the morning of the 5th, and by the greatest exertion, by hanging,

flogging, etc, etc, in the course of that day I restored order among the troops, and I hope I have gained the confidence of the people. . . . but the property of every one is gone.[7]

He tried to uphold a semi-legalistic distinction between acceptable and unacceptable plunder. Houses captured during the attack and houses inhabited by employees of Tipu's government or by those possessing public property were subject to prize. In effect, they could legitimately be plundered, though they were supposed to be guarded – for prize – by designated sentries. But all houses which were not 'taken' or guarded when the town's surrender was proclaimed were not subject to prize. Wellington (to use his later title) insisted that civilians' status changed when a flag was raised over the town indicating that a written surrender and grant of amnesty or cowle had been agreed. This effort failed. On 8 May, he wrote to the Governor General that the East India Company army – whose troops he dismissed as 'plunderers' – and the army sent by the Nizam of Hyderabad should leave Seringapatam as soon as possible. They 'still occasion great confusion and terror among the inhabitants, and tend to obstruct our settlement of the country'. Two weeks later the army had still not left, becoming instead 'very inflammable' over disputed prize money; 'There is nothing about which an army is in general so jealous (particularly an Indian army) as its prize . . .'.[8]

Wellington tried in 1799 to maintain a distinction crucial to establishing the laws of warfare. Throughout the eighteenth century, rulers who had just claims to territory currently controlled by others could resort to war, if those claims were rejected. In the absence of supra-national bodies, princes acquired titles and/or territory by exercising the accepted right to secure such territory through just wars. In turn, their armies were rewarded with booty taken during a justifiable campaign. But, of course, plundering had to be regulated to prevent invading armies rapidly descending into roaming gangs of thieves.[9] A campaign whose objective was a major town offered the advantage that the prospect of plundering a large and/or wealthy town restrained soldiers from absconding to plunder as they advanced through enemy territory.

Plunder had long been expected as a necessary and just reward for armies pursuing just causes. When the Maratha War of 1803 began, the very first success achieved by Wellington's army in early August was to force the capitulation of Ahmednaghar after six days of blockade. The fact that the fortified town surrendered without being stormed did not inhibit plundering. One officer present later noted: 'Two sepoys . . . were, by orders of the General, hung up on each side of the gateway; a measure which, it must be confessed, created some disgust at the moment, but which, at the outset of a campaign, was perhaps a necessary example for the sake of discipline . . .'.[10]

Unlike Ahmednaghar, the next objective, Gawilgarh (Gwalighur), had to be besieged and stormed. Wellington's orders for the storming of Gawilgarh on 15 December 1803 included the instruction 'that the soldiers and sepoys may not be allowed to quit their ranks and go in search of plunder, as is but too commonly the practice'.[11] Such orders failed to limit violence or plundering, as Captain Blakiston noted:

I saw a party of the Scotch brigade bring out some of the enemy, whom they had found concealed in a house, saying that they would give the rascals a chance. Then, taking them out one by one like basket-hares, they called to them, in Hindostanee, to run, and, when they got to the distance of about thirty yards, they levelled and brought them down. It was with difficulty that they could be persuaded to give up this cruel diversion.[12]

Despite Wellington's orders preceding the assault, Blakiston recounted how he had been threatened with violence when he remonstrated with 'several of our soldiers in the act of plundering and ill-using the inhabitants'. He later in part explained such behaviour: 'During the siege . . . we were all buoyed up with the hope of making our fortunes, as immense treasures were reported to be deposited in the fort'.[13] Little was found and disappointment may have spurred an ever more aggressive search for loot.

It is obvious, therefore, that the violence unleashed in Ciudad Rodrigo in 1812 should have been foreseen by Wellington. He knew full well how civilian populations and his own forces would be affected by the storming of a well-defended town. Equally importantly, such awareness was not confined to officers who had served in distant India. Many officers in the Peninsula had served in the major assaults launched by the British immediately before the Peninsular War, against Copenhagen and Buenos Aires.

In September 1807, British officers differed over the acceptability of bombarding the city of Copenhagen. Believing that Napoleon intended to seize the Danish fleet, the British intervened to force the government to surrender its warships in Copenhagen harbour. The British did not wish to destroy the ships and they did not have the time to starve the city's 100,000 people into submission in order to induce the Danish government to negotiate. They chose therefore to bombard the city until the authorities agreed to transfer the fleet. The bombardment, mainly at night, occurred during 2–5 September and led to the exodus from the city of about 20,000 people, the death of about 2,000 civilians, the destruction of about one-twelfth of the central city and extensive damage to many more buildings.[14]

Many officers in 1807 expressed reservations about the action and sympathy for the Danish civilians. For example, Captain William Gomm, then an Assistant Quarter Master General and later a battalion commander at San Sebastian, noted how the fires spread when a timber-yard was hit and high winds worked their effect throughout the bombardment. By the third night the sky resembled 'a volcano during a violent eruption'. He assured his sister that 'the women and children, and most of those incapable of bearing arms, had flocked in great numbers' to the farther part of town 'where our fire had no effect'. But he continued:

The idea of a bombardment is shocking to humanity. It has been the practice among nations of late to open a siege by this measure; it was done at Valenciennes; it was done at Dantzic; it is always done. But though it is sanctioned by the laws of war, it is always more becoming, and a measure of more enlightened warfare, to attack a town in any other way than by distressing the inhabitants. . . . But in many instances the time and means necessary for a regular attack are wanting, as in the present one, where time is everything to us.

According to Gomm, who was on the staff, the commander of the expedition, Lord Cathcart, was especially distressed at having to proceed in this way.[15] The general's reluctant decision to bombard followed the advice of George Murray, his Deputy Quartermaster General, that it was the only feasible option. Murray, however, conceded that 'the bombardment of the town itself was generally held to be improper' by British officers.[16]

Murray was closely involved in the preparations for the siege of San Sebastian, since he was Wellington's Quarter Master General, or effectively his chief of staff, in 1813. It seems inconceivable that senior officers failed to assess the probable effects of assaulting San Sebastian. Lieutenant Colonel Francis Brooke, who commanded the 4th in the reserve at the second assault, had served at Copenhagen, as well as Badajoz.[17] Wellington commanded the reserve at Copenhagen, and, although he was not involved, as a relatively junior Major General, in strategic decision-making, he initially expressed strong reservations about a bombardment and accepted it as the option of last resort.[18] From the evidence of previous behaviour, one can only assume that the attack on San Sebastian was regarded as a regrettable necessity.

Gomm continued to comment on the effects of subjugating towns. Witnessing the ruins of burnt-out houses after the capture of Ciudad Rodrigo, he lamented: 'I have been too much used to such scenes for some time past for you to expect a very feeling account of them now. Like Macbeth, we "have supp'd so full of horrors" they scarcely move us'. At San Sebastian, Gomm commanded the 9th in both assaults. As the second bombardment was being prepared, he remarked that 'We have sadly marred' the town and its surroundings, adding that 'I am afraid we shall be obliged to destroy a great part of the town'. In the event, he was saddened by the destruction of such a fine place, although he stressed that 'many of the excesses committed at Badajos were avoided here'.[19]

In the same year that Copenhagen and its inhabitants were bombarded, many senior officers later at San Sebastian were directly involved in close-quarter urban fighting in Buenos Aires. Thousands of troops had entered the city, which did not possess fortified walls, by five parallel roads. Meeting intense and prolonged resistance, these columns suffered heavy casualties and were forced to surrender. This capitulation led to a widely reported court martial lasting 32 days in January–March 1808. The commander-in-chief, Lieutenant General John Whitelocke, was cashiered for his incompetence.

It is remarkable how many officers serving at Buenos Aires were present in the Peninsula in 1813. Of course, it is difficult to demonstrate how the events in Buenos Aires shaped subsequent thinking, because officers rarely exchanged stories, reminiscences or tactical assessments in writing. But it is equally unlikely that aspects of so notorious a campaign were not informally discussed. Senior officers serving in the Peninsula in 1812–13 who had been at Buenos Aires included: Alexander Dickson, who headed the Royal Artillery in the Peninsula in 1812–13; Augustus Frazer, who

led the Royal Horse Artillery there in 1813; and the senior military representative at
La Coruña in 1813 when it became a busy, much-visited transhipment point, Thomas
Bourke. Frazer, who commanded the artillery of twenty-eight mostly small-calibre
guns at Buenos Aires, and Bourke, who was military secretary in the expedition to
Buenos Aires, testified at the court martial. Other senior officers involved in 1807
included: Major General Robert Crauford, who testified at great length in 1808 and
died of wounds at Ciudad Rodrigo; Major General Dennis Pack, who commanded a
Portuguese brigade at Ciudad Rodrigo, at Burgos and at Vitoria; Major General
Thomas Bradford, whose long service in the Peninsula included command of a
Portuguese brigade at San Sebastian; Lieutenant Colonel John Nugent, who was at
Badajoz; Lieutenant Colonel Samuel Whittingham, who had been one of Whitelocke's
aides-de-camp and served in the Portuguese army's Quarter Master General's
department from 1809; and Lieutenant Colonel Henry Cadogan, whose death from
wounds at Vitoria deeply affected Wellington.[20] There were ample opportunities for
the experience at Buenos Aires to be discussed in the Peninsula.

While one can only speculate whether lessons were deduced from Buenos Aires,
the main messages were obvious. First, according to Lieutenant Colonel Bourke, 'it
was quite impossible to prevent a great deal of butchery' in attacking an 'open town'.[21]
Secondly, urban fighting exposed the assailants to ferocious ambushes. For example,
one column of 225 rank and file from the 88th advanced to a church which needed to
be seized. On reaching the church gateway, the column came under fire from houses
opposite. In failing to break open the church door and gain cover, it lost nearly thirty
casualties. Forced to take refuge in nearby houses, the men fought on for about 4 hours
before surrendering at around midday. The battalion's other column was 'continually
assailed from the houses on both sides of the streets with musketry, hand grenades, tin
pots, brickbats and all sorts of missiles they could throw upon us'. Virtually half the
450 men of the 88th engaged that day were killed or wounded.[22] On the right wing of
the force marching into the town, according to Lieutenant Colonel Pack, 'The first
remarkable thing that attracted my notice, was the extraordinary stillness of the town.
. . . Some intelligent men of the advanced guard, observed the sound of voices in
several of the houses as we passed'. But Pack decided that his orders required him to
move forward rather than assess the situation in the houses. As he approached his
objective, he was attacked by 'an enemy almost invisible and certainly inassailable
[*sic*]'. The front divisions of his column of 600 men were devastated by enemy fire.[23]
It was extraordinarily difficult for the assailants to counter musket fire from roof tops
screened by parapets.

The third lesson was that urban fighting required, therefore, the destruction of
houses. The British at Buenos Aires did not possess enough or adequate tools to enter
the houses. As Brigadier General Lumley complained, 'The pick axes which had been
delivered to the columns were useless in breaking open the strong massy doors and
windows which is the same throughout the town; but by the united efforts of the
soldiers, we at length forced open some few houses.'[24] But to avoid what degenerated
into mini sieges of individual buildings, the British ideally needed to bombard the
town. This proved impossible. The Royal navy's larger warships could not sail near

enough to the town to deliver a significant bombardment. In addition, the buildings were so solidly built of stone that they could not readily be destroyed by artillery. Captain Frazer claimed that he could have erected an artillery battery to bombard the town. But he met the response that 'the City could not be set on fire. I replied that the experiment might be made; and that in all events the enemy must be dislodged' from one part of the city.[25]

The lead battalions pressing through Buenos Aires suffered heavy losses and humiliating surrender before a general capitulation and British withdrawal were negotiated. No one who remembered that experience would have wished to engage again in street fighting before bombarding the town being entered. Nor would remembrance of Buenos Aires have encouraged restraint in the use of force by troops fighting their way into a hostile town.

If the dangers of urban warfare were not obvious from these prominent British undertakings at Seringapatam, Gawilgarh, Copenhagen and Buenos Aires, then French campaigning in Spain offered even more recent evidence of the savage nature of urban fighting. The evidence from the most dramatic examples – Zaragoza, Tarragona and Gerona – was accessible to British officers serving in the Peninsula, and each merits attention.

The two sieges of Zaragoza, during June–August 1808 and then from 20 December 1808 to 20 February 1809, cost 54,000 Spanish lives and 10,000 French military casualties. The city's population was only 43,000, but the extraordinary scale of its religious life – sustained by over 110 monasteries, convents and churches – drew Spanish soldiers and local peasants into the city once it declared its opposition to the French. Marshal Lannes, deploying some 3,000 sappers and artillerymen, relied upon their specialist activities supported by artillery fire to destroy rows of houses and other buildings. About one-third of the houses and churches were demolished. Lannes avoided street fighting as much as possible because the city's defenders proudly regarded their cause as a matter of life and death. Fierce hostility in the surrounding countryside to the presence of French imperial troops encouraged the flow of reinforcements into the city, while the clergy stirred the civilian population with a will to resist. But heavy death tolls, terrible sickness, lack of food and sheer exhaustion eventually forced the defenders to agree terms. Unusually, a city which had been stormed was allowed to capitulate without being sacked, although the destruction and rampant disease scarcely made Zaragoza an enticing place in which to linger.[26]

The scale of destruction was widely reported in England. Such information was familiar to those British officers who avidly read and commented on the latest newspapers from home, 'gaping for news like trout on a summer evening as we are', as one of them put it.[27] The *Morning Chronicle* insisted that the 'great part of the town was reduced by the batteries and mines to a heap of ruins'.[28] *The Times* in 1809 reported the intensity of the conflict. The sheer numbers of people in the city – said to be 120,000 including 40,000 armed men – underscored the challenge of feeding so many. The ceaseless French bombardment steadily eroded resistance, so that the city seemed 'to have been wrung from the hands of the defenders, house by house', with the French taking thirty or forty houses per day.[29] The 33rd bulletin issued by the French Army of

Spain was quoted extensively, with its grim warning: 'the calamities which have befallen this unhappy town, are a terrifying example to the people'. The bulletin stressed that the French would have to mine buildings used as centres of resistance within the city and that they would deploy three companies of miners and eight companies of sappers to destroy such obstacles. The French eventually took and occupied one-third of the houses; 'The enemy defended *every house* [*sic*] . . . every day several houses were blown up . . .'. Monasteries and public buildings were destroyed by mortar fire and the church containing the image of Our Lady of Pilar, which was used to boost Spanish morale, 'was battered down by bombs, and no longer inhabitable'.[30]

Significantly for contemporary evaluations of San Sebastian's fate, the story of Zaragoza's destruction was repeated in *The Military Panorama or Officers' Companion* in August 1813. A central lesson of urban conflict was emphasized yet again; 'the French had been taught by experience, that the only means of conquering Zaragoza was to destroy it house by house, and street by street'. Even before the French entered the city, their bombardment had reputedly reduced two-thirds of it to ruins. Further resistance was undermined by the ravages wrought by disease.[31] Such accounts made contemporaries fully aware of the grim consequences of urban fighting.

Yet early nineteenth-century writers erected a conceptual barrier against analysing the effects of such conflict. Although British journalistic accounts of the siege of Zaragoza spelled out the horrendous human casualties briefly and factually, they used them as glowing evidence of the defenders' extraordinary patriotism rather than as grim reminders of what should be avoided in urban combat. According to *The Times*, 'No event of equal importance has in fact occurred since the commencement of the Spanish war'.[32] The newspaper printed a letter from an officer serving in the Peninsula insisting that the defence of Zaragoza and Gerona were 'the two most heroic and splendid examples of persevering courage in the history of the world'.[33] The *Morning Chronicle* skipped details of the human suffering during the siege, stressing instead that the 'glorious resistance' staged by 'the brave inhabitants' furnished 'one of the most splendid instances of courage and patriotism that stand upon record'.[34]

The French general Maximilien Foy, in memoirs published in the 1820s, offered unusually explicit reflections on the challenges of urban warfare. In describing the French advance into the city at the first siege in the summer of 1808, Foy claimed that, after initially retreating, the 'The inhabitants of Sarragossa and the garrison did what had never been done before' in rallying and attacking the French in concentrated numbers. French troops 'were dispersed through the houses, and occupied in plundering'. This sudden and unanticipated counter-attack forced them to retreat and take up defensive positions within the city's buildings. 'The French soldiers, unaccustomed to this defensive warfare, were much inferior in it to the Spaniards'. Under pressure on other fronts, the French then pulled out of Zaragoza and lifted the siege.

Foy recognized that the defenders of Zaragoza defeated regular, disciplined troops in a way that was 'next to impossible' on the battlefield. He acknowledged the magnitude of the achievement: 'The defence of Saragossa set a great example to Spain;

it will re-echo through future ages'. But he did not probe the tactical lessons to be learned. Instead, as did others reflecting on the siege, he stressed the triumph of 'moral nature' over 'physical nature', inspired by 'religious fervour' and a 'sublime indifference to life and death'. 'In Spain', he insisted, 'the sieges have always been heroic'.[35]

The Spanish had a similar public interest in turning the horrors of urban fighting into heroic narrative. In 1808 when Goya was invited to return to his native city of Zaragoza he was asked not to commemorate its defenders' acute suffering but 'to see and study the ruins of the city, in order to paint the glorious deeds of her citizens'. As a fledgling artist in 1780–1, Goya had completed a commission at the El Pilar cathedral, which became in 1808–9 a symbol of civic resistance to the French. He was asked to return there by Jose Palafox, the charismatic leader of the city's defence.[36]

There was little publicly articulated sense that civilian suffering in urban conflict was aberrant. Even when British commentators had every reason to emphasize civilian suffering at French hands, they tended instead to focus on civilian sacrifice as evidence of Spanish resilience. Both British commentaries and the leaders of Zaragoza's defence promoted the impact of Spanish patriotism instead of stressing the extent of French brutality.

Zaragoza's suffering did not end with the French expulsion from the city in 1813. Having stood as a beacon of fervent Spanish patriotism in 1808–9, it simply became in 1813 what cities had long been, a type of treasure trove whose resources were available to incentivize and reward ill-paid soldiers. When Francisco Espoz y Mina's insurgent Navarre Division attacked the town in March, they plundered it, and his guerrilla troops continued to rob and terrorize the inhabitants until they finally left in November. Since Wellington in November 1813 was aware of the power struggles within the city, he almost certainly knew of the guerrilla bands' excesses.[37]

While Zaragoza provided the most devastating example of urban warfare during the Peninsular War, the French siege of Tarragona, an important and well-fortified port on the east coast, offered more direct comparisons to the British conduct of sieges.[38] The operation, from 3 May to 28 June 1811, was no faster and no more strikingly 'efficient' than British siege operations in 1812–13, other than the failed attempt at Burgos. Moreover, the comparison was one from which contemporaries might have benefited, since *The Times* reported events at Tarragona and an account by the Spanish commander, Don Juan Senen de Contreras, was published in London on 14 August 1813.

The French made slow progress and military and civilian casualties mounted. Marshal Suchet arrived outside the town on 3–4 May 1811, leading 46,000 troops with plentiful artillery; 22,000 men were assigned to the siege. The French failed to prevent the Spanish from strengthening their garrison by introducing 4,000 extra troops on 10 May. They failed to take the outlying Fort Olivo on 29 May, suffering 2,000 casualties in the process. They did not begin an artillery bombardment until 1 June, finally assailing the lower city on the 21st, when five storming parties took the lower city. On 28 June breaches in the inner city's walls were stormed. The consequences proved dire for civilian life and property. Half the 4,000 dead in the city were civilians and there was widespread destruction. Extensive pillaging was unsurprising since Tarragona had served as the base for the Spanish army of Catalonia for three years and was a major depot and trading centre. The French lost 924 killed and 3,372 wounded in capturing Tarragona. In comparison, British casualties throughout the siege of San Sebastian totalled 965 killed and 2,800 wounded and missing. Granted, the Spanish garrison at Tarragona was three times the size of the French garrison which the British attacked at San Sebastian, but the costs in manpower of assaulting a well-defended city were high for both.[39]

The time taken in preparing the assault on Tarragona, the intensity of the fighting, and the damage inflicted on the city indicate that the British sieges did not differ markedly from French ones. One obvious criticism of British practice centred on the insufficient number of 24-pounders with which they opened their bombardments. But Napoleon was sceptical of reliance simply on massive artillery bombardments. He stressed that fighting within cities should focus on houses and avoid committing large numbers of troops to contesting exposed streets. At Zaragoza, mining buildings took priority over the artillery assault.[40] The French did not therefore deploy more artillery guns in their sieges than the British did. The French deployed sixty siege guns and eighty-four field artillery guns at the start of their formal siege of Zaragoza. This certainly exceeded the ordnance available to Wellington, but Zaragoza was far bigger than the towns Wellington assaulted. According to Oman, the artillery used at Zaragoza was also 'far more than the French had turned against many of the first-class fortresses of Germany'. Despite such firepower, the French took over a month before storming into the city and then spent twenty-four days fighting within the walled city.[41] This underscored the scale of the challenge posed by a large town fanatically defended. One tactical difference was that the British were ready to storm breaches earlier than the French.

Yet *The Times* in commenting on the siege of Tarragona in August 1813 made light of technical and tactical issues, concentrating instead on the siege's wider implications. The events of 1811 had demonstrated Spanish 'gallantry' and military determination in contrast to the persistent 'crimes' and 'the atrocious conduct which has so universally characterised the modern Frenchmen'.[42] This became a recurrent theme by 1813. In early September, the newspaper claimed that Tarragona's capture cost 12,000 French casualties. More widely, it insisted that 500,000 Frenchmen had died in the attempt to conquer Spain, evidence of the intense national resistance to French criminality and tyranny.[43] In such commentary, the scale of French destructiveness made Spanish accusations of British misbehaviour at San Sebastian seem minor by comparison, as well as being morally and politically unacceptable criticisms of an ally's occasional lapses.

Following the controversy over British excesses at San Sebastian and with the siege of Bayonne about to begin, in March 1814 the *Royal Military Panorama* (as the periodical had become) published a long two-part account of the French siege of Gerona in 1809.[44] The French made two separate efforts to seize Gerona in June and in July–August 1808, but were forced to withdraw. Under pressure at many points in their campaigns in Spain, they had inadequate manpower to stage an effective siege.

The siege of May–December1809 was of a different order of magnitude. But the attempts of 1808 and the prolonged siege of 1809 offer striking lessons and a comparative yardstick for assessing British behaviour in San Sebastian.

According to the account printed in the *Royal Military Panorama*, 17,000 French troops besieged Gerona in May 1809, while an army of 18,000 gave protective cover to the besieging force. The French tried first to break open the defences by bombarding the small castle with twenty 24-pounders. They attempted to take a narrow breach rather than spend time (as the British did at San Sebastian) on creating a wide one. But they failed to seize a breach which could take 40 men abreast on 4–5 July, and failed again in 3 attempts on 8 July with 6,000 men, suffering 1,600 casualties in the process. Switching tack to attrition, a steady French bombardment forced the Spanish in August to withdraw from the castle, though not from the town, once the castle's main defences were reduced to ruins. Meanwhile, the Spanish bought time through two classic defenders' responses. They occasionally sallied out in strength and broke up the attackers' works and guns. Secondly, General Joaquin Blake on 1 September advanced upon Gerona and marched 4,500 troops into the town with 15 days' supplies. Some 3,000 of these men allegedly 'volunteered' to remain and reinforce the defences. On 26 September, further, modest supplies were delivered by force.

As Napoleon had stressed, this siege, protracted for over six months, demonstrated the costliness of starving defenders into surrender. The besieged exploited opportunities to strike out against their enemy, while hoping that fresh supplies might be secured. This had been the overwhelming lesson learned from the extraordinary British defence of Gibraltar in 1779–83, when the garrison was replenished on three occasions by large convoys escorted by Royal Navy fleets. As previously noted, senior officers involved in the Peninsular sieges of 1812–13 were fully aware of Gibraltar's successful resistance and the heavy costs it imposed upon the Franco-Spanish besiegers.

But the second siege of Gerona was notable – unlike Gibraltar – for the suffering, sickness, starvation and death it inflicted upon civilians. While the Spanish defenders were commended for their determination and bravery, they found that safe refuge against French artillery in basements and cellars became increasingly difficult to secure. An account of the siege, published in August 1809 but referring to events in late June, stressed that French artillery fire directed at the castle inevitably hit houses, with some being hit over twenty times by the second week.[45] Temporary hospitals were exposed to bombardment and had constantly to be shifted. With a garrison of 3,400 at the beginning of the siege, the defenders raised 8 companies, about 800 men, from among the town's 14,000 people. After General Blake re-supplied the town, the French, making a second attempt to take it, launched a wide-ranging assault on 19 September, at one point advancing four times upon their objective, but still without success. By 29 November sewage waste was overwhelming; starvation was commonplace; 500 troops had died in hospital in the previous 3 weeks; fuel for cooking had disappeared; and all the buildings in Gerona were destroyed or ruined. The town capitulated on 12 December 1809. Although the terms of the surrender were generous – the French were not to be quartered on what remained of the city – the sick and wounded were left uncared for, with many dying as a result.

No figures for civilian deaths were given in 1814. Much later, Charles Oman concluded that only 4,248 Spanish soldiers of the 9,371 troops in the main contingents of defenders survived, and that 6,000 of the 14,000 inhabitants died, mainly from starvation and disease.[46] A recent study suggests that half the town's population of about 9,000 people died during the course of the wars of independence, with the town's economy ruined.[47] The evidence was plain. Sieges, however conducted or resolved, involved the horror of collateral damage. Such a conclusion could be drawn in 1814 from earlier reports of Peninsular sieges but more immediately from the story of the siege of Gerona, addressed to a military readership and published soon after accusations were aired that the British had intentionally destroyed San Sebastian.

The typical, rather than exceptional, destructiveness of sieges has been overlooked because limited attention has been given to siege warfare by historians of the Napoleonic wars. Even when sieges have been examined recent accounts do not focus on the nature of urban warfare. A recent evaluation of the siege of Gerona concentrated on its impact later in the nineteenth century as a symbol of Spanish resistance to the French, arguing that ideological nationalism dominated Spanish descriptions of the siege and the city's history.[48]

Returning to the lessons that might have been learned by 1813, the long siege of Gerona in 1809 absorbed about 30,000 French imperial troops, of whom only 10,000 were involved directly in the siege work.[49] The rest were committed to blockading the city. Although the town's population was about 50 per cent larger than San Sebastian's, it tied down substantially more besieging troops. Yet if the French blockade protected their lines of communication with France to the north, it failed to seal off access by the Spanish from the south and south-east.[50] The first 'lesson' to be drawn from Gerona was that Wellington did not have the manpower for a long siege. He could not have blocked off San Sebastian for months by land and sea with the military and naval forces available to him in July–August 1813 while also committing his main army to preventing the French from relieving and replenishing Pamplona, as they had attempted to do at Sorauren. The French could only advance through the mountains via Roncesvalles and the British were well placed to block them there. But that defensive line absorbed much of Wellington's forces.

A second 'lesson' from Gerona was that British preparations for and implementation of the bombardment of San Sebastian were not slow by contemporary standards. Although French military resources far exceeded British resources in Spain, their siege operations were no more swift or effective. At their first attempt on Zaragoza in June–July 1808, the French took a month to bring a siege train of forty-six guns, including howitzers and mortars, from Bayonne and Pamplona and deployed insufficient troops to prevent Spanish reinforcements and supplies getting through the blockade. As for Gerona in June–August 1808, General Foy bemoaned the fact that 'The labours of the siege were carried on with extreme slowness; every thing was wanting'.[51]

Finally, the destruction wrought in assaulted towns was fearsome given the practical impossibility of distinguishing civilian from military targets. A clear distinction was made between bombarding a town to force its surrender and storming prepared breaches. This distinction was emphasized in the short campaign after Waterloo to suppress the border fortresses still held by French garrisons. According to Henegan, commanding the military train, the Prussian 2nd Corps, under Prince Augustus, and a British siege train subjected the fortress towns to: 'the unnecessary horrors of bombardment, which was the mode of attack adopted by the Prussians, to the great injury of the inhabitants and houses, especially at Philippeville, where the conflagration destroyed nearly half the town'.[52]

Prince Augustus, a nephew of Frederick the Great, had been involved for some years in re-organizing the Prussian artillery and perhaps had a particular interest in the bombardments' impact. The garrisons in Maubeuge, Landrecy, Philippeville, Marienbourg and Rocroy knew the war was lost and capitulated after five, two, four, three and five days' resistance respectively. Although the towns were not randomly plundered, they were subjected to the heavy burden of re-supplying the Prussian Corps and re-clothing the troops from the ample stocks held by the towns' tailors and shoemakers.[53] Cambrai was less 'fortunate' in 1814; according to one inhabitant, 'Our city received a bombardment that went exactly by the book. Three hours of heavy shelling then the assault, and twenty-four hours of pillaging'.[54]

These towns were bombarded, assaulted and plundered because they refused to capitulate. Campaigning armies customarily subordinated concern for civilian suffering to the quest for strategic gain. The underlying objective remained the defeat of the enemy's army. But where resistance occurred and force was needed to overcome it, then civilians were punished as members of victorious armies plundered and raped. Such excesses resulted from a combination of pressures. A minority of soldiers no doubt resorted to extreme violence as part of what they regarded as 'normal' behaviour. Others presumably 'compensated' in moments of intense pressure for their own hardships and the extreme conditions of assaulting breaches and fighting inside towns by punishing those who had resisted for so long. Many were probably mentally numbed by weeks of tense or draining campaigning or trench duties. But this was nothing new or revolutionary in warfare. The sacking of defended cities did not essentially differ in the 1810s from such actions before the 1790s. In 1527 troops under or allied to the Emperor Charles V marched south upon Rome, seized the city and systematically sacked it. The inhabitants of whatever age or sex were put to the sword and the Pope was held to ransom. Religious anti-Catholicism inspired some of the invaders, but for many the incentive was lack of regular pay.[55] In 1631, during the Thirty Years War, religious antagonism and power politics lay behind the destruction of Magdeburg following a 6-month siege which led to 20,000 civilian deaths and reduced the city to 200 houses and 449 people in 1632.[56] News of this disaster was 'carried across all of Europe', while the 'wholesale slaughter would go down in history as synonymous with the atrocities of the war'.[57] Soldiers' reactions to urban warfare in the 1810s were not, as David Bell contended, the outcome of new ideological fervour and the separation of the military from their own populations.[58] Their recurrence more accurately reflected the sheer pace of Revolutionary and Napoleonic campaigning, with pressure to deal quickly with pockets of enemy resistance, and a sense that soldiers deserved rewards in their role as soldiers unconnected with any higher calling as representatives of national principles or aspirations.

Notes

1. Wollocombe (ed.), *With the Guns in the Peninsula*, 51, 70, 101, 153.
2. Hew Strachan, *Wellington's Legacy: the Reform of the British Army 1830–54* (Manchester, 1984), 64–8, 89–93.
3. This is a powerful theme in a widely reviewed account: William Dalrymple, *The Last Mughal: the Fall of a Dynasty, Delhi, 1857* (London, 2007 edn), 358–64, 374, 385–8.
4. Oman, *A History of the Peninsular War*, v, 183–4.
5. Drinkwater, *The Siege of Gibraltar*, 166–7.
6. 'Narrative of the Siege of Gibraltar', *Weekly Miscellany* (21 September 1781), 603.
7. Wellesley to Mornington, 8 May 1799, Wellington (ed.), *Supplementary Despatches*, i, 212.
8. 'Memorandum about the Cowle'; Wellesley to Mornington, 8, 23 May 1799; Wellington (ed.), *Supplementary Despatches*, i, 211, 215, 222.
9. There is a trenchant analysis of these issues in James Q. Whitman, *The Verdict of Battle: the Law of Victory and the Making of Modern War* (Cambridge MA, 2012), 18–21, 114–32, 184–6.
10. Anon. [Blakiston], *Twelve Years' Military Adventure*, i, 141.
11. Memorandum, 14 December 1803, Wellington (ed.), *Supplementary Despatches*, iv, 297.
12. Anon. [Blakiston], *Twelve Years' Military Adventure*, i, 228–9.
13. Anon. [Blakiston], *Twelve Years' Military Adventure*, i, 229–30, 234–5.
14. Munch-Petersen, *Defying Napoleon*, 199–200.
15. Carr-Gomm (ed.), *Letters and Journals*, 85–6.
16. Munch-Petersen, *Defying Napoleon,* 195–7.
17. *Royal Military Calendar*, iv, 330.
18. Munch-Petersen, *Defying Napoleon*, 180, 196; Muir, *Wellington. The Path to Victory*, 212, 509.
19. Carr-Gomm (ed.), *Letters and Journals*, 248, 317, 319.
20. Those present, and key testimonies, are noted in An Eminent English Barrister, *Buenos Ayres*, 34, 54–64, 83–9, 108, 111–13, 117, 161, 183–5; biographical information is taken from the *Royal Military Calendar*, iii, 269–74, 297; iv, 171, 236; Hall, *A History of the Peninsular War: VIII*, 94, 145; Wellington to Henry Wellesley, 22 June 1813, *WD*, x, 454.
21. An Eminent English Barrister, *Buenos Ayres,* 40.
22. An Eminent English Barrister, *Buenos Ayres*, 149–52.
23. An Eminent English Barrister, *Buenos Ayres*, 156, 161.
24. An Eminent English Barrister, *Buenos Ayres*, 145, also 143, 164, 169.
25. An Eminent English Barrister, *Buenos Ayres*, 152, 184.
26. Oman, *A History of the Peninsular War*, ii, 90–2, 104–5, 123, 139–40; Bell, *The First Total War*, 283; Pedro Rújula, 'Zaragosa (1808–1809) El Mito de la Resistancia Popular', in Gonzalo Butrón and Pedro Rújula (eds), *Los Sitios en la Guerra de la Independencia: la Lucha en las Ciudades* (Madrid, 2012), 15–37.
27. Glover (ed.), *A Gentleman Volunteer*, 115, 130, 133, 135, 142.
28. *Morning Chronicle*, 16 March 1809.
29. *The Times*, 4 March 1809, p. 4; 16 March 1809, p. 4.
30. *The Times*, 15 March 1809, p. 3.
31. *Military Panorama*, 461–2.
32. *The Times*, 16 March 1809, p. 4.
33. *The Times*, 28 October 1809, p. 2.
34. *Morning Chronicle*, 16 March 1809.
35. Foy, *History of the War*, ii, 287–90.
36. Xavier Bray, *Goya: The Portraits* (London, 2015), 163, 164; Sarah Symmonds (ed.), *Goya; A Life in Letters* (London, 2004), 10, 15–16, 271.
37. Esdaile, *Fighting Napoleon*, 179–83.
38. Esdaile, The *Peninsular War*, 360–2.
39. *The Times*, 14 August 1813, p. 2; Oman, *A History of the Peninsular War*, iv, 499–512, 524–6.

40. Colson, *Napoleon on War,* 333, 344.

41. Oman, *A History of the Peninsular War*, ii, 104–5.

42. *The Times*, 14 August 1813, p. 2.

43. *The Times*, 6 September 1813, p. 3; the newspaper reinforced this claim by noting that the Austrian government joined the alliance against France to reflect the people's 'impatience to live in independence, and under their own laws' while being inspired by 'the sentiment of wounded national honour, and the hatred of a foreign dominion', 15 September 1813, p. 4.

44. The details in the next paragraphs are drawn from this account: 'Campaigns in the Peninsula', *Royal Military Panorama,* iii (March 1814), 541–8; supplementary number to iii (March 1814), 644–53.

45. *The Times*, 11 August 1809, p. 2.

46. Oman, *A History of the Peninsular War*, iii, 60.

47. Jordi Canal, 'Gerona (1808–1809) 'El Baluarte Sacrasanto de Nuestra Nacionalidad' in Butrón and Rújula (eds), *Los Sitios en la Guerra de la Independencia*, 53.

48. Canal, 'Gerona', 39–63, esp. 49, 52, 62–3.

49. Canal, 'Gerona', 50.

50. Canal, 'Gerona', 46.

51. Foy, *History of the War*, ii, 266–7, 410.

52. Henegan, *Seven Years Campaigning*, ii, 181.

53. Henegan, *Seven Years Campaigning*, ii, 181–2.

54. Thoral, *From Valmy to Waterloo*, 203.

55. Michael Mallett and Christine Shaw, *The Italian wars 1494–1559* (Harlow, 2012), 158–63.

56. Mark Greengrass, *Christendom Destroyed: Europe 1517–1648* (London, 2015 edn), 613.

57. Richard Bassett, *For God and Kaiser: The Imperial Austrian Army* (New Haven CT, 2015), 29.

58. Bell, *The First Total War*, 190–1.

Chapter 16

Conclusions

The siege of San Sebastian demonstrated both positive and negative characteristics of the British military campaign in the Peninsula. Five possible criticisms of the British conduct of sieges were discussed at the beginning of this study. In re-assessing the siege of San Sebastian, it is clear that those criticisms were unjustified or were applicable more generally to siege warfare in the period. First, British experience and expertise in this specialist aspect of war has been dismissed as defective. In fact, senior officers involved in the siege of San Sebastian had been involved in numerous siege operations and had plentiful opportunities to study or discuss sieges in the recent British military past. Secondly, Wellington was criticized for providing inadequate artillery for major sieges. In fact, the number of heavy guns was not out of line with the quantity of firepower deployed by the French in their Peninsular sieges. If there were shortfalls in what was desirable, these flowed not from any systemic failures in British military practice but from the variable and often improvised nature of the campaign which placed particular strains on transport. Thirdly, the British were viewed as lacking appropriate mental commitment to the prolonged rigours of siege operations. In reality, the impatience to end sieges quickly by storming breaches resulted more from pressures of time and Wellington's limited manpower than from any specific mind-set. The British had insufficient troops to detach a corps to undertake a prolonged blockade while also fielding an army big enough to deter, deflect or defeat a major French relieving force. There was nothing peculiarly British about this dilemma. General Maximilien Foy made a similar criticism of French approaches to siege warfare in 1808. He argued that, under pressure from Napoleon for quick results, French commanders frequently ignored 'the first principle of the attack of fortresses'. This, he urged, was 'never to employ men against them when you have the material means at command, and even to wait until these material means are completely collected before you employ them'. Unfortunately, this principle was ignored through 'the petulance and impatience which form the basis of the French character'.[1]

Fourthly, Wellington and his subordinate commanders were accused of miscalculating the risks of attacking breaches and entering well-defended towns when they might have learned sobering lessons from examples of French urban fighting. Yet Napoleon commented that Wellington probably assessed the balance correctly between high immediate casualties suffered to gain breaches and the likelihood of even higher losses from sickness and recurrent, lower-intensity fighting during prolonged sieges.[2] Fifthly, the criticism of British troops' undoubted misconduct in San Sebastian needs to be placed in the grim context of the challenges posed by urban warfare and by soldiers' aggression when fortified towns were stormed.

Comparisons with major French sieges suggest that the British moved no more slowly than the French in establishing their batteries and creating breaches. For example, at Zaragoza in 1808–9, the French took five days to install nine batteries in the third and final parallel which they constructed and then another ten days for the batteries to create practicable breaches. At the far smaller town of Gerona, which was not much larger than San Sebastian, the French took three weeks moving into and consolidating their positions around their target. They then spent nearly a month from beginning to dig the trenches to creating a breach in the fortifications dominating Gerona.[3] While the British failed to achieve the speedy gains expected by Wellington in early July, they progressed at a rate which certainly matched that of French siege operations in the Peninsula.

More significantly, the siege of San Sebastian illuminated three broad developments, each of which requires further reflection. First, the British war in the Peninsula and especially the shift of campaigning to Spain's north coast required the adaptation of the Royal Navy's role, an adaptation which Wellington judged to be slow and inadequate. The difficulties of inter-service planning and co-operation shaped his later assessment of the limitations of sea power in projecting military forces directly into operations on land. Secondly, although the tactics employed in the siege and assault were closely assessed and discussed both before and after the event, the conduct of the siege demonstrated the limitations of scientific warfare in this period. Sieges were allegedly the most scientifically determined form of war-fighting, but concluding a siege by assault involved extensive improvisation as much as it entailed the 'scientific' application of predetermined principles and methods. Thirdly, the siege occurred in the testing circumstances of July–September 1813, when Wellington's triumph at Vitoria increased British politicians' and the British public's expectations of further stunning successes against the French and when the French withdrawal from most of Spain increased Spanish self-confidence in dealing with their British allies. But the relationship between national political determination to fight the war and the argument that national mobilization indicated the emergence of 'modern', ideologically driven warfare remains nebulous. The challenges which Wellington faced and the campaign issues with which he dealt were organizational and managerial rather than ideological. Competing national interests occasionally shaped his strategy, but his thinking and actions were overwhelmingly directed to the organization of his army and that army's fighting capabilities and the political and military management of his campaign.

The Royal Navy's Role
Peninsular sieges shaped Wellington's thinking about the Royal Navy's ability to support major land operations. Although navalists write of Britain's 'command of the ocean' in this period, the Royal Navy's ability to work closely with his army along a difficult coast did not impress Wellington. Fundamentally, of course, the British presence in the Peninsula depended upon sea power, which ensured that a significant

British force could be transported there and supplied and reinforced once safely landed and operational.[4] The navy's role in supply and trade was impressive and vital. During British military operations in the Peninsula in 1808–14, 404 convoys, comprising from 1 or 2 vessels to as many as 100 ships, sailed from Britain to Portugal and Spain. The navy protected those shipments and made possible a large increase in exports to Iberia, which in 1812 absorbed about 20 per cent of Britain's exports. Substantial food supplies from North America and, beginning in 1812, from the Baltic could be conveyed to Wellington's army because of naval power. These supplies had the added bonus of easing the burden on the Portuguese and Spanish economies created by the British military presence, although much food, especially meat, had to be purchased locally. Munitions and weapons similarly flowed across the seas to the British and their allies in Iberia.[5] But Wellington's reservations about the navy's role in the projection of power were more nuanced. They concerned the scale, flexibility and speed with which the navy could support operations on land in shifting and specific contexts. The late-Victorian and Edwardian writer on warfare, Colonel Charles Callwell, distinguished between 'command of the sea' and the ability to control all sea routes and to project power locally with naval support. He stressed that, even after Trafalgar, individual French warships and armed merchant ships were able to disrupt and damage British interests at sea. With the war against America after 1812, 'that security enjoyed by transports and by merchant vessels when command of the sea is absolute and complete, was no longer enjoyed under the Union Jack even in the Bay of Biscay and on the coast of Portugal'. It was important therefore to distinguish between control and preponderance when considering British naval power.[6] Wellington's experience confirmed that distinction. It shaped his longer term scepticism about Britain's ability to project its power in places where it did not already possess secure and substantial land bases, and to adapt quickly to the vicissitudes of campaigning in distant theatres of war.

The siege of San Sebastian played an important part in influencing Wellington's assessment of sea power's limitations. It provoked a great deal of friction between Wellington and the Royal Navy. Wellington's frustrations spanned a wide range of practical matters concerning the naval resources available to support his campaign and the effectiveness of those vessels assigned to the Peninsula. Thus the events of July and August 1813 demonstrated the difficulty of translating Britain's global dominance of the high seas into local maritime control. The navy was accused of failing to deliver the siege train and supplies more promptly, failing to blockade rigorously and failing to provide for the evacuation of the wounded.

Arguably this siege appeared so minor to the Royal Navy that what Wellington insisted was deficient performance had limited significance in any broader assessment of naval power projection. But the delays and difficulties in projecting power on land from naval vessels were far from being unprecedented. One glaring case familiar to Wellington occurred at Copenhagen in 1807. On that occasion the Royal Navy had a strategic interest in securing the Danish fleet. The British expedition sent to the Danish capital included 27,000 troops, 25 ships of the line, 40 smaller warships from frigates to brigs and 377 transports. A large contingent of troops arrived at Elsinore, well north of its objective, by 8 August and Copenhagen was invested on 17 August. Yet this vast force deployed only forty mortars and ten howitzers, supported by thirty 24-pounders to suppress the Danes' defences and open a breach if an assault had to be mounted. Even so, not all the guns and supplies had been landed by 28 August. Moreover, the bombardment did not start until 2 September, nearly one month after the troops' landing. Admittedly, in this case the delay was attributed, probably unfairly, to the caution and indeed hesitation of the army commander, Lord Cathcart.[7] Yet, despite the facts that the navy brought a large fleet and accessed relatively unchallenging landing-points, the deployment of siege guns whose numbers were small in relation to the force deployed was far from swift. The significance of events there was not lost on two participants in the siege: Wellington, who served as a junior Major General, and the talented Richard Fletcher, who became Wellington's chief engineer for most of the Peninsular War until he was killed at the second assault on San Sebastian.[8] Thus the particular lesson from San Sebastian was not unique in Wellington's career.

We have seen how Wellington periodically blamed the Royal Navy for delaying his progress. Some, at the very least, of that criticism was unfair because Wellington did not spell out in the early months of 1813 the direction he intended to follow. Nor did he anticipate being delayed by a siege of San Sebastian. Naval commanders could scarcely plan for events for which they had no forewarning. As Christopher Hall has indicated, even such a local tactical initiative as the capture of Isla Santa Clara was decided only relatively late in August.[9] However, once the French were removed from San Sebastian, the town's importance in supporting Wellington's invasion of France became obvious. The Royal Navy worked effectively in conveying fleets of transports to the northern Spanish coast, especially after the removal of the local French threat made the full utilization of nearby Pasajes possible. The new supply route from southern England functioned effectively by September. Captain Collier, the squadron commander, estimated that 131 transports had entered, were about to enter or had left Pasajes in a four-week period to the end of that month.[10] A further convoy left Plymouth on 28 September for San Sebastian only a week or so after news of its final surrender had reached England.[11] While this convoying role remained fundamental to Wellington's operations, convoys were often slow to assemble. And getting men, munitions and materiel to northern Spain was a quite different task from assisting in projecting power along Spain's northern coast.

Although relations with the Royal Navy squadron appeared more satisfactory in early 1814, Wellington continued to complain of inadequate naval resources. This was not unreasonable. The Channel fleet, responsible for the Bay of Biscay, had at its disposal only 13,518 men in 1813. That amounted to 10 per cent of the Royal Navy's total manpower, which itself was lower than it had been in the four years from 1807–11 inclusive.[12] Wellington not unreasonably questioned the logic of a naval command system organized so that the squadrons covering the northern coast of Spain and the coast of Portugal belonged to two different fleets, with different commanders-in-chief and widely dispersed and separate areas of responsibility.[13] He also bemoaned the shortage of warships available for the extensive duties required. Wellington wanted all transport ships to proceed first to Santander and then to sail on to Pasajes or St Jean de Luz. Convoys, however, were sometimes so large that individual merchant ships were picked off by French raiders. Such losses meant that the number of transports in each convoy had to be restricted, with the result that loaded transports lingered in port. In addition, Wellington wanted a warship to collect money from Gibraltar whenever the Commissary had 50,000 dollars available for his army, and to call at Cádiz whenever 200,000 dollars was available there. The two visits could be co-ordinated, with the monies being taken to Lisbon. From Lisbon, Wellington sought naval protection for one convoy per week. He wanted such cover for two convoys per week from La Coruña and Santander.[14] In early March he ascribed the lack of troop reinforcements to the fact that 'we have never been able to get a sufficient quantity of shipping to attend the army'.[15]

This appreciation of the constraints on Britain's ability to project power in depth and with local adroitness influenced Wellington's strategic assessments long after 1815. It helps to explain his cautious approach in the decades after 1815 to British interventions in Europe and his insistence that Britain work in close concert with Continental allies if it contemplated using military leverage in European diplomacy.

For example, Wellington's caution shaped his responses to crises in Spain in the 1820s and 1830s. When, in the spring of 1820, an army mutiny threatened instability and possibly revolution in Spain, Wellington, as a member of the Cabinet, advised firmly against British intervention. Landing an army on the Mediterranean coast or in Portugal would be pointless because advancing inland posed so many difficulties; 'there are no navigable rivers or other means of communication by water; and but few roads in the country practicable for military operations'. Transporting the numbers of cavalry horses needed would be extremely difficult, while suitable horses were in short supply in the Peninsula. The absence of very large towns increased the challenges of securing the food required by a large army. Co-operation was not eased by the xenophobia which the British frequently ascribed to the Spanish.[16]

Again, in 1823, British intervention was discussed when the French appeared likely to send an army into Spain. Wellington cautioned that even naval measures against France might provoke the Holy Alliance powers – notably Russia and Prussia, and possibly also Austria – to retaliate against Britain by seizing George IV's German kingdom of Hanover and attacking Britain's Continental ally, the Netherlands. The French would be tempted to invade Portugal, Britain's other European ally. He added:

> It is the greatest mistake to suppose that if we enter this or any war, we can do it by halves, or confine our operations to one branch of our military power and resource. We must deploy our whole force, by land, as well as by sea. And after all we should scarcely have enough to defend all that we are bound to protect.

Wellington dismissed the value of naval intervention in Spain. Naval power alone might make the French capture of Barcelona and other ports on the coast of Catalonia and Valencia difficult, 'but not impracticable, as the events of the late war shew'. It would help the Spaniards opposing the absolutist monarchy to hold Cádiz, if they constructed defensive works on the lines adopted in the 1810s. But naval power would be worthless against the French themselves. Using the navy to seize distant French colonies would achieve nothing: 'no additional colony would be of any use to us, and I know that the French government are very doubtful whether the possession of any colony is advantageous to them'. The classic application of British sea power in capturing enemy colonies to use later as bargaining chips in peace settlements was, in Wellington's eyes, anachronistic.[17]

Finally, Wellington was scathing about 'our petty warfare' in 1837 when the British government supported the military operations of a British Legion based on San Sebastian by deploying a Royal Navy squadron off the coast. Permitted to campaign against the Carlist insurgents in a civil war, the volunteer Legion could not maintain contact with the ships at sea or establish effective military co-ordination with Spanish forces at Pamplona and Bilbao. Small expeditions supported by British sea power would gain nothing in Spain.[18] These examples demonstrated how Wellington's experience in the Peninsular War made him sceptical about the viability of 'limited' interventions and conscious of the difficulties of projecting British power in detail despite the Royal Navy's unchallenged access to the high seas.

Tactical Assessments

If the navy's role periodically angered Wellington, it was artillery tactics and the conduct of the assaults which provoked controversy within the army. Who made the final decisions on tactics remains unclear. Rory Muir has most recently placed the responsibility squarely with the senior engineer and artillery officers. He notes that Wellington approved the selection of the town wall facing the Urumea River as the site for the main breach. Breaching would be easier there and entering the town's centre would be easier than from the isthmus wall. The lengthy bombardment during 20 to 24 July and the decision to attack early in the morning on 25 July, postponed from the previous day, were both against Wellington's advice. Muir stresses that Wellington delegated decisions to those on the spot and left San Sebastian on 23 July to respond to French advances elsewhere along his wide front. When preparations for the second assault were resumed, Wellington and Graham again, according to Muir, accepted the advice of the 'ordnance officers' concerning the direction of the attack. Wellington's main contribution was to goad the 5th Division by publicly doubting their ability to take the breach. He only confirmed the division's leading role in the second assault after the return of Lieutenant General Leith, an energetic and offensive-minded officer, to its command. Muir concludes that 'there was nothing preventing Fletcher and the engineers proceeding slowly and methodically according to the rules of their craft'. But he also notes that senior British commanders were becoming frustrated and impatient at the delays.[19]

The distinction between consulting in order to take informed decisions and simply bowing to expert advice is necessarily a fine one. Some light was cast upon this process by Sir John Burgoyne, who served at San Sebastian, during the Indian Mutiny-Rebellion:

That there is nothing derogatory in a General-in-Chief considering it desirable to consult such officers professionally in the peculiar branches, we have the instance of the late Duke of Wellington in the Peninsula, who consulted them invariably on all engineering matters, frequently gave up his opinions to them, and always desired to have those of superior station [i.e. rank] near him.[20]

Unfortunately, it is not entirely clear from 1813 how far the balance of advice ran in any particular direction.

Given the well-publicized difficulties the French faced in besieging Spanish towns, Wellington might be criticized for his readiness to commit in 1812–13 to four different sieges, particularly after the second siege, at Badajoz, proved far more costly than he probably expected. An obvious explanation is that Wellington regarded the towns he besieged as relatively minor, if tactically challenging, impediments on his lines of advance rather than as major objectives in themselves.

As we have seen in Chapter 10, Sir John Jones and Sir John May later criticized the conduct of the siege in considerable detail while asserting that a more rigorous scientific approach would have yielded speedier results at far less cost in casualties. They were partly inspired by the belief, as Jones expressed it, that British siege operations should have been far more successful given 'our natural advantages, great resources, and liberal military expenditure'.[21] Their concerns, and other officers' analyses described in the chapters on the assaults, indicate that the conduct of the siege was open to four main criticisms.

The first goes to the heart of the nature of battle in this period. Wellington has been credited in his defensive battles, but even on the attack, with forming his battalions into lines of infantry two soldiers deep. This formation when pitched against French columns maximized the firepower of each battalion. Assaults on major breaches could not, self-evidently, conform to that practice. Hundreds of men were squeezed into narrow fronts where they were exposed to intense fire from above. Infantry were trained simply to fire in the direction of their massed opponents, not to aim at individual targets. In battle they created an extensive field of fire. If their firing did not directly incapacitate their enemies, neither did an enemy's infantry musket fire disproportionately wound or kill them. One contemporary calculation from the allied attack at Vitoria suggested that only 1 musket shot in every 459 wounded or killed a Frenchmen; and that estimate over-estimated the impact of infantry fire since it took no account of the losses inflicted on the French by the allies' bayonets or by their 90 artillery guns.[22] The infantry at the breach must have felt frustratingly ineffective; the narrow column formation was alien to them and they were not trained as sharp-shooters. Firing upwards at French defenders was far harder than firing down at British infantry struggling up the breach.[23] The assailants knew they would suffer far higher casualties at a breach than their opponents.

The second concerned the quality and quantity of the artillery used, the targets chosen for the bombardment, the order in which they were attacked, and the timing of the assault. The problems the British faced in selecting their tactics were generic rather than specific. An unofficial assessment in the *Royal Military Panorama* made this point indirectly in describing one challenge at San Sebastian. It noted that the chief engineer 'was killed by a musket-ball in one of the many showers that issued from the horn-work, until the curtain was carried'. The lesson was that engineers had to understand 'the necessity of attacking places regularly – of first destroying the defences, and of having at least two points of assault, a feint, or an escalade'. The planned assault had been too narrowly focused, since 'one breach, however large, with a good garrison, is always a very strong position' from which to mount a robust defence.[24] As for the quantity of guns, mortars and howitzers deployed, the British siege trains in the Peninsular War conformed to the standard complement of thirty to sixty such weapons constituting eighteenth-century siege trains.[25]

The third was the failure to take account of the challenges of urban fighting as demonstrated by French experience in the Peninsula. Their assault on Gerona, according to the commentary cited earlier and published in 1814, demonstrated how determined resistance could drain a well-led army. But that account said nothing about the adequacy or otherwise of the weaponry or tactics used by the French. In fact, the French deployed in one section twenty 24-pounders, the same number used at the first assault on San Sebastian. This artillery failed, not surprisingly, to create a wide breach quickly. The storming parties could not overcome intense barrages of small-arms fire when they assaulted the walls.[26] This was despite their expenditure of 11,000 cannon balls, 7,000 grenades and 80,000 musket balls.[27] The French at Gerona repeatedly failed to take the main breach at the Monjuich castle, which overlooked and commanded the town in the valley below. They first closed upon the town on 8 May, but did not start entrenching until 6 June and their bombardment of the castle, their main objective, began only on 3 July. An opportunistic attempt was made to take the newly formed breach on the night of 4–5 July and a more concerted attempt was made shortly before sunrise on 7 July. About 2,500 troops thrown at the breach and at a failed escalade of a flanking demi-lune suffered 1,079 casualties, including 77 officers. This severe loss occurred despite the French having thought long and hard about their tactics and having planned their approach with precision. Oman drew a more general conclusion from such a reversal: 'A broad breach by itself does not necessarily make a place untenable, if the spirit of the defenders is high, and if they are prepared with all the resources of the military art for resisting the stormers'.[28]

A fourth line of criticism, therefore, concerned the need to make tactical choices based upon the defenders' morale. Oman argued that the French at Gerona, despite their expert engineers' assessments, made the same error as the British were to make at San Sebastian; they 'attacked before the garrison was demoralized'.[29] Even after the Spanish eventually withdrew from the castle, once it was destroyed by the bombardment, they defended the town of Gerona with equal vigour. On 19 September, the French suffered 624 casualties, including 3 colonels, in failing to take breaches in the town walls. The commanding officer was criticized for excessive optimism about his ability to take a breach simply because one had been made.[30] Yet such precedents had little apparent impact on British planning. British accounts of San Sebastian praised the spirit and commitment of the British attackers; but the senior commanders proved less perceptive in assessing the likely initiative and determination of the French defenders.

A judgement on the British performance is therefore bound to be mixed. Much thought went into tactical dispositions and the timing of initiatives. There was no single view taken by senior officers in any one branch; Royal Engineers and Royal Artillery officers, as well as battalion commanders, differed as to which decisions proved to be misguided and which measures seemed to them inadequate. Senior officers adapted to circumstances and learning-by-doing occurred. But the bigger issues concerning siege operations and urban fighting were not systematically aired. Whether contemporaries would have expected them to be discussed formally in the midst of a fast-moving campaign remains unclear.

The Significance of the Siege

There has been a long-standing debate over whether the wars of 1792–1815 marked the beginning of modern warfare. This naturally begs the question of what defines 'modern'. Weapons and tactics did not change dramatically, but the availability of manpower, the size of armies, the scale of some, though by no means all, battles and the geographical reach of campaigning all dwarfed what had gone before. Another, more recent approach has been to re-emphasize how mass mobilization depended upon a transformation in political thinking and rhetoric. International conflict was viewed increasingly in 'modern' ideological terms as involving a commitment to waging something approaching total war. Modern wars became contests between conflicting political, social and cultural values rather than disputes over territory.[31]

This case-study of one particular campaign casts doubt on ideas that warfare in the 1810s required the commitment of a full spectrum of resources, involved an increasingly rigorous application of scientific assumptions and methods, and depended upon 'modern' notions of national mobilization to sustain prolonged and complex operations. Ideas concerning national identities and external threats to 'national' independence may have been important rhetorically in creating domestic political support for war. But the study of an individual campaign indicates that the practice of warfare remained a largely self-contained professional activity.[32] Senior and middle-ranking officers worked within very severe constraints – of manpower, munitions, transport, food, space, distance and politics – which repeatedly tested their professional abilities. The specific military challenges of managing a campaign in all its frustrating complexity absorbed far more of their time and energy than any thoughts about the ideological stakes at issue. Of course, British officers opposed the Napoleonic system and repudiated the French Revolution and its associated principles. But they did not hate the French. Their overriding commitment was to manage the campaign and defeat their opponent. This case-study therefore casts doubt on the value of grand theory in understanding the conduct of war in the 1810s.

The siege of San Sebastian also, more specifically, illuminates controversial aspects of Wellington's conduct of operations. It demonstrated the tension in Wellington's generalship between his strategic caution and his capacity for opportunistic and risky initiatives. Strategically, the siege was intended to be a short sweeping-up operation subordinate to the allies' drive towards France. French determination, under Napoleon's orders, to hold the allies at San Sebastian turned a subsidiary venture into a substantial conflict which cost Wellington time, considerable effort and very heavy casualties. Wellington probably expected his base by autumn 1813 to be inside south-west France, using the port of St Jean de Luz, rather than being dependent upon the ports of northern Spain.

Wellington's reluctance to invade France in August 1813 is usually explained by his concern that peace might be agreed between Napoleon and Russia and Prussia. While that fear clearly restricted Wellington's operations, other factors prevented an advance across the Pyrenees during August. Wellington's ability to advance was weakened by the fighting in the last week of July and by the need to besiege San Sebastian. In addition, substantial Spanish forces were tied down in blockading Pamplona. The French, by holding the line of the Pyrenees, obliged the British to fight hard for San Sebastian since their defence of the Pyrenees left Wellington with little option but to take control of the town. In this way, Wellington was boxed in, and forced to pay dearly to consolidate his position.

The focus on San Sebastian followed from the central importance of Pasajes to the logistical support for the invasion of south-west France. Even when the British took St Jean de Luz, they still used Pasajes as a safer harbour. But Pasajes was impossible to use unless the British either bottled up the French in San Sebastian with a long-term and rigorous blockade or removed them from it. The two ports together therefore acquired high strategic importance in defending the front on the Bidassoa River and in preparing an invasion of France. There is no evidence that such a strategic assessment existed before July 1813 when Wellington's offensive ground to a halt.

At the operational level, San Sebastian raised further questions about the British conduct of sieges. Wellington as commanding general did not assess the difficulties posed by San Sebastian. His campaign of 1813 was based on an approach well described by Huw Davies as 'Light and Quick'. But Wellington in July did not predict the speed and effectiveness of the French recovery after Vitoria. And he repeatedly asserted that San Sebastian would be seized very readily. If his written comments of July were reflected in his conversations with, and oral instructions to, his subordinate commanders, then the message of impatient optimism about moving forward and sweeping aside pockets of French resistance would have sent a clear signal that San Sebastian was a sideshow to be resolved without much trouble. Of course, once Soult's presence was felt, Wellington switched to a defensive mode and conducted protracted, complex and successful blocking operations from the last week in July until the first week in October. But that had not been his original intention.

Managing the Campaign
Given these shortcomings, the operation against San Sebastian demonstrated how scientific warfare degenerated into a test of the sheer fighting grit of attacking infantrymen. May and Jones, in their efforts to extract lessons from Wellington's Peninsular sieges, implicitly joined a long line of writers who argued that sieges in particular were subject to 'scientific' analysis and prescription. Careful and scholarly treatises on fortifications and sieges had been published since at least the late sixteenth century, and the French in the late eighteenth century had debated the technical

challenges of siege operations at great length and with considerable passion. Some senior artillery and engineer officers offered thoughtful assessments of the operations they undertook. French scientific debate on such matters was far more extensive and sophisticated in the late eighteenth century than any such discourse occurring in Britain. That did not mean that French artillery was superior to British artillery by the 1810s. In fact, the example of San Sebastian supports Rothenberg's view that the British compared well with the French in that arm.[33] Yet the failure of scientifically judged bombardments to deliver carefully calibrated military solutions was disguised at the time either by claims that the provision of artillery was consistently inadequate or by an emphasis on character and courage as decisive ingredients in assaulting breaches.

The critiques we have noted were tactical and practical in their focus. Senior officers assessed what did and what did not work in managing the siege. We know that the senior officers who managed the assaults – and not simply the specialist artillery and engineer officers – were all acquainted with fortifications and sieges. Their letters and journals demonstrate that they reflected on what happened at San Sebastian, while coming to divergent conclusions as to what went wrong.

The decision to besiege San Sebastian and the conduct of the siege therefore fell to senior officers who had some knowledge of siege warfare. If their actions bore a limited relationship to theoretical prescriptions, they were subject in practice to local and immediate conditions which required extemporizing. At virtually every stage of the process of mounting first the attack and then the assault, an extremely challenging effort was required to bring the appropriate type and number of guns, and the ammunition to sustain them, first to San Sebastian itself and then to the firing lines. Transporting weapons and equipment by land or sea was difficult. Moving them onshore and then on to their designated emplacements required considerable ad hoc organization, and patience. Translating British domination over the world's sea lanes into a more detailed control along the coast of the Bay of Biscay depended upon deploying the appropriate type and number of warships and transport vessels. The greatest naval power in the world struggled to meet this specialist challenge. The bombardment itself was neither as quick nor as straightforward as anticipated. Experts disagreed about where the breach should be made and about the requisite breadth of the breach. At critical points, aspersions were cast upon particular infantry battalions' ability to do their job.

The success of the siege operation ultimately depended upon the co-ordination of many small component parts: the mix of brigs and frigates off-shore, the arrival of transport ships, the work of local women and allied soldiers at Pasajes harbour, the requisition of mules to get the materiel of war from Pasajes to the siege, the emplacement and correct mix of guns of different types and calibre, the accuracy of artillery targeting, the choice of how many and which troops to engage in the assaults, the balancing of British and Portuguese forces in selecting troops for the assaults, the decisions about continuing or breaking off the assaults, the choice of commanding officers for this multitude of functions and, of course, the ordering and shaping of the whole. Assembling this mosaic of components occurred against a background of pressures involving time, and the uncertain movements of the French, as well as the dependability of the Spanish armies.

In so far as the siege operation was managed by interlocking and overlapping clusters of experts – among engineers, artillerymen, infantrymen and those charged with providing logistical support and transport – then Wellington liaised effectively with the heads of those different clusters, especially in planning the second assault.[34] Within the artillery, engineers and infantry, however, objectives were typically accomplished through experimentation, adaptation and learning-by-doing rather than through the application of strictly laid-out precepts derived from well-formulated, scientific principles of siege warfare. This approach hardly made senior officers unprofessional. In adapting pragmatically to diverse challenges, they operated no differently from most drivers of Britain's contemporaneous industrial transformation. Moreover, they had plentiful opportunities to exchange information and insights both within their separate services and between the services based upon widespread experiences of other sieges. But the strong and recurrent tactical criticisms voiced by some senior officers suggest that limited efforts to achieve consensus were made within each service. Planning meetings of, notably, senior engineer and artillery officers either did not occur, or such meetings were so contentious that no agreed plans were finalized. We know that Wellington consulted the expert heads, but we do not know how far the expert heads consulted or even fully informed their subordinates. The picture emerging from letters, journals and later treatises is not one of amateurism, but one where divergent assessments and proposals were vigorously developed. Such differing views were not, however, reconciled in formal and well-attended meetings. This phenomenon is neither surprising nor peculiarly 'pre-modern' or amateurish.

It follows therefore that the operation against San Sebastian, unplanned when the campaign of 1813 began, challenged the managerial capacities of Wellington's senior command. Wellington visited the front frequently at the height of preparations for the assaults and spent a significant amount of time there. He had a remarkable capacity to focus on particular problems and then to move on. As Captain Blakiston remarked in 1829,

> My old commander, Sir Samuel Auchmuty, used to say, that Job wanted one more trial of his patience, and that was the command of an army. Not that this kind of responsibility affected Lord Wellington much. If any thing went wrong he vented his spleen at once, and, it must be confessed, in no very measured terms; but, as far as regarded himself, there was an end of it. He had, what I have rarely seen in any one, the power of dismissing a subject from his mind whenever he chose . . .[35]

Despite this enviable facility, Wellington spent long periods concentrating on the details of siege preparations. For the second assault and its follow-up, he visited the siege site on 26, 29 and 30 August and 1 September. Even so, he and his subordinate commanders did not develop clear, agreed and replicable plans for the conduct of the siege and the direction and nature of the assaults. Much was improvised and success depended upon opportunistic initiatives and extraordinary courage. A good case can be made that the breakthrough at San Sebastian depended upon the explosion of munitions on the curtain wall at the height of the second assault. That was scarcely the predicted outcome of the scientific application of prolonged artillery fire. This conclusion reminds us of the sobering truism that at some point in a campaign the result may well hinge on a clash of arms whose outcome cannot be certain.

This case-study has shown that senior artillery, engineer and infantry officers had contradictory ideas about tactics and priorities. There were strong differences of opinion not only between but also among senior officers within the several arms. Wellington's stature as a commander is not diminished by such divergences of professional opinion, even when he erred in deciding upon particular options over the alternatives. Instead, his decisiveness was the more impressive in the light of the tactical choices available to him and the strength of feeling with which tactical options were canvassed and operational post-mortems were offered.

In August 1914 when Britain went to war with Germany the subject of military management as distinct from battlefield leadership emerged in stark terms. There was a public discussion over who might take charge of the War Office. The post was a political appointment held for 250 years by civilians. But *The Times* argued that the position should go to a serving officer, Field Marshal Lord Kitchener of Khartoum, because his 'long and varied experience of the work of organizing warfare is unequalled among British soldiers'. His successes were achieved 'not so much by directing his troops in battle as by his laborious, indomitable, unceasing organization of the means which led to victory'.[36] In examining transformations in late nineteenth-century and twentieth-century warfare, some of which Kitchener experienced, Williamson Murray has identified adaptation in war as a separate skill from innovation in peacetime, with an emphasis on the extreme challenge of adapting tactics and operational planning to rapid technological and industrial change.[37] While the siege of San Sebastian did not involve adaptation to new technology, nevertheless the conduct of the siege and the lack of any firm guiding tactical plans meant that rapid adaptation to geographical and military circumstances was essential to success. Wellington, in contrast to Kitchener, was remarkable both for managing battles and for managing the details of a complex campaign. But siege operations did little, if anything, to burnish Wellington's reputation as a battlefield commander. His military genius was not abundantly in evidence at San Sebastian. His soldiers' extraordinary fighting determination played a vital role in the struggle. But equal weight needs to be given to the collective effort of a highly experienced team of senior officers to manage in a sustained, sometimes incisive and consistently adaptable manner the myriad elements shaping military operations which, eventually, brought victory.

Notes

1. Foy, *History of the War*, ii, 283.
2. Colson, *Napoleon on War*, 360.
3. Oman, A *History of the Peninsular War*, ii, 115, 121; iii, 27–9.

4. N.A.M. Rodger, *Command of the Ocean: A Naval History of Britain, 1649–1815* (London, 2004), 563–4, 574–5, 582–3; James Davey, *In Nelson's Wake* (London, 2016), 297–8.

5. Hall, *Wellington's Navy*, 112, 116–17, 137–41; Roger Knight and Martin Wilcox, *Sustaining the Fleet, 1793–1815: War, the British Navy and the Contractor State* (Woodbridge, 2010), 53–4.

6. Colonel C.E. Callwell, *Military Operations and Maritime Preponderance* (Edinburgh,1905), 2–4.

7. Munch-Petersen, *Defying Napoleon*, 145, 170–1, 173, 200–1.

8. 'Sir Richard Fletcher' entry, *ODNB.*

9. Hall, *Wellington's Navy*, 215–19.

10. Hall, *Wellington's Navy*, 220.

11. *The Times*, 13 October 1813, p. 2.

12. Knight and Wilcox, *Sustaining the Fleet*, 222.

13. Wellington to Penrose, 11 February 1814, *WD*, xi, 514.

14. Memorandum for Colonel Bunbury, 1 February 1814, *WD*, xi, 493.

15. Wellington to Hope, 8 March 1814, *WD*, xi, 563.

16. 'Memorandum from . . . Wellington to Lord Castlereagh . . .', 16 April 1820, WP1/644/7.

17. 'Memorandum from . . . Wellington to George Canning . . .', 10 February 1823, WP1/757/6.

18. *House of Lords Debates*, 21 April 1837, Vol. 3, cc 137–150, esp c 150.

19. Muir, *Wellington. The Path to Victory*, 539–40, 547–9.

20. General Collinson and General Webber (eds), *General Sir Henry Drury Harness* (London, 1903), 159.

21. Jones, *Journals*, i, v.

22. David Gates, *The British Light Infantry Arm, c1790–1815* (London, 1987), 140.

23. This point is made in relation to attacking up-hill by Muir, *Salamanca 1812*, 172.

24. *Royal Military Panorama*, iii (February 1814), 449.

25. Langins, *Conserving the Enlightenment*, 129.

26. *Royal Military Panorama*, iii, 542, 544–5, 645–6.

27. Canal, 'Gerona', 50.

28. Oman, *A History of the Peninsular War*, iii, 25, 27–9, 31–3.

29. Oman, *A History of the Peninsular War*, iii, 33.

30. Oman, *A History of the Peninsular War*, iii, 47–8.

31. These issues are incisively assessed by Roger Chickering, 'Introduction' in Roger Chickering and Stig Forster (eds), *War in an Age of Revolution, 1775–1815* (Cambridge, 2010), 1–17. The argument for transformation is advanced by Bell, *The First Total War*. A contrary view, that the French themselves and Europe more generally were exhausted by war and its looting armies by 1815, is graphically put in Esdaile, *Napoleon's Wars*, 495, 518–22; Richard J. Evans, *The Pursuit of Power: Europe 1815–1914* (London, 2016), 1–5.

32. The case for the commonality of military developments in late eighteenth-century Europe is made by Stephen Conway: 'The British Army, "Military Europe", and the American War of Independence', *William and Mary Quarterly*, 67 (2010), 69–100; 'The eighteenth-century British army as a European institution', in Kevin Linch and Matthew McCormack (eds), *Britain's Soldiers: Rethinking War and Society 1715–1815* (Liverpool, 2014), 17–38.

33. Rothenberg, *The art of warfare*, 177,183.

34. There is a great deal of interest in the nature of networks. I make a general point from the sophisticated model offered by Ronald S. Burt, *Brokerage and Closure: An Introduction to Social Capital* (Oxford, 2005).

35. Anon. [Blakiston], *Twelve Years' Military Adventure*, ii, 316.

36. *The Times*, 5 August 1914, p. 7.

37. Williamson Murray, *Military Adaptation in War: With Fear of Change* (Cambridge, 2011).

Guide to Reading

Guide to Reading

The basic source is the core collection of Wellington's correspondence in Lieutenant Colonel Gurwood (ed.), *The Dispatches of Field Marshal the Duke of Wellington*, 12 vols (London, 1838); abbreviated in the notes as *WD*.

An enlarged edition is John Gurwood (ed.), *The Dispatches of Field Marshal the Duke of Wellington*, 8 vols (London, 1845; repr. Cambridge, 2010)

There is occasional use of Duke of Wellington (ed.), *Supplementary Despatches and Memoranda of . . . Arthur, Duke of Wellington*, 9 vols (London, 1858)

To supplement the printed letters, I have made use of material in the Wellington Papers at the Hartley Library, University of Southampton:

WP 9/1/1/8
WP 9/2/2/10
WP 9/2/2/12
WP 9/2/2/15
WP 9/2/2/17
WP 12/1/8

WP 1/372 (folder 1)
WP 1/373 (folder 4)
WP 1/373 (folder 5)
WP 1/374 (folder 1)
WP 1/374 (folder 2)
WP 1/374 (folder 6)
WP 1/376 (folder 6)
WP1/644/7
WP1/757/6
WP1/759/1

Some topics have been explored further in the War Office archives at The National Archives, Kew:

WO 1/253
'Return of Ordnance taken 21 January 1812' WO 1/253; 'Return of Ordnance and Ammunition taken at Badajoz 8 April 1812' WO 1/254
'Abstract Account of the Valuation of Ordnance . . . Captured in the Peninsula 1808–
     April 1814', WO 44/503

WO55/ 981
WO 55/1316
WO 55/1278
WO 55/1545
WO 55/1544
WO 55/1561

This study concerns the British campaign. But use has been made of records of the Napoleonic armies in Spain in the French military archives, Service historique de la Défense, Château De Vincennes:

SHAT C^8 142
SHAT C^8 149
SHAT C^8 156
SHAT C^8 213
SHAT C^8 218
SHAT C^8 221
SHAT C^8 248
SHAT C^8 343
SHAT C^8 372
SHAT C^8 385

For events covering a short chronological period, limited value was found in consulting unpublished papers:

Orders for the VI Division 28 October, 3, 4 November 1812, Order book 12 February–6 November 1812, Clinton Papers, Box G13, John Rylands Library, University of Manchester
    Order Oct 1, 1812, 'Orders for the VI Division 12 Feb – 6 Nov 1812', Clinton papers, Box G13
    Papers of Maxton Graham Family of Cullquhey, Perthshire GD155/1102, National Records of Scotland

Biographical material was found in:

Oxford Dictionary of National Biography
John A. Hall, *A History of the Peninsular War: Volume VIII* (London, 1998)
The Royal Military Calendar or Army Service and Commission Book, 5 vols (3rd edn, London: 1820)

Contemporary Published Accounts and Letters
An Eminent English Barrister, *Buenos Ayres: the Trial of Lieut. Gen. Whitelocke* (Dublin, 1808)

Anon. [Blakiston], *Twelve Years' Military Adventure in Three Quarters of the Globe*, 2 vols (London, 1829)

Batty, Robert, *Campaign of the Left Wing of the Allied Army, in the Western Pyrenees and South of France, in the Years 1813–14* (London, 1823)

Beatson, Alexander, *A View of the Origin and Conduct of the War with Tippoo Sultaun* (London, 1800)

Bunbury, Sir Henry, *Narratives of Some Passages in the Great War with France (1799–1810)* (London, 1927)

Carr-Gomm, Francis Culling (ed.), *Letters and Journals of Field Marshal Sir William Maynard Gomm* (London, 1881)

Clausewitz, Carl von, *On War*, ed. and trans. Michael Howard and Peter Paret (Princeton NJ, 1989)

Drinkwater, John, A *History of the Late Siege of Gibraltar* (London, 1785)

Fischer, Frederick Augustus, *Travels in Spain in 1797 and 1798*, trans. from the German (London, 1802)

Foy, General, *History of the War in the Peninsula under Napoleon*, 2 vols (London, 1827)

Gleig, George, *The Subaltern: A Chronicle of the Peninsular War* (London, 1825)

Glover, Gareth, *An Eloquent Soldier* (Barnsley, 2011)

Glover, Michael (ed.), *A Gentleman Volunteer: The Letters of George Hennell from the Peninsular War, 1812–13* (London, 1979)

Hayter, Alethea (ed.), *The Backbone: Diaries of a Military Family in the Napoleonic Wars* (Durham, 1993)

Henegan, Sir Richard D., *Seven Years Campaigning in the Peninsula and the Netherlands 1808–1815*, 2 vols (Stroud, 2005 repr. of 1846 edn)

Jones, Lieutenant Colonel Harry (ed.), *Journals of the Sieges Carried on by the Army under The Duke of Wellington, in Spain . . .*, 3 vols (London, 1846, 3rd edn repr. 1998)

Larpent, Sir George (ed.), *The Private Journal of F. S. Larpent, Esq, Judge Advocate General of the British Forces in the Peninsula*, 3 vols (London, 1853)

Leith Hay, Major, *A Narrative of the Peninsular War*, 2 vols (Edinburgh, 1931)

Liddell Hart, B.H. (ed.), *The Letters of Private Wheeler 1809–1828* (Moreton-in-Marsh, 1993 repr.)

May, Sir John, *A Few Observations on the Mode of Attack, and Employment of the Heavy Artillery* (London, 1819)

Memoir of Field Marshal Sir Hew Dalrymple Ross (Woolwich, 1871)

Sabine, Edward (ed.), *Letters of Colonel Sir Augustus Simon Frazer, K.C.B.* (Uckfield, 2001 repr.)

Schaumann A.L.F., *On the Road with Wellington: Diary of a War Commissary in the Peninsular War* (London, 1999)

Smith, Harry, *The Autobiography of Sir Harry Smith 1787–1819* (London, 1999 repr.)

Somerville, Alexander, *History of the British Legion, and War in Spain* (London, 1839)

Surtees, William, *Twenty-Five Years in the Rifle Brigade* (London, repr. 1833)
Thompson, W.F.K. (ed.), *An Ensign in the Peninsular War* (London, 1981)
Wollocombe, Richard Henry (ed.), *With the Guns in the Peninsula* (London, 1991)
Wrottesley, George, *Life and Correspondence of Field Marshal Sir John Burgoyne*, 2 vols (London, 1873)

Journals and Newspapers
'A Picture of War', *Chambers's Edinburgh Journal*, 16 February 1839
'Three Modern Sieges', *All the Year Round*, 5, 25 February 1871, 296
Caledonian Mercury (Edinburgh)
Colburn's United Service Magazine (1844, Part I; 1845, Part II)
The *Critic*, 6.149 (6 November 1847)
Edinburgh Annual Register, Vol. 8 (January 1815)
Gentleman's Magazine (April 1823)
House of Commons *Debates*, 18 March 1824, Vol. 10, c 1233; 1 July 1825, Vol. 13, c 1472
House of Lords *Debates*, 8 November 1813, Vol. 27
House of Lords *Debates*, 21 April 1837, Vol. 3
Liverpool Mercury
(London) *Examiner*
London Journal
The Military Panorama or Officers' Companion / *The Royal Military Panorama or Officers' Companion* (1812–15)
Monthly Magazine, or British Register (December 1831)
The *Morning Chronicle*
The *Morning Post*
New Annual Register for 1813
Saturday Review
Theatrical Journal
The Times
(Truro) *Royal Cornwall Gazette*

Secondary Works
Atkinson, C.T., 'A Peninsular Brigadier', *Journal of the Society of Army Historical Research*, XXXIV (1956)
Bachrach, Bernard S., 'Medieval Siege Warfare. A Reconnaissance', *Journal of Military History*, 58 (1994), 119–33
Bamford, Andrew, *A Bold and Ambitious Enterprise: the British Army in the Low Countries, 1813–1814* (London, 2013)
Barbaro, Alessandro, *The Battle. A History of the Battle of Waterloo* (London, 2006 edn)
Bassett, Richard, *For God and Kaiser: The Imperial Austrian Army* (New Haven CT, 2015)
Beales, Derek, *Joseph II: II Against the World, 1780–1790* (Cambridge, 2009)

Beamish, North Ludlow, *History of the King's German Legion*, 2 vols (London, 1837)

Bell, David A., *The First Total War: Napoleon's Europe and the Birth of Modern Warfare* (London, 2008 edn)

Belmas, Jacques Vital, *Journaux des sièges faits ou soutenus par les Français dans la péninsula, de 1807 à1814*, 4 vols (Paris, 1836–7)

Best, Geoffrey, *Humanity in Warfare* (London, 1983 edn)

Bew, John, *Castlereagh. Enlightenment, War and Tyranny* (London, 2011)

Blanning, T.C.W., *The French Revolutionary Wars 1787–1802* (London, 1996)

Bond, Brian, *The Pursuit of Victory from Napoleon to Saddam Hussein* (Oxford, 1996)

Bourne, Kenneth, *Palmerston: the Early Years 1784–1841* (London, 1982)

Bray, Xavier, *Goya: The Portraits* (London, 2015)

Brown, David, *Palmerston: A Biography* (New Haven CT, 2010)

Burt, Ronald S., *Brokerage and Closure: An Introduction to Social Capital* (Oxford, 2005)

Callwell, Colonel C.E., *Military Operations and Maritime Preponderance* (Edinburgh,1905)

Canal, Jordi, 'Gerona (1808–1809) El Baluarte Sacrasanto de Nuestra Nacionalidad', in Gonzalo Butrón and Pedro Rújula (eds), *Los Sitios en la Guerra de la Independencia: la Lucha en las Ciudades* (Madrid, 2012), pp. 39–63

Chandler, David, *The Campaigns of Napoleon* (London, 1966)

Checkland, S.G., *The Rise of Industrial Society in England, 1815–1885* (London, 1964)

Chickering, Roger and Stig Forster (eds), *War in an Age of Revolution, 1775–1815* (Cambridge, 2010)

Clowes, William Laird, *The Royal Navy*, 6 vols (London 1997, repr. 1900 edn)

Collins, Bruce, 'Siege Warfare in the Age of Wellington', in C.M. Woolgar (ed.), *Wellington Studies IV* (University of Southampton, 2008), 22–53

Collins, Bruce, *War and Empire: the Expansion of Britain, 1790–1830* (Harlow, 2010)

Collinson, General and General Webber (eds), *General Sir Henry Drury Harness* (London, 1903)

Colson, Bruno, *Napoleon on War* (Oxford, 2015)

Conway, Stephen, 'The British Army, "Military Europe", and the American War of Independence', *William and Mary Quarterly*, 67 (2010), 69–100

Conway, Stephen, 'The eighteenth-century British army as a European institution', in Kevin Linch and Matthew McCormack (eds), *Britain's Soldiers: Rethinking War and Society 1715–1815* (Liverpool, 2014), 17–38

Coss, Edward J., *All for the King's Shilling. The British Soldier under Wellington, 1808–1814* (Norman OK, 2010)

Cowper, Colonel L.I. (ed.), *The King's Own. The Story of a Royal Regiment,* 2 vols (Oxford, 1939)

Creveld, Martin van, *Command in War* (Cambridge MA, 1985)

Dalrymple, William, *The Last Mughal: the Fall of a Dynasty, Delhi, 1857* (London, 2007 edn)

Daly, Gavin, *The British Soldier in the Peninsular War: Encounters with Spain and Portugal, 1808–1814* (Houndsmill, 2013)

Davey, James, *In Nelson's Wake* (London, 2016)

Davies, Huw J., *Wellington's Wars. The Making of a Military Genius* (New Haven CT, 2012)

Duffy, Christopher, *The Fortress in the Age of Vauban and Frederick the Great 1660–1789*, Vol. II, *Siege Warfare*, 2 vols (London, 1985)

Duncan, Captain Francis, *History of the Royal Regiment of Artillery*, 2 vols (London, 1872–3)

Esdaile, Charles, *The Duke of Wellington and the Command of the Spanish Army* (London, 1990)

Esdaile, Charles, *The Peninsular War. A New History* (London, 2002)

Esdaile, Charles J., *Fighting Napoleon: Guerrillas, Bandits and Adventurers in Spain 1808–1814* (New Haven CT, 2004)

Esdaile, Charles, *Napoleon's Wars: An International History 1803–1815* (London, 2007)

Esdaile, Charles J. and Philip Freeman, *Burgos in the Peninsular war, 1808–1814* (Houndsmill, 2015)

Evans, Richard J., *The Pursuit of Power: Europe 1815–1914* (London, 2016)

Forrest, Alan, *Great Battles. Waterloo* (Oxford, 2015)

Fortescue, J.W., *A History of the British Army*, 13 vols (London, 1900–30)

Gat, Azar, 'What Constituted the Military Revolution of the Early Modern Period?', in Roger Chickering and Stig Forster (eds), *War in an Age of Revolution, 1775–1815* (Cambridge, 2010), 21–48

Gates, David, *The Spanish Ulcer* (London, 1986)

Gates, David, *The British Light Infantry Arm, c1790–1815* (London, 1987)

Gleig, Revd G.R., *The Life of Major-General Sir Thomas Munro, Bart*, 3 vols (London, 1830)

Greengrass, Mark, *Christendom Destroyed: Europe 1517–1648* (London, 2015 edn)

Griffith, Paddy, *The art of war of revolutionary France, 1789–1802* (London, 1998)

Halévy, Elie, *England in 1815*, trans. E.I. Watkin and D.A. Barker (London, 1961 edn)

Hall, Christopher, *Wellington's Navy. Sea Power and the Peninsular War, 1807–1814* (Manchester, 2004)

Hall, John A., *A History of the Peninsular War: Volume VIII* (London, 1998)

Harrington, Peter, *British Artists and War: The Face of Battle in Paintings and Prints, 1700–1914* (London, 1993)

Haythornthwaite, Philip, 'Sieges in the Peninsular War' and 'A List of Peninsular War Sieges', in Paddy Griffith (ed.), *A History of the Peninsular War: Volume IX* (London, 1999) 213–29, 419–23

Hibbert, Christopher (ed.), *The Wheatley Diary* (London, 1964)

Horward, Donald D., *Napoleon and Iberia: The Twin Sieges of Ciudad Rodrigo and Almeida, 1810* (London, 1994 repr.)

Horward, Donald D., 'Napoleon and the mighty fortresses of Europe', in R.

Caldwell, D. Horward et al. (eds), *The consortium on revolutionary Europe 1750–1850: selected papers 1994* (Tallahassee FL, 1994), 306–14

Howard, Michael, *War in European History* (Oxford, 1976)

Howard, Michael, *Captain Professor* (London, 2006)

Keegan, John, *The Mask of Command* (London, 1988 edn)

Knight, Roger, *Britain Against Napoleon: the Organization of Victory 1793–1815* (London, 2013)

Knight, Roger and Martin Wilcox, *Sustaining the Fleet, 1793–1815: War, the British Navy and the Contractor State* (Woodbridge, 2010)

Langins, Janis, *Conserving the Enlightenment. French Military Engineering from Vauban to the Revolution* (Cambridge MA, 2004)

Leggatt, Don, *Shaping the Royal Navy: Technology, authority and naval architecture, c1830–1906* (Manchester, 2015)

Leggiere, Michael V., *The Fall of Napoleon: Volume 1 The Allied Invasion of France, 1813–1814* (Cambridge, 2007)

Lepage, Jean-Denis G.G., *Vauban and the French Military under Louis XIV* (Jefferson NC, 2010)

Lewis, Robert C., *The British Industrial Revolution in Global Perspective* (Cambridge, 2009)

Lynn, John A., *The Wars of Louis XIV 1667–1714* (London, 1999)

McCranie, Kevin D., *Admiral Lord Keith and the Naval War Against Napoleon* (Gainesville FL, 2006)

Mallett, Michael and Christine Shaw, *The Italian wars 1494–1559* (Harlow, 2012)

Mallinson, Allan, *The Making of the British Army* (London, 2009)

Moorsom, M.S., *History of the 52ⁿᵈ Regiment 1755–1816* (Felling, 1996 repr. 1860 edn)

Moran, Daniel and Arthur Waldron (eds), *The People in Arms: Military Myth and National Mobilization since the French Revolution* (Cambridge, 2003)

Muir, Rory, *Britain and the Defeat of Napoleon, 1807–1815* (New Haven CT, 1996)

Muir, Rory, *Tactics and the experience of Battle in the age of Napoleon* (New Haven CT, 1998)

Muir, Rory, *Salamanca 1812* (New Haven CT, 2001)

Muir, Rory, *Wellington: The Path to Victory, 1769–1814* (New Haven CT and London, 2013)

Munch-Petersen, Thomas, *Defying Napoleon: How Britain Bombarded Copenhagen and Seized the Danish Fleet in 1807* (Stroud, 2007)

Murray, Williamson, *Military Adaptation in War: With Fear of Change* (Cambridge, 2011)

Olavide, Juan, Braulio Albrellos, Juan Vigon, 'San Sebastian el Sito de 1813',16–17, 21 mss, bvpb.mcu.es/es/consulta/registro.crud?id

Oman, Carola, *Sir John Moore* (London, 1953)

Oman, Charles, *A History of the Peninsular War*, 7 vols (London, 1900–30)

Painting, Vivienne, *John Boydell* (London, 2005)

Planert, Ute, 'Innovation or Evolution? The French Wars in Military History', in

Roger Chickering and Stig Forster (eds), *War in an Age of Revolution, 1775–1815* (Cambridge, 2010), 69–84

Pollak, Martha D., *Turin 1564–1680: Urban Design, Military Culture, and the Creation of the Absolutist Capital* (Chicago IL, 1991)

Price, Munro, *Napoleon. The End of Glory* (Oxford, 2014)

Rait, Robert S., *The Life and Campaigns of Hugh First Viscount Gough Field Marshal*, 2 vols (Oxford, 1903)

Robertson, Ian C., *Wellington Invades France* (London, 2003)

Rodger, N.A.M., *Command of the Ocean: A Naval History of Britain, 1649–1815* (London, 2004)

Rothenberg, Gunther E., *The art of warfare in the age of Napoleon* (Bloomington IN, 1980)

Rújula, Pedro, 'Zaragosa (1808–1809) El Mito de la Resistancia Popular', in Gonzalo Butrón and Pedro Rújula (eds), *Los Sitios en la Guerra de la Independencia: la Lucha en las Ciudades* (Madrid, 2012), pp. 15–37

Shadwell, Lieutenant General, *The Life of Colin Campbell, Lord Clyde*, 2 vols (Edinburgh, 1881)

Sherwig, John M., *Guineas and Gunpowder* (Cambridge MA, 1969)

Showalter, Dennis E., *The Wars of Frederick the Great* (Harlow, 1996)

Smyth, Major B., *A History of the Lancashire Fusiliers*, 2 vols (Dublin, 1903), Vol. I

Somerville, Alexander, *History of the British Legion, and War in Spain* (London, 1839)

Strachan, Hew, *Wellington's Legacy: the Reform of the British Army 1830–54* (Manchester, 1984)

Strachan, Hew, *From Waterloo to Balaclava. Tactics, Technology, and the British Army 1815–1854* (Cambridge, 1985)

Sun Tzu, *The Art of War*, trans. and with an introduction by Samuel B. Griffith (Oxford, 1963)

Symmonds, Sarah (ed.), *Goya; A Life in Letters* (London, 2004)

Thompson, Mark, 'The Rise of the Scientific Soldier as seen through the Performance of the Corps of Royal Engineers during the early 19th Century' (PhD thesis, University of Sunderland, 2008)

Thoral, Marie-Cecile, *From Valmy to Waterloo: France at War, 1792–1815* (Houndsmill, 2011)

Thorne, R.G., *The House of Commons 1790–1820*, 5 vols (London, 1986)

Tone, John Lawrence, *The Fatal Knot: The Guerrilla War in Navarre and the Defeat of Napoleon in Spain* (Chapel Hill NC, 1994)

Weigley, Russell F., *The Age of Battles: the Quest for Decisive Warfare from Breitenfeld to Waterloo* (London, 1991)

Weller, Jac, *Wellington in the Peninsula* (London, 1999 edn)

Whitman, James Q., *The Verdict of Battle: the Law of Victory and the Making of Modern War* (Cambridge MA, 2012)

Index